St ‖‖‖‖‖‖‖ de

D0947376

pany

Macroeconomics

8th Canadian Edition

McConnell / Brue / Barbiero

Prepared by

William B. Walstad
University of Nebraska, Lincoln

Robert C. Bingham

Torben Andersen
Red Deer College

McGraw-Hill
Ryerson

Toronto   Montréal   New York   Burr Ridge   Bangkok
Bogotá   Caracas   Lisbon   London   Madrid   Mexico City
Milan   New Delhi   Seoul   Singapore   Sydney   Taipei

McGraw-Hill
Ryerson Limited
A Subsidiary of The McGraw-Hill Companies

Study Guide
to accompany
MACROECONOMICS
Eighth Canadian Edition

ISBN: 0-07-560461-2

1 2 3 4 5 6 7 8 9 10 MP 8 7 6 5 4 3 2 1 0 9

Printed and bound in Canada

Statistics Canada information is used with the permission of the Ministry of Industry, as Minister responsible for Statistics Canada. Information on the availability of the wider range of data from Statistics Canada can be obtained from Statistics Canada's Regional Offices, its World Wide Web site at *http://www.statcan.ca* and its toll-free access number 1-800-263-1136.

Care has been taken to trace ownership of copyright material contained in this text. The publishers will gladly take any information that will enable them to rectify any reference or credit in subsequent editions.

Senior Sponsoring Editor: *Lynn Fisher*
Senior Supervising Editor: *Kelly Dickson*
Production Coordinator: *Madeleine Harrington*
Formatter: *Jay Tee Graphics, Ltd.*
Printer: *Maracle Press*

CONTENTS

Preface

Preface

Welcome to the study of economics. This *Study Guide* is intended to accompany and complement the textbook, *Macroeconomics*, 8th Canadian edition, by McConnell, Brue and Barbiero. The design of the *Study Guide* is based on the conviction that active study is superior to passive study. To benefit from an aerobics class, you must not only watch the instructor's demonstrations — you must do the exercises yourself. To learn carpentry you cannot merely read a book — you must practise using the tools. Learning economics is a lot like aerobics or carpentry: you must do exercises, and you must handle the tools.

The *Study Guide* lets you practise using the tools of economics, and gives you feedback along the way. It provides a range of questions that require verbal, numerical, and graphical answers. These are the three main modes of analysis in economics, and skill in all three areas will likely be expected of you on your economics exams.

I hope that you will work extensively with this *Study Guide*, and that as a result, you have more success, and more fun, in your economics course.

■ WHAT THE STUDY GUIDE IS

For each chapter in the text there is a chapter in the *Study Guide*. Each *Study Guide* chapter has twelve sections. The first five sections identify and explain the basic content of each chapter.

1. An introduction relates the chapter to other chapters, and identifies what topics are of special importance.
2. A checklist states your learning objectives.
3. A chapter outline summarizes all of the essential points in the chapter.
4. A list of terms and concepts that you will learn about in the chapter.
5. Selected hints and tips alert you to common pitfalls and points you cannot afford to overlook.

The final sections provide questions and answers:

6. Fill-in questions.
7. Problems and projects.
8. True-false questions.
9. Multiple-choice questions.
10. Discussion questions.
11. Answers to all fill-in questions, true-false questions, multiple-choice questions, and most of the problems.
12. Answers to key questions from the textbook can be found at the back of the *Study Guide*.

■ A BIT OF ADVICE

Try to work several times each week with both the text and the *Study Guide*. Economics is absorbed most effectively in small, frequent doses.

You might find it useful to preview the *Study Guide* introduction, chapter outline, and checklist before tackling a new chapter in the textbook. However, most of your time with the *Study Guide* should come after reading the chapter in the textbook, and probably after your instructor has dealt with the material in class.

Make a serious attempt to answer a question before looking at its solution. Evaluate your results to assess your areas of strength and weakness. If you don't have time to do all of the questions, choose ones that seem more important given your instructor's emphasis.

When reviewing for exams, you will not have time to re-read all of the textbook chapters. Use the compact summaries in the *Study Guide* for quick review and to focus on key areas that you might need to review in more detail in the textbook.

■ ACKNOWLEDGEMENTS

I thank Cyril Grant, William Walstad, and the late Robert Bingham, whose work on earlier editions of the *Study Guide* made my work much easier. Thanks to Tom Barbiero for preparing a fine text for Canadian students, and to my colleague, Syed Ahmed, for the encouragement. The McGraw-Hill Ryerson team was very helpful: especially Daphne Scriabin, Joseph Gladstone, Gail Marsden, and Jennifer Burnell.

Sheila, Niels, Kate and Alison, I appreciate your patience. Finally, I am grateful to my students at Red Deer College who have taught me a great deal about what is important in introductory economics.

Torben Andersen

CHAPTER 1

The Nature and Method of Economics

Chapter 1 introduces you to economics — the social science concerned with the efficient use of scarce resources to achieve maximum satisfaction of human material wants. You are given a sense of the kinds of topics economists study, how economists analyze these topics, and why economics is useful and important. You are also given "Ten Key Concepts" that will be reinforced throughout the textbook because they represent the set of core concepts that we hope you will take with you for life.

At the heart of economics is the idea of scarcity: the fact that our limited resources are insufficient to produce all the material goods we want. Accordingly, we must make choices about how to allocate our resources, and in these choices we face tradeoffs. When we choose to allocate resources to producing one thing we sacrifice the production of something else. This sacrifice is known as an opportunity cost.

Economic explanations of human behaviour are based on the assumption of "rational self-interest" and on "marginal analysis." People make rational decisions to maximize their fulfillment of their own goals. These goals differ between individuals and are not limited to material goals or to selfish goals. When people make decisions they weigh the marginal benefits and marginal costs of different courses of action. It is rational to do more of an activity if the marginal benefit exceeds the marginal cost.

An understanding of economics will help you to be a well-informed citizen who can participate intelligently in the democratic process. The study of economics will also give you analytical skills to use as a manager, as a worker, or as a consumer. However, economics is primarily an academic subject, and its objective is to examine topics from a social, rather than a personal, point of view.

The discipline of economics uses the scientific method. In theoretical economics we derive principles or theories that are generalizations about economic behaviour. While these generalizations may be somewhat abstract and simplified representations, they must be based on facts in the real world. Economic generalizations can be derived through induction or deduction. In either case, a vital part of the scientific method is to test theories by comparing their predictions with actual data. Policy economics entails the application of theories and data to formulate policies, solve economic problems, or help us achieve certain economic goals.

In Canada we have six economic goals for our society: economic growth, full employment, economic efficiency, price level stability, equitable distribution of income, and a balance in foreign trade. Policy questions often centre on how these goals should be interpreted, and on the relative importance of different goals when there are tradeoffs between goals. Such questions move us from economic theory and positive economics, which investigates *what is,* to normative economics, which incorporates subjective or value-laden views of *what ought to be.*

Economics is divided into two broad categories: microeconomics and macroeconomics. Microeconomics studies the behaviour of individual economic units. Macroeconomics studies economy-wide aggregates. Though they focus on different sorts of questions, both microeconomics and macroeconomics use the scientific method and are based on the scarcity principle.

Clear thinking about economic questions requires that we avoid many common pitfalls. Errors in thinking can occur from bias, loaded terminology, imprecise definitions, fallacies of composition, and confusing correlation with causation. Awareness of these pitfalls will help you think more objectively about economic issues.

■ CHECKLIST

When you have studied this chapter, you should be able to:

☐ Define economics.

☐ Describe the economic perspective and how it is based on scarcity, rational self-interest, and marginal costs and marginal benefits.

☐ Identify which three of the *Ten Key Concepts* are discussed in this chapter.

☐ Explain why scarcity gives rise to opportunity costs.

☐ Give two reasons for studying economics.

☐ Distinguish between theoretical economics and policy economics.

☐ Explain what an economic principle is and what its purpose is.

☐ Discuss how economic principles are generalizations and abstractions.

☐ Distinguish between induction and deduction as methods of developing economic principles.

☐ Explain the "other things equal" assumption and why this assumption is employed in economics.

☐ Outline the three steps in formulating economic policy.

☐ List six economic goals that are widely accepted in Canada.

☐ Distinguish between macroeconomics and microeconomics.

☐ Distinguish between positive economics and normative economics and provide examples of both.

☐ Recognize the "pitfalls to straight thinking" when confronted with examples.

■ CHAPTER OUTLINE

1. Economics is the social science concerned with the efficient use of scarce resources to achieve maximum satisfaction of human material wants.

2. *Ten Key Concepts* are listed in Chapter 1 and later developed and reinforced throughout the textbook. The concepts are divided into three categories:

    (a)   those pertaining to the individual

    (b)   those explaining interaction among individuals

    (c)   those dealing with the economy as a whole and the standard of living.

3. The economic perspective on human behaviour is described in three interrelated ideas:

    (a)   Scarcity of resources forces people to make choices and incur opportunity costs.

    (b)   People make rational decisions based on their own self-interest.

    (c)   People make choices by comparing marginal costs and marginal benefits.

4. Many modern ideologies and policy debates are informed by the ideas of prominent economists. Some knowledge of economics is therefore essential to be a well-informed citizen. Economics also has personal applications for business executives, consumers and workers.

5. Economists develop economic principles (also called theories, laws or models) to help us to understand the economy and formulate policies which will solve economic problems.

    (a)   The object of economic theorizing is to systematically arrange and analyze facts so that we may discover regularities or trends. Without bringing such order to facts we could not discover the relationships between facts.

    (b)   Induction is a method which distills theories from facts. Deduction is a method where hypotheses are derived by logic, and then tested against the facts.

    (c)   Economic theories are generalizations which are expressed as tendencies or trends. These tendencies need not hold true in every single case in order for theories to be useful.

    (d)   Economic theories are abstractions from reality because they are simplifications designed to omit irrelevant facts.

    (e)   As an analytical tool, economists use the assumption of *ceteris paribus*, or "other things equal," in order to focus on only the variables of main interest.

6. Economic policy involves the application of economic principles to reach specific goals. The three steps in policy design are stating the goals, determining the policy options for achieving the chosen goals, and implementing and evaluating the effects of the selected policy.

7. At least six major economic goals are widely accepted in Canada: economic growth, full employment, economic efficiency, price level stability, equitable distribution of income, and balance of trade. Economic goals may be complementary or conflicting. When goals conflict, the tradeoffs must be assessed and value judgments made about how to balance them.

8. Economists derive principles of economic behaviour at the macroeconomic and the microeconomic level. Macroeconomics deals with the economy as a whole by examining aggregate measures (such as employment at the national level). Microeconomics looks at specific economic units (such as the real estate market in a particular city).

9. Economists deal with both positive economics and normative economics. Positive economics concerns the study of facts to determine *what is,* whereas normative economics involves value judgments to determine *what ought to be.* Sound economic policy decisions involve both because solutions cannot be implemented before the current situation is understood and value judgments are made about the desired situation.

10. Common pitfalls to avoid in order to think clearly and logically using the economic perspective include:
  (a)   bias or preconceptions not warranted by facts
  (b)   loaded terminology that appeals to emotions and leads to nonobjective analysis of issues
  (c)   careless use of terms that have precise technical definitions
  (d)   the fallacy of composition, or the assumption that what is true for one is necessarily true for the group
  (e)   the *post hoc* fallacy, or the mistaken belief that if event A precedes event B, A is the cause of B
  (f)   confusion of correlation with causation

■   **TERMS AND CONCEPTS**

after this, therefore
   because of this fallacy
aggregate
deduction
economics
economic perspective
fallacy of composition
generalizations
induction
macroeconomics

marginal analysis
microeconomics
normative economics
other things equal
   assumption
policy economics
positive economics
principles
theoretical economics
tradeoffs

■   **HINTS AND TIPS**

1.   You may have difficulty accepting the claim that economics is a science, especially because its theories are inexact. Economics is a science by virtue of its methodology. That economic generalizations are inexact does not disqualify economics from being a science, nor does it negate the value of these generalizations. Think of generalizations from cancer research, or from meteorology. Scientists have demonstrated an important link between smoking and lung cancer, even though the knowledge is not exact enough to identify which specific smokers will get cancer. Meteorologists' weather forecasts are not always correct, but most follow these forecasts because they are generally better than the forecasts we could generate ourselves without the benefit of the inexact science of meteorology.

2.   A way to remember the pitfalls to objective thinking in economics is to associate each with a specific example. Choose examples that are funny, or that have personal application. For example: "The day I ate ice cream at the lake it was really hot, so next time it gets too cool I will eat some ice cream." Which fallacy is this an illustration of?

3.   You will not yet fully understand the *Ten Key Concepts* because most of them are not explained in this chapter, but the first three you should understand after reading this chapter. All of the concepts will show up in various chapters, so return to the list from time to time throughout the course to check your progress in learning these important concepts.

■   **FILL-IN QUESTIONS**

1. Economics is concerned with the _____ use of _____ resources to attain the _____ satisfaction of human material wants.

2. Deriving principles or theories is called _____ economics, whereas applying economic principles to solve problems is called _____ economics.

3. When an economist develops economic principles from a study of the facts, she is using the (inductive, deductive) _____ method; whereas when she uses facts to test hypotheses or predictions derived from economic theories she is using the _____ method.

4. Economic principles (often called _____ or _____) derived from facts are all _____ about human economic behaviour and, as such, necessarily involve _____ from reality.

5. Economists hypothesize that how many cigarettes a consumer will purchase depends upon the price of cigarettes, and several other factors such as income and tastes. To isolate the relationship between the price of cigarettes and the quantity purchased economists often assume that these other factors are constant. This is termed the _____ assumption.

6. Studying the economy in aggregate is called (microeconomics, macroeconomics) _____, whereas studying a specific business or market is called _____.

7. The three steps involved in the formulation of economic policy are:

(a) _____
(b) _____
(c) _____

8. Six economic goals that are widely accepted in Canada include:

(a) _____
(b) _____
(c) _____
(d) _____
(e) _____
(f) _____

9. Two different types of statements can be made about economic topics. A (positive, normative) _____ statement explains *what is* by offering a scientific proposition about economic behaviour that is based on theory and facts. A _____ statement includes a value judgment that suggests *what ought to be*. Many of the reported disagreements among economists usually involve _____ statements.

10. There are many obstacles to logical consistency in economic reasoning. For example, the conclusion that "what is true for an individual must necessarily be true of the group" is known as the fallacy of _____.

11. The economic perspective is a _____ perspective that has three interrelated features: (1) It recognizes that scarcity requires _____; (2) that people make decisions in a _____ manner based on their _____; and (3) that weighing the costs and benefits of a decision is based on _____ analysis.

■   PROBLEMS AND PROJECTS

1. Below are five statements, each containing an example of a common pitfall in thinking about economics. Indicate, in the space following each statement, the type of pitfall involved.

(a)   The Second World War resulted in forty-five years of economic expansion in Canada. _____

(b)   "An unemployed worker can find a job if he or she looks diligently and conscientiously for employment; therefore, all unemployed workers can find employment if they search diligently and conscientiously." _____

(c)   "Just tell me when rain will be needed and I will schedule my vacation for that week." _____
_____

(d)   "The players, not the team owners, deserve to benefit from the recent explosion in revenues experienced by the National Basketball Association; after all, it is the players that fans pay to see." _____

(e)   "The North American Free Trade Agreement is making Canadian workers pawns of the powerful corporations who can move their sweat shops to Mexico." _____

2. Indicate in the space beside each statement whether it is positive (P) or normative (N).

(a)   Tuition fee increases are causing university enrolments to decrease. __P__

(b)   The supply management system in agriculture protects our small family farms from unfair competition by large corporate agricultural enterprises. __N__

(c)   Higher income tax rates reduce the number of people willing to be employed. __P__

(d)   The Employment Insurance program is too generous because it gives people the incentive to quit their jobs. __N__

(e)   Free trade can improve the standard of living of a country. __P__

(f)   The federal government should do more to eliminate regional disparity in Canada. ___N___

■ TRUE-FALSE

Circle T if the statement is true, F if it is false.

1. Economics deals with the activities by which people earn their living and try to improve their standard of living.   **Ⓣ F**

2. The main objective of the study of economics is to provide specific job-related skills.   **T Ⓕ**

3. In economics, the terms "law," "principle," and "theory," mean essentially the same thing.   **Ⓣ F**

4. The "other things equal" or *ceteris paribus* assumption is made in order to simplify the reasoning process.   **Ⓣ F**

5. Abstraction in economic theory is useful because it eliminates unnecessary complexity and irrelevant facts.   **Ⓣ F**

6. A common reason that individuals disagree on what economic policy should be chosen is that they disagree on the goal or desired result.   **Ⓣ F**

7. Making value judgments as to preferred goals of an economy is known as positive economic analysis.   **T Ⓕ**

8. The statement: "Increased patent protection for the Canadian pharmaceutical industry will result in increased research and development activity in Canada" is a positive statement.   **Ⓣ F**

9. Rational self-interest is the same thing as being selfish.   **T Ⓕ**

10. If two variables are correlated with one another, changes in one must be causing changes in the other.   **T Ⓕ**

11. Microeconomic analysis is concerned with the behaviour of individual households and business firms.   **Ⓣ F**

12. Scarcity is caused by the fact that people make choices.   **T Ⓕ**

13. In economics the word "marginal" means additional, or extra.   **Ⓣ F**

■ MULTIPLE-CHOICE

Circle the letter that corresponds to the best answer.

1. Which statement is the best one to complete a short definition of economics? "Economics is the study of:
  (a)   how businesses maximize profits."
  (b)   the triumph of the capitalistic system over communism."
  (c)   monetary transactions."
  (d)   the efficient use of scarce resources."

d.

2. The statement that "there is no free lunch" refers to what economic concept?
  (a)   correlation does not imply causality
  (b)   everything has an opportunity cost
  (c)   nothing is free because government taxes everything
  (d)   individuals have different tastes and preferences

b

3. One economic principle states that, *ceteris paribus*, the lower the price of a commodity the greater will be the quantity of the commodity consumers will wish to purchase. On the basis of this principle alone, it can be concluded that:
  (a)   if the price of mink coats falls, more mink coats will be purchased by consumers
  (b)   if the price of mink coats falls, there must have been a decrease in the demand for clothes made of fur
  (c)   if the price of mink coats falls and there are no important changes in the other factors affecting their demand, consumers will purchase more mink coats
  (d)   if more mink coats are purchased this month than last month, it is because the price of mink coats has fallen

c

4. An economic model is *not*:
  (a)   an ideal type of economy or economic policy that we should strive to achieve
  (b)   a tool economists employ to enable them to predict
  (c)   an abstract representation of the economy or some part of the economy
  (d)   an explanation of how the economy or a part of the economy functions in its essential details

a

5. Which of the following is *not* among the dangers encountered when constructing or applying an economic model?

(a)   it may contain irrelevant facts and be more complex than necessary

(b)   it may come to be accepted as "what ought to be" rather than as "what is"

(c)   it may be overly simplified and so be a very poor approximation of the reality it explains

(d)   it may result in a conclusion that is unacceptable to people

6. A theory in economics:

(a)   is useless if simplifying assumptions are used

(b)   is of little use if it is abstract

(c)   is useful if the predictions of the theory usually correspond to actual economic occurrences

(d)   is useless if its predictions are not always correct

7. The method of reasoning in which economic principles are derived from an analysis of historical data is called:

(a)   descriptive economics

(b)   hypothesis testing

(c)   induction

(d)   deduction

8. Which of the following would not be contained in an economic theory?

(a)   predictions that are deduced from that theory

(b)   definitions that clearly set out the variables included in the model

(c)   statements of the relationships among the variables in the model

(d)   normative statements as to the most preferred outcomes

9. During World War II, Canada employed price controls to prevent inflation; this was referred to as "a fascist and arbitrary restriction of economic freedom" by some and as "a necessary and democratic means of preventing ruinous inflation" by others. Both labels are examples of:

(a)   economic bias

(b)   the fallacy of composition

(c)   misuse of common-sense definitions

(d)   loaded terminology

10. If one individual decides to consume less beef, there will be little or no effect on beef prices. To argue, therefore, that if all individuals consume less beef there should be little or no effect on beef prices is an example of:

(a)   the *post hoc, ergo propter hoc* fallacy

(b)   the fallacy of composition

(c)   an oversimplified generalization

(d)   using loaded terminology

11. The Great Depression that began in 1929 was preceded by a stock market crash. To conclude that the depression was then caused by the decline in the stock market is an example of:

(a)   the *post hoc, ergo propter hoc* fallacy

(b)   the fallacy of composition

(c)   the *ceteris paribus* assumption

(d)   using loaded terminology

12. Which of the following would be studied in microeconomics?

(a)   the output of the entire economy

(b)   the national unemployment rate

(c)   the effect of money supply changes on the Consumer Price Index

(d)   the price and output of apples

13. If economic growth tends to produce a more equitable distribution of income among people in a nation, then the goals of growth and equitable income distribution seem to be:

(a)   deductive

(b)   conflicting

(c)   complementary

(d)   mutually exclusive

14. To say that two economic goals are conflicting means that:

(a)   there is a tradeoff in the achievement of the goals

(b)   these goals are not accepted as goals

(c)   the achievement of one goal results in achievement of the other goal

(d)   it is impossible to quantify both goals

15. Which of the following is a macroeconomic topic?

(a)   the effect of cigarette tax reductions on cigarette consumption

(b)   the effect of government set stumpage fees on the amount of lumber being exported to the United States

(c)   the effect of the cod fishery closure on the unemployment rate in Halifax

(d) the effect of the falling Canadian dollar on Canada's exports and imports

■ DISCUSSION QUESTIONS

1. What are some issues that you face in your personal or work life for which a knowledge of economics could provide you with useful skills?

2. What is a "laboratory experiment under controlled conditions?" Why are such experiments not normally possible in economics? What does economics have instead of a laboratory?

3. What is the relationship between facts and theory?

4. Why are economic principles and models necessarily generalizations and abstractions?

5. Sketch a map showing me how to get from your home to the nearest grocery store. In what ways is your map realistic, and in what ways is it unrealistic (abstract)? Would your map necessarily be more helpful to me in finding the store if it was more realistic? Would it be worth making it more realistic? How do these issues concerning your map relate to issues concerning economic theories?

6. What does it mean to say that economic principles can be used for prediction and control?

7. Explain each of the following:
 (a) fallacy of composition
 (b) loaded terminology
 (c) the *post hoc, ergo propter hoc* fallacy.

8. Explain briefly the difference between:
 (a) macroeconomics and microeconomics
 (b) deduction and induction
 (c) correlation and causation.

■ ANSWERS

FILL-IN QUESTIONS

1. efficient, scarce, maximum

2. theoretical, policy

3. inductive, deductive

4. theories, laws (or models), generalizations, abstractions

5. "other things equal" (*ceteris paribus*)

6. macroeconomics, microeconomics

7. (a) stating goals; (b) analyzing policy options; (c) evaluating policy effectiveness

8. (a) full employment; (b) economic growth; (c) price stability; (d) balance of trade; (e) equitable distribution of incomes; (f) economic efficiency

9. positive, normative, normative

10. composition

11. cost-benefit; choices; rational; self-interest; marginal

PROBLEMS AND PROJECTS

1. (a) *post hoc ergo propter hoc* fallacy; (b) the fallacy of composition; (c) confusing correlation and causation; (d) bias; (e) loaded terminology

2. (a) P; (b) N; (c) P; (d) N; (e) P; (f) N

TRUE-FALSE

1. T	**2.** F	**3.** T	**4.** T	**5.** T	**6.** T
7. F	**8.** T	**9.** F	**10.** F	**11.** T	**12.** F
13. T					

MULTIPLE-CHOICE

1. (d)	**2.** (b)	**3.** (c)	**4.** (a)	**5.** (d)	**6.** (c)
7. (c)	**8.** (d)	**9.** (d)	**10.** (b)	**11.** (a)	**12.** (d)
13. (c)	**14.** (a)	**15.** (d)			

APPENDIX TO CHAPTER 1
Graphs and Their Meaning

The old saying that "a picture is worth a thousand words" is true in economics because economists use graphs to "picture" relationships between economic variables. A graph can display a lot of information in a manner that is precise yet quick to comprehend. Because we rely so much on these "pictures," you need to be skilled in constructing and interpreting graphs. Even if you are already familiar with the fundamentals of graphing, perhaps from previous classes in math and sciences, you should review this appendix. If none of this material seems familiar, relax: all of the basics that you need are explained in this appendix.

The appendix shows how to construct a graph from a table of data on two variables (using the example of income and consumption). Each variable is represented on one of the two axes, so each axis should be labelled with the variable name, its units of measurement, and marked off with a consistent measurement scale. Once the data points are plotted and a line drawn to connect the plotted points, one can determine whether there is a direct or inverse relationship between the variables.

Economists usually, but not always, measure the independent variable (income) on the horizontal axis and the dependent variable (consumption) on the vertical axis of the graph. The curve plotted to illustrate the relationship between the two variables is drawn based on the *ceteris paribus* condition. If any other variable that influences the dependent variable happens to change, then we must plot a whole new curve through a different set of points. This is termed a shift in the curve.

A relationship that is linear (a straight line on the graph) can be defined by two simple elements: the slope and the vertical intercept of the line. The slope is the ratio of the vertical change (rise) to the horizontal change (run). The slope often has economic meaning, because slopes measure effects of mar-ginal changes. As discussed in Chapter 1, marginal analysis is central to economics. For graphs involving nonlinear curves the slope is not constant; it varies as one moves along the curve. This slope at a particular point can be estimated by determining the slope of a straight line drawn tangent to the curve at that point. The vertical intercept of a line is the value on the vertical axis when the horizontal axis variable is zero. A linear relationship is easily expressed in equation form once the slope and the vertical intercept are found from a graph or table of data.

■ **CHECKLIST**

When you have studied this appendix, you should be able to:
□ Understand why economists use graphs.
□ Construct a graph of two variables using numerical data from a table.
□ Construct a table with two variables from an algebraic function or from data on a graph.
□ Determine whether a graph shows a direct or an inverse relationship between two variables.
□ Identify dependent and independent variables in economic examples and graphs.
□ Calculate the slope of a straight line between two points and determine the vertical intercept for the line.
□ Write a linear equation using the slope of a line and the vertical intercept, and when given values for the independent variable, determine values for the dependent variable.
□ Estimate the slope of a nonlinear curve at a point using a line that is tangent to the curve at that point.

■ APPENDIX OUTLINE

1. A graph is a visual representation of the relationship between variables and is helpful in describing economic theories and models.

2. To construct a simple graph, plot numerical data about two variables from a table. Sometimes the tabular data must be found first by using an equation relating the two variables.

(a)   Each graph has a horizontal and a vertical axis that can be labelled for each variable and then scaled for the range of the data points that will be measured on the axis. Along a given axis a certain increment of distance represents a consistent increment in the variable.

(b)   Data points are plotted on the graph by drawing perpendiculars from the scaled points on the two axes to the place on the graph where the perpendiculars intersect.

(c)   A line or curve can then be drawn to connect the points plotted on the graph. If the line is straight the relationship is "linear."

3. The slope of the line on a graph shows the nature of the relationship between the two variables.

(a)   A line that is upsloping to the right indicates a positive or direct relationship between the two variables: an increase (a decrease) in one is associated with an increase (a decrease) in the other.

(b)   A line that is downsloping to the right indicates a negative or inverse relationship between the two variables because the variables are changing in opposite directions: an increase (a decrease) in one is associated with a decrease (an increase) in the other.

4. Economists are concerned with determining cause and effect in economic events.

(a)   An independent variable is the variable that changes first, and "causes" another variable to change.

(b)   A dependent variable is the variable "effected" by a change in another variable.

(c)   Economists do not always follow the convention used in mathematics whereby an independent variable is placed on the horizontal axis and a dependent variable on the vertical axis.

5. A two-variable graph is a simplified representation of an economic relationship. In such a graph there is an implicit assumption that all other factors are being held constant. This "other things equal" or *ceteris paribus* assumption is a simplification that helps us focus on the two variables of interest. If another variable that influences the dependent variable does change, then the curve on the graph will shift to a new position.

6. A slope and vertical intercept can be calculated for a linear relationship (straight line graph). These values also define the equation of the line.

(a)   The slope of a straight line is the ratio of the vertical change to the horizontal change between two points.

(b)   The slope reflects the marginal effect on one variable of a small change in the other.

(c)   A positive (negative) slope indicates a direct (inverse) relationship between the two variables.

(d)   The vertical intercept is the value where the line intersects the vertical axis of the graph.

(e)   A linear equation is written as $y = a + bx$. Once the values for the intercept a and the slope b are calculated, then given any value of variable x, the value of variable y can be determined.

7. A straight line has a constant slope, but a nonlinear curve has a continually changing slope. To estimate the slope of a nonlinear curve at a point, calculate the slope of a line tangent to the curve at that point.

■ APPENDIX TERMS AND CONCEPTS

dependent variable   **inverse relationship**
direct relationship   **slope of a straight line**
horizontal axis   **vertical axis**
independent variable   **vertical intercept**

■ HINTS AND TIPS

1. Some students are comfortable with economic graphs right away, whereas others initially have a strong aversion to the graphs. If you are in the first group, you are fortunate because economics will come more easily to you. If you are in the second group, do not run because you cannot hide! It is incredibly important that you quickly develop basic skills with graphing. If you find this appendix very difficult you should seek extra help with these tools.

2. The text includes a number of graphs of real world data showing relationships between two variables. These graphs often take the form of a "scatter diagram" with a "best-fitting line." That is, the

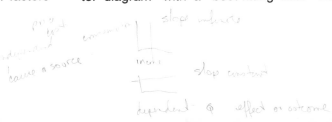

data points may be somewhat scattered, rather than lying exactly on a curve. In many of these graphs no precise relationship is evident in the data, but there is a discernible tendency or pattern in the data, indicating that the variables are related. The best-fitting line is indicated to show this pattern. If you take a statistics course you will learn the proper techniques for determining such best-fitting lines, and for judging when you can be reasonably sure that the points in a scatter diagram do indicate some relationship. To understand this textbook you need only have a rough idea of a "best-fitting line."

3. All of the graphs in this appendix have actual numerical values marked on the axes. Later in the text you will see some graphs without any numbers on the axes. In such cases the specific numbers are not necessary for the explanation, but you should recognize that there are numbers implicit on the axes. If at first you have difficulty comprehending such graphs you could pencil in arbitrary values on the axes until you get used to these abstract graphs.

■   **FILL-IN QUESTIONS**

1. The relationship between two economic variables can be visualized with a two-dimensional graph.
   (a)   By convention, the (dependent, independent) _____ variable is placed on the horizontal axis and the _____ variable is placed on the vertical axis. The _____ variable is said to change because of a change in the _____ variable. In economics the axis designations (always, sometimes) _____ follow convention.
   (b)   The vertical and horizontal (scales, ranges) _____ on the graph are calibrated to reflect the _____ of values in a table of data points on which the graph is based.
   (c)   Other variables, apart from the two in the graph, that might affect the economic relationship are assumed to be (changing, held constant) _____. The Latin phrase meaning "other things remaining constant" is: _____.

2. The graph of a straight line that slopes downward to the right indicates that there is (a direct, an inverse) _____ relationship between the two variables. A graph of a straight line that slopes upward to the right tells us that the relationship is (direct, inverse) _____. When the value of one variable increases and the value of the other variable increases, then the relationship is _____; when the value of one increases, while the other decreases, the relationship is _____.

3. The slope of a straight line between two points is defined as the ratio of the (vertical, horizontal) _____ change over the _____ change. When two variables move in the same direction, the slope will be (negative, positive) _____; when the variables move in opposite directions, the slope will be _____. The point at which the line meets the vertical axis is called the _____.

4. We can express the graph of a straight line with a linear equation that can be written as $y = a + bx$.
   (a) a is the (slope, intercept) _____ and b is the _____.
   (b)   If a was 2, b was 4, and x was 5, then y would be _____. If the value of x changed to 7, then y would be _____. If the value of x changed to 3, then y would be _____.

5. The slope of a (straight line, nonlinear curve) _____ is constant throughout; the slope of a _____ varies from point to point. The slope of a nonlinear curve at a point can be estimated by calculating the slope of a straight line that is _____ to the point on the curve.

■   **PROBLEMS AND PROJECTS**

1. The data below represent the relationship between the mortgage interest rate and the number of new houses built.

Mortgage Rate (% per year)	Housing Starts (thousands per year)
12	70,000
10	90,000
8	110,000
6	130,000
4	150,000

   (a)   Which variable is dependent? _____ Which is independent? _____
   (b)   On the axes of the graph below, set up the scales to best suit these data. Label each axis of the graph (including the units of measurement).
   (c)   Plot the five data points given in the table.

(d) The curve is (up-, down-) _____ sloping, meaning that the relationship between the mortgage interest rate and housing starts is (direct, inverse) _____.

2. (a) Based on the relationship found in question 1, if the mortgage rate increases by 1%, *ceteris paribus*, then housing starts will (decrease, increase) _____ by _____ thousands per year.

(b) If household incomes rise, new homes would become (more, less) _____ affordable, so there would be (more, fewer) _____ new housing starts at the same interest rate as before. On the graph, this would cause a (leftward, rightward) _____ shift of the curve in question 1.

(c) If lumber prices increase, new homes would become (more, less) _____ affordable, so there would be (more, fewer) _____ new housing starts at the same interest rate as before. On the graph, this would cause a (leftward, rightward) _____ shift of the initial curve.

3. The Hammerheads, a very mediocre club band, have just released a CD. They will immediately sell 10 copies to their parents and friends. Thereafter, they can sell 4 copies for each performance they give in a club.

(a) Based on this information, complete the table below.

Performances	CD Sales
0	_____
5	_____
10	_____
15	_____
20	_____

(b) Which variable is dependent? _____ Which is independent? _____

(c) Plot the data on the graph below.

CD Sales

Performances

(d) The vertical intercept value is _____.

(e) The slope value is _____.

(f) Write the equation for this relationship:

_____.

4. An economist is hired to determine the relationship between real estate value and proximity to the waterfront in a Manitoba lakeshore resort community. The table below gives selling prices for undeveloped building lots sold in 1998.

(a) On the graph provided, create a "scatter diagram" with lot prices on the vertical axis and distance to shore on the horizontal axis.

Lot	Distance to Shore (m)	Price ($)
A	200	9,000
B	0	18,000
C	50	16,000
D	100	15,000
E	50	17,000
F	150	10,000
G	200	7,000
H	125	12,000

Price (thousand $)

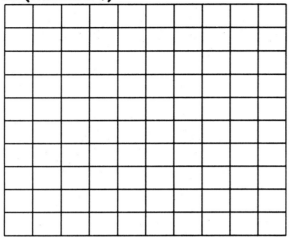

Distance to shore (m)

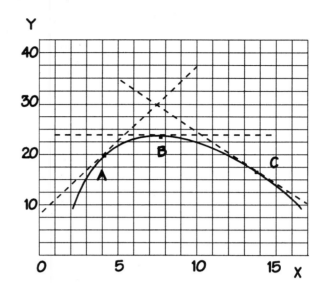

(b)   The scatter diagram suggests that lot prices are (directly, inversely, not) _____ related to their proximity to the waterfront.

(c)   With a ruler, draw in what appears to be the "best-fitting" line through these data points.

(d)   The value of the vertical intercept is _____. This value indicates price for a lot that is _____.

(e)   The value of the slope is _____. This value indicates that price (falls, rises) _____ by $_____ for each metre from the waterfront.

(f)   The expression for the equation of this line is: _____.

5. This question is based on the graph below.

(a)   The function has a negative slope between the X values of _____ and _____. Over this range the relationship between X and Y is (direct, inverse) _____.

(b)   Find the slope of the curve at the following points:

A: _____, B: _____, C: _____

■   **TRUE-FALSE**

Circle T if the statement is true; F if it is false.

1. Graphs provide a visual representation of the relationship between two variables.   **T** F

2. If the straight line on a two-variable graph is upward sloping to the right, then there is a positive relationship between the two variables.   **T** F

3. A variable that changes as a consequence of a change in another variable is considered to be a dependent variable.   **T** F

4. *Ceteris paribus* means that the value of all other variables is set equal to zero.   **T** F

5. In the ratio for the calculation of the slope of a straight line, the horizontal change is divided by the vertical change.   T **F**

6. If the slope of the linear relationship between consumption (on the vertical axis) and income (on the horizontal axis) is 0.90, then it tells us that for every $1 increase in income there will be a $0.90 increase in consumption.   **T** F

7. The slope of a straight line is 0.   T **F**

8. If a linear equation is $y = 10 + 5x$, the vertical intercept is 10.   **T** F

9. A function with a constant slope becomes steeper as the independent variable increases.   **T** F

10. If the slope of a straight line on a two-variable (x, y) graph is 2 and the vertical intercept was 6, then if the value for x is 10, the value for y is 22.   **T** F

11. A slope of 4 for a straight line in a two-variable graph indicates that there is an inverse relationship between the two variables.   **T** F

12. If there is an inverse relation between price and quantity demanded, the graph of this function will be downward sloping.   **T** F

13. In the relationship between snowfall and demand for snowblowers, snowfall is the dependent variable.   T **F**

14. If the line tangent to a nonlinear curve is up-sloping, this indicates that the slope of the curve is positive at that point.   **T** F

15. If two points described by the (x, y) combinations of (13, 10) and (8, 20) lie on a straight line, then the slope is 2.   T **F**

16. On a graph relating the number of visitors to Canada's national parks to the price of admission to the parks, an increase in levels of rainfall would likely shift the curve to the left.   **T** F

■ **MULTIPLE-CHOICE**

Circle the letter that corresponds to the best answer.

1. If an increase in one variable is associated with a decrease in another variable, then we can conclude that the variables are:

(a) nonlinear
(b) directly related
(c) inversely related
(d) positively related

2. Economists:
(a) always put the independent variable on the vertical axis
(b) always put the independent variable on the horizontal axis
(c) sometimes put the dependent variable on the horizontal axis
(d) use only linear functions

3. If the curve in a two-variable graph shifts, what does this indicate?
(a) the two variables are positively related
(b) the two variables are negatively related
(c) the relationship between the two variables must be nonlinear
(d) some third variable must have changed

4. If y is plotted on the vertical axis and x is on the horizontal axis, which of the following is a false statement regarding the equation $y = 100 + 0.4 x$?
(a) the vertical intercept is 100
(b) the slope is 0.4
(c) when x is 20, y is 108
(d) the graph is nonlinear

5. If a straight line drawn tangent to a nonlinear curve has a slope of zero, then at the point of tangency the curve is:
(a) vertical
(b) horizontal
(c) upsloping
(d) downsloping

6. Consider a graph relating gasoline consumption (on the vertical axis) to population (on the horizontal axis). All of the following will affect gasoline consumption, but which one will **not** shift the curve?
(a) increased consumer incomes
(b) increased availability of public transit
(c) increased population
(d) more efficient gasoline engines

Answer questions 7 through 10 on the basis of the following diagram.

Price

80

60

40

20

0   100   200   300   400

Quantity Supplied

7. The graph indicates that price and quantity supplied are:
   (a) positively related
   (b) negatively related
   (c) indirectly related
   (d) nonlinear

8. The slope of the line is:
   (a) 0.15
   (b) 0.20
   (c) 1.50
   (d) 6.67

9. The vertical intercept is:
   (a) 0
   (b) 10
   (c) 20
   (d) 80

10. The linear equation for the function is:
   (a) $p = 20 + 0.15q$
   (b) $q = 20 + 6.67p$
   (c) $p = 20 + 6.67q$
   (d) $q = 20 + 0.15p$

11. Which of the following statements is true?
   (a) a vertical line has a slope of zero
   (b) a horizontal line has a slope of infinity
   (c) a nonlinear curve has different slopes at different points
   (d) an upsloping line has a negative slope

■ **DISCUSSION QUESTIONS**

1. Why do economists use graphs? Give two examples of a graph that illustrates the relationship between two economic variables.

2. If the vertical intercept increases in value but the slope of a straight line stays the same, what happens to the graph of the line? If the vertical intercept decreases in value, what will happen to the line?

3. When you know that variables X and Y are inversely related, what does this tell you about the slope of a line showing the relationship between these two variables? What do you know about the slope when X and Y are positively related?

4. Which variable is the dependent and which is the independent in the following economic statement: "A decrease in business taxes gave a big boost to investment spending."? How do you tell the difference between a dependent and independent variable when examining economic relationships?

5. Why is an assumption made that all other variables are held constant when we construct a two-variable graph of the price and quantity of a product?

6. If you were to plot a two-variable graph of the price of gasoline versus per capita use of gasoline, using the data for a variety of nations, what sort of graph would you expect, and what sort of relationship would this represent? In all likelihood the data points would be somewhat scattered, rather than consistently located along a precise line or curve. Give some reasons why the data points might be somewhat scattered.

7. How do the slopes of a straight line and a nonlinear curve differ? How do you estimate the slope of a nonlinear curve?

■ **ANSWERS**

FILL-IN QUESTIONS

1. (a) independent, dependent; dependent, independent; sometimes (b) scales, ranges (c) held constant; *ceteris paribus*

2. an inverse; direct; direct, inverse

3. vertical, horizontal; positive, negative; vertical intercept

4. (a) intercept, slope; (b) 22; 30; 14

5. straight line, nonlinear curve, tangent

PROBLEMS AND PROJECTS

1. (a) housing starts; mortgage interest rates; (d) down; inverse; (b) and (c):

2. (a) decrease, 10,000; (b) more, more, rightward; (c) less, fewer, leftward

3. (a) see table
(b) CD sales; performances; (d) 10; (e) 4; (f) CD Sales = 10 + 4 Performances; (c) see graph

Performances	CD Sales
0	10
5	30
10	50
15	70
20	90

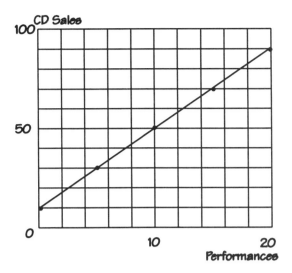

4. (a) see graph; (b) inversely; (c) see graph; (d) about $19,000; on the waterfront; (e) about -55; falls; about $5500. (f) Price = 19,000 − 55 Distance.

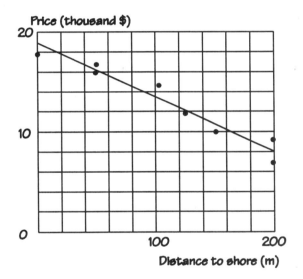

5. (a) 8; 17; inverse; (b) 3.0; 0; -2.1.

TRUE-FALSE

1. T	**2.** T	**3.** T	**4.** F	**5.** F	**6.** T
7. F	**8.** T	**9.** F	**10.** F	**11.** F	**12.** T
13. F	**14.** T	**15.** F	**16.** T		

MULTIPLE-CHOICE

1. (c)	**2.** (c)	**3.** (d)	**4.** (d)	**5.** (b)	**6.** (c)
7. (a)	**8.** (a)	**9.** (c)	**10.** (a)	**11.** (c)	

CHAPTER 2

The Economic Problem: Scarcity, Wants and Choices

The field of economics is based on two fundamental facts: our wants are unlimited or insatiable, and the resources available for satisfying these wants are limited, or scarce. Consequently, we face the economizing problem, or the need to make choices about how to allocate our scarce resources in order to satisfy our wants as much as possible. The main categories of these resources are land, capital, labour and entrepreneurial ability.

Given the condition of scarcity, satisfaction of wants can only be maximized if all resources are fully employed and used efficiently. Efficiency has two elements: productive efficiency is achieved if resources are used in the least cost manner, and allocative efficiency is achieved if resources are used to produce those goods society wants most.

The production possibilities table and the production possibilities curve are useful for illustrating many concepts in this chapter: scarcity, choice, the law of increasing opportunity cost, allocative and productive efficiency, unemployment and economic growth. The production possibilities model is both one of the most basic and one of the most important economic models that you will study.

Every economy is faced with the problem of scarcity and must find ways to allocate resources for the production of different goods and services. No two economies arrive at exactly the same system for addressing their fundamental economic problems. Between the extreme systems of pure (or *laissez-faire*) capitalism and the command economy are various mixed systems. Canada's economy is a mixed system that relies mainly on the market system. Some less developed countries operate as traditional economies.

The circular flow model illustrates how businesses and households interact in economies, such as Canada's, that rely on market systems. These economic agents interact in resource markets (where households sell and businesses buy), and in product markets (where households buy and businesses sell).

■ **CHECKLIST**

When you have studied this chapter, you should be able to:

☐ Write a definition of economics that incorporates the two basic facts on which economics is grounded.

☐ Explain why choices are necessary.

☐ Identify the four categories of economic resources and the type of income associated with each.

☐ Distinguish between full employment and full production and explain why both are necessary for efficient use of resources.

☐ Distinguish between productive efficiency and allocative efficiency.

☐ State the four assumptions made when a production possibilities table or curve is constructed.

☐ Construct a production possibilities curve when you are given the appropriate data.

☐ Define opportunity cost.

☐ Calculate opportunity cost from a production possibilities table or curve.

☐ State the law of increasing opportunity costs and present the economic rationale for this law.

☐ Explain why marginal benefit must equal marginal cost at the point of allocative efficiency.

☐ Use a production possibilities curve to illustrate situations of underemployment of resources, expanding resource supplies, and technological advance.

☐ Come up with your own examples of situations to illustrate with the production possibilities model.

☐   Describe some economic characteristics of pure capitalism, the command economy, mixed systems, and traditional economies.
☐   Draw the circular flow diagram complete with labels.

■   **CHAPTER OUTLINE**

1. The study of economics rests on two facts:
   (a)   Society's material wants are essentially unlimited and insatiable.
   (b)   Economic resources that are the means of producing goods and services are limited or scarce.

2. There are four categories of economic resources: land, capital, labour, and entrepreneurial ability. The payments received by those who provide the economy with these four resources are, respectively: rental income, interest income, wages, and profits.

3. Economics is the social science that studies how society's scarce resources are used (allocated) to attain the greatest possible fulfillment of society's unlimited wants. To achieve this goal society must use its resources efficiently, achieving both full employment and full production.
   (a)   Full employment occurs when all available resources are being used.
   (b)   Full production occurs when the resources are being used as efficiently as possible. Two kinds of efficiency must be achieved:
      (i)   productive efficiency — where any particular mix of goods and services is produced in the least-costly way.
      (ii)   allocative efficiency — where the resources are devoted to production of that particular mix of goods and services most wanted by society.

4. The production possibilities table, or a production possibilities curve, indicates the alternative combinations of goods and services an economy is capable of producing when it has achieved full employment and productive efficiency.

5. Four assumptions are made when constructing a production possibilities table or curve:
   (a)   full employment and productive efficiency
   (b)   fixed resources
   (c)   fixed technology
   (d)   two goods are being produced

6. Any point on the production possibilities curve is attainable. Society must choose one particular combination of goods (i.e., one attainable point). If the chosen combination provides the greatest satisfaction, the economy is said to be allocatively efficient.

7. Because points outside the curve are unattainable, no matter how desirable, the production possibilities curve illustrates the condition of scarcity.

8. Given full employment and full production, society can produce more of one good only by producing less of the other good. This foregone output is termed the opportunity cost and arises because resources must be shifted from producing one good to producing the other.

9. The marginal opportunity cost of producing additional units of a product usually increases as more of that product is produced. This generalization is the law of increasing opportunity costs.
   (a)   Opportunity costs are increasing because resources are not perfectly adaptable from one production use to another.
   (b)   Increasing opportunity costs cause the production possibilities curve to be concave (bowed out from the origin).

10. The amount of resources allocated to the production of a good is optimal where the marginal benefit received from the last unit produced equals its marginal cost. This marginal cost is the opportunity cost in terms of other goods that could have been produced with the same resources.
   (a)   The optimal production level corresponds to the point of allocative efficiency.
   (b)   Marginal benefit falls as more is produced.
   (c)   Marginal cost rises as more is produced.

11. Relaxing the assumptions underlying the production possibilities model gives some additional results.
   (a)   An economy experiencing unemployment and productive inefficiency is operating at a point inside its production possibilities curve, and is therefore failing to meet its productive potential.
   (b)   Economic growth occurs through improvements in technology or expansions in resource supplies, leading to an expanded production possibilities curve.
   (c)   Resource allocation decisions made today help to determine production possibilities in the future; the more capital or other future goods we produce today, the more the production possibilities curve will expand in the future.

12. Many contemporary and historical events and problems can be analyzed with the production possibilities model. These include: economic transition during war, discrimination, land-use controversies, labour force participation rates, African famine, and emerging technologies.

13. Different societies use different economic systems for addressing the fundamental economic problem of scarcity. These systems differ mainly in who owns the economic resources, and in the method used to coordinate and direct economic activity.

(a)   At one extreme is pure capitalism, which relies upon the private ownership of resources, the profit motive, and the market system.

(b)   At the other extreme, the command economy uses public ownership of its resources and makes decisions by central planning.

(c)   Most real-world economies — including Canada — lie between these two extremes and can be described as mixed systems.

(d)   Some less developed nations have traditional economies in which resource allocation and income distribution are directed by customs and traditions.

14. The circular flow model illustrates the interaction between businesses and households in resource markets and product markets. In exchange for resources that households supply to firms, firms pay incomes that households in turn use to demand goods and services produced by firms.

■ **TERMS AND CONCEPTS**

allocative efficiency	labour
capital	land
capital goods	law of increasing
circular flow model	opportunity costs
command economy	market systems
consumer goods	opportunity cost
economic growth	product market
economic resources	production
economic system	possibilities table
economizing problem	and curve
entrepreneurial ability	productive efficiency
factors of production	pure capitalism
full employment	resource market
full production	traditional economies
investment	utility

■ **HINTS AND TIPS**

1. The production possibilities curve is the first instance where graphing skills are needed. If you have serious difficulty mastering the graphical analysis you may have a general weakness in graphing that you should address immediately. Graphs are used constantly in the chapters that follow. Spend extra time on the graphical questions in this study guide, the relevant sections of the chapter, and with Appendix 1A of this study guide. Your instructor may also have additional resources or advice for you.

2. A movement from one point on the production possibilities curve to another point on the same curve indicates a change in what combination of products society *chooses*. In contrast, a shift of the whole production possibilities curve indicates a change in the *set of choices* available to society.

3. Many students initially confuse the coordinates of a point on the production possibilities curve with the intercepts of the curve. The intercepts indicate the *maximum*, or *potential*, production for each good (if all resources are dedicated to producing that good), whereas the coordinates of the production point show *actual* production for each good.

■ **FILL-IN QUESTIONS**

1. The two fundamental facts that provide the foundation of economics are:

(a)   Society's material wants are __unlimited__.

(b)   Society's   economic   resources   are __scarce__.

2. Consumer goods satisfy human wants (directly, indirectly) __directly__ and capital goods satisfy these wants __indirectly__.

3. Economic efficiency requires that there be both full __employment__ of resources and full __production__.

4. What four functions does an entrepreneur serve?

(a) __takes initiative__

(b) __makes decisions__

(c) __takes risks__

(d) __innovative__

5. Below is a production possibilities curve for tractors and suits of clothing.

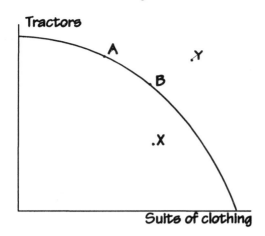

(a)   If the economy moves from point *A* to point *B*, it will produce (more, fewer) ___fewer___ tractors and (more, fewer) ___more___ suits.
(b)   If the economy is producing at point *X*, some of the resources of the economy are either ___unemployed___ or ___under employed___
(c)   If the economy is to produce at point *Y*, it must either expand its supply of ___resources___ or improve its ___efficiency___. technology

6. The quantity of other goods and services an economy must go without in order to produce more low-cost housing is the ___opportunity cost___ of producing the additional low-cost housing.

7. If Canada attempts to expand her apple industry, the opportunity cost per apple produced will tend to increase because resources are not completely ___adaptable___ to different uses. This is an example of the generalization known as the law of ___increasing opportunity costs___

8. For each situation below, indicate whether there is overallocation, underallocation, or optimal allocation of resources to the production of the good in question.
(a)   marginal benefit is greater than marginal cost at the current output level ___underallocation___
(b)   marginal benefit equals marginal cost at the current output level ___optimal___
(c)   marginal benefit is less than marginal cost at the current output level ___overallocation___

9. If some available resources are unemployed, productive efficiency (is, is not) ___is not___ met, and the economy is (inside, outside, on) ___inside___ its production possibilities curve.

10. Productive efficiency means that the ___least costly___ production techniques are used in the production of wanted goods and services.

11. Production is allocatively efficient when, given the distribution of resources, the economy produces that combination of goods ___wanted___ by society.

12. All points on the production possibilities curve are ___productively___ efficient but some points are not ___allocatively___ efficient.

13. Full production implies that two kinds of efficiency, ___productive___ and ___allocative___, are achieved.

14. Improvements in oil drilling technology would shift Canada's production possibilities curve to the (right, left) ___right___. Depletion of forest resources would shift our production possibilities curve to the ___left___.

15. In pure capitalism property resources are (publicly, privately) ___privately___ owned; in a command economy resources are ___publicly___ owned.

16. The term "laissez-faire" can be roughly translated as ___leave it be___ and means a ___passive___ role for government in the economy.   ___limited___

17. The Canadian economy leans toward the system known as ___pure capitalism___, but the government plays an active role in some sectors, so our system is considered a ___mixed___ system.

■   **PROBLEMS AND PROJECTS**

1. Match the resources on the left with the corresponding resource payments on the right.

labour	rental income
capital	profits
land	wages
entrepreneurial ability	interest income

2. Below is a list of resources. Indicate in the space to the right of each whether the resource is land (Ld), capital (K), labour (L), or entrepreneurial ability (EA).

(a) fishing grounds in the North Atlantic _____
(b) a farmer's inventory of wheat _____
(c) Maple Leaf Gardens in Toronto _____
(d) the work performed by the late Henry Ford _____
(e) Cavendish beach in Prince Edward Island _____
(f) Stelco's steel plant in Hamilton, Ontario ___
(g) the tasks accomplished in making the Apple Computer a commercial success _____
(h) the work done by a welder on an assembly line _____

3. An economy produces two products, timber (T) and fish (F), according to the production possibilities table below. The usual assumptions apply.

(a) Plot the data from the production possibilities table on the graph provided. Place T on the vertical axis and F on the horizontal axis.
(b) Can the economy produce 4 of F and 22 of T? _____ If not, why? _____ What is the maximum amount of T that can be produced in combination with 4 of F?_____

Combination	Timber	Fish
a	0	6
b	7	5
c	13	4
d	18	3
e	22	2
f	25	1
g	27	0

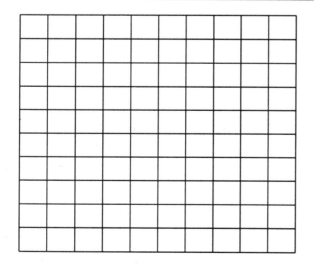

(c) If the economy is producing 2F and 15T, what problem is being experienced? _____
(d) Assuming that the economy is productively efficient, what is the opportunity cost of producing 1F instead of none? _____ What is the opportunity cost of the second unit of F? _____ And the third F? _____
(e) As the number of units of F produced increases, what is the trend in the number of units of T that must be given up to get the extra F? _____. Because of this trend, the shape of the production possibilities curve is _____ to the origin.

4. For each case below you are given an initial production possibilities curve between timber and fish. Sketch a new curve to show the result of the events given.

(a) The nation's supplies of labour and capital expand.

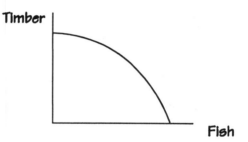

(b) New tree-planting techniques improve the success of reforestation operations.

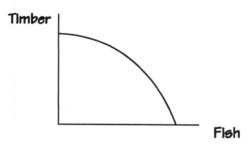

(c) An ecological disaster wipes out a large part of the fish stocks.

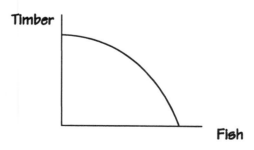

5. An economy is achieving full production, producing a combination of automobiles and food. Now a technological advance occurs which enables this economy to produce automobiles with fewer resources than previously. How is it possible for the society to consume more automobiles *and* more food as a result? Illustrate below using the production possibilities diagram.

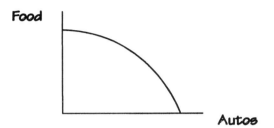

6. Below is a list of economic goods. Indicate in the space beside each whether the good is a consumer good (C), a capital good (K), or that it depends (D) upon who is using it and for what purpose.

(a)   a dairy cow   _____
(b)   a tractor   _____
(c)   a shopping mall parking lot _____
(d)   a telephone pole   _____
(e)   a telephone   _____
(f)   your refrigerator   _____
(g)   a refrigerator in a restaurant _____

7. A department store is installing video cameras to reduce shoplifting. The marginal costs and marginal benefits of additional cameras are:

Camera	MB ($/month)	MC ($/month)
1	300	100
2	250	125
3	160	150
4	50	175

(a)   If the store must choose one of the numbers shown in the table, the optimal number of cameras is _____.
(b)   How much better off is the store with the optimal number than with one camera fewer? ____
(c)   How much better off is the store with the optimal number than with one camera more? ____

■ **TRUE-FALSE**

Circle T if the statement is true, F if it is false.

1. If you must stand in line for six hours to get into a free concert by the Tragically Hip, there is no opportunity cost to you for seeing the concert.   T **F**

2. Money is a resource and is classified as "capital."   T **F**

3. A Canada Savings Bond is classified as a capital good.   T **F**

4. Profit is the reward paid to those who provide the economy with capital.   **T** F

5. The payment to Quebec Hydro for electricity service by a resident of Montreal is a rent payment.   T **F**

6. If the main opportunity cost of going to college is the foregone earnings, university enrolment should increase during periods of high unemployment, other factors remaining constant.   **T** F

7. The opportunity cost of producing wheat tends to increase as more wheat is produced because land less suited to its production must be reallocated from other uses.   **T** F

8. Drawing a production possibilities curve concave to the origin is the geometric way of stating the law of increasing opportunity costs.   **T** F

9. An economy cannot produce outside its production possibilities curve because resources are limited.   **T** F

10. The problem of scarcity is likely to be solved by technological progress.   T **F**

11. Every person in a society would prefer any point on the production possibilities curve to every point off the curve.   T **F**

12. An economy that is employing the least cost productive methods has achieved allocative efficiency.   T **F**

13. Given full employment and full production, it is not possible for an economy that can produce only two goods to increase its production of both.   **T F**

14. Economic growth can be represented by a shift of the production possibilities curve to the right.   **T F**

15. The more capital goods an economy produces today, the greater will be its ability to produce all goods in the future, *ceteris paribus.*   **T F**

16. Most nations use economic systems some-where between the extremes of pure capitalism and command economy.   **T F**

17. In a command economy most resources are privately owned and are allocated by the market system.   **T F**

18. In the circular flow model, households function on the demand side of the resource and product markets.   **T F**

■   **MULTIPLE-CHOICE**

Circle the letter that corresponds to the best answer.

1. In her role as an "innovator" an entrepreneur:
   (a)   makes basic policy decisions in a business firm
   (b)   combines factors of production to produce a good or service
   (c)   invents a new product or production proc-ess
   (d)   takes risks in the market place

2. An economy is efficient when it has achieved:
   (a)   full employment
   (b)   full production
   (c)   either full employment or full production
   (d)   both full employment and full production

3. When a production possibilities schedule is written (or a production possibilities curve is drawn), four assumptions are made. Which of the following is **not** one of those assumptions?
   (a)   only two goods are produced
   (b)   wants are unlimited
   (c)   the economy has both full employment and full production
   (d)   the quantities of all resources available to the economy are fixed

Answer the next four questions on the basis of the following diagram.

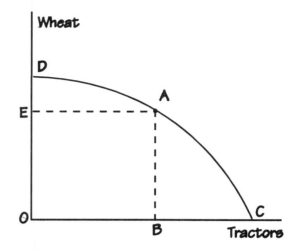

4. At point *A* on the production possibilities curve:
   (a)   less wheat than tractors is being produced
   (b)   fewer tractors than wheat are being pro-duced
   (c)   the economy is employing all its resources
   (d)   the economy is not employing all its re-sources

5. The opportunity cost of producing *0B* of tractors is:
   (a)   *0D* of wheat
   (b)   *0E* of wheat
   (c)   *ED* of wheat
   (d)   *0C* of tractors

6. If there occurred a technological improvement in the production of tractors but not wheat:
   (a)   point *D* would remain fixed and point *C* shift to the left
   (b)   point *C* would remain fixed and point *D* shift upward
   (c)   point *D* would remain fixed and point *C* shift to the right
   (d)   point *C* would remain fixed and point *D* shift inward

7. From one point to another along the same pro-duction possibilities curve:
   (a)   resources remain fixed but are reallocated between the production of the two goods
   (b)   resources are increased and are reallo-cated between the two goods

(c) resources are increased and production of both goods increased

(d) idle resources are put to work to increase the production of one good

8. If opportunity costs are constant, instead of increasing, the production possibilities curve will be:
  (a) concave to the origin
  (b) convex to the origin
  (c) a downward sloping straight line
  (d) parallel to the horizontal axis

9. Which of the following would cause a nation's production possibilities curve to shift inward toward the origin?
  (a) more people in the labour force
  (b) increased international trade
  (c) rising unemployment of workers
  (d) not replacing the capital stock as it wears out

10. Which of the following will slow down the rate at which Canada's production possibilities curve shifts rightward?
  (a) increasing rate of technological change
  (b) increased immigration
  (c) decrease in the birth rate
  (d) decreased impediments to the interprovincial flow of goods and services

11. The opportunity cost of providing a governmentally financed stadium for a city's baseball team is:
  (a) the interest on the money borrowed to finance the stadium
  (b) the future tax increase the public will be forced to bear to pay for the stadium
  (c) the other goods and services that must be sacrificed so that resources can be used for stadium construction
  (d) there is no opportunity cost since Ottawa will finance the stadium under a regional development program

12. Private ownership of property resources, use of the market system to direct and coordinate economic activity, and the presence of the profit motive are characteristic of:
  (a) pure capitalism
  (b) the command economy
  (c) market socialism
  (d) the traditional economy

13. An economy with some public ownership and numerous governmental regulations together with an emphasis on private ownership, profit motive, and market determined prices can be described as a:
  (a) pure capitalistic system
  (b) market socialism
  (c) mixed system
  (d) command economy

14. Productive efficiency is attained when:
  (a) resources are all employed
  (b) output is produced at least possible cost
  (c) there is no government involvement in the economy
  (d) the production possibilities curve is concave

15. The term "laissez-faire" refers to:
  (a) the absence of government intervention in markets
  (b) the absence of monopoly
  (c) the absence of competition in markets
  (d) efficient use of employed resources

■ **DISCUSSION QUESTIONS**

1. Explain what is meant by the "economizing problem." Why are resources scarce?

2. When is a society economically efficient? What is meant by "full production," and how does it differ from "full employment"?

3. What four assumptions are made in drawing a production possibilities curve? How do technological progress and an increased supply of resources in the economy affect the curve?

4. Why cannot an economist determine which combination in the production possibilities table is "best"? What determines the optimum product-mix?

5. What is opportunity cost? What is the law of increasing opportunity costs? Why do opportunity costs increase?

6. Would the economic problem disappear if the affluent countries, including Canada, offered to pay more for the products of the Third World countries? Explain.

7. During the Cold War, Russia seemed to be quite competitive with the United States in terms of military might, despite the fact that Russia's overall production capabilities were much lower than America's. How can these observations be intepreted using production possibility curves for the two nations?

8. If resources in an economy are fully employed, what would be the effect on living standards if the government decided to increase the output of goods for the future? Explain using the production possibilities curve.

9. Explain why you agree or disagree with the statement: "The opportunity cost of allocating large numbers of people to clean up Ontario's lakes during a recession is different from the opportunity cost during a period of full employment."

10. Explain the difference between productive and allocative efficiency.

11. How is the "what to produce" question solved under the pure capitalistic system as compared to a mixed system?

12. What are the roles of households and of businesses in the resource market and the product market?

■ **ANSWERS**

FILL-IN QUESTIONS

1. (a) unlimited; (b) scarce (or limited)

2. directly; indirectly

3. employment, production

4. takes initiative, makes business-policy decisions, innovates, bears risk

5. (a) fewer, more; (b) unemployed, underemployed; (c) resources, technology

6. opportunity cost

7. adaptable; increasing opportunity costs

8. (a) underallocation; (b) optimal allocation; (c) overallocation

9. is not; inside

10. least costly

11. most wanted

12. productively, allocatively

13. productive, allocative

14. right; left

15. privately, publicly

16. let it be, limited

17. pure capitalism; mixed

PROBLEMS AND PROJECTS

1. labour: wages; capital: interest income; land: rental income; entrepreneurial ability: profits

2. (a) Ld; (b) K; (c) K; (d) EA; (e) Ld; (f) K; (g) EA; (h) L

3. (b) No; this combination lies outside the production possibilities curve; 13 T; (c) productive inefficiency (unemployment or underemployment); (d) 2T, 3T, 4T; (e) increasing, concave

4. (a) Both T and F intercepts shift out; (b) T intercept shifts out, F intercept is unchanged; (c) F intercept shifts in, T intercept is unchanged

5. More automobiles can now be produced with a given amount of resources, so the automobiles intercept shifts out. By moving some resources from autos to food, the society can produce more food and more automobiles. Show this on your diagram by shifting production possibilities curve, then showing a movement to a new point that is northeast of the original point.

6. (a) K, (b) K, (c) K, (d) K, (e) D, (f) C, (g) K

7. (a) 3 cameras; (b) $10/month is the net benefit for the 3rd camera; (c) $125/month is the net loss for the 4th camera

TRUE-FALSE

1. F	2. F	3. F	4. F	5. F	6. T
7. T	8. T	9. T	10. F	11. F	12. F
13. T	14. T	15. T	16. T	17. F	18. F

MULTIPLE-CHOICE

1. (c) **2.** (d) **3.** (b) **4.** (c) **5.** (c) **6.** (c)
7. (a) **8.** (c) **9.** (d) **10.** (c) **11.** (c) **12.** (a)
13. (c) **14.** (b) **15.** (a)

CHAPTER 3

Overview of the Market System

Chapter 2 outlined the central economic problem faced by every economy. The nature of the problem is reflected in five fundamental questions: (1) how much of society's resources should be used; (2) what is to be produced; (3) how is that output to be produced; (4) who is to receive the output; and (5) can the system adapt to change? Chapter 3 explains how these questions are answered within a market system.

The market system or capitalism has six defining characteristics: the institution of private property; freedom of choice for consumers and freedom of enterprise for suppliers; the pursuit of self-interest; competition; coordination through markets and prices; and a very limited role for government. Households exercise choice over the supply of the resources that they own, and then spend the incomes from these resources on those goods and services that will best satisfy their wants. Firms employ resources to produce goods that seem to them likely to yield the greatest profit. The profits depend on producing goods that consumers are willing to pay for, and on producing these goods using the most efficient techniques. These demand and supply decisions determine prices in the market economy. The prices provide incentives and signals to consumers and producers, thereby providing a coordinating mechanism that determines the allocation of society's resources.

Consumers and producers have the freedom to follow their self-interest as they exchange resources, money, and goods over which they have property rights. Where these interactions occur in competitive markets with large numbers of independent buyers and sellers, and where there is easy entry and exit, no individual will have significant power or control in the market. The discipline of competition ensures that self-interested choices made by individual consumers or producers are also in the interests of society — as though individuals are guided by an "invisible hand" to serve the public interest. Accordingly, the role of government is quite limited.

All modern economies have three other characteristics that increase dramatically the amount of goods and services that modern economies can produce: (1) extensive use of advanced technology and capital goods; (2) specialization in production; and (3) use of money. Specialization stimulates the creation of new technology and capital goods, and creates the need for a monetary system that can facilitate exchanges by eliminating the reliance on barter.

The chapter closes with a thumbnail sketch of the structure of the Canadian economy and its evolution over time. Over recent decades the tertiary sector (or service sector) has been growing as a share of Canada's employment and output while the primary sector (e.g., agriculture, forestry, mining) and secondary sector (e.g., manufacturing, construction, transportation) have been declining. Many of our industries are highly concentrated and foreign ownership is prevalent in many sectors (e.g., manufacturing).

■ CHECKLIST

When you have studied this chapter, you should be able to:

☐ Identify the six key institutional characteristics of the market system of capitalism and discuss the importance of each.
☐ Identify and explain the three other characteristics of all modern economies.

26

☐ List the Five Fundamental Questions every economy must answer and explain how the answers are determined in a market economy.
☐ Explain what is meant by the "invisible hand."
☐ Explain the case for the market system.
☐ Explain how the use of money facilitates trade.
☐ List some of the main structural features of the Canadian economy.

■ **CHAPTER OUTLINE**

1. The market system, or capitalism, is an economic system having six defining tenets: private property, freedom of enterprise and choice, self-interest as the dominant motive, competition, reliance on self-regulating markets, and a limited role for government.

(a) Under private property, resources are owned by households and firms, and resource owners are free to obtain, control, employ and dispose of their property as they see fit.

(b) Freedom of enterprise means that firms are free to choose what resources to employ, how to use the resources, what goods to produce, and where to sell these goods. Freedom of choice means that consumers can spend their incomes on whatever goods they want, and resource owners can supply their land, labour, etc. as they see fit.

(c) Self-interest is assumed to be the driving force behind decisions. For example, consumers try to maximize their satisfaction, and entrepreneurs try to maximize their firms' profits.

(d) Because each market has many independent buyers and sellers, all of whom have freedom to enter or exit the market, competition is pervasive and economic power is diffused rather than concentrated in the hands of a few.

(e) In the market system signals and incentives are conveyed through prices. Because buyers and sellers respond spontaneously to price changes, resource allocation is coordinated in a decentralized and spontaneous fashion.

(f) Markets create a sufficiently self-regulating, self-adjusting and efficient allocation of resources that there is little economic role for the government to play.

2. All modern economies, not just market economies, have three other main characteristics:

(a) There is extensive use of state-of-the-art technologies and complex capital goods (e.g., tools, machinery, computers, factories). Effi-ciency is improved through roundabout production whereby capital goods are produced in order to produce more efficiently the goods that consumers ultimately want.

(b) Specialization prevails at all levels. Division of labour among individual workers means that each person produces only a very narrow range of goods, and relies on the existence of markets and prices to be able to trade for goods that others have specialized in producing. The same is true of regions and nations. Specialization creates efficiencies by making use of ability differences, by allowing learning by doing, and by saving time.

(c) In order to overcome the inconvenience and transactions costs of organizing barter transactions, some system of money emerges in every modern society. It is impossible to sustain a highly specialized economy without some form of money to facilitate exchanges. Anything that is generally accepted by sellers in exchange for goods and services is considered money.

3. The competitive market system functions with two primary groups of decision makers: households (consumers) and firms (businesses). Households are the ultimate suppliers of resources, and firms are the suppliers of goods purchased by consumers with the incomes from their resources. The market system communicates the decisions of millions of individual households and firms, and coordinates these decisions in a coherent allocation of resources.

4. Faced with unlimited wants and scarce resources, every economy must find answers for the Five Fundamental Questions: how much of our society's resources to use; what goods and services to produce; how to produce that output; who is to receive the output; and how the system can adapt to change.

5. The market system, or price mechanism, provides answers to the last four Fundamental Questions.

(a) Consumer demands for products and firms' desires for profits determine what and how much of each good is produced, and at what price. Those goods that can be produced at a profit will be produced, and those whose production would lead to loss will not be produced.

(b) The desires of businesses to maximize profits motivates them to utilize production technologies that economize on resources, especially those resources that are relatively expensive.

(c)   Goods are distributed to consumers on the basis of their willingness and ability to pay the existing market prices for these goods. Consumers' incomes are determined by the quantities and prices of the labour, property and other resources they supply in resource markets. The market system does not guarantee an equitable distribution of income and consumer goods.

(d)   Changes in consumer tastes, technology, and resource supplies are signaled by price changes that give households and firms incentives to adjust their choices; thus the economy spontaneously accommodates changes.

6. Competition in the economy compels firms and households acting in their own self-interest to promote (as though led by an "invisible hand") the interests of society as a whole. This concept was first noted by Adam Smith in his 1776 book, *The Wealth of Nations*.

7. The market system has a number of merits. The two economic virtues of the system are the efficient allocation of resources and the incentives for productive efficiency in the use of resources. The personal freedom allowed in a market economy is its major noneconomic virtue.

8. Any economy can be divided into three major sectors: primary, secondary, and tertiary (service sector). In Canada the tertiary sector (including wholesale, retail, services, finance, public administration, etc.) is a growing share of the economy; whereas the primary sector (including agriculture, forestry, fishing, mining, and oil) and the secondary sector (including manufacturing, construction, transportation, and utilities) are shrinking.

9. The Canadian economy is also characterized by high levels of foreign ownership and control and by high levels of concentration in the sense that many markets are dominated by only a few producers.

■   **TERMS AND CONCEPTS**

barter	Five Fundamental
competition	Questions
consumer sovereignty	freedom of choice
division of labour	freedom of enterprise
dollar votes	"invisible hand"
economic costs	medium of exchange

money	self-interest
private property	specialization
roundabout production	

■   **HINTS AND TIPS**

1.   The crux of the market system is the dual role played by prices: to provide both signals and incentives. An increase in the price of a product signals that for some reason this product has become relatively more scarce. The price increase gives consumers the incentive to reduce their consumption (as they ration their limited incomes) and gives producers the incentive to produce more (in order to maximize profits).

2.   Think about what an amazing thing it is that a market system works at all! How can millions of independent decisions by consumers and producers possibly add up to a coherent allocation of resources that virtually guarantees that your neighbourhood store will have milk and bread every time you come to buy them? The system coordinates resource allocation in a spontaneous and decentralized manner. Nobody is in control of the whole economy; nobody has the responsibility to coordinate the allocation of resources. Yet, as if guided by an "invisible hand" the economy is coordinated.

■   **FILL-IN QUESTIONS**

1. The ownership of resources by private individuals and organizations is the institution of _____.

2. Under capitalism private businesses have freedom of _____ and consumers have freedom of _____.

3. Competition is present if two conditions prevail; these two conditions are

(a)   _____

(b)   _____

4. In a market system, an increase in the scarcity of a product is signaled by a(n) (increase, decrease) _____ in the _____ of the product. This change gives consumers and producers the incentive to revise their choices in furthering their own _____.

5. The concept of the pure market system as a self-regulating economy precludes any significant role for _____.

6. List the six characteristics of the market system.
(a) _____
(b) _____
(c) _____
(d) _____
(e) _____
(f) _____

7. If Robinson Crusoe spends time building a canoe to enable him to catch more fish, he is engaging in _____ production.

8. Economic units seeking to further their own self-interest and operating within the capitalistic system will simultaneously, as though directed by an _____, promote the _____ interest.

9. Firms are forced by competition to use the _____ production methods.

10. List the Five Fundamental Questions to which every society must respond.
(a) _____
(b) _____
(c) _____
(d) _____
(e) _____

11. Division of labour means essentially the same as _____ of labour.

12. Three ways in which division of labour enhances a society's output are:
(a) _____
(b) _____
(c) _____

13. In an economy where specialization of labour is extensive, individuals are extremely (independent, interdependent) _____, and in order to benefit from the specialization these individuals must _____ with each other.

14. A system of trading goods directly for goods is known as _____.

15. An economy based on specialization and trade cannot operate efficiently without a system of _____.

16. International specialization and exchange requires a system of exchanging _____.

17. Exchange by barter requires a _____ of wants.

18. For an item to serve as money it simply needs to be _____ by sellers in exchange for goods and services.

19. The economist who first wrote about the "invisible hand" was _____.

■ **PROBLEMS AND PROJECTS**

1. Consider a college with fewer parking spots than students who would like to drive to school. At present the college offers free parking on a first-come-first-served basis. They are considering charging for parking, setting the fee high enough that there would always be a few spots open.
(a) Why would the system of charging for parking change the allocation of parking spots?
(b) Why would some students be in favour of the change while others would not?
(c) What socially beneficial incentives would be created by the proposed parking fee?

2. Suppose that a firm can produce 100 units of product X by combining labour, land, capital, and entrepreneurial ability in three different ways as shown in the table below. It can hire labour at $2 per unit, land at $3 per unit, capital at $5 per unit, and entrepreneurial ability at $10 per unit.

Resource	Method		
	1	2	3
Labour	8	13	10
Land	4	3	3
Capital	4	2	4
Entrepreneurial ability	1	1	1

(a) Which is the least cost method of producing 100 units of X? _____
(b) If the wage for labour rises from $2 to $3 per unit, which is the least cost method to produce 100 units of X? _____
(c) If the firm produces 100 X, the increase in the wage rate gives the firm the incentive to (increase, decrease) its use of labour from _____ units to _____ units.

3. The grade that you earn in your economics course this term will be the product of your work, and you probably consider this grade your private property.

(a) How would your incentives change if you did not have the right to communicate your grade to potential employers or other colleges or universities?

(b) How would your incentives change if you had to share your "output" on exams with your classmates (i.e., everybody is awarded the class average grade)?

(c) Are there any reasons for restricting your property rights in your grade? Should you be able to transfer your grade to somebody else?

■ **TRUE-FALSE**

Circle T if the statement is true, F if it is false.

1. The Canadian economy can be classified as "pure capitalism." **T F**

2. Self-interest and selfishness are the same thing. **T F**

3. In the real world there are usually legal limits placed on the rights of private property. **T F**

4. In a competitive market every seller has significant influence over the market price. **T F**

5. In the market system prices are set by a government agency. **T F**

6. If property rights did not exist for intellectual property, individuals would have less incentive to create music, books and computer programs. **T F**

7. In the market system prices serve as signals for the allocation of resources. **T F**

8. The market system promotes productive efficiency. **T F**

9. Because the market system is efficient in resource use, it follows that every individual is better off under this form of economic organization than any alternative. **T F**

10. The distribution of output in the market economy depends upon the distribution of resources. **T F**

11. In a purely capitalist economy, firms make the ultimate decisions about what to produce. **T F**

12. In a market system competition serves to regulate self-interest for the benefit of society. **T F**

13. The employment of capital to produce goods and services implies that there will be roundabout production. **T F**

14. Specialization allows for a more efficient use of resources. **T F**

15. Money is a device for facilitating the exchange of goods and services. **T F**

16. "Coincidence of wants" means that two persons desire to acquire the same good or service. **T F**

17. The market system ensures that all households will receive an equitable share of the economy's output of goods and services. **T F**

18. The "invisible hand" refers to government intervention in the market. **T F**

■ **MULTIPLE-CHOICE**

Choose the letter that corresponds to the best answer.

1. Which of the following is not one of the six characteristics of capitalism?
 (a) competition
 (b) freedom of enterprise and choice
 (c) self-interest
 (d) central economic planning

2. To decide how to use its scarce resources to satisfy human wants capitalism relies on:
 (a) central planning
 (b) roundabout production
 (c) a price system together with the profit motive
 (d) the coincidence of wants

3. The "invisible hand" is used to explain how in the market system:
 (a) property rights are defined
 (b) resources are allocated
 (c) the self-interest of individuals is harnessed for the benefit of society
 (d) allocative efficiency is achieved

4. In the market system a decrease in the demand for a good should result in all but:

(a)   an increase in the price of the resources producing the good

(b)   a decrease in the profitability of producing the good

(c)   a movement of resources out of the production of the good

(d)   a decrease in the price of the good

5. Roundabout production refers to:

(a)   the use of resources by government

(b)   the use of resources to produce consumer goods directly

(c)   the use of resources to produce services

(d)   the use of resources to produce capital goods that in turn are used to produce other goods

6. Which of the following is **not** an example of a capital good?

(a)   money

(b)   a warehouse

(c)   a forklift

(d)   a computer

7. The basis for competition entails all but:

(a)   the presence of a large number of buyers

(b)   the freedom to enter or leave a particular market

(c)   the presence of a large number of sellers

(d)   a fair price determined by a public agency

8. Which of the following is among the reasons that specialization in production increases efficiency?

(a)   trade is rendered unnecessary

(b)   barter transactions are rendered unnecessary

(c)   individuals usually possess very similar resources and talents

(d)   experience or "learning-by-doing" results in increased output

9. Barter:

(a)   is the main method of trading in capitalist economies

(b)   is the main method of trading in socialist economies

(c)   is the exchange of a good for money

(d)   is the exchange of a good for a good

10. Which of the following is **not** a necessary consequence of specialization?

(a)   people will barter

(b)   people will engage in trade

(c)   people will be dependent upon each other

(d)   people will produce more of one thing than they would produce in the absence of specialization

11. Which of the following is **not** a disadvantage of specialization?

(a)   increased interdependence among economic units

(b)   the performance of repetitive and boring tasks

(c)   increased production

(d)   need for exchange

12. Which of the following is **not** a virtue of the market system?

(a)   allocative efficiency

(b)   productive efficiency

(c)   equitable distribution of income

(d)   ability to adapt to changes in tastes, technologies and resource supplies

13. The term "division of labour" means the same as:

(a)   specialization

(b)   barter

(c)   economies of scale

(d)   coincidence of wants

14. All modern economies have the following characteristics except for:

(a)   specialization

(b)   limited government interference

(c)   use of money

(d)   roundabout means of production

■   **DISCUSSION QUESTIONS**

1. List the Five Fundamental Questions that all economies must answer. Which of these questions does the market system answer, and how so?

2. What property rights does the owner of a motor vehicle have? What restrictions or limits are there on those rights, and why do these restrictions exist? Do these restrictions increase or decrease the value of owning a vehicle?

3. How does the pursuit of self-interest by all economic units in the market system model ultimately benefit society? Give an example of a choice you make that is in your self-interest, but not selfish.

4. If the economic decisions in a capitalist economy are not made by a central authority, how are they made?

5. At one time the world price of oil was expected to hit $100 a barrel by the 1990s. If so, the Canadian economy would presumably have allocated more resources to oil production. How would market forces have produced such a result? How would market forces have changed the gasoline consumption habits of Canadian households?

6. If housing prices are rising in Vancouver and falling in the neighbouring municipality of Burnaby, what does this signal? What incentives do these price changes create?

7. What are the advantages of "indirect" or "roundabout" production?

8. In order for a market to be competitive, why must there be many buyers and many sellers? What might be some consequences of a lack of large numbers of buyers or sellers?

9. How does an economy benefit from specialization and division of labour?

10. What are the disadvantages of barter, and how does money overcome these disadvantages?

■ ANSWERS

FILL-IN QUESTIONS

1. private property

2. enterprise, choice

3. large number of buyers and sellers; freedom of exit from and entry to any market

4. increase, price, self-interest

5. government

6. private property; freedom of enterprise and choice; self-interest; markets and prices; competition; limited government

7. roundabout

8. "invisible hand," social (or public)

9. least cost

10. How much of society's resources should be used?; What goods and services should be produced?; How is the output to be produced?; Who is to receive the output?; How can the system adapt to change?

11. specialization

12. making use of ability differences, allowing learning by doing, saving time

13. interdependent, trade

14. barter

15. money

16. currencies

17. coincidence

18. accepted

19. Adam Smith

PROBLEMS AND PROJECTS

1.   (a) Some students currently willing and able to arrive early or to spend time hunting for a spot may be unwilling to pay for a spot, whereas others may be willing and able to pay; (b) differences in availability of money and time; (c) students who place a low value on parking would have incentive to walk, bus, carpool; firms seeking profit would have more incentive to provide near campus parking for a fee.

2.   (a) 2 at $55; (b) 1 at $66; (c) decrease, 13, 8.

3.   (a) If you could not use a good grade to help you get jobs, scholarships, etc. you may have less incentive to learn the course material; (b) If you get a better mark on an exam, your share of that mark would be very small, so you would have less incentive to learn the course material; (c) Restricted property rights in grades are probably justified because if students could sell their grades to other people then good grades would no longer indicate what they are supposed to, and would therefore cease to have value.

TRUE-FALSE

1. F	**2.** F	**3.** T	**4.** F	**5.** F	**6.** T
7. T	**8.** T	**9.** F	**10.** T	**11.** F	**12.** T
13. T	**14.** T	**15.** T	**16.** F	**17.** F	**18.** F

MULTIPLE-CHOICE

1. (d)	**2.** (c)	**3.** (c)	**4.** (a)	**5.** (d)	**6.** (a)
7. (d)	**8.** (d)	**9.** (d)	**10.** (a)	**11.** (c)	**12.** (c)
13. (a)	**14.** (b)				

CHAPTER 4

Demand and Supply

This chapter presents the most important tool of economic analysis: the demand and supply model. This model is used to analyze how various events affect the market price and quantities traded in competitive markets. Although many real world markets do not exactly correspond to the assumptions of the basic demand and supply model, the model is widely used because its predictions have proven to be correct in a wide variety of situations.

Demand is an inverse relationship between price and quantity demanded, *ceteris paribus*. Supply is a positive relationship between price and quantity supplied, *ceteris paribus*. The demand and supply relationships can be expressed in the form of algebraic equations, schedules in tables, or in graphs. Given the demand and the supply, there is only one price at which the quantity demanded by consumers exactly equals the quantity supplied by sellers. This is the equilibrium price, or market clearing price. The equilibrium quantity is the quantity demanded and supplied at the equilibrium price.

Starting from an equilibrium, a change in any demand or supply determinant will shift the demand or supply curve, and throw the market out of equilibrium — creating either a shortage or a surplus. To eliminate the shortage (or surplus) the price must rise (or fall) to restore the balance between how much consumers are willing and able to buy and producers are willing and able to sell.

In order to analyze how an event affects the market equilibrium one must first determine whether it is supply or demand that is directly affected by the event. Secondly, one must determine whether the affected curve increases or decreases. From there it is a simple matter to decide the direction of change for the equilibrium price and quantity.

Mastery of the supply and demand model requires clear understanding of the definitions of demand and supply, and of the crucial distinctions between "demand" and "quantity demanded" and between "supply" and "quantity supplied." Practice with the graphical model of demand and supply will greatly help clarify these concepts.

- **CHECKLIST**

When you have studied this chapter, you should be able to:

☐ Define a market.
☐ Define demand and state the law of demand.
☐ Give reasons for the inverse relation between price and quantity demanded.
☐ Graph a demand curve from a demand schedule.
☐ Derive a market demand from individual demands.
☐ List the major determinants of demand and explain how each one shifts the demand curve.
☐ Distinguish between a change in demand and a change in quantity demanded.
☐ Define supply and state the law of supply.
☐ Graph a supply curve from a supply schedule.
☐ List the major determinants of supply and explain how each one shifts the supply curve.
☐ Distinguish between a change in supply and a change in quantity supplied.
☐ Explain the concept of equilibrium.
☐ Determine, when you are given data on demand and supply, what the equilibrium price and quantity will be.

☐ Determine, when you are given data on demand and supply, how much shortage or surplus will exist at nonequilibrium prices.

☐ Explain, when there is a shortage or a surplus, the actions of consumers and business firms that restore price to an equilibrium.

☐ Predict the effects of changes in demand and supply on equilibrium price and equilibrium quantity.

☐ Explain the meaning of the rationing function of prices.

■ CHAPTER OUTLINE

1. A market is any institution or mechanism that brings together the buyers and the sellers of a particular good or service. In this chapter it is assumed that markets are highly competitive.

2. Demand is the relationship between the price of a product and the amount of that product the consumer is willing and able to purchase in a specific time period. The relationship can be expressed in a table, a graph, or an equation.

3. The law of demand states that, other things being equal, as price falls, the quantity demanded rises. That is, there is an inverse relationship between price and quantity demanded.

4. There is plenty of strong evidence for the law of demand, but there are also several analytical reasons:

(a) If consumption is subject to *diminishing marginal utility* consumers are willing to buy additional units of a good only if the price is reduced.

(b) When price falls there is an *income effect*: the consumer's overall buying power increases so the consumer buys more of the good.

(c) When price falls there is a *substitution effect*: the consumer is motivated to buy more of the good that is now relatively less expensive instead of other goods for which it is a substitute.

5. The demand curve is a graphic representation of demand and the law of demand.

(a) The graph has price on the vertical axis, and quantity demanded on the horizontal axis.

(b) A change in price leads to a movement along the demand curve. This is termed a change in quantity demanded.

6. The market demand is derived by "adding up" the individual consumer demands. At each price,

the market quantity demanded is the sum of the quantities demanded for all individual consumers in the market. The law of demand applies to both individual and market demand curves.

7. The price determines the quantity demanded for a good, but factors other than price determine the location of the whole demand curve. These factors are known as the demand determinants:

(a) tastes and preferences of consumers;

(b) the number of consumers in the market;

(c) the money incomes of consumers;

(d) the prices of related goods (substitutes and complements);

(e) consumer expectations (regarding future prices and incomes).

8. A change in any one of the determinants will shift demand to the left (a decrease) or the right (an increase), creating an entirely different demand curve. This is termed a change in demand.

(a) If preferences shift in favour of a good, its demand will increase.

(b) If the number of consumers of a good increases, its demand will increase.

(c) If consumer incomes increase, demand will increase if the good is normal (or superior), and demand will decrease if the good is inferior.

(d) If an increase in the price of one good causes the demand for another good to decrease, the two goods are complements; if the price increase causes demand for the other good to increase, the two goods are substitutes.

(e) If consumers expect higher prices or incomes in the future they may increase their demand now.

9. A change in demand and a change in the quantity demanded are not the same thing. The difference is most obvious on a graph. A change in the price of the good itself causes a change in the quantity demanded, which on the graph is a movement to a different point on the same demand curve.

10. Supply is the relationship between the price of a product and the amount of that product that suppliers will offer to sell in a specific time period. The law of supply states that, other things being equal, as price rises, the quantity supplied rises. That is, there is a positive relationship between price and quantity supplied. The quantity supplied rises with price because the supplier can profitably produce more output at a higher price.

11. The supply curve is a graphic representation of supply and the law of supply.

   (a)   The graph has price on the vertical axis, and quantity supplied on the horizontal axis.

   (b)   A change in price leads to a movement along the supply curve. This is termed a change in quantity supplied.

12. The determinants of supply are:

   (a)   resource prices;

   (b)   production technology;

   (c)   taxes and subsidies;

   (d)   prices of other goods;

   (e)   expectations;

   (f)   number of sellers.

13. A change in any of the determinants will shift supply to the left (a decrease) or the right (an increase), creating an entirely different supply curve. This is termed a change in supply.

   (a)   If prices of production resources fall, supply will increase.

   (b)   A technological change will improve the efficiency of production and increase the supply.

   (c)   A new tax will raise the producer's costs and reduce the supply; a new subsidy will increase the supply.

   (d)   Producers may reallocate their resources if the price of a related good changes: we cannot generalize about the direction of change in supply.

   (e)   It is also difficult to generalize about how a change in expectations about the future price will change today's supply.

   (f)   An increase in the number of suppliers will increase the supply.

14. A change in supply and a change in the quantity supplied are not the same thing. The difference is most obvious on a graph. A change in the price of the good itself causes a change in the quantity supplied, which on the graph is a movement to a different point on the same supply curve.

15. The market-clearing or equilibrium price of a good is that price at which quantity demanded and quantity supplied are equal; the equilibrium quantity is equal to the quantity demanded and supplied at the equilibrium price.

   (a)   If price is above the equilibrium, there is a surplus (quantity demanded is less than quantity supplied), which will cause the price to fall.

   (b)   If price is below the equilibrium, there is a shortage (quantity demanded is greater than quantity supplied) which will cause the price to rise.

   (c)   The only sustainable price is the equilibrium price.

   (d)   The rationing function of price is the elimination of shortages and surpluses in a market.

16. Any change in a determinant of demand or supply will cause the curve to shift, and result in a new equilibrium price and quantity.

   (a)   Most changes shift only one of the two curves.

   (b)   When there is a change in demand, and the supply is unchanged, equilibrium price and quantity change in the same direction as the change in demand.

   (c)   When there is a change in supply, and the demand is unchanged, quantity moves in the same direction as the supply change, but equilibrium price moves in the opposite direction.

   (d)   In situations where both supply and demand change, both curves will shift; either the direction of price change or quantity change will be predictable, the other will be indeterminate.

■   **TERMS AND CONCEPTS**

change in demand (or supply) versus change in the quantity demanded (or supplied)	**income and substitution effects**
complementary goods	**inferior good**
demand	**law of demand**
demand curve	**law of supply**
demand schedule	**market**
determinants of demand	**normal good**
determinants of supply	**rationing function of prices**
diminishing marginal utility	**shortage**
equilibrium price and quantity	**substitute goods**
	supply
	supply curve
	supply schedule
	surplus

■   **HINTS AND TIPS**

   1. This chapter is the most important one in the book. Be sure to spend extra time on it, and to return to it for review of the fundamentals if you run into difficulties when studying later chapters.

2. You have not mastered the chapter until you can clearly distinguish between a change in demand and a change in quantity demanded; the same for supply vs. quantity supplied. You should be able to articulate the difference verbally, and graphically.

3. More than any of the previous chapters, this chapter requires active practice. Pick up your pencil and draw graphs. Begin by plotting demand and supply schedules onto graphs. Study carefully the examples in the text and study guide to learn the appropriate labels for such graphs. Once you are confident of working with graphs with concrete numbers, go to the next step of drawing abstract graphs where numbers are implied on the axes, but not explicitly given.

4. If algebraic work with demand and supply is relevant in the economics course you are studying, please look at the Appendix to Chapter 4.

■ FILL-IN QUESTIONS

1. A market is the institution or mechanism that brings together the _____ and the _____ of a particular good or service.

2. The demand schedule reflects a (positive, negative) _____ relationship between price and quantity demanded. The supply schedule reflects a _____ relationship between price and quantity supplied.

3. Factors which shift the demand curve when they change are called demand _____.

4. The Latin phrase meaning "all other things being equal" is _____.

5. When demand or supply is graphed, price is placed on the _____ axis and quantity on the _____ axis.

6. The graph of the demand schedule is called the demand _____ and according to the law of demand is _____ sloping.

7. A change in price causes a change in (demand, quantity demanded) _____, and results in a (movement along, shift in) _____ the demand curve. A change in consumer incomes causes a change in (demand, quantity demanded)

_____, and results in a (movement along, shift in) _____ the demand curve.

8. Marianne tends to buy more books when the price of books falls because:
    (a)   her purchasing power is increased, so she can afford to buy more books and other goods; this is called the _____ effect.
    (b)   books become less expensive relative to magazines, so Marianne tends to buy more books and less magazines; and this is called the _____ effect.

9. Don likes to have spare drill bits for various projects around the house. He is willing to pay less for each successive drill bit because he is successively less likely to actually need each extra one he buys. This is an example of the principle known as diminishing _____.

10. A change in price causes a change in (supply, quantity supplied) _____, and results in a (movement along, shift in) _____ the supply curve. A change in resource costs causes a change in (supply, quantity supplied) _____, and results in a (movement along, shift in) _____ the supply curve.

11. An increase in supply is shown by a shift of the entire supply curve to the (left, right) _____. A decrease in supply is shown by a shift of the entire supply curve to the _____.

12. The equilibrium price of a commodity is the price at which _____ equals _____.

13. If quantity demanded exceeds quantity supplied, price is (above, below) _____ the equilibrium price. This creates a (shortage, surplus) _____ that will cause the price to (rise, fall) _____.

■ PROBLEMS AND PROJECTS

1. (a) Plot the demand and supply schedules below on the graph provided. Indicate on the graph the equilibrium price and quantity by drawing lines from the intersection of the demand and supply curves to the price and quantity axes, and label the values P* and Q*.

Price per Unit	Quantity Demanded	Quantity Supplied	Shortage (-) or Surplus (+)
$13	18	54	_____
12	21	48	_____
11	24	42	_____
10	27	36	_____
9	30	30	_____
8	33	24	_____
7	36	18	_____
6	39	12	_____

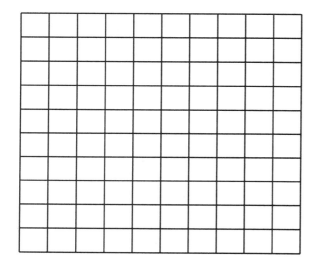

(b)   At equilibrium, P* = _____, and Q* = _____.
(c)   Fill in the last column of the table showing the amount of shortage or surplus that would exist at each price shown.

2. (a) Three individuals' demand schedules for bread are shown below. Assuming these are the only buyers in the market, fill in the market demand schedule for bread.

Price (per loaf)	Quantity Demanded (loaves of bread per month)			
	Doug	Leslie	Chong	Total
$1.20	10	6	8	_____
1.10	12	8	10	_____
1.00	15	11	12	_____
0.90	19	15	14	_____
0.80	24	18	16	_____

(b)   If the market supply of bread is 40 loaves per month if price is $1.10, then Doug will end up consuming 12 loaves per month. True or false, and why?

3. Below are some events that affect the market for wine. In each space, indicate whether the event shifts demand (D) or supply (S), and whether it is an increase (+) or decrease (-) in the curve.
(a)   Increase in the price of grapes   _____
(b)   Increase in population of consumers _____
(c)   Increase in the price of cheese   _____
(d)   Improvement in production technology   _____
(e)   New subsidies for wine production   _____
(f)   Increase in the price of beer   _____
(g)   Consumers expect a new tax on wine _____

4. Suppose that the demand and supply model is applicable to the Canadian beef market. For each of the following events, sketch a demand and supply graph showing the effect on the equilibrium price and quantity of beef in Canada.
(a)   A popular singer remarks that red meat in the diet may be a contributing factor in heart and circulatory diseases.
(b)   The East coast cod fishery is closed due to depleted fish stocks.
(c)   The United States government lifts an embargo that has until now prevented the importation of beef from Canada.
(d)   The price of livestock feed grains falls sharply due to a record harvest.
(e)   Agriculture Canada discovers a new growth hormone that will increase the weight of beef cattle by 20% with the same feed intake.
(f)   Hamburger restaurants experience a jump in costs as provincial governments raise the minimum wage rate.

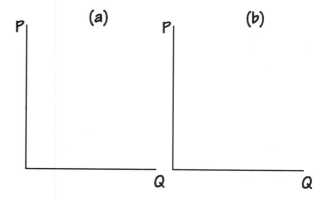

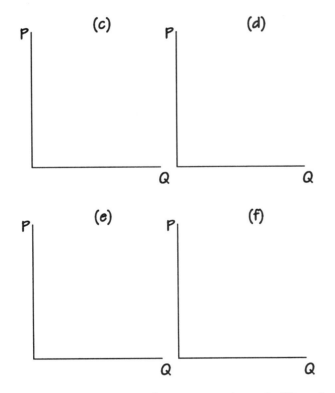

(c)

(d)

(e)

(f)

5. The table below shows a number of different cases where this is a change in demand and/or supply. In the columns for price change and quantity change, fill in the direction in which the equilibrium will change: increase (+), decrease (-), or indeterminate (?).

Case	Demand	Supply	Price change	Quantity change
a	increases	constant	_____	_____
b	constant	increases	_____	_____
c	decreases	constant	_____	_____
d	constant	decreases	_____	_____
e	increases	increases	_____	_____
f	increases	decreases	_____	_____
g	decreases	decreases	_____	_____
h	decreases	increases	_____	_____

6. In the 1990s, most golf courses in Canada raised their green fees (the price of playing golf), but also had more golfers coming to play at their courses. This case (is, is not) _____ a violation of the law of demand. Three possible reasons for the observed behaviour are:

(a) _____

(b) _____

(c) _____

7. The graph below shows the demand and supply for daily parking spots in the downtown core of a Canadian city.

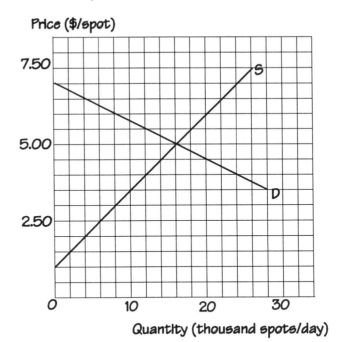

Price ($/spot)

Quantity (thousand spots/day)

(a) The current equilibrium price is _____ per spot, and _____ spots are rented each day.

(b) Suppose that the city government levies a new tax on parking lot operators in order to raise revenue to pay for a rapid transit system. The tax is set at $1.50 per spot rented. If the consumer pays $6.00, the supplier keeps $6.00-$1.50=$4.50. If the consumer pays $5.00, the supplier keeps _____.

(c) Show the new supply curve reflecting the tax. (The supply curve will shift upward by the amount of the tax because suppliers require this much extra in order to be willing to maintain the same supply as before).

(d) The new equilibrium price is _____ per spot, and _____ spots are rented each day. Accordingly, the price consumers pay for one spot has (fallen, risen) _____ by $_____ , and the price that suppliers keep has _____ by $_____. Therefore, the consumers' burden of the tax is _____ percent, and the suppliers' burden is _____ percent.

8. The table below shows the demand and supply schedules for firewood in two small towns, Eastwick and Westwood. Initially each town exists as a separate competitive market because there is no passage across the river that separates the towns.

	Eastwick		Westwood		Total	
Price	Qd	Qs	Qd	Qs	Qd	Qs
$225	80	100	45	105	____	____
200	90	90	55	95	____	____
175	100	80	65	85	____	____
150	110	70	75	75	____	____
125	120	60	85	65	____	____

(a) In Eastwick the equilibrium price is _____ per cord, and the equilibrium quantity is _____ cords per year.

(b) In Westwood the equilibrium price is _____ per cord, and the equilibrium quantity is _____ cords per year.

Now a bridge is built across the river, turning Eastwick and Westwood into one combined market.

(c) Fill in the market demand and supply schedules.

(d) The new equilibrium price is _____ per cord. This represents an increase in (Westwood, Eastwick) _____ and a decrease in _____.

(e) In Westwood quantity demanded is now _____ cords per year, and quantity supplied is now _____ cords per year. In Eastwick quantity demanded is now _____ cords per year, and quantity supplied is now _____ cords per year. Therefore, the town of _____ must import _____ cords per year from the town of _____.

■ **TRUE-FALSE**

Circle T if the statement is true, F if it is false.

1. A market is any arrangement that brings together the buyers and sellers of a particular good or service.　　**T F**

2. Demand is the amount of a commodity a buyer will purchase at a particular price.　　**T F**

3. The law of demand states that as price increases, the demand for the product decreases, *ceteris paribus*.　　**T F**

4. In graphing supply and demand schedules, supply is put on the horizontal axis and demand on the vertical axis.　　**T F**

5. A fall in the price of a good will cause the demand for goods that are substitutes for it to decrease.　　**T F**

6. If two goods are complements, an increase in the price of one will cause the demand for the other to decrease.　　**T F**

7. A change in buyers' tastes will cause the demand curve to shift.　　**T F**

8. An increase in income increases the demand for normal goods.　　**T F**

9. Diminishing marginal utility refers to the phenomenon that the consumer gets less additional satisfaction from one more unit of a product the more of the product he already has.　　**T F**

10. Since the amount purchased must equal the amount sold, demand and supply must always equal each other.　　**T F**

Questions 11-13 are based on the accompanying graph.

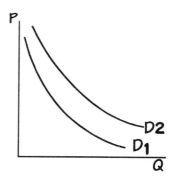

11. If the demand curve moves from D_1 to D_2 demand has increased.　　**T F**

12. The shift of the demand curve from D_1 to D_2 could be caused by a decrease in the price of complements.　　**T F**

13. The shift of the demand curve from D_1 to D_2 could be caused by a decrease in supply.　　**T F**

14. A normal good is also termed a superior good.　　**T F**

15. A decrease in quantity supplied can be caused by an increase in production costs. **T** F

16. If the supply curve for green lipstick shifts to the right, the supply of green lipstick has decreased. T (F)

17. If the market price of a commodity is momentarily below its equilibrium, the price will tend to rise because demand will decrease and supply will increase. T (F)

18. When quantity demanded exceeds quantity supplied, the market price will tend to fall. T (F)

19. The equilibrium price is also referred to as the market-clearing price. (T) F

20. The rationing function of prices is the elimination of shortages and surpluses. (T) F

21. There is an inverse relationship between a change in supply and the resulting change in equilibrium price. (T) F

■ **MULTIPLE-CHOICE**

Circle the letter that corresponds to the best answer.

1. An increase in the quantity demanded of oranges can be caused by:
   (a) a shift to the left of the supply curve of oranges
   (b) a shift to the right of the supply curve of oranges
   (c) a decline in the demand for orange juice
   (d) a rise in the demand for orange juice

2. A decrease in the quantity demanded:
   (a) shifts the demand curve to the left
   (b) shifts the demand curve to the right
   (c) is a movement down along the demand curve
   (d) is a movement up along the demand curve

3. If skiing at Banff and skiing at Whistler are substitutes, an increase in the price of skiing at Banff will:
   (a) decrease the demand for skiing at Whistler
   (b) increase the demand for skiing at Whistler
   (c) decrease the quantity demanded of skiing at Whistler
   (d) increase the quantity demanded of skiing at Whistler

4. Which pair of goods would most consumers regard as complementary goods?
   (a) coffee and tea
   (b) hockey sticks and skates
   (c) hamburger meat and bus rides
   (d) books and televisions

5. Which of the following is **not** among the determinants of demand?
   (a) consumer incomes
   (b) consumer expectations of future prices
   (c) prices of substitute goods
   (d) cost of resources

6. If an increase in income causes the demand for a particular good to decrease, then that good is:
   (a) normal
   (b) inferior
   (c) substitute
   (d) complement

7. According to the law of supply:
   (a) equilibrium quantity will always increase when equilibrium price increases
   (b) equilibrium quantity will always decrease when equilibrium price increases
   (c) the supply curve has a negative slope
   (d) if other things remain the same, the quantity supplied increases whenever price increases

8. A supply curve indicates:
   (a) the profit-maximizing quantities sellers place on the market at alternative prices
   (b) the minimum quantities sellers place on the market at alternative prices
   (c) the maximum quantities sellers will place on the market at different prices for inputs
   (d) the quantities sellers place on the market in order to meet consumer demand at that price

9. The supply curve of the firm slopes upward in the short run because:
   (a) the increased production requires the use of inferior inputs
   (b) hiring more inputs for the extra production requires the payment of higher input prices

(c) the increased technology to produce more output is expensive

(d) productive efficiency declines because certain productive resources cannot be expanded in a short period of time

10. A movement along a supply curve for a good would be caused by:

(a) an improvement in the technology of production

(b) an increase in the price of the good

(c) an increase in the number of suppliers of the good

(d) a change in expectations

11. Which of the following would increase the supply of books?

(a) an increase in the demand for books

(b) an increase in the price of books

(c) an increase in the cost of paper

(d) a decrease in the wages paid to printers

12. A market is in equilibrium when:

(a) inventories of the good are not rising

(b) suppliers can sell all of the good they decide to produce at the prevailing price

(c) quantity demanded equals quantity supplied

(d) demanders can purchase all of the good they want at the prevailing price

13. When the price of toothpaste falls, what will happen?

(a) quantity demanded decreases

(b) demand increases

(c) supply decreases

(d) quantity supplied decreases

Questions 14 to 17 are based on this diagram.

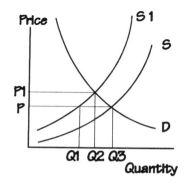

14. Given the original demand and supply curves are *D* and *S*:

(a) the equilibrium price and quantity were P and Q_1

(b) the equilibrium price and quantity were P and P_1

(c) the equilibrium price and quantity were P_1 and Q_1

(d) the equilibrium price and quantity were P and Q_3

15. The shift of the supply curve from *S* to S_1 is termed:

(a) an increase in supply

(b) an increase in quantity supplied

(c) a decrease in supply

(d) a decrease in quantity supplied

16. The shift in the supply curve from *S* to S_1 could be caused by:

(a) an increase in the price of the good

(b) a technological improvement in the production of the good

(c) a decrease in demand

(d) an increase in the cost of the resources used in the production of the good

17. If the price was prevented from adjusting when the supply shifted from *S* to S_1 the result would be:

(a) a surplus of $Q_3 - Q_1$

(b) a shortage of $Q_2 - Q_1$

(c) a shortage of $Q_3 - Q_1$

(d) a surplus of $Q_3 - Q_2$

18. Which of the following events would likely cause a furniture manufacturer to increase his supply of oak tables:

(a) an increase in the price of oak tables

(b) an increase in the cost of oak lumber

(c) a decrease in the demand for pine tables

(d) an increase in wages paid to staff

19. An increase in supply and an increase in demand will:

(a) increase price and increase the quantity exchanged

(b) decrease price and increase the quantity exchanged

(c) affect price in an indeterminate way and decrease the quantity exchanged

(d) affect price in an indeterminate way and increase the quantity exchanged

20. If scalping NHL playoff game tickets is profitable, this is a sign that the initial price at which the tickets were issued was:
 (a) below the equilibrium price
 (b) equal to the equilibrium price
 (c) above the equilibrium price
 (d) unreasonably high

21. A shortage of paper would cause the price of paper to go up. This would in turn alleviate the shortage by:
 (a) giving buyers incentives to use less paper
 (b) giving producers incentives to find ways to supply more paper
 (c) increasing the amount of paper being recycled
 (d) all of the above

■ **DISCUSSION QUESTIONS**

1. What is a market? For what kinds of goods does a laundromat bulletin board, or classified pages in a student newspaper, often serve as a market?

2. Carefully state the law of demand and explain the three reasons put forth in this chapter to justify downward sloping demand curves.

3. The last time OPEC succeeded in sharply increasing the price of oil, drivers reacted by significantly reducing their gasoline consumption. Explain this in terms of the income effect and substitution effect.

4. Explain the difference between an increase in demand and an increase in quantity demanded. What are the factors that cause a change in demand?

5. Define supply and explain why supply curves are upward sloping.

6. Explain the differences between a change in supply and a change in quantity supplied. What are the factors that cause a change in supply?

7. Neither demand nor supply remains constant for long. Economic circumstances are always changing so the actual prices we see are often not equilibrium prices. Why then do economists spend so much time trying to determine the equilibrium price and quantity if these magnitudes change so frequently?

8. How are normal, inferior, substitute, complementary, and independent goods defined? During a recession, who would fare better, firms that sell normal goods, or firms that sell inferior goods?

9. Analyze the following quotation and explain the fallacies contained in it. "An increase in demand will cause price to rise; with a rise in price, supply will increase and the increase in supply will push price down. Therefore, an increase in demand may or may not result in a price increase."

10. Following the Kyoto accord on emissions of greenhouse gases, Canada wants to reduce the burning of fossil fuels. Explain why a new tax on automobiles and/or a subsidy for bicycles would help the pursuit of this goal.

■ **ANSWERS**

FILL-IN QUESTIONS

1. buyers, sellers (either order)

2. negative, positive

3. determinants

4. *ceteris paribus*

5. vertical, horizontal

6. curve, downward (negative)

7. quantity demanded, movement along; demand, shift in

8. (a) income; (b) substitution

9. marginal utility

10. quantity supplied, movement along; supply, shift in

11. right, left

12. quantity demanded, quantity supplied

13. below; shortage, rise

PROBLEMS AND PROJECTS

1. (b) $9, 30; (c) from top to bottom: +36, +27, +18, +9, 0, -9, -18, -27.

2. (a) 24, 30, 38, 48, 58; (b) False. The price is not in equilibrium at $1.10; because Qd = 30 and Qs = 40, price must fall. At a price below $1.10 Doug will demand more than 12.

3. (a) S-; (b) D+; (c) D- (complements); (d) S+; (e) S+; (f) D+ (substitutes); (g) D+

4. (a) D shifts left: P -, Q -; (b) D shifts right: P +, Q +; (c) S shifts left: P +, Q -; (d) S shifts right: P -, Q +; (e) same as (d); (f) same as (c).

5. (a) +, +; (b) -,+; (c) -,-; (d) +,-; (e) ?,+; (f) +,?; (g) ?,-; (h) -,?

6. is not; (a) population growth, (b) increased incomes, (c) increased preferences for golf, or increased prices for substitutes, etc.

7. (a) $5.00, 16,000; (b) $3.50; (d) about 5.50, 12,000, risen, 0.50, fallen, 1.00, 33, 67.

8. (a) $200, 90; (b) $150, 75; (c) Qd = 125, 145, 165, 185, 205; Qs = 205, 185, 165, 145, 125; (d) $175, Westwood, Eastwick; (e) 65, 85; 100, 80; Eastwick, 20, Westwood.

TRUE-FALSE

1. T	**2.** F	**3.** F	**4.** F	**5.** T	**6.** T
7. T	**8.** T	**9.** T	**10.** F	**11.** T	**12.** T
13. F	**14.** T	**15.** F	**16.** F	**17.** F	**18.** F
19. T	**20.** T	**21.** T			

MULTIPLE-CHOICE

1. (b)	**2.** (d)	**3.** (b)	**4.** (b)	**5.** (d)	**6.** (b)
7. (d)	**8.** (a)	**9.** (d)	**10.** (b)	**11.** (d)	**12.** (c)
13. (d)	**14.** (d)	**15.** (c)	**16.** (d)	**17.** (c)	**18.** (c)
19. (d)	**20.** (a)	**21.** (d)			

APPENDIX TO CHAPTER 4

The Mathematics of Market Equilibrium

This appendix shows how the demand and supply model can be represented mathematically. The demand curve and the supply curve can be expressed in equation form as functions of price. Only at the equilibrium price do both functions generate the same value for quantity. Therefore, given the equations for demand and supply, we can set the two equal to solve for equilibrium price and quantity.

This appendix deals with only straight-line demand and supply curves, so their equations can be represented as simple linear equations. Demand is given by $P = a - bQd$, and supply is given by $P = c + dQs$. Each parameter in the equations has an economic meaning. If the price reaches a or higher, the amount demanded will be zero. If the price reaches c or lower, the amount supplied will be zero. The value b indicates the number of units by which quantity demanded will fall for every one unit rise in price. The value d indicates the number of units by which quantity supplied will rise for every one unit rise in price.

Normally the values for a, b, c, and d are known. With these parameters known, P and Qd are unknown in the demand equation, and P and Qs are unknown in the supply equation. There appear to be three unknowns (P, Qd, and Qs), but at the equilibrium price where negotiations between buyers and sellers have concluded, Qd and Qs are equal. Therefore the only unknowns are equilibrium price and quantity, which can be represented as Q^* and P^*.

■ CHECKLIST

When you have studied this appendix, you should be able to:
☐ Understand how demand and supply curves can be represented in equations.
☐ Solve supply and demand equations to find equilibrium price and quantity.

■ APPENDIX OUTLINE

1. A market equilibrium can be expressed as a price and quantity pair (Q^*, P^*) and occurs where quantity demanded equals quantity supplied $(Qd = Qs)$.

2. The market equilibrium results from the negotiating process that brings together the sellers' behaviour and the buyers' behaviour.

3. The buyers' behaviour is represented in the equation: $P = a - bQd$. Buyers will buy only at prices below a, and b shows the rate at which their quantity demanded falls if price rises.

4. The sellers' behaviour is represented in the equation: $P = c + dQs$. Sellers will sell only at price above c, and d shows the rate at which their quantity supplied rises if price rises.

5. The equilibrium values are solved from the parameter values as follows:
$$P^* = (ad + bc)/(a + d)$$
$$Q^* = (a - c)/(b + d)$$

■ HINTS AND TIPS

1. Solving for the equilibrium price at which a demand equation and a supply equation are equal is no different from examining a demand and supply graph to find the equilibrium price. There is only one value for price at which the two equations, or the two curves, have the same value for quantity.

2. If price is not at the equilibrium value there will be a shortage or a surplus, which can also be determined from the equations by substituting the given price into both equations and then comparing

45

the resulting values for quantity demanded and quantity supplied.

■ FILL-IN QUESTIONS

1. The maximum price that buyers are willing to pay for a product is given by the (slope, intercept) _____ term in the (demand, supply) _____ equation.

2. The extent to which the producers are willing to supply more when price increases is reflected in the (slope, intercept) _____ term in the (demand, supply) _____ equation.

3. If demand is given by $P = a - bQd$, an increase in the value of parameter a indicates that the demand curve shifts to the (left, right) _____, and equilibrium price will (decrease, increase) _____.

4. If supply is given by $P = c + dQs$, a decrease in the value of parameter c indicates that the supply curve shifts to the (left, right) _____, and equilibrium price will (decrease, increase) _____.

■ PROBLEMS AND PROJECTS

1. Suppose that the market for lemons can be characterized by the following equations:
$P = 4 - 0.01\ Qd$
$P = 1 + 0.02\ Qs$
  (a) Solve for the equilibrium quantity: _____
  (b) Solve for the equilibrium price: _____
  (c) If price was fixed by government policy at $P = 2$, would there be a shortage or a surplus, and what would the amount be?
  (d) If price was fixed by government policy at $P = 3.5$, would there be a shortage or a surplus, and what would the amount be?

2. The data below represents the market for computer printers.

Price ($/printer)	Qd (printers/yr)	Qs (printers/yr)
100	4000	0
200	3000	0
300	2000	1000
400	1000	2000
500	0	3000

  (a) Based on the demand schedule, what is the demand equation? _____
  (b) Based on the supply schedule, what is the supply equation? _____
  (c) Use the supply and demand equations to solve for equilibrium: P* = _____, Q* = _____

■ TRUE-FALSE

Circle the T if the statement is true; the F if it is false.

1. If the demand curve is given by $P = 12 - 2\ Qd$, then quantity demanded will be 3 if price is 6. **T F**

2. If the supply curve is given by $P = 5 + 4\ Qs$, then price will be 7 if quantity supplied is 2. **T F**

3. A change in either of the parameters in the demand equation will change the market equilibrium price. **T F**

4. A change in either of the parameters in the supply equation will change the market equilibrium price. **T F**

5. A change in either of the parameters in the demand equation will change the parameters in the supply equation. **T F**

■ MULTIPLE-CHOICE

Circle the letter that corresponds to the best answer.

Answer questions 1 through 6 on the basis of the following demand and supply equations:
$P = 100 - 2\ Qd$
$P = 40 + 4\ Qs$

1. The equilibrium price, P^*, will be:
  (a) 50
  (b) 60
  (c) 70
  (d) 80

2. The equilibrium quantity, Q^*, will be:
  (a) 10
  (b) 20
  (c) 30
  (d) 40

3. The lowest price at which producers are willing to begin selling output is:
- **(a)** 10
- **(b)** 20
- **(c)** 30
- **(d)** 40

4. Quantity demanded would become zero if the price rises above what level?
- **(a)** 70
- **(b)** 80
- **(c)** 90
- **(d)** 100

5. If price is 60, what would the situation be in this market?
- **(a)** a surplus of 15
- **(b)** a shortage of 15
- **(c)** a surplus of 20
- **(d)** a shortage of 20

6. The demand equation given could also be re-written as:
- **(a)** $Qd = 100 - 2P$
- **(b)** $P = 50 - Qd$
- **(c)** $Qd = 100 - 0.5 Qd$
- **(d)** $Qd = 50 - 0.5 P$

■ DISCUSSION QUESTIONS

1. What aspect of a demand equation shows that the equation is consistent with the law of demand? What aspect of the supply equation ensures that there is a positive relation between price and quantity supplied?

2. In the demand equation, what is the meaning of an increase in the parameter a, or b? In the supply equation, what is the meaning of an increase in the parameter c, or d?

■ ANSWERS

FILL-IN QUESTIONS

1. intercept, demand

2. slope, supply

3. right, increase

4. right, decrease

PROBLEMS AND PROJECTS

1. (a) 100; (b) 3; (c) shortage of 150; (d) surplus of 75

2. (a) $P = 500 - 0.1 Qd$; (b) $P = 200 + 0.1 Qs$; (c) $P^* = 350$, $Q^* = 1500$

TRUE-FALSE

1. T   2. F   3. T   4. T   5. F

MULTIPLE-CHOICE

1. (d)   2. (a)   3. (d)   4. (d)   5. (b)   6. (d)

CHAPTER 5

The Public Sector

This chapter explores the five main economic functions of government in a market economy. The Canadian economy is dominated by markets, but our governments play significant roles to strengthen and facilitate the working of the market system, and to achieve economic and social goals. In fact, all economies around the world that are primarily market-based also use some elements of the command system for addressing the Five Fundamental Questions. Following are the key roles for government:

(a) Government must provide a legal and social framework. Effective production, specialization and exchange all depend on government establishing a legal system, property rights, systems of weight and measures, a monetary system, etc.

(b) A decentralized and spontaneously coordinated market system depends on competition. Without adequate competition among sellers, consumers will not be sovereign and too much power will be held by sellers who can exploit monopoly power to increase their profits and misallocate society's resources. Government attempts to maintain competition through regulation of businesses, laws prohibiting anti-competitive behaviours, and direct government ownership.

(c) The market system does not necessarily distribute its output equally, or according to need. Because distribution strictly according to market forces would leave many people with unacceptably low incomes, there is a role for government to redistribute incomes. This may be accomplished through transfer payments, taxes, price controls and other market interventions.

(d) Competitive markets may, under various circumstances, fail to produce an efficient allocation of resources. When spillovers or externalities exist, some of the costs or benefits of production or consumption of a good affect someone other than the immediate producer or consumer. Since these "external" costs or benefits are ignored by those choosing the levels of production or consumption, the levels will end up being too high or too low. Goods which everyone can benefit from collectively, and which non-payers cannot be excluded from enjoying, are called public goods. Users' incentives to "free ride" rather than pay may make it impossible for private firms to supply such goods. Inefficiencies of externalities and public goods may be solved by taxes, subsidies, regulations, or direct government involvement in providing the good.

(e) Government tries to stabilize the economy's level of activity to achieve full employment and stable prices. Government can manipulate its spending, taxation, and interest rates in an effort to offset fluctuations in the private economy.

The chapter revisits the circular flow model from Chapter 2. Now the model is modified to include linkages between governments and businesses and households. Twelve linkages among the household, business, and government sectors are explained.

The next section describes the size and the roles of federal, provincial, and municipal governments in Canada. Government outlays involve both government purchases (which directly absorb or employ resources) and transfer payments (which do not directly absorb resources). By almost any measure, the government sector has grown massively as a proportion of the nation's economy since World War II. Governments' expenditures have grown faster than their revenues, which has created persistent problems with deficits. Consequently, the ratio of our public debt to our national output has grown to alarming levels. The federal government gets nearly half of its revenues from personal income taxes, and spends over half of its revenue on social services and interest payments on debt. The provinces raise the bulk of their revenues from a variety of taxes, and spend two-thirds of their revenues on health, education and social services. For municipal governments, transfers from other levels of government and property taxes are the biggest revenue sources, and education is the single biggest expenditure category.

The last part of the chapter mentions the debate over the proper size of government: a debate provoked by ballooning government debt and concerns over the effectiveness of government actions in the economy.

■ CHECKLIST

When you have studied this chapter, you should be able to:

□ Briefly explain why Canada is a mixed economy rather than a pure market economy.
□ List the five economic functions of government in Canada.
□ Give examples of institutions and services that government must maintain to provide an appropriate "legal and social framework."
□ Define monopoly and explain why government strives to prevent monopoly and to preserve competition.
□ Explain the case for redistribution of income.
□ List the principal methods government may use to redistribute income.
□ Explain what is meant by a "market failure."
□ Define a spillover cost and a spillover benefit, and explain why a competitive market fails to allocate resources efficiently when there are spillovers.
□ List the strategies government may use to reduce spillovers and improve the allocation of resources.
□ Define a public good (and a quasi-public good), and explain why a competitive market fails to allocate enough resources to producing such goods.
□ List the strategies government may use to ensure provision of appropriate quantities of public and quasi-public goods.
□ Explain why the private economy may require stabilization.
□ List the steps government may take to stabilize the economy.
□ Draw and carefully label a circular flow diagram that includes businesses, households, and government.
□ Use the circular flow diagram to explain how government alters the distribution of income, the allocation of resources, and the level of activity in the economy.
□ Distinguish between government purchases and transfer payments.
□ Identify the largest revenue source and the largest expenditure category for each of the three levels of government in Canada: federal, provincial, municipal.
□ Summarize the views of those in favour of cutting the size of government and the views of those in favour of maintaining the size of government.

■ CHAPTER OUTLINE

1. Like other economies in the real world, Canada is neither a pure market economy nor a purely planned economy. Canada uses a mixed system in which markets dominate but government has significant roles.

2. Government in the Canadian economy performs five economic functions:
   (a) provides the legal and social framework needed for the economy to operate effectively
   (b) maintains competition to prevent abuse of monopoly power
   (c) redistributes income to reduce income inequality
   (d) reallocates resources to take account of spillover costs or benefits, and of public goods
   (e) stabilizes the economy to keep the price level stable and maintain full employment

3. By providing a legal and social framework, government sets the "rules of the game" governing the relationships between consumers, businesses, and resource suppliers. Such "refereeing" of economic relationships gives people greater confidence in markets and lowers their costs of making market transactions. Therefore, the volume of trade expands.

4. Examples of the legal and social framework include the systems established for money, weights and measures, property rights, police force and judiciary, etc.

5. When a market is competitive, sellers are forced by competition to respond to consumer preferences, and to keep prices as low as possible. When a market is monopolized, the seller has the power to raise prices by reducing output. This restriction of output benefits the monopolist who enjoys higher profits,

but is not in the social interest. Output is restricted, so too few of society's economic resources are allocated to producing the good in question.

6. In Canada, government attempts to control monopoly by: (a) regulation or direct public ownership (especially for "natural monopolies"), or (b) anti-combines laws that prohibit certain monopolizing behaviours.

7. The market system yields high incomes to some and low incomes to others. This unequal distribution of income leads to poverty and other unacceptable results. Government redistributes income by transfer payments, income taxes and other taxes, and by direct market interventions such as price controls.

8. Market failure can arise from externalities or spillovers, situations where a third party incurs a cost or benefit from the consumption or production of a good or service. The immediate buyer and seller ignore the external benefit or cost because they affect somebody else.
    (a)   When spillover costs occur, resources are overallocated to production. For example, a mill may produce too much steel because the costs of environmental pollution are ignored by the mill operator.
    (b)   When spillover benefits occur, resources are underallocated to production. For example, people may acquire too little education because they ignore the benefits that their education provides for the rest of society.

9.   Government can correct for the misallocation of resources that results from spillover costs or benefits.
    (a)   For spillover costs, government may implement legislation to directly limit or prohibit the activity, or levy specific taxes that pass back to the producer a cost equal to the spillover cost.
    (b)   For spillover benefits, government may provide subsidies to consumers or producers to encourage the activity, or government may supply the activity directly.

10. Market failure can also arise in the case of public or quasi-public goods.
    (a)   A public good, such as national defence, is indivisible and is not subject to the exclusion principle. Therefore, its benefits are available to everybody, not only those who pay. This creates a free-rider problem: because people can enjoy the good without contributing to its cost, there is no economic incentive for anybody to supply the good.
    (b)   Quasi-public goods, such as streets and parks, could be made exclusive, but are provided by government because they entail substantial spillover benefits.

11. Since private markets would not allocate enough resources to the production of public goods and quasi-public goods, government provides these goods on the basis of group, or collective, choices. Through the political process we decide what to tax, at what level to set taxes, and how to spend our tax revenues. Ultimately, this process diverts from the private sector the resources needed for public and quasi-public goods.

12. The newest function of government is to stabilize the economy at full employment, and at a stable price level. Without government intervention, the level of aggregate expenditures fluctuates. If there is demand for more goods than the economy can produce, then there will be inflation. If too little is demanded, there will be unemployment among workers and other resources. Government can use its power to spend and to tax to manipulate the level of aggregate expenditures.

13. A circular flow diagram that includes the private sector and the public sector reveals that government purchases public goods from private businesses, collects taxes from and makes transfer payments to these firms, purchases labour services from households, and collects taxes from and makes transfer payments to these households. As well, government can alter the distribution of income, reallocate resources, and change the level of economic activity by affecting the six flows in the diagram.

14. Government outlays, which include purchases and transfers, represent about 45% of Canada's annual production.
    (a) Government purchases of goods and services are considered "exhaustive" because they directly absorb or use up resources.
    (b)   Transfer payments are considered "non-exhaustive" because they transfer purchasing power (e.g., to households and firms) but do not absorb resources.

15. Federal expenditures fall into three key areas: social services, protection of persons and property, and interest on the public debt. The federal government's main revenue source is personal income taxes; corporate income taxes, the GST, and employment insurance contributions are also important.

16. Provincial governments spend more on health than anything else; education and social services are next. The provinces' main source of revenues is income tax. General sales taxes and transfers from the federal government are also important.

17. Municipal governments' top spending category is education. Their revenues come mainly from property taxes and transfers from provincial governments.

18. The appropriate size for Canada's government is constantly debated. Critics of government are very concerned about the growing public debt, the ineffectiveness of some government programs, and detrimental effects of high taxes. Their views are opposed by those who believe that many of our social and economic goals can be achieved only through extensive involvement in the economy by a government that has adequate tax revenue to work with.

■ **TERMS AND CONCEPTS**

corporate income
  taxes
exclusion principle
free-rider problem
government purchases
monopoly
personal income tax
principal-agent
  problem

property taxes
public good
quasi-public goods
sales and excise tax
spillover costs and
  spillover benefits
transfer payments

■ **HINTS AND TIPS**

1. The key thing to get out of this chapter is an understanding of the five functions of government in the economy. Be sure that you understand the circumstances that create "market failure" and in what cases markets will either underallocate or overallocate resources to producing a good.

2. You should be able to construct from memory the circular flow diagram with households, firms and the government sector. To help fix it in your mind, try to think of a concrete example for each of the twelve types of flows. For example, to remember the

flow from resource markets to the government sector, you might think of school teachers' labour.

■ **FILL-IN QUESTIONS**

1. All actual economies are "mixed" because they combine elements of a _____ economy and a _____ economy.

2. List the five economic functions of government:
(a) _____
(b) _____
(c) _____
(d) _____
(e) _____

3. To control monopoly in Canada, government has: (a) created commissions to _____ the prices and the services of _____ monopolies; (b) enacted _____ laws to maintain competition.

4. Government frequently reallocates resources when it finds instances of _____ failure. The two major cases of such failure of the competitive market involve _____ and _____ goods.

5. Spillovers occur when benefits or costs associated with the production or consumption of a good are incurred by a _____ party. Spillovers are also called _____.

6. Governments can resolve the problem of spillover costs through the use of _____ or _____.

7. If spillover benefits accompany the production of a good, then resources will be _____ to the production of that good by the market economy.

8. Governments can resolve the problem of spillover benefits through _____ paid to the _____ or the _____ of the good.

9. Public goods are not subject to the _____ principle. Once a public good is produced, the benefits from the good cannot be confined to the purchaser. This results in a _____ effect.

10. A _____ good is a good that could be made exclusive, but is commonly provided by gov-

ernment because it has substantial spillover benefits.

11. To stabilize the economy when there is less
than full employment, government must (increase,
decrease) _____ aggregate expenditures by
(increasing, decreasing) _____ government
expenditures for goods and services, and by (increasing, decreasing) _____ taxes.

12. To stabilize the economy when there are inflationary pressures, government must (increase, decrease) _____ aggregate expenditures by
(increasing, decreasing) _____ government
expenditures for goods and services, and by (increasing, decreasing) _____ taxes.

13. In the expanded circular flow model, the net tax
flow is obtained by subtracting all government
_____ to business firms and _____ to
households from the taxes paid by firms and households.

■ **PROBLEMS AND PROJECTS**

1. The circular flow diagram below includes business firms, households, and government (the public
sector). Also shown are the product and resource
markets.
    (a)   Identify the sector that corresponds to each
box:
                a. _____
                b. _____
                c. _____
                d. _____
                e. _____
    (b) Supply a label or an explanation for each of
the twelve flows in the model:
                1: _____
                2: _____
                3: _____
                4: _____
                5. _____
                6: _____
                7: _____
                8: _____
                9: _____
                10: _____
                11: _____
                12: _____

(c)   If government wished to increase the production of public goods and decrease the production of private goods in the economy, which
flows could it increase? _____, _____, _____.

2. Below is a list of various government activities.
Indicate which of the five government functions the
activity represents. Hint: some activities fall under
more than one function.
    (a)   Maintaining an army. _____
    (b)   Providing an employment insurance sys-
tem. _____
    (c)   Establishing the Bank of Canada. _____
    (d)   Providing equalization payments to the
poorer provinces in Canada. _____
    (e)   Barring a merger of two large banks. _____
    (f)   Providing drought relief payments to farm-
ers. _____
    (g)   Cutting income taxes during a recession.
_____
    (h)   Taxing cigarettes. _____
    (i)   Regulating the Vancouver Stock Exchange.
_____
    (j)   Setting tax rates higher for large incomes
than for smaller ones. _____
    (k)   Developing environmental programs to fight
the greenhouse effect. _____

3. Match each example on the right with the type
of situation on the left:
    (a)   spillover cost   (1) a radio broadcast
    (b)   spillover benefit   (2) a noisy house party
    (c)   public good   (3) safe driving

■ TRUE-FALSE

Circle T if the statement is true, F if it is false.

1. Among governments in Canada, only the federal government has a role in affecting resource allocation.   T (F)

2. A monopoly has the power to restrict supply and raise price above the competitive level.   (T) F

3. An economy in which strong and effective competition is maintained may need programs designed to redistribute income.   T F

4. Competitive product and input markets do not always ensure an optimal allocation of an economy's resources.   (T) F

5. Market forces ensure that aggregate expenditures are always sufficient to generate full employment.   T (F)

6. A spillover or externality is a cost or benefit that is imposed upon an individual or group external to the market transaction.   (T) F

7. The market system will overallocate resources to the production of goods that confer spillover benefits.   T (F)

8. Pollution is a cause of market failure because the price of the polluting product does not reflect all the resource costs used in its production.   (T) F

9. A government subsidy could be used to correct the misallocation of resources that results when spillover benefits are present.   (T) F

10. Taxes imposed on products that create pollution will lower the marginal cost of production and increase supply.   T (F)

11. A public good is any good or service that is provided free by the government.   T (F)

12. For public goods the free-rider problem occurs when people can receive benefits without contributing to the cost of providing the good.   (T) F

13. Governments provide environmental protection services because these services provide spillover benefits and private producers of environmental protection services would encounter the free-rider problem.   (T) F

14. A government purchase of a snowplow truck is "non-exhaustive" while a government transfer payment to single parents is "exhaustive."   T (F)

15. Over the last several decades, government expenditures and government revenues in Canada have grown at almost the same rate.   T (F)

16. In the 1980s and 1990s, the growth of public debt was much the same in Canada as in other OECD countries.   T F

■ MULTIPLE-CHOICE

Circle the letter that corresponds to the best answer.

1. The functions of government include all of the following except:
   (a) maintaining competition
   (b) redistributing wealth and income
   (c) promoting growth and stabilizing the economy
   (d) determining the least cost method of production

2. Which of the following is not one of the methods utilized by government to control monopoly?
   (a) laws to make all monopolies illegal
   (b) government ownership of monopolies
   (c) government regulation of monopolies
   (d) anti-combines laws

3. One of the following is not presently employed by government to redistribute income. Which one?
   (a) the negative income tax
   (b) direct market intervention
   (c) income taxes that take a larger part of the incomes of the rich than the poor
   (d) transfer payments

4. In a pure market economy, the distribution of income will be unequal because of:
   (a) unequal distribution of talents
   (b) unequal inheritances
   (c) unequal luck
   (d) all of the above

5. If external benefits accompany the production of a good:

(a) resources will be overallocated to the production of the good

(b) resources will be underallocated to the production of the good

(c) a tax on the production of the good will result in the optimum production of the good

(d) the good is exported to foreign countries

6. In the case where producing a good results in spillover costs, government could promote the optimal output by:

(a) enforcing anticombines laws

(b) taxing the producers of the good

(c) subsidizing consumers of the good

(d) subsidizing producers of the good

7. Which of the following is an example of government provision of a legal and social framework?

(a) police enforcement of speed limits on the Trans-Canada Highway

(b) establishment of regulations for product packaging

(c) inspection of pumps at gas stations and scales at butcher shops

(d) all of the above

8. Which of the following is a good example of a good or service providing spillover benefits?

(a) a video game

(b) landscaping

(c) a sofa

(d) an oil change for a car

9. Suppose that in order to relieve traffic congestion, user charges are imposed on drivers using urban expressways. This would be a response to what economic problem?

(a) spillover benefits

(b) spillover costs

(c) the free-rider problem

(d) inequitable income distribution

10. Public goods differ from private goods in that public goods are:

(a) divisible

(b) subject to the exclusion principle

(c) not subject to the free-rider problem

(d) *not* divisible and *not* subject to the exclusion principle

11. Quasi-public goods are goods and services:

(a) to which the exclusion principle could be applied

(b) that have large spillover benefits

(c) that private producers would overproduce

(d) that have large spillover benefits, and to which the exclusion principle could be applied

12. If the market system tends to overallocate resources to the production of good X:

(a) good X could be a public good

(b) good X could involve spillover benefits

(c) good X could involve spillover costs

(d) good X could be prone to the free-rider problem

13. Government expenditures, taxes, and transfer payments in the circular flow affect:

(a) the distribution of income

(b) the allocation of resources

(c) the level of economic activity

(d) all of the above

14. Property taxes are the largest source of revenue for which level of government in Canada?

(a) federal

(b) provincial

(c) municipal

(d) no level of government

15. Employment insurance contributions are a revenue source for which level of government in Canada?

(a) federal

(b) provincial

(c) municipal

(d) no level of government

16. The largest expenditures category for provincial governments in Canada is:

(a) education

(b) highways

(c) social services

(d) health care

17. The largest expenditures category for Canada's municipal governments is:

(a) debt interest

(b) education

(c) social services

(d) police

■ DISCUSSION QUESTIONS

1. What are the five economic functions of government in Canada's mixed economy? Explain what the performance of each of these functions requires government to do.

2. Would you like to live in an economy in which government undertook only the first two functions listed in the text? What would be the advantages and disadvantages of living in such an economy?

3. What is "market failure" and what are the two major kinds of such failures?

4. If the person living down the hall from you plays her music very loudly, is there a spillover cost or spillover benefit? If a homeowner builds an extra high fence between his house and his neighbours', is there a spillover cost or spillover benefit?

5. Based on ideas from this chapter, what is the case for government supporting needle exchange programs for intravenous drug users?

6. What principles from this chapter seem relevant to understanding the Internet?

7. How do private goods and public goods differ? Why does there tend to be underallocation of resources to public goods in the absence of government intervention?

8. What basic method does government employ in Canada to reallocate resources away from the production of private goods and toward the production of public goods?

9. What are the some of the key trends in expenditures and revenues for federal, provincial and municipal governments in Canada? What are some of the most contentious issues?

■ ANSWERS

FILL-IN QUESTIONS

1. market, command

2. (a) provide legal and social framework; (b) maintain competition; (c) redistribute income; (d) reallocate resources; (e) stabilize the economy

3. (a) regulate, natural; (b) anti-combines

4. market; spillovers (or externalities), public

5. third; externalities

6. specific taxes, regulations

7. underallocated

8. subsidies, consumers, producers

9. exclusion; free-rider

10. quasi-public

11. increase, increasing, decreasing

12. decrease, decreasing, increasing

13. subsidies, transfer payments

■ PROBLEMS AND PROJECTS

1. (a) a: business firms, b: resource markets, c: government, d: households, e: product markets;
(b) 1: businesses pay costs for resources that become money income for households, 2: households provide resources to businesses, 3: household expenditures become receipts for businesses, 4: businesses provide goods and services to households, 5: government spends money in product market, 6: government receives goods and services from product market, 7: government spends money in resource market, 8: government receives resources from resource market, 9: government provides goods and services to households, 10: government provides goods and services to businesses, 11: businesses pay net taxes to government, 12: households pay net taxes to government;
(c) (1) 9, 10, 11

2. (a) reallocates resources; (b) redistributes income and stabilizes the economy; (c) provides a legal foundation and social environment and stabilizes the economy; (d) redistributes income and wealth; (e) maintains competition; (f) redistributes income; (g) stabilizes the economy; (h) reallocates resources; (i) provides a legal foundation and social environment; (j) redistributes income and wealth; (k) reallocates resources.

3. a=2, b=3, c=1

■ TRUE-FALSE

1. F	2. T	3. T	4. T	5. F	6. T
7. F	8. T	9. T	10. F	11. F	12. T
13. T	14. F	15. F	16. F		

■   **MULTIPLE-CHOICE**

1. (d)   **2.** (a)   **3.** (a)   **4.** (d)   **5.** (b)   **6.** (b)
7. (d)   **8.** (b)   **9.** (b)   **10.** (d)   **11.** (d)   **12.** (c)
13. (d)   **14.** (c)   **15.** (a)   **16.** (d)   **17.** (b)

CHAPTER 6

Canada in the Global Economy

As members of the global economy, Canadian consumers depend entirely on many goods produced in other nations, and many Canadian workers and businesses depend on selling goods in foreign markets. Why does international trade occur, and how does trade benefit us? These are the fundamental questions of this chapter.

Canada's imports and exports have mushroomed in the last three decades. Today our exports and imports each total over $200 billion annually, and represent about 30% of our economy. We trade many different products, and many of our major exports are also our major imports (e.g., automotive products, machinery, and equipment). The United States is our most important trading partner, and we trade mainly with industrialized countries. World trade has increased mainly because of improved transportation and communications technologies, relative peace, and many policy initiatives around the world that have cut tariffs and other trade barriers. The number of important players in world trade has increased, especially among the newly industrializing Asian nations.

The circular flow model is easily amended to add the "rest of the world" sector to the product market. Export flows are paid for by foreign expenditures, and import flows are paid for by expenditures from the domestic economy. From this diagram it is easy to understand how instability in foreign economies can introduce instability into the Canadian economy, and vice versa.

The principle of comparative advantage shows why nations trade. In the simplest scenario, there are two nations, each producing two goods at constant opportunity cost ratios. If the opportunity costs differ between the two nations, each should specialize in producing that good for which their domestic opportunity cost is below the other nation's. If

both nations follow this rule, both goods will be produced and traded, and both nations can end up with more output than they could produce if they remained self-sufficient. Perhaps surprisingly, these benefits are available to all nations that trade, even nations that are absolutely less productive than their trading partners.

In reality, nations usually do not barter goods with one another, as represented in the simplified scenario of the comparative advantage model. Instead, international trade is conducted through monetary transactions between households and firms in different countries acting as buyers and sellers. Such transactions require a foreign exchange market where currencies may be traded. The exchange rate, or equilibrium price of one currency in terms of another, is determined by the supply and the demand for the currency. The basic principles of supply and demand that you studied in Chapter 4 apply to foreign exchange markets also. Shifts in the supply or demand for a currency will change its price. If the currency's price rises (falls) in terms of another currency it has appreciated (depreciated) relative to the other currency.

Despite the important benefits from specialization and international trade, many nations try to limit trade. The major barriers to world trade are: (1) protective tariffs, (2) import quotas, (3) nontariff barriers, and (4) export subsidies. But why do governments seek to reduce imports and/or increase exports? One reason may be the mistaken yet common belief that exports are beneficial because they create jobs, whereas imports are harmful because they destroy jobs at home. Another explanation is found by examining who gains and who loses from policies that limit trade. Domestic firms facing tough competition from imports often lobby governments to impose tariffs or quotas. Domestic consumers would lose from the resulting higher prices. However, even if the benefits of protection for the domestic firms are less than the costs for domestic consumers, the costs are obscure and dispersed. Therefore, government may enjoy more political success by imposing tariffs and quotas than by supporting free trade.

Protectionist measures taken by one nation may lead other nations that lose exports to retaliate with protectionist measures of their own. In order to prevent such conflicts and to reduce existing trade barriers, various bilateral and multilateral trade agreements have evolved. The most important one is the General Agreement on Tariffs and Trade (GATT), and its successor, the World Trade Organization (WTO). Important regional trade blocs include the European Union (EU), and the North American Free Trade Agreement (NAFTA). A trade bloc enables member nations to enjoy freer trade with other member nations, but has uncertain effects on trade with other nations. Benefits of membership may attract more members (for example, NAFTA added Mexico), or the world may fragment into a number of hostile trading blocs. Canada's membership in NAFTA has provoked strong public reaction; both for and against the agreement.

■ **CHECKLIST**

When you have studied this chapter, you should be able to:

□ Explain why international trade is important to the Canadian economy, and describe the volume and pattern of our trade.

□ Describe four factors that have facilitated growth in world trade since World War II.

□ Identify some of the world's key trading nations, and nations whose importance is growing.

□ Draw the circular flow diagram including the international trade dimension.

□ Explain the basic principle of comparative advantage.

□ Explain how international trade can help to lessen the scarcity problem.

□ Compute the comparative costs of production from a numerical example with data on production possibilities for two goods for two producers.

□ Determine from the example which producer has the comparative advantage in each good.

□ Indicate the range in which the terms of trade will be found in the example.

□ Compute the gains from specialization and trade in the example.

□ Describe the main characteristics of the foreign exchange market.

□ Draw a demand and supply graph of the foreign exchange market.

□ Distinguish between appreciation and depreciation of a currency.

□ Identify four types of government interferences with free trade.

□ Discuss two reasons why governments interfere with international trade.

□ Explain the lesson of Bastiat's Petition of the Candlemakers.

□ Describe the nature and purpose of GATT, and list some of the highlights of the Uruguay round provisions.

□ Describe the history, goals and results of the European Union.

□ Describe the features of NAFTA, including the arguments for and against Canada's participation.

□ Discuss the ability of Canadian firms to compete in the world economy.

■ **CHAPTER OUTLINE**

1. The volume of international trade is now so large, and national economies so interdependent, that the world can be thought of as a "global economy."

2. Compared to most other nations, Canada relies relatively heavily on trade.

(a) The market in Canada is too limited to allow for efficient production of the full range of goods and services, so we must import many goods, and therefore export others to pay for the imports.

(b) Exports and imports are about 30% of our national output.

(c) The bulk of Canada's trade is with other industrialized nations, particularly the United States.

(d) Canada's three major exports, in order, are automotive products, machinery and equipment, and industrial goods and materials. Our major imports, in order, are machinery and equipment, automotive products, industrial goods and materials.

3. Several factors have facilitated rapid growth of world trade since World War II:

(a) improved transportation technology,

(b) improved communications technology,

(c) general decline in tariffs,

(d) peace in most industrialized nations.

4. In sheer volume of trade, the world's major players are the United States, Japan, and Western Europe. Despite very recent problems, a number of Asian nations are becoming more important in world trade: Hong Kong, Singapore, South Korea, Taiwan, and China. Eastern European countries are also building trading relationships.

5. The circular flow model reflects the international trade dimension once we add the "rest of the world" box. This box is connected to the Canadian product market through flows of imports and exports, and the Canadian and foreign expenditures on these goods.

6. Specialization and trade among economic units (individuals, firms, provinces, regions, or nations) are based on the principle of comparative advantage. Specialization and trade increase productivity and output. Adam Smith wrote about this in 1776, and the idea was fully explained by David Ricardo in the early 1800s.

7. The basic principle of comparative advantage is shown with an example of two individuals able to do two jobs, or with an example of two nations producing two goods.

(a)   A chartered accountant (CA) needing her house painted can paint it herself, or can hire a house painter. The CA will try to minimize her opportunity cost. By comparative advantage, even if the CA can do the job in less time than the painter can, if the CA incurs a lower opportunity cost by hiring the painter, the CA will specialize in accounting. Likewise, the painter will specialize in painting, and hire a CA to prepare his tax return, if this minimizes his opportunity costs.

(b)   Mexico and Canada both can produce corn and soybeans. Assuming each nation has a straight line production possibilities curve (or constant cost ratio), then each nation has the lower opportunity cost — and therefore comparative advantage — in producing one of the two goods. By specializing in producing one good, each nation can trade for the other nation's good. The terms of trade, or ratio at which one good is traded for another, lies between the cost ratios for the two nations.

(c)   When two nations specialize and trade according to their comparative advantage, both nations can consume more of both goods than their domestic production possibilities curves would permit. This reduces the scarcity problem.

8. National currencies are traded in highly competitive foreign exchange markets. Such markets establish the exchange rates — the rates at which various national currencies are traded for one another. Exchange rates link all domestic prices with all foreign prices.

9. Supply and demand for a currency determine its exchange rate. Shifts in the supply and demand cause exchange rate appreciation or depreciation.

(a)   Increased demand or decreased supply for a currency will cause it to appreciate, or rise in price as measured in other currencies.

(b)   Decreased demand or increased supply for a currency will cause it to depreciate, or fall in price as measured in other currencies.

10. Governments implement policies that restrict trade between nations:

(a)   Such policies include protective tariffs, import quotas, nontariff barriers, and export subsidies.

(b)   Trade restrictions may be imposed because the nature of the gains from trade is misunderstood, or because governments have strong political incentives to protect domestic businesses from international competition.

(c)   Regardless of governments' motives, restrictive trade policies impose costs that outweigh the benefits. Consumers pay higher prices, exporters have less access to foreign markets, and the nation makes less efficient use of its resources.

11. To prevent protectionism and to promote trade, various national policies and international institutional arrangements have evolved. Nations have signed bilateral agreements extending tariff reductions to one another through most-favoured-nation clauses.

(a)   The General Agreement on Tariffs and Trade (GATT) has been the most comprehensive forum for reducing tariffs on a multilateral basis.

(b)   GATT has existed since 1947, now has one hundred and twenty-five member states, and has been the vehicle for eight rounds of negotiations to reduce trade barriers.

(c)   Through the recent Uruguay round, major changes are being phased in between 1995 and 2005: reductions in thousands of tariffs, inclusion of services, reduced farm subsidies, protection of intellectual property, reduced quotas on textiles and apparel, and the establishment of the World Trade Organization (WTO).

12. The European Union (EU) is a regional trade bloc that has abolished tariffs between EU countries, enabled free movement of labour and capital within the EU, and developed some common economic policies (such as tariffs that will apply to nonmember countries). The EU has increased trade and efficiency of production within the bloc, but has also created frictions with nonmember nations (including Canada).

13. In 1989 Canada and the United States signed the Free Trade Agreement (FTA). In 1993 the bloc formed by the FTA was extended to include Mexico under the terms of the North American Free Trade Agreement (NAFTA). Critics fear that jobs will be lost to Mexico where wages are low and the workplace is less regulated than Canada. Proponents argue that the typical advantages from freer trade outweigh any drawbacks.

14. There is concern that the world may be splitting into potentially hostile trading blocs. On the other hand, some nations (including Canada) belong to more than one bloc, and there are also incentives for linking free-trade zones such as the NAFTA and EU.

15. Globalization of trade intensifies competition for Canadian producers. Many succeed by keeping costs low, using new technology, and offering superior products to retain market shares in Canada and capture new markets abroad. Other firms are unable to compete, and have lost market share or even folded. Many of the unsuccessful firms previously enjoyed long periods of protection from imports (via tariffs or quotas). These results of increasing world trade are consistent with the principle of comparative advantage: with freer trade Canadian producers who have a comparative advantage will expand output, whereas Canadian producers who do not have a comparative advantage will shrink.

■ **TERMS AND CONCEPTS**

absolute advantage	comparative
appreciation	advantage
"Asian tigers"	depreciation
Canada-U.S. Free Trade	European Union (EU)
Agreement (FTA)	exchange rates

export subsidies	nontariff barriers
foreign exchange	North American Free
market	Trade Agreement
General Agreement on	(NAFTA)
Tariffs and Trade	protective tariffs
(GATT)	terms of trade
import quotas	trade bloc
most-favoured-nation	World Trade
clauses	Organization
multinational	
corporations	

■ **HINTS AND TIPS**

1. Finding which producer of a good has the comparative advantage depends on being able to compare opportunity costs across producers. If the data on production possibilities reflects constant costs, opportunity costs can be found easily by dividing a producer's maximum outputs of each of the two goods. For example, suppose Norway's maximum outputs are 100 fish or 20 tables. What is the cost of 1 table? Divide the number of tables into the number of fish: 100 fish/20 tables = 5 fish per table. What is the cost of 1 fish? Divide the number of fish into the number of tables: 20 tables/100 fish = 1/5 table per fish.

2. Foreign exchange rates are confusing because they can be expressed in two ways. Is Canada's exchange rate the amount of foreign currency that one Canadian dollar can buy, or the amount in Canadian dollars that it takes to buy one unit of foreign currency? Surprisingly, either form is correct, as long as you specify which one you are using. For example, our exchange rate with Mexico could be 4 pesos for $1, or $0.25 for 1 peso. These are reciprocal expressions of exactly the same rate! Always be clear on which form of the exchange rate you are using.

■ **FILL-IN QUESTIONS**

1. A nation is more likely to rely on international trade the more (diversified, limited) _____ its resource base is and the (larger, smaller) _____ its domestic market is.

2. In recent decades Canada's trade has (increased, decreased) _____ in absolute terms, and _____ as a percentage of our national income. Canada trades mainly with (developing, developed) _____ nations. Our major trading partner is _____.

3. Factors that have facilitated growth in trade since World War II include improvements in _____ and _____ technology, a general decline in _____, and _____ between the major trading nations in the world.

4. In the circular flow model, imports and exports are added as flows to the _____ market. Canadian expenditures pay for (exports, imports) _____, and foreign expenditures pay for _____.

5. If Nigeria can produce 10 kg of coffee at a cost of 1 barrel of oil, and Kenya can produce 25 kg of coffee at a cost of 1 barrel of oil, then _____ has the lower cost for producing oil, and _____ has the lower cost of producing coffee. The comparative advantage for oil lies with _____ and for coffee lies with _____.

6. The amount of one product that a nation must export in order to import one unit of another product is the _____.

7. When the dollar price of foreign currency increases, the dollar has (appreciated, depreciated) _____, while foreign currency has _____.

8. In the market for Japanese yen, an increase in the (demand for, supply of) _____ yen will decrease the dollar price of yen, while an increase in the _____ yen will increase the dollar price of yen. If the dollar price of yen increases, then Japanese goods imported into Canada will be (more, less) _____ expensive to Canadians, while Canadian goods exported to Japan will be _____ expensive for Japanese.

9. The major government policies that restrict trade include protective _____, import _____, _____ barriers, and _____ subsidies.

10. Governments may mistakenly intervene in trade with other nations because they mistakenly think of (exports, imports) _____ as helpful, and _____ as harmful for their own economy.

11. Tariffs and quotas (benefit, cost) _____ domestic firms and their employees in the protected industries but _____ domestic consumers of their products in the form of (lower, higher) _____ prices than would exist if there were free trade.

12. The three cardinal principles established in the GATT are:
   (a) _____ treatment for all member nations;
   (b) reduction of _____ by multilateral negotiations; and
   (c) the elimination of import _____.

13. The major provisions of the Uruguay round of GATT negotiations include _____ reductions, coverage of _____ by GATT, cuts in subsidies to _____ producers, protection of _____ property, phased reduction of _____ on textiles and apparel, and the formation of a _____ Organization.

14. The trade bloc first formed as the Common Market in 1958 is now known as the _____. The specific aims of the Common Market were to abolish tariffs and quotas among (member, non-member) _____ nations, to establish common tariffs on goods imported from _____ nations, to permit free movement of capital and _____ within the Common Market nations, and to adopt common policies on other matters.

15. The FTA joined Canada in a trade bloc with _____ in the year _____. Under the name NAFTA, the FTA was extended in the year _____, when _____ joined the bloc.

■ **PROBLEMS AND PROJECTS**

1. Julius and Murray are tailors. Their production possibilities tables for trousers and jackets are given below. Initially they work independently, with Julius choosing production alternative D, and Murray choosing E from his alternatives.

JULIUS: Production Possibilities Table

Product	Production Alternative					
	A	B	C	D	E	F
Trousers	75	60	45	30	15	0
Jackets	0	10	20	30	40	50

MURRAY: Production Possibilities Table

			Production Alternative				
Product	A	B	C	D	E	F	G
Trousers	60	50	40	30	20	10	0
Jackets	0	5	10	15	20	25	30

(a) For Julius 1 pair of trousers costs _____ jackets, and 1 jacket costs _____ pairs of trousers.

(b) For Murray 1 pair of trousers costs _____ jackets, and 1 jacket costs _____ pairs of trousers.

(c) The comparative advantage in making trousers lies with _____ because his opportunity cost is (lower, higher) _____. The comparative advantage in making jackets lies with _____ because his opportunity cost is (lower, higher) _____.

(d) If Julius and Murray form a partnership, Julius should specialize in making the _____, and Murray should specialize in making the _____.

(e) Working independently Julius and Murray would produce a total of 50 pairs of trousers and 50 jackets. If each specializes fully, their combined output will be _____ pairs of trousers, and _____ jackets. Thus, the gain from specialization is _____ pairs of trousers and _____ jackets.

2. The nations of Venezuela and Costa Rica have the production possibility tables shown below.

(a) Find the opportunity costs:

Venezuela: 1 apple costs _____

1 banana costs _____

Costa Rica: 1 apple costs _____

1 banana costs _____

(b) Determine which country has the comparative advantage in each good:

Apples: _____

Bananas: _____

VENEZUELA: Production Possibilities Table

			Production Alternative			
Product	A	B	C	D	E	F
Apples	40	32	24	16	8	0
Bananas	0	4	8	12	16	20

COSTA RICA: Production Possibilities Table

			Production Alternative			
Product	A	B	C	D	E	F
Apples	75	60	45	30	15	0
Bananas	0	5	10	15	20	25

(c) From the information given we cannot determine specifically what the terms of trade will be. However, the terms of trade must be greater than _____ apples per banana, and less than _____ apples per banana.

(d) Suppose that each nation would choose production alternative C if specialization and trade were impossible. The combined production in the two countries would be _____ apples and _____ bananas.

(e) If each nation specializes completely according to comparative advantage, their combined production will be _____ apples and _____ bananas.

(f) Their combined gains from specialization will be _____ apples and _____ bananas.

(g) Suppose that the nations specialize and then agree to trade 25 apples for 10 bananas. This trade will leave Venezuela consuming _____ apples and _____ bananas. Costa Rica will consume _____ apples and _____ bananas.

(h) Compared to production alternative C, this leaves Venezuela with a gain of _____ apples and _____ bananas. Compared to production alternative C, this leaves Costa Rica with a gain of _____ apples and _____ bananas.

3. The table below shows four different currencies and how much of each can be purchased with 1 Canadian dollar.

(a) In the blanks indicate whether the Canadian dollar appreciated (A) or depreciated (D) against these currencies from Year 1 to Year 2.

Currency per Canadian $

Country	Currency	Year 1	Year 2	A or D
France	Franc	3.4	3.3	_____
Germany	Mark	1.10	1.14	_____
Kuwait	Dinar	.20	.18	_____
Japan	Yen	84	86	_____

(b) Compute the amount of Canadian currency one would have to exchange to get 100 units of each of the four foreign currencies. Use Year 1 exchange rates.

100 Francs = $ _____

100 Marks = $ _____

100 Dinar = $ _____

100 Yen = $ _____

■ TRUE-FALSE

Circle T if the statement is true, F if it is false.

1. Canada is completely dependent on other nations for many products that we do not produce domestically.   **T F**

2. No nation in the world has a higher percentage of GDP represented by exports and imports than Canada does.   **T F**

3. The first economists to explain the principle of comparative advantage were Adam Smith and David Ricardo.   **T F**

4. The principle of comparative advantage applies just as well to individuals or regions as it does to nations.   **T F**

5. If two nations produce only coal and lumber, one of the nations could have the comparative advantage over the other in both coal and lumber. **T F**

6. If two nations have identical cost conditions for producing two goods, neither nation will have a comparative advantage.   **T F**

7. A nation that has resources that are more productive in every good than another nation's resources will be unable to gain by trading with the less productive nation.   **T F**

8. Specialization and trade according to comparative advantage will enable a nation to have combinations of goods that lie outside the nation's production possibility curve.   **T F**

9. In the foreign exchange market graph, if the British pound price of Japanese yen is plotted on the vertical axis, on the horizontal axis must be the quantity of British pounds.   **T F**

10. An increase in incomes of Canadian households would tend to increase the supply of Canadian dollars in the exchange market.   **T F**

11. If the supply of Canadian dollars in the foreign exchange market increases, the Canadian dollar will appreciate relative to foreign currencies, *ceteris paribus*.   **T F**

12. If the U.S. dollar price of the Canadian dollar is $0.80, then the Canadian dollar price of the U.S. dollar must be $1.20.   **T F**

13. An appreciation of the Canadian dollar will make our imports less expensive to Canadian consumers, and our exports more expensive to foreign consumers.   **T F**

14. Export subsidies are government payments to domestic producers to encourage them to export more.   **T F**

15. Bastiat's purpose in the Petition of the Candlemakers was to satirize the arguments of producers who seek protection from competition.   **T F**

16. The formation of a trade bloc encourages efficiency in production because access to larger markets enables producers to benefit from large-scale production.   **T F**

17. The 1989 Free Trade Agreement has benefited some Canadian firms and has harmed others.   **T F**

18. NAFTA includes Canada, the United States, Mexico and some Central American nations.   **T F**

■ MULTIPLE-CHOICE

Circle the letter that corresponds to the best answer.

1. As of the late 1990s, our imports and exports amount to approximately what fraction of Canada's GDP?
  (a)   1/10
  (b)   1/6
  (c)   1/4
  (d)   1/3

2. Based on the data in the text, which sector represents the largest percentage of Canadian exports?
  (a)   agricultural products
  (b)   automotive products
  (c)   energy products
  (d)   forest products

3. Based on recent data in the text, which sector represents the largest percentage of Canadian imports?
(a) agricultural products
(b) automotive products
(c) consumer products
(d) machinery and equipment

Questions 4 through 7 are based on the data in the table which shows maximum production levels for the regions of Heath and Cliff, both of which have constant costs of production, and are able to trade with one another.

Heath		Cliff	
Wool	Peat	Wool	Peat
100	20	120	40

4. In Heath, the domestic opportunity cost of:
(a) 1 wool is 5 peat
(b) 1 wool is 1/5 peat
(c) 1 wool is 1.2 wool
(d) 1 peat is 1/5 wool

5. In Cliff, the domestic opportunity cost of:
(a) 1 peat is 3 wool
(b) 1 peat is 2 peat
(c) 1 wool is 3 peat
(d) 1 peat is 1/3 wool

6. Which of the following statements is **not** true?
(a) Heath has the comparative advantage in wool
(b) Cliff should specialize in peat
(c) both Heath and Cliff could gain from trading with one another
(d) Heath has the comparative advantage in both wool and peat

7. The terms of trade will be:
(a) more than 3 wool for 1 peat
(b) less than 5 wool for 1 peat
(c) between 3 and 5 wool for 1 peat
(d) not between 3 and 5 wool for 1 peat

8. The foreign exchange market is a market for:
(a) imports and exports
(b) shares in multinational corporations
(c) bonds sold by foreign government
(d) currencies

9. If the equilibrium exchange rate changes so that the dollar price of Japanese yen increases:
(a) the dollar has appreciated
(b) the yen has depreciated
(c) Canadians will be able to buy more Japanese goods
(d) Japanese will be able to buy more Canadian goods

10. If the United States begins to demand more Mexican goods:
(a) the demand for the peso will increase, causing the peso to appreciate
(b) the demand for the peso will increase, causing the peso to depreciate
(c) the supply of U.S. dollars will decrease, causing the dollar to appreciate
(d) the supply of U.S. dollars will decrease, causing the dollar to depreciate

11. Which of the following is designed to restrict trade?
(a) export subsidies
(b) NAFTA
(c) GATT
(d) import quotas

12. Why do governments often restrict international trade?
(a) to expand their nation's production possibilities
(b) to protect domestic industries from foreign competition
(c) to encourage efficiency in production
(d) to benefit consumers

13. One important outcome of the Uruguay round of GATT was:
(a) elimination of services from the agreement
(b) greater restrictions on patents and copyrights
(c) increasing tariffs on manufactured products
(d) reductions in agricultural subsidies

14. The European Common Market:
(a) helped to abolish tariffs and import quotas among its members
(b) aimed for the eventual free movement of capital and labour within the member nations
(c) imposed common tariffs on products imported from countries outside the Common Market
(d) did all of the above

15. One potential problem with the European Union is that:
  (a) a free flow of labour and capital within the EU is likely to create mass unemployment
  (b) economies of large-scale production will result in higher consumer prices
  (c) trade with nonmember nations may diminish
  (d) all of the above   c

16. A trade bloc is the same thing as a:
  (a) nontariff barrier
  (b) import quota   c
  (c) free-trade zone
  (d) trade restriction

17. For Canada, one advantage of NAFTA is:
  (a) higher prices for consumer goods   b
  (b) access for Canadian producers to larger markets
  (c) the opportunity to reduce our reliance on imports
  (d) more low wage job opportunities for Canadians

18. Which Canadian firms will be most able to compete effectively under a system of freer world trade?
  (a) firms that were previously protected by tariffs and quotas   b
  (b) firms in industries where Canada has a comparative advantage
  (c) firms that had monopoly power in the Canadian market
  (d) very few Canadian firms will be able to compete

■ **DISCUSSION QUESTIONS**

1. What are Canada's principal exports and imports? Why does Canada trade so much with the United States? Why does international trade represent a bigger part of Canada's economy than of the U.S. economy?

2. What are some factors contributing to the growth in international trade since World War II?

3. Sketch how the international trade component can be built into the circular flow model.

4. Explain how comparative costs determine which producer has the comparative advantage. What determines the terms of trade? What is the gain that results from specialization and trade according to comparative advantage?

5. Suppose that Dr. Ocula is an outstanding eye surgeon with good enough hand-eye coordination that he keyboards faster than anyone else in town. Use the principle of comparative advantage to explain why he hires someone else to do the word-processing in his office, even though he could do it faster himself.

6. How might an appreciation of the value of the Canadian dollar relative to the American dollar depress the Canadian economy? Which Canadians would be harmed, and which would benefit?

7. What are the major types of trade barriers, and how do they work to restrict international trade?

8. Hypothetically, suppose that Canada has a 20% import tariff on shoelaces. Also suppose that there are only about twenty Canadian manufacturers of shoelaces. If the tariff raises shoelace prices in Canada by 25 to 50 cents a pair, how much would this tariff cost you each year? Estimate the annual benefit of the tariff to each Canadian manufacturer. Do you know whether in fact there is a shoelace tariff? Do you think that Canadian shoelace manufacturers know? How do you explain the difference in the knowledge, and how does this help explain why the government might have implemented this tariff?

9. What does Canada gain from participating in GATT? Which kinds of Canadian industries would be most likely to support the GATT initiatives? And which would be most likely to oppose them?

10. Is it possible that both Canada and the United States can gain from the NAFTA? If so, how?

11. "Canadian firms cannot compete in the global economy because wages are too high in Canada." Discuss this assertion.

■ **ANSWERS**

FILL-IN QUESTIONS

1. limited, smaller

2. increased; increased; developed; United States

3. transportation, communications, tariffs (trade barriers), peace

4. product; imports, exports

5. Nigeria, Kenya; Nigeria, Kenya

6. terms of trade

7. depreciated, appreciated

8. supply of, demand for; more, less

9. tariffs, quotas, nontariff, export

10. exports, imports

11. benefit, cost, higher

12. equal or non-discriminatory; tariffs; quotas

13. tariff, services, agricultural, intellectual, quotas, World Trade

14. European Union; member, nonmember, labour

15. United States, 1989; 1993, Mexico

PROBLEMS AND PROJECTS

1. (a) 2/3, 1 1/2; (b) 1/2, 2; (c) Murray, lower, Julius, lower; (d) jackets, trousers; (e) 60, 50; 10, 0.

2. (a) 1/2 banana, 2 apples, 1/3 banana, 3 apples; (b) Costa Rica, Venezuela; (c) 2, 3; (d) 69, 18; (e) 75, 20; (f) 6, 2; (g) 25, 10, 50, 10; (h) 1, 2, 5, 0.

3. (a) D,A,D,A; (b) 29.4, 90.9, 500, 1.19

TRUE-FALSE

1. T	**2.** F	**3.** T	**4.** T	**5.** F	**6.** T
7. F	**8.** T	**9.** F	**10.** T	**11.** F	**12.** F
13. T	**14.** T	**15.** T	**16.** T	**17.** T	**18.** F

MULTIPLE-CHOICE

1. (d)	**2.** (b)	**3.** (d)	**4.** (b)	**5.** (a)	**6.** (d)
7. (c)	**8.** (d)	**9.** (d)	**10.** (a)	**11.** (d)	**12.** (b)
13. (d)	**14.** (d)	**15.** (c)	**16.** (c)	**17.** (b)	**18.** (b)

CHAPTER 7

Measuring Domestic Output and the Price Level

Macroeconomics deals with the working of the overall economy. Therefore, we need measures of such variables as the overall levels of output, income, and prices. This chapter discusses why such measures are important, defines the key measures, and discusses what the measures can and cannot tell us about the overall economy.

The measurement of the economy's overall production is known as national income accounting. The key measure is gross domestic output (GDP), which measures the total market value of all final goods and services produced in the country in a year. GDP can be determined through either the "income approach" or the "expenditure approach." In total, incomes and expenditures must be equal because the value of the nation's output equals the total expenditures on this output, and these expenditures become the incomes of those in the nation who have produced this output.

By the expenditures approach, GDP consists of four categories: personal consumption (C), gross investment (I_g), government purchases (G), and net exports (X_n). This same total GDP (after a few adjustments) is also distributed as incomes to households as: wages, rent, interest, and profit. The chapter also explains the relationship of GDP to other national income accounting measures: gross national product (GNP), personal income (PI), and disposable income (DI). The circular flow model (first encountered in Chapter 2) is useful for illustrating the relationship between the income flows and the expenditure flows.

GDP is the market value of the nation's output, so it is measured in dollar terms. GDP measured in this way is known as "nominal GDP" and can fluctuate from year to year either because of variation in the amount of output (real variation in GDP), or because of changes in the value of a dollar (inflation or deflation). To enable us to draw reliable conclusions about changes in the economy's real output, economists have developed a constant dollar measure, known as "real GDP," which is found by deflating nominal GDP by the GDP price index. Another important price index, or measure of the average price level of goods and services, is the consumer price index (CPI). Canada's reported inflation rate is based on movements in the CPI.

The final section of Chapter 7 points out some of the limitations of the real GDP measure. Even if GDP is adjusted for inflation, it is dangerous to assume that GDP is a good measure of the well-being of the society.

■ CHECKLIST

When you have studied this chapter, you should be able to:

☐ State three purposes of national income accounting.

☐ Define GDP (gross domestic product).

☐ Explain why GDP is a monetary measure.

☐ Explain what is meant by "final goods and services," describe how double counting is avoided in constructing the accounts, and describe what "value added" means.

☐ Provide some examples of transactions that are excluded from GDP.

☐ Explain why GDP must be the same total whether calculated from the expenditure approach or the income approach.

☐ Describe the four basic expenditure components that comprise GDP.

☐ Compute GDP using the expenditure approach when you are provided with appropriate data.

☐ Explain: (1) the difference between gross and net investment; (2) why changes in inventories are investment; and (3) the relation between net investment and economic growth.

☐   Identify the four income components and the two adjustments utilized in the income approach to determining GDP.

☐   Compute GDP using the income approach when you are provided with appropriate data.

☐   Define each of the following and, when you are given the needed data, compute: GNP, PI, and DI.

☐   Explain the difference between nominal GDP and real GDP.

☐   Given the relevant data, derive real GDP from nominal GDP by two methods.

☐   Given any two of real GDP, nominal GDP, GDP price index, solve for the third.

☐   Explain the concept of a price index, and discuss the differences between the CPI and GDP price index.

☐   Give four reasons why the CPI tends to overstate the rate of inflation.

☐   Present seven reasons why GDP may not be a good measure of social welfare.

■   CHAPTER OUTLINE

1. National income accounting consists of concepts that enable economists to: (a) measure the economy's output, (b) measure changes and trends in the economy's output over time, and (c) formulate policies designed to improve the economy's performance.

2. The gross domestic product (GDP) is the total market value of all final goods and services produced within the country during a year.

   (a)   GDP is a monetary measure.

   (b)   To avoid double counting, GDP includes only final goods and services (goods and services that are not for resale or further processing). Value added represents the contribution made to final output by the individual firm that may be supplying either final or intermediate outputs.

   (c)   GDP excludes nonproductive transactions such as purely financial transactions and second-hand sales.

3. Measurement of GDP can be accomplished by either the expenditure or the income approach, but the same result is obtained by the two methods.

4. In the expenditure approach, GDP is computed by adding the total amounts of the four types of spending for final goods and services:

   (a)   Personal consumption expenditures (C) are the expenditures of households for durable and nondurable goods and for services.

   (b)   Gross investment (I_g) is the sum of all final purchases by governments and business firms for machinery, equipment, and tools; all construction spending; and changes in inventories.

   (1) A change in inventories is included in investment because it is part of the year's output (even though it was not sold during the year).

   (2) Investment does not include expenditures for stocks or bonds or for second-hand capital goods.

   (3) Net investment equals gross investment less the amount of investment in replacement capital.

   (4) An economy in which net investment is positive (zero, negative) is an expanding (a static, a declining) economy.

   (c)   Government purchases of goods and services (G) are the current expenditures (that is, excluding investment) made by all governments in the economy on products of businesses and for resource services from households.

   (d)   Net exports (X_n) equal the expenditures made by foreigners for goods and services produced in the economy less the expenditures made by the consumers, government, and businesses of the economy for goods and services produced in foreign nations.

   (e)   The sum of the four major expenditure categories gives aggregate expenditures, or Gross Domestic Product. In symbols, $C + I_g + G + X_n = GDP$.

5. Computation of GDP by the income method requires the addition of the eight uses for the income derived from the production and sale of final goods and services:

   (a)   wages, salaries, and supplementary labour income;

   (b)   corporation profits before taxes;

   (c)   interest and miscellaneous investment income;

   (d)   farmers' income;

   (e)   net income of nonfarm unincorporated business, including rent;

   (f)   inventory valuation adjustment;

   (g)   indirect taxes;

   (h)   capital consumption allowances (depreciation).

6. In addition to GDP, several other national income measures are useful.

(a) Gross national product (GNP) measures the total of all final goods and services produced during a year by resources supplied by Canadians (whether in Canada or abroad).

(b) Personal income (PI) is the total income received by households, earned or unearned.

(c) Disposable income (DI) is PI less personal taxes and other transfers to government; and is equal to PI less personal taxes.

(d) Figure 7-3 is a more realistic and complex circular flow diagram that shows the flows of expenditures and incomes among households, businesses, governments, and the rest of the world.

7. The value of different years' outputs (GDP levels) can be usefully compared only if the value of money itself does not change.

(a) The value of money changes whenever there is inflation or deflation.

(b) GDP calculated at current prices, and unadjusted for price level changes, is called *nominal* GDP. GDP calculated to adjust for price level changes, or measured in constant dollars, is called *real* GDP.

8. We construct a price index to measure the overall trend in prices, to enable us to measure inflation and deflation, and to adjust nominal GDP for price changes.

(a) The price level is stated as an index number that measures the ratio of the combined price of a market basket of goods in a given year to the combined price of a market basket of goods in a base year, with that ratio multiplied by 100.

(b) To adjust nominal GDP figures for inflation, divide the year's nominal GDP by that year's price index (expressed in hundredths). The result is the real GDP.

(c) When the price index in a year is below (above) its base year level of 100, the nominal GDP figure for that year is inflated (deflated) by this adjustment.

(d) An alternative method of finding real GDP is to calculate the value of the current year's output using base year prices. The GDP price index can then be found by dividing nominal GDP by real GDP.

9. Another important price index is the consumer price index (CPI).

(a) The CPI measures the prices of a fixed market basket of some 600 consumer goods and services purchased by "typical" urban Canadian consumers.

(b) The CPI for a given year is found as the price of the market basket in the given year divided by the price of the same basket in the base year, all multiplied by 100.

(c) The rate of inflation or deflation is computed by taking the annual percentage change in the CPI.

(d) The GDP price index measures the prices of *all* goods and services produced in the economy, and uses the current composition of output to determine the relative importance (or weight) of each item in the basket.

10. Inflation rates calculated from the CPI overstate the rate of inflation by up to about 0.5% per year because the CPI does not account for:

(a) consumers shifting their spending to buy less of goods that are becoming *relatively* more expensive, and more of goods that are becoming *relatively* less expensive;

(b) new products;

(c) quality improvements;

(d) consumers shopping to take advantage of discounts or special sale prices at particular stores.

11. GDP is reasonably accurate and useful for measuring domestic production, but is not, for the following reasons, a measure of society's overall well-being.

(a) It excludes the value of goods and services produced but not bought and sold in markets.

(b) It excludes leisure time.

(c) It does not record product quality improvements.

(d) It does not measure changes in the composition and the distribution of society's output.

(e) It does not account for population change. (However, the per capita GDP measure overcomes this criticism.)

(f) It does not record the environmental pollution costs associated with producing final goods and services.

(g) It does not measure the market value of final goods and services produced in the underground economy.

■ **TERMS AND CONCEPTS**

capital consumption
allowances
(depreciation)

consumer price index
(CPI)

corporate income
   taxes
depreciation
disposable income
dividends
double counting
expenditure and
   income approaches
final and intermediate
   goods
government current
   purchases of goods
   and services
gross and net
   investment
gross domestic
   product (GDP)
gross national product
   (GNP)

indirect taxes
national income
   accounting
net domestic income
   at factor costs
net exports
nominal GDP
personal consumption
   expenditure
personal income
personal saving
price index
real GDP
undistributed
   corporate profits
value added

■ HINTS AND TIPS

1. This is a fairly difficult chapter, mainly because of the number of new concepts introduced. Some memorization is inevitably required in this chapter, but the more you understand this chapter, the less you will have to rely on memorization.

2. Accounting, in the sense used in this chapter, is really a process of adding-up. It is up to you to learn which elements to add up to arrive at each of the several income measures in this chapter.

3. Of all income measures, GDP is the most important. You must know exactly what it means, and what component parts are included in GDP. Figure 7-1 shows the components from both the expenditure approach and the income approach. Understanding of GDP is also enhanced by considering what is omitted from GDP.

4. Another crucial concept in this chapter is the distinction between real GDP and nominal GDP. Make sure that you clearly understand the distinction, and that you know how to convert from one to the other.

■ FILL-IN QUESTIONS

1. National income accounting is valuable because it provides a means of tracking the level of _____ in the economy and the course it has followed over the long run; it also provides the in-

formation required to devise and put into effect the public _____ that will improve the performance of the economy.

2. GDP is the abbreviation for _____, and measures the total market _____ of all final goods and services (produced, sold) _____ in an economy in a year. The goods and services are valued at their _____ prices.

3. GNP is the abbreviation for Gross _____ Product. Suppose that in 1999 Danish resources produce 500 billion kroner worth of final goods and services in Denmark, and 40 billion worth of final goods and services in other countries. Meanwhile, 30 billion worth of final goods and services are produced in Denmark by foreign owned resources. Denmark's GDP is _____ billion kroner, and Denmark's GNP is _____ billion kroner.

4. In measuring GDP, only final goods and services are included; if intermediate goods and services were included, the accountant would be committing the error of _____.

5. Value added is the difference between the market value of a firm's _____ and its _____ from other firms. The total value added to a product at all stages of production equals the _____ of the final product; and the total value added to all final products produced in the economy during a year is the

_____.

6. GDP can be computed by adding up all spending on final goods and services produced this year. This method is the _____ approach. GDP can also be computed by adding all incomes derived from the production of this year's output. This method is the _____ approach.

7. In using the expenditures approach, national income accountants divide expenditures on final goods and services into four categories or expenditure streams:
   (a) _____
   (b) _____
   (c) _____
   (d) _____

8. In symbols, the GDP by the expenditures approach = _____ + _____ + _____ + _____

9. Gross investment includes all the final purchases of _____ goods (such as machinery, equipment and tools) by businesses and governments, all _____ of new buildings and houses, and changes in _____.

10. Net investment is less than gross investment by an amount equal to _____.

11. If gross investment is less than depreciation, net investment is (positive, zero, negative) _____ and the economy's stock of capital is (constant, declining, increasing) _____.

12. Government transfer payments are not counted as part of government purchase of goods and services because transfer payments do not represent a payment for goods _____.

13. An economy's net exports equal its _____ less its _____.

14. In the income approach, GDP is computed by adding the incomes earned by inputs to the productive process to two nonincome charges: _____ and _____.

15. The net incomes of _____ businesses represent a mixture of labour income and investment income that is impossible to segregate.

16. Supplementary labour income consists of some components of employers' labour costs that are sometimes called "_____."

17. Corporation profits are distributed in three ways:
(a) _____
(b) _____
(c) _____

18. Disposable income equals _____ income minus personal _____ and other personal _____ to government.

19. A price index is the ratio of the combined price of a market basket of goods and services in a given year to the combined _____ of the _____ basket of goods and services in the _____ year, with the ratio being multiplied by 100.

20. The price index used to adjust the nominal GDP for changes in the price level is called the _____. To obtain real or _____ dollar

GDP, _____ the year's nominal GDP by that year's price index expressed in hundredths.

21. For several reasons the real GDP is not a measure of social welfare in an economy.
(a) It excludes both _____ transactions that result in the production of goods and services, and the amount of _____ enjoyed by the citizens of the economy.
(b) It fails to record improvements in the _____ of the products produced, changes in the composition and distribution of the economy's total _____, the _____ costs that are an undesirable side-effect of producing the GDP, and the goods and services produced in the _____ economy.

22. When the population of an economy grows at a faster rate than its real GDP grows, GDP per _____ falls, and the standard of living in the economy (rises, falls, remains constant) _____.

■ **PROBLEMS AND PROJECTS**

1. Below are hypothetical data for the economy in a particular year. There is no statistical discrepancy.

	Billions of $
Exports	169
Corporate profits before taxes	46
Capital consumption allowances (depreciation)	76
Government current purchases of goods and services	133
Accrued net income of farm operators from farm production	4
Indirect taxes (less subsidies)	75
Wages, salaries, supplementary labour income	373
Gross investment	139
Personal saving	49
Corporate income taxes	17
Government transfer payments	149
Interest and miscellaneous investment income	59
Net income from nonfarm unincorporated businesses, including rent	36
Personal consumption expenditures	398
Imports	170
Undistributed corporate profits	7
Personal taxes	136

Compute each of the following:

(a) Dividends $_____
(b) Net Exports $_____
(c) Net Investment $_____
(d) Gross Domestic Product $_____

2. In 1998 a steel company purchased $100 million worth of new machinery, $25 million worth of used machinery, and spent $113 million building new corporate headquarters. The company had $520 million worth of inventory of steel products at the beginning of the year and $482 million worth of inventory at year end. Depreciation was $30 million in 1998.

(a) Determine this company's contribution to the nation's gross investment for 1998.

(b) Determine the company's contribution to net investment for 1998.

3. Suppose the toy industry consists of only three firms: a wood producer, a toy manufacturer, and a toy retailer. The tables below show their financial data.

Wood Producer			
Purchases of material inputs	$0	Sales to toy manufacturer	$84
Wages	65		
Profits	19		

Toy Manufacturer			
Purchases from wood producer	$84	Sales to toy retailer	$110
Wages	16		
Profits	10		

Toy Retailer			
Purchases from toy manufacturer	$110	Sales to consumers	$150
Wages	30		
Profits	10		

(a) Based on the firms' data, complete the table below:

Firm	Gross Value of Production	Purchases from other Firms	Value Added
Wood producer	$_____	$_____	$_____
Toy manufacturer	_____	_____	_____
Toy retailer	_____	_____	_____
TOTALS	_____	_____	_____

(b) Compute the total incomes, or factor payments:

Wages $_____
Profits $_____
Total Incomes $_____

(c) Explain why the totals in (a) and (b) should be the same.

4. The next table contains data on Canada's nominal GDP, constant dollar GDP, and the GDP price index for a number of years. Complete the missing entries.

Year	Nominal GDP (Billion $)	Real GDP (Billion $)	GDP Price Index
1984	$444.7	$_____	95.2
1985	477.9	489.6	_____
1986	_____	505.7	100.0
1987	551.6	526.8	_____
1988	605.9	_____	109.5
1989	_____	565.6	114.9

5. In the table below are nominal GDP figures for three years and the price indices for each of the three years. (The GDP figures are in billions.)

(a) Which of the three years appears to be the base year? _____.

(b) Between:
(1) 1929 and 1933 the economy experienced (inflation, deflation) _____.
(2) 1933 and 1939 the economy experienced (inflation, deflation) _____.

Year	Nominal GDP	Price Index	Real GDP
1929	$104	121	$_____
1933	56	91	_____
1939	91	100	_____

(c) Use the price indices to compute the real GDP in each year (rounding your answer to the nearest billion dollars).

(d) The nominal GDP figure:
(1) for 1929 was (deflated, inflated, neither) _____.
(2) for 1933 was _____.
(3) for 1939 was _____.

(e) The price level:
(1) fell by _____% from 1929 to 1933;
(2) rose by _____% from 1933 to 1939.

6. Use the information below to calculate for 2000 and 2001 the nominal GDP, the real GDP, and the GDP price index. 1986 is the base year.

Good	Out-put in 2000	Out-put in 2001	Price in 1986	Price in 2000	Price in 2001
Books	20	22	$8	$10	$12
Cards	1000	900	$1	$1	$1
Dolls	8	10	$15	$20	$21
Grain	100	80	$2	$2	$3

(a) 2000 nominal GDP $_____
(b) 2001 nominal GDP $_____
(c) 2000 real GDP $_____
(d) 2001 real GDP $_____
(e) 2000 GDP price index _____
(f) 2001 GDP price index _____
(g) The economy experienced (deflation, inflation) _____ of _____% from 2000 to 2001.
(h) The economy produced (less, more) _____ goods in 2001 than in 2000.

7. Assume that the objective of the gross domestic product measure is to reflect the value of all final goods and services produced in the nation during a year. Given this, and what you have learned in this chapter about how GDP accounting works, classify each of the following as: Included, Correctly Excluded, or Incorrectly Excluded.

(a) the transfer from Burke to Solomon of shares in a mining company
(b) gardening services that Slade performs in his own backyard
(c) the increase in inventories held by Canadian Tire stores
(d) health care provided in a provincially-funded hospital in Prince Edward Island
(e) construction services provided in Indonesia by a Canadian-based firm
(f) Wilson's purchase of a second-hand radio from Pickett

8. In each case below, explain whether it is real GDP or nominal GDP that the speaker is discussing.

(a) "Last year the nation's GDP rose by 3.5%, but this did not translate into much growth since the Consumer Price Index was up 2.8%."
(b) "If GDP begins growing faster than population there will be more goods and services per capita, tending to improve our standard of living."

■ **TRUE-FALSE**

Circle T if the statement is true, F if it is false.

1. Gross domestic product measures the total market value of all final goods and services produced in the economy in one year. Ⓣ **F**

2. Both the nominal GDP and the real GDP of the Canadian economy are measured in constant dollars. **T** Ⓕ

3. The total market value of the wine produced in Canada during a year is equal to the number of bottles of wine produced in that year multiplied by the average price at which a bottle is sold during that year. Ⓣ **F**

4. Value added is the market value of a firm's output less the value of the inputs it has purchased from others. Ⓣ **F**

5. If the value added by all firms in an economy were summed, the resulting figure would be equal to gross domestic product. Ⓣ **F**

6. The gross domestic product would be understated if intermediate goods were included in its calculation. **T** Ⓕ

7. Goods purchased with public transfer payments are not included in the gross domestic product. **T** Ⓕ

8. If a car was produced in 1991 and sold in 1992, it would be included in 1992's gross domestic product. **T** Ⓕ

9. The two approaches to the measurement of the gross domestic product yield identical results because one approach measures the total amount spent on the products produced by business firms during a year, while the second approach measures the total income of business firms during the year. **T** Ⓕ

10. The expenditure approach to computing GDP is also known as the factor payment approach. **T** Ⓕ

11. The expenditure made by a household to have a new home built is a personal consumption expenditure. **T** Ⓕ

12. In national income accounting any increase in the inventories of business firms is included in gross investment.   **T** F

13. The revenue from the sale of new issues of stocks is included in gross investment but not in net investment.   **T** F

14. If gross investment is greater than capital consumption during a given year, the economy's stock of capital has increased.   **T** F

15. Gross investment cannot be a negative amount.   **T** F

16. The net exports of an economy equal its exports of goods and services less its imports of goods and services.   **T** F

17. Dividends are the only part of corporate profits that are included in calculating gross domestic product by the income approach.   **T** F

Use the data in the following table to answer true-false questions 18 to 21 and multiple-choice questions 10 to 16. There is no statistical discrepancy.

	Billions
Personal consumption expenditure	$50
Net investment	10
Capital consumption allowance	7
Government purchases of goods and services	31
Exports	8
Imports	6
Wages, salaries, and other labour income	40
Interest	9
Corporation income taxes	8
Dividends	11
Undistributed corporation profits	3
Net farm incomes	2
Net nonincorporated business incomes	12
Inventory evaluation adjustment	-1
Indirect taxes less subsidies	18
Government transfers to households	9
Personal taxes	20

18. The stock of capital goods in the economy has expanded.   **T** F

19. Gross investment is equal to $17 billion.   **T** F

20. This is a static economy.   T **F**

21. Net exports are equal to $2 billion.   **T** F

22. A price index measures the combined price of a particular collection of goods and services in a given period relative to the combined price of identical or similar goods and services in a reference period. **T** F

23. The base year of a price index must always be the first year of the period covered.   T **F**

24. Comparison of a gross domestic product with the gross domestic product of an earlier year when the price level has risen between the two years necessitates the "inflation" of the GDP figure in the later year.   **T** F

25. In a year when nominal GDP rises, real GDP must also rise, though not necessarily by the same percentage.   T **F**

26. If the price index for 1990 is 126 and the price index for 1991 is 130, the price level rose by 4% between 1990 and 1991.   **T** F

27. The inflation rate calculated from the consumer price index tends to overstate the increases in the cost of living.   **T** F

28. A GDP value that reflects current prices is called current dollar or nominal GDP.   **T** F

29. Nominal GDP figures are adjusted for price changes over time by expressing each year's price index in hundredths and dividing it into the nominal GDP of that year.   **T** F

30. GDP is an accurate measure of the social welfare of society.   T **F**

31. The presence of an underground economy results in an overstatement of the GDP value.   T **F**

■ **MULTIPLE-CHOICE**

Circle the letter that corresponds to the best answer.

1. Which of the following is not an important purpose for national income accounting?
 (a) to provide a basis for the formulation and application of policies designed to improve the economy's performance

(b) to permit measurement of the economic efficiency of the economy

(c) to permit the estimation of the output of final goods and services in the economy

(d) to enable the economist to chart the growth of the economy over a period of time

2. In the computation of GDP, to include both the value of a loaf of bread and the value of the flour that goes into the bread would be an example of:

(a) including a nonmarket transaction

(b) including a nonproductive transaction

(c) including a noninvestment transaction

(d) double counting

3. In the definition of GDP the term "final goods and services" refers to:

(a) goods and services that are in the final stage of production

(b) goods and services that have been produced and purchased this year

(c) goods and services purchased this year for final use and not for resale or further processing

(d) goods and services produced in prior years and finally sold this year

4. Excluded from the measurement of GDP are all of the following with the exception of:

(a) government transfer payments

(b) purchases of stocks and bonds

(c) second-hand sales

(d) investment expenditures by business firms

5. Net investment equals gross investment less:

(a) gross national product

(b) net inventory change

(c) capital consumption allowances

(d) government investment expenditure

6. If net investment is a positive value, a nation's stock of capital is:

(a) increasing

(b) declining

(c) staying constant

(d) not enough information provided to reach a conclusion

7. Which of the following does not represent investment?

(a) an increase in the quantity of shoes on the shelves of a shoe store

(b) the construction of a house that will be occupied by its owner

(c) the purchase of newly issued shares of stock in Canadian Pacific Limited

(d) the construction of a factory building using money borrowed from a bank

8. A refrigerator is produced by its manufacturer in 1991, sold during 1991 to a retailer, and sold by the retailer to a final consumer in 1992. The refrigerator is:

(a) counted as consumption in 1991

(b) counted as investment in 1992

(c) counted as investment in 1991

(d) not included in the gross domestic product of 1991

9. The income approach to GDP sums the total income earned by resource suppliers and adds two nonincome charges:

(a) saving and investment

(b) depreciation and indirect taxes less subsidies

(c) indirect business taxes and undistributed corporate profits

(d) depreciation and net investment

Questions 10 to 16 use the national income accounting data given in the table in the true-false section.

10. Gross domestic product is equal to:

(a) $90 billion

(b) $100 billion

(c) $107 billion

(d) $109 billion

11. Corporate profits are equal to:

(a) $15 billion

(b) $17 billion

(c) $19 billion

(d) $22 billion

12. Net exports are equal to:

(a) $3 billion

(b) $2 billion

(c) -$32 billion

(d) $32 billion

13. The net domestic income is equal to:

(a) $70 billion

(b) $75 billion

(c) $80 billion

(d) $83 billion

14. Personal income is equal to:
  (a) $70 billion
  (b) $74 billion
  (c) $77 billion
  (d) $81 billion

15. Personal disposable income is equal to:
  (a) $50 billion
  (b) $54 billion
  (c) $57 billion
  (d) $63 billion

16. Personal saving is equal to:
  (a)   -$8 billion
  (b)   -$3 billion
  (c) $4 billion
  (d) $8 billion

17. In national income accounting personal income is:
  (a)   income earned by the factors of production for their current contribution to production
  (b)   income received by households before personal taxes
  (c)   income received by households less savings
  (d)   income received by households less personal consumption expenditure

18. If both nominal GDP and the level of prices are rising, it is evident that:
  (a)   real GDP is constant
  (b)   real GDP is rising but not as rapidly as prices
  (c)   real GDP is declining
  (d)   no conclusion can be drawn concerning the real GDP of the economy on the basis of this information.

19. In 1971 the Canadian nominal GDP was $97 billion and in 1991 the nominal GDP was $674 billion. The GDP price index (1986 = 100) was 33.8 in 1971 and 122 in 1991. The percentage change in real GDP was approximately:
  (a)   22%
  (b)   67.2%
  (c)   93%
  (d)   594%

20. The real GDP in Canada in 1989 was $566 billion and in 1991 it was $553 billion. It can be concluded that:
  (a)   the price level in Canada declined between 1989 and 1991
  (b)   the price level in Canada rose between 1989 and 1991

  (c)   the quantity of goods and services produced in Canada fell between 1989 and 1991
  (d)   the quantity of goods and services produced in Canada increased between 1989 and 1991

21. In an economy, the total expenditure for a market basket of goods in year 1 (the base year) was $400 million. In year 2, the total expenditure for the same basket of goods was $450 million. What was the GDP price index for year 2?
  (a)   88
  (b)   112.5
  (c)   188
  (d)   103

22. Changes in the real GDP from one year to the next do not reflect:
  (a)   changes in the quality of the goods and services produced
  (b)   changes in the size of the population of the economy
  (c)   changes in the average length of the work week
  (d)   any of the above changes

23. A price index one year was 145 and the next year it was 167. What is the approximate percentage change in the price level from one year to the next as measured by that index?
  (a)   12%
  (b)   13%
  (c)   14%
  (d)   15%

24. GDP is deficient as a measure of social welfare because GDP does not reflect:
  (a)   increased leisure enjoyed by members of society
  (b)   the composition and distribution of output
  (c)   transactions in the underground economy
  (d)   all of the above

25. Which of the following is **not** another term for nominal GDP?
  (a)   current dollar GDP
  (b)   unadjusted GDP
  (c)   real GDP
  (d)   money GDP

26. The consumer price index tends to overstate the rate of inflation because:

(a) the quality of products tends to increase over time

(b) consumers switch their purchases in favour of goods that have become relatively less expensive

(c) consumers tend to buy more from those stores that offer special sale prices

(d) all of the above reasons

■ DISCUSSION QUESTIONS

1. Of what use are national income accounts to the economist and to the government's economic policy makers?

2. Why is GDP a monetary measure, and why is it necessary that it be a monetary measure?

3. Why does GDP exclude nonproductive transactions? What are the two principal types of nonproductive transactions? List some examples of each.

4. Why are there two ways, both of which yield the same answers, of computing GDP?

5. Why are transfer payments excluded from GDP but included in PI?

6. Is residential construction counted as investment or consumption? Why? Why is a change in inventories counted as an investment?

7. How do you define a static, an expanding, and a declining economy? What is the relationship between gross investment and the capital consumption allowances in these three economic situations?

8. Why do economists find it necessary to inflate and deflate GDP when comparing GDP in different years? How do they do this?

9. Why is GDP not a measure of the social welfare of society? Are there any omissions from GDP that are likely to be particularly problematic if you are trying to use GDP data to compare social welfare in the Bahamas with social welfare in Canada? Or if you are trying to compare social welfare in modern day Canada with Canada a century ago?

■ ANSWERS

FILL-IN QUESTIONS

1. production, policies

2. gross domestic product, value, produced; market

3. national, 530, 540

4. double counting

5. output, purchases; market price, GDP

6. expenditure; income

7. (a) personal consumption expenditure (b) gross investment (c) government current purchase of goods and services (d) net exports

8. C; I_g; G; X_n

9. capital; construction; inventories

10. depreciation

11. negative, declining

12. produced

13. exports, imports

14. indirect taxes, depreciation

15. unincorporated

16. fringe benefits

17. (a) corporation income tax (b) dividends (c) undistributed corporate profits

18. personal, taxes, transfers

19. price, identical, base

20. GDP price index; constant, divide

21. (a) nonmarket, leisure (b) quality, output, environment, underground

22. capita, falls

PROBLEMS AND PROJECTS

1. (a) $22, (b) $-1, (c) $63; (d) Expenditure Approach: 398 + 139 + 133 + (-1) = $669; Income Approach: 373 + 46 + 59 + 4 + 36 + 75 + 76 = $669

2. (a) 100 + 113 + (520 - 482) = $175 million
(b) 175 - 30 = $145 million

3. (a) Wood producer: $84; 0; $84
Toy manufacturer: $110; $84; $26
Toy retailer: $150; $110; $40
Totals: $344; $194; $150
(b) 111; 39; 150
(c) Total incomes = total expenditures

4. 1984: $467.1; 1985: 97.6; 1986: $505.7; 1987: 104.7; 1988: $553.3; 1989: $649.9

5. (a) 1939; (b) (1) deflation, (2) inflation; (c) 86, 62, 91; (d) (1) deflated, (2) inflated, (3) neither; (e) (1) 24.8, (2) 9.9

6. (a) (20 x 10) + (1000 x 1) + (8 x 20) + (100 x 2) = $1560; (b) $1614; (c) (20 x 8) + (1000 x 1) + (8 x 15) + (100 x 2) = $1480; (d) $1386; (e) ($1560/$1480) x 100 = 105.4; (f) 116.4; (g) inflation, 10.5%; (h) less

7. (a) correctly excluded; (b) incorrectly excluded; (c) included; (d) included; (e) correctly excluded; (f) correctly excluded

8. (a) Most of the 3.5% increase in **nominal** GDP is accounted for by price increases; (b) **Real** GDP must grow faster than population for output per capita to increase.

TRUE-FALSE

1. T	**2.** F	**3.** T	**4.** T	**5.** T	**6.** F
7. F	**8.** F	**9.** F	**10.** F	**11.** F	**12.** T
13. F	**14.** T	**15.** T	**16.** T	**17.** F	**18.** T
19. T	**20.** F	**21.** T	**22.** T	**23.** F	**24.** F
25. F	**26.** F	**27.** T	**28.** T	**29.** T	**30.** F
31. F					

MULTIPLE-CHOICE

1. (b)	**2.** (d)	**3.** (c)	**4.** (d)	**5.** (c)	**6.** (a)
7. (c)	**8.** (c)	**9.** (b)	**10.** (d)	**11.** (d)	**12.** (b)
13. (b)	**14.** (b)	**15.** (b)	**16.** (c)	**17.** (b)	**18.** (d)
19. (c)	**20.** (c)	**21.** (b)	**22.** (d)	**23.** (d)	**24.** (d)
25. (c)	**26.** (d)				

CHAPTER 8

Macroeconomic Instability: Unemployment and Inflation

In Chapter 7 you learned how to define and how to compute the nominal and real value of GDP. Chapter 8 deals with how macroeconomic instability is manifested in fluctuations in real GDP, unemployment, and the price level. The chapters that follow will provide fuller explanations for how these variables are determined, why they are subject to fluctuation, and what policies may be used to control them for the benefit of society.

Over the long haul, Canada's real GDP has shown a clear trend of growth (giving us a rising standard of living), but we see continual short-run deviations from the long-run trend. Sometimes we enjoy the prosperity that comes with rapidly growing output and employment, while at other times we suffer through hard times of shrinking output and employment. We refer to such periodic fluctuations in output, employment, and price levels as "business cycles." The first section of the chapter describes the four phases of a typical business cycle and the impact on the production of different kinds of goods.

Unemployment fluctuates significantly during the business cycle, but some types of unemployment persist even when the economy is operating at full capacity. Currently, if Canada is at "full employment" we would expect about 7-8% of the labour force to be unemployed. In fact, our unemployment rate has rarely been this low in recent years. Careful examination of how unemployment is defined and measured reveals several problems that may lead to overstatement or understatement of the unemployment problem. As well as the hardship experienced by unemployed workers themselves, unemployment costs society the lost production that the unemployed could have produced. The relationship between unemployment and lost production is captured in Okun's Law. The burden of unemploy-

ment is not borne equally: unemployment rates vary between men and women, between provinces, between younger and older workers, and between occupations.

Inflation is a second problem that can result from economic instability. Inflation is measured as an annual percentage increase in the general (or average) level of prices in an economy. In the 1990s Canada has experienced mild inflation, but we experienced inflation of over 10% per year as recently as the early 1980s. Inflation can be caused by factors on either the demand side or the supply side of the economy. If inflation is not extreme, its most significant effects are arbitrary redistributions of income and wealth, particularly when the inflation is unanticipated. Some individuals suffer while others benefit. But inflation may not only affect how the pie is divided, it may also affect the size of the pie. The fear of inflation in Canada is rooted in the lesson of history that extremely rapid inflation can lead to a severe breakdown in the economy which can devastate almost everyone's living standard.

■ **CHECKLIST**

When you have studied this chapter, you should be able to:

□ Explain what "macroeconomic stability" means for prices, employment, and growth.

□ Explain what is meant by the business cycle; describe the four phases of a typical cycle; and identify the two sources of noncyclical fluctuations.

□ Identify the phase of the business cycle the Canadian economy is presently passing through.

□ Identify the immediate cause of most cyclical changes in the levels of output and employment.

□ Provide two explanations for why industries producing capital goods and consumer durables are more vulnerable to the business cycle than industries producing services and consumer nondurables.

☐   Distinguish between frictional, structural, and cyclical unemployment; and explain the causes of each kind of unemployment.

☐   Define full employment and the full-employment unemployment rate (the natural rate of unemployment).

☐   Describe the definitions and process used by Statistics Canada to measure the levels of employment, unemployment, labour force, and unemployment rate.

☐   List three criticisms of the data collected from the StatsCan survey.

☐   Given the necessary data, calculate employment, unemployment, labour force, and the unemployment rate.

☐   Define the GDP gap, and state Okun's law.

☐   Identify the economic cost of unemployment and the groups that usually bear larger burdens of unemployment.

☐   Define inflation and the rate of inflation.

☐   Summarize Canada's unemployment experience (since the 1970s) and inflation experience (since the 1920s); and compare Canada's recent experience with the experience of other major nations.

☐   Distinguish between demand-pull and cost-push inflation.

☐   Describe how inflation can arbitrarily redistribute income and wealth among groups, and explain why these effects depend on whether the inflation is anticipated or not.

☐   Give examples of groups that lose from inflation and groups that benefit from inflation.

☐   Describe how labour contracts and loan contracts can be designed to eliminate redistributive effects when inflation is correctly anticipated.

☐   Explain the relationship between nominal and real income, and between nominal and real interest rates.

☐   Discuss how inflation can stimulate real output, and how it can reduce real output.

☐   Explain what hyperinflation is, and how it can create macroeconomic breakdown.

■   **CHAPTER OUTLINE**

1. Canada has experienced a long-run trend of growth in real output, but around this trend we have experienced many business cycles (periods of short-term economic instability).

(a)   A business cycle entails alternating periods of prosperity and recession (or depression). Cycles are of irregular duration and intensity but typically follow a four-phase pattern: peak, recession, trough, and recovery to the next peak.

(b)   The single most important cause of fluctuations in the levels of output and employment in a market economy is fluctuation in the level of total spending or demand.

(c)   Not all changes in employment and output are cyclical; some are due to seasonal and secular influences.

(d)   The business cycle affects the entire economy, but it does not affect every industry or every province in the same way or to the same degree.

(e)   During a cycle, the output of capital goods and consumer durables fluctuates more than the output of services and consumer nondurables because: (1) the purchase of capital and durable goods can be postponed, and (2) the industries producing these goods are largely dominated by a few large firms that hold prices constant and let output decline when demand falls.

2. Full employment does not mean that everyone in the labour force is employed and that unemployment is zero; some unemployment is normal. There are at least three kinds of unemployment:

(a)   Frictional unemployment arises when workers are searching for jobs, or are waiting to take jobs very soon. Such unemployment is inherent in a dynamic economy and is generally desirable for workers and society as a whole.

(b)   Structural unemployment is the result of changes in technology and in the type of goods and services consumers prefer to buy. A mismatch between the skills or location of workers compared to the skills or location required for available jobs makes structural unemployment a serious and longer term problem.

(c)   Cyclical unemployment is the result of insufficient aggregate spending in the economy.

3. Because some frictional and structural unemployment is unavoidable, the full-employment unemployment rate (the natural rate of unemployment) is the sum of frictional and structural unemployment. It is achieved when cyclical unemployment is zero (real output of the economy is equal to its potential output).

(a)   The economy does not usually operate at full employment, so the unemployment rate is not usually at its natural rate. Usually unemployment is above the natural rate, but it is sometimes below.

(b) Canada's current natural rate of unemployment is estimated to be around 7 to 8 percent. Demographic and institutional changes can cause the natural rate to change.

4. Based on the monthly Labour Force Survey of 55,000 households, Statistics Canada finds the unemployment rate by dividing the number of persons in the civilian labour force who are unemployed by the total number of people in the civilian labour force.

(a) Some adults are neither employed nor seeking work, so they are not counted in the labour force.

(b) The estimated unemployment rate tends to understate true unemployment because part-time workers who want full-time jobs are classified as employed, and because discouraged individuals who have abandoned active job search are not counted among the unemployed. Incentives for some people to give false information in the survey leads to overstatement of true unemployment.

(c) Unemployment results in an economic cost of lost output (or a GDP gap). Okun's law is that for every 1% which the actual unemployment rate exceeds the natural rate of unemployment, there is a 2% GDP gap.

(d) The burden of unemployment is unequally distributed among different groups in the labour force. Younger workers, blue-collar workers, less-educated workers, and workers in the Maritimes and Quebec have suffered higher than average unemployment rates in recent years.

(e) Unemployment has also been linked to a number of serious social problems.

(f) As compared to the United States, United Kingdom, Japan and Germany, in Canada the unemployment rate over the last eleven years has been relatively high.

5. Since the falling prices of the 1930s, the general level of prices in Canada has risen almost every year. During some periods (such as the 1970s) prices have risen fairly quickly, while at other times (such as the late 1990s) prices have been fairly stable.

(a) Inflation is defined as a rising general level of prices; deflation is a falling general level of prices.

(b) The rate of inflation in any year is the percentage change in the consumer price index (CPI) between that year and the previous year.

The rule of 70 can be used to calculate how many years it would take for the price level to double at any given rate of inflation.

(c) Canada's inflation rate accelerated in the 1960s and 1970s, reaching a peak yearly rate of increase of 12.4% in 1981, and has since declined irregularly to about 2% per year in the late 1990s.

(d) Canada's inflation rate is now low relative to rates in other industrialized countries.

6. As a provisional theory of inflation, we distinguish between demand-pull inflation, which results from an excess aggregate demand for goods compared to the economy's capacity to produce, and cost-push or supply-side inflation, which results from increasing per unit production costs.

7. Even if the total output of the economy is constant, **unanticipated** inflation arbitrarily redistributes real income and wealth, benefitting some groups and hurting others.

(a) The percentage change in real income can be approximated by subtracting the percentage change in the price level from the percentage change in nominal income.

(b) Unanticipated inflation redistributes income away from fixed-income receivers.

(c) Unanticipated inflation injures savers because it decreases the real value of any savings, the nominal value of which is fixed.

(d) Unanticipated inflation benefits debtors and hurts creditors because it lowers the purchasing power or the real value of the debt when it is repaid.

(e) When the inflation is anticipated, and people can adjust their nominal incomes to reflect the expected rise in the price level, the redistribution of income and wealth is lessened. This occurs with COLA clauses in labour agreements, and with adjustments to nominal interest rates in financial agreements.

(f) The real interest rate equals the nominal interest rate less the inflation rate premium.

8. There are several scenarios in which inflation rate and the real output level are related.

(a) Some economists believe that the economy can only reach full employment if there is enough demand to create some demand-pull inflation. If so, there may be some trade-off between inflation and unemployment.

(b) If costs of production begin to rise in an economy that previously had full employment and price stability, the existing level of spending will then buy less real output as the prices rise (cost-push inflation). If so, inflation and unemployment may be positively related.

(c) If there is very rapid inflation (hyperinflation), this will lead people to expect yet further price increases, so they will spend more in order to stay ahead of the anticipated price increases, and they will demand higher nominal wages to compensate for the anticipated price increases. The resulting inflationary spiral has the potential to cause economic collapse (such as in Weimar Germany).

9. Major increases or decreases in prices on the stock market do not directly create macroeconomic instability. However, since stock prices reflect investors' expectations of corporations' future profits, the stock price index is one useful predictor of future changes in business activity.

■ **TERMS AND CONCEPTS**

anticipated inflation	nominal income
business cycle	nominal interest rate
cost-of-living	Okun's law
adjustment	peak
cost-push inflation	per-unit production
cyclical unemployment	costs
demand-pull inflation	potential output
discouraged workers	real income
frictional	real interest rate
unemployment	recession
full-employment	recovery
unemployment rate	rule of 70
GDP gap	seasonal variations
hyperinflation	secular trend
inflation	structural
inflation premium	unemployment
labour force	trough
natural rate of	unanticipated inflation
unemployment	unemployment rate

■ **HINTS AND TIPS**

1. The term business cycle is misleading if it implies to you a sense of regularity or predictability. Neither the duration nor the depth of a recession is likely to be consistent from one recession to the next. Therefore, some economists prefer to use the term "business fluctuations" rather than "business cycles."

2. Even when the economy is at full employment there is some unemployment; this is the natural rate of unemployment. Therefore, it is also possible — such as occurred during World War II — for the economy to exceed its full employment level of output for a period of time.

3. Many people falsely assume that the categories of "the employed" and "the unemployed" account for everyone. In fact, some people are in neither category and therefore are not counted as members of the labour force. Movements in and out of this group can explain many otherwise puzzling changes in labour market statistics. For example, with a fixed population of adults, it is possible for both unemployment and employment to rise if the labour force grows.

4. How inflation affects the distribution of wealth and income depends crucially on whether or not the inflation is correctly anticipated. Learn to ask, whenever you are confronted with an inflation scenario: "what level of inflation had been anticipated?"

■ **FILL-IN QUESTIONS**

1. Macroeconomic stability refers to steady _____, full _____ and price _____.

2. The history of the Canadian economy is a long-term trend of (steady, unsteady) _____ economic growth, with the growth at times accompanied by price _____ and at other times interrupted by low levels of _____ of goods and services and _____ of labour.

3. The term "business cycle" refers to the recurrent _____ in the level of business activity around the long-run growth trend in the economy. The four phases of a typical business cycle are _____, _____, _____, and _____. The duration and magnitude of the fluctuation in output during the cycle (are, are not) _____ much the same from one cycle to another.

4. In addition to the changes brought about by the business cycle, changes in output and employment may be due to _____ variations and to a _____ trend.

5. Production and employment in the (durable, nondurable) _____ and (capital, consumer) _____ goods industries are especially susceptible to fluctuation when the economy expands or contracts. On the demand side, the purchase of these goods can be _____, while on the supply side the exercise of _____ power results in producers lowering _____ rather than _____.

6. The three types of unemployment are:
(a) _____
(b) _____
(c) _____

7. Frictional unemployment refers to that group of workers who are _____ for jobs or _____ to take jobs in the near future. Structural unemployment means the lack of job opportunities due to changes in product _____ or _____. Cyclical unemployment arises in the _____ - phase of the business cycle.

8. Full employment (does, does not) _____ - mean a zero unemployment rate. The full-employment unemployment rate is: (a) sometimes called the _____ rate of unemployment; (b) equals the total of the _____ and the _____ unemployment in the economy; (c) realized when the _____ unemployment in the economy is equal to zero and when the _____ output of the economy is equal to its _____ output; and (d) currently estimated to be about _____% in Canada.

9. When the economy achieves its natural rate of unemployment, the number of job seekers is (greater than, less than, equal to) _____ the number of job vacancies.

10. The unemployment rate is found by dividing _____ by the _____, and multiplying by 100%.

11. The cost to society of unemployment is the lost _____ that the unemployed resources could have produced. The GDP gap is equal to _____ GDP minus _____ GDP; and for every percentage point the unemployment rate rises above the natural rate of unemployment the GDP gap will, according to Okun's law, (increase, decrease) _____ by _____%.

12. (a) An unemployed worker who is searching for work (is, is not) _____ classified as unemployed, and (is, is not) _____ classified as a member of

the labour force. (b) An unemployed worker who has no job prospects and who is not actively seeking work (is, is not) _____ classified as unemployed, and (is, is not) _____ classified as a member of the labour force.

13. The burdens of unemployment are borne more heavily by (adult, teenage) _____ and (blue-collar, white-collar) _____ workers.

14. Inflation means a _____ in the general level of _____ in the economy. The rate of inflation in year 1999 is equal to the price index for year _____ less the price index for year _____ all divided by the price index for year _____, and multiplying by 100%.

15. The amount of goods and services one's nominal income can buy is called _____ income. If one's nominal income rises by 10% over the same period that the price level rises by 7%, the percentage increase in _____ income would be _____%.

16. Inflation:
(a) hurts those whose money incomes are relatively (fixed, flexible) _____;
(b) penalizes savers when the inflation is (anticipated, unanticipated) _____, and benefits (borrowers, lenders) _____.

17. The redistributive effects of inflation are less severe when it is (anticipated, unanticipated) _____.
(a) Clauses in labour contracts that call for automatic adjustments of workers' income from the effects of inflation are called _____.
(b) The percentage increase in purchasing power that the lender receives from the borrower is the (real, nominal) _____ rate of interest; the percentage increase in money that the lender receives is the _____ rate of interest.

18. Real income measures the _____ power of nominal income. To obtain real income for a year divide the _____ income by a _____ index (expressed in hundredths) for that year. If nominal income increases at a faster rate than the price index, real income will _____; if the price index is increasing at a faster rate, real income will _____.

■ PROBLEMS AND PROJECTS

1. The solid line in the chart below shows twenty years of history of real output for some nation. The points labelled as years refer to the beginning of the years. The broken line shows potential real output for this nation.

Real GDP

1980   1985   1990   1995   2000

(a)   During this period the nation experienced six full business cycles. Identify the six peaks that marked the beginnings of these cycles.
(b)   Which cycle lasted the longest from peak to peak?
(c)   In which recession did real output fall the farthest?
(d)   Which recovery was the quickest?
(e)   What does the slope of the broken line indicate?
(f)   In what year was the output gap the largest? What does this indicate?
(g)   Were there any years when the output gap was negative? What does this indicate?
(h)   In what year was the level of cyclical unemployment probably highest? Why?

2. In the following table are Canadian labour force statistics for 1989 and 1990. (Numbers of persons are in thousands.)

	Year	
	1989	1990
Civilian noninstitutional population (15+)	20,141	20,430
Civilian labour force	13,503	13,688
Not in labour force	___	___
Employed	___	12,486
Unemployed	1,108	___
Unemployment rate (%)	___	___

(a)   Fill in the missing entries in the table.
(b)   How is it possible that both employment and unemployment increased in 1990?
(c)   Would you say that 1989 or 1990 was a year of full employment?
(d)   Why is the task of maintaining full employment over the years more than just a problem of finding jobs for those who happen to be unemployed at any given time?

3. Janice consumes only one good, "Pepsi," and measures purchasing power in terms of litres of "Pepsi."
(a)   At the beginning of the year when "Pepsi" was $1 a litre Janice loaned $100 interest free for one year to a friend. During the course of the year the price of "Pepsi" increased to $1.25.
(1) How many litres of "Pepsi" did Janice lend to her friend?
(2) How many litres of "Pepsi" were returned to Janice when the loan was paid back?
(3) By how much did the unanticipated inflation reduce Janice's wealth?
(b)   Suppose that Janice knew that the price of "Pepsi" would increase to $1.25. What nominal interest rate would she charge in order to keep the purchasing power of the loan constant?
(c)   Suppose that Janice wants to receive a 3% increase in purchasing power from the loan. Given that she knows that the price of "Pepsi" will increase to $1.25, how much money must she receive when the loan is repaid? What nominal interest rate will she charge?

4. Chikara is thinking of purchasing a $1000 Canada Savings Bond, which carries a 6% nominal interest rate. Chikara anticipates annual inflation will be 4%.
(a)   If Chikara is correct, what is the approximate real rate of return he would receive on the Savings Bond?
(b)   Now consider income taxes. Chikara is in the 45% marginal tax bracket so that 45 cents of

every extra dollar of nominal income is paid in taxes. If he is correct about the inflation rate, approximately what real rate of return after taxes would he receive on the Savings Bond?

5. The nation whose GDP data appears in the following table had a natural rate of unemployment of 5% throughout the three years shown.

Year	Potential Real GDP	Actual Real GDP	Real GDP Gap
1994	600	600	_____
1995	618	_____	28
1996	630	_____	_____

(a) In 1994 the nation's real GDP gap was ___, and the unemployment rate was _____%.
(b) In 1995 actual real GDP was _____, and the unemployment rate must have been (above, below) _____ the natural rate of 5%.
(c) Suppose that in 1996 the nation had 7% unemployment. By Okun's law, actual real GDP must have been approximately _____% below potential real GDP. Therefore, the real GDP gap was about _____, and actual real GDP was about _____.

6. The following table shows the price index in the economy at the end of four different years.

Year	Price Index	Rate of Inflation
1	100.00	
2	112.00	_____%
3	123.20	_____%
4	129.36	_____%

(a) Compute and enter in the table the rates of inflation in years 2, 3, and 4.
(b) Employing the "rule of 70," how many years would it take for the price level to double at each of these three inflation rates?
(c) If nominal income increased by 15% from year 1 to year 2, what was the approximate percentage change in real income?
(d) If nominal income was $25,000 in year 2, what was real income (measured in year 1 $)?
(e) If the nominal interest rate was 14% to borrow money from year 1 to year 2, what was the approximate real rate of interest over that period?

7. Mr. Diamond drove a milk truck for Island Dairies from 1963, when his wage was $1.50 per hour, until his retirement in 1991, when his wage rate was $10.00 per hour. If the CPI was 25 in 1963 and 125 in 1991, did his real wage increase or decrease over these years? By how much?

8. The Atlantic Bank lends Ms. Theberge $100,000 at a nominal interest rate of 11%. Both parties to the loan expect that this will yield a real interest rate of 8%.
(a) What inflation rate do the bank and Theberge expect?
(b) Suppose that inflation turns out to be 5%. What is the error in the inflation prediction, what does the error do to the real interest rate, and to whose benefit is this surprise?

■ **TRUE-FALSE**

Circle T if the statement is true, F if it is false.

1. The long-term trend of economic growth in Canada has been interrupted by periods of unemployment and recession. **T** F

2. The business cycle is best defined as alternating periods of increases and decreases in the rate of inflation in the economy. T (**F**)

3. Individual business cycles tend to be of roughly equal duration and intensity. **T** F

4. Not all changes that occur in output and employment in the economy are due to the business cycle. (**T**) F

5. During a recession, industries that are highly concentrated tend to show relatively small decreases in output and relatively large decreases in prices. T (**F**)

6. One reason for structural unemployment is a mismatch between worker skills and the skills required to fill vacant jobs. (**T**) F

7. The essential difference between frictionally and structurally unemployed workers is that the former do not have and the latter do have saleable skills. **T** (**F**)

8. Cyclical unemployment is sometimes termed deficient-demand unemployment. (**T**) F

9. Full employment means zero unemployment.   T **F**

10. The full-employment unemployment rate is equal to the total of the frictional and structural unemployment rates.   **T** F

11. If unemployment in the economy is at its natural rate, the actual and potential outputs of the economy are equal.   **T** F

12. The natural rate of unemployment in the Canadian economy has remained a constant 6% of the labour force since the 1950s.   T **F**

13. At the natural rate of unemployment, the number of job vacancies is equal to the number of job seekers.   **T** F

14. It is possible for the unemployment rate and the number of people employed to rise at the same time.   **T** F

15. By not counting discouraged workers as unemployed, the official unemployment data tends to overstate the unemployment rate.   T **F**

16. If some people who report themselves as "unemployed" are employed in the underground economy, the reported unemployment rate may be overstated.   **T** F

17. The economy's GDP gap is measured by deducting actual GDP from potential GDP.   **T** F

18. An economy cannot produce an actual real GDP that exceeds its potential real GDP.   T **F**

19. Teenagers, because they will work for lower wages, have a lower unemployment rate than persons 25 years of age and older.   T **F**

20. The economic costs of cyclical unemployment are the goods and services that are not produced.   **T** F

21. If over a one year interval the consumer price index rises from 114.0 to 119.5, the rate of inflation is 5.5%.   T **F**

22. If the price level increases by 10% each year, the price level will double every ten years.   T **F**

23. A person's real income is the amount of goods and services that the person's nominal income can purchase.   **T** F

24. If the rate of inflation is greater than the percent increase in nominal income, real income will decline.   **T** F

25. Inflation lowers the living standard of those individuals living on a fixed nominal income.   **T** F

26. Unanticipated deflation would benefit creditors (lenders) and hurt debtors (borrowers).   **T** F

27. The real interest rate equals the nominal interest rate plus the expected rate of inflation.   T **F**

28. Whether the inflation is anticipated or unanticipated, the effects of inflation on the distribution of income are much the same.   T **F**

29. The redistribution impact of inflation is somewhat reduced by the fact that many individuals simultaneously gain and lose from inflation.   **T** F

■   **MULTIPLE-CHOICE**

Circle the letter that corresponds to the best answer.

1. Which one of the following is not one of the four phases of an idealized business cycle?
- **(a)**   inflation
- **(b)**   recession
- **(c)**   recovery
- **(d)**   trough

2. Changes in business activity may be the result of:
- **(a)**   seasonal variation
- **(b)**   the business cycle
- **(c)**   secular trend
- **(d)**   any of the above

3. Total employment in December of this year was greater than total employment in December 1928. This is no doubt due to the effect of:
- **(a)**   seasonal variations
- **(b)**   secular trend
- **(c)**   the business cycle
- **(d)**   business fluctuations

4. If employment in the forest products sector of the Canadian economy during last summer was 12% above what it normally is in that season, this is likely due to:
- **(a)** seasonal variations
- **(b)** secular trend
- **(c)** the business cycle
- **(d)** both seasonal variations and the business cycle

5. Since 1945, the deepest recession experienced in Canada occurred in:
- **(a)** 1954
- **(b)** 1973
- **(c)** 1982
- **(d)** 1991

6. Production and employment in which of the following industries would be least affected by a depression?
- **(a)** dairy products
- **(b)** furniture
- **(c)** factory equipment
- **(d)** construction

7. A worker who loses his job at a petroleum refinery because electricity is being generated by using a nuclear reactor rather than the burning of oil is an example of:
- **(a)** frictional unemployment
- **(b)** structural unemployment
- **(c)** cyclical unemployment
- **(d)** disguised unemployment

8. A worker who has quit one job and is taking two weeks off before reporting to a new job is an example of:
- **(a)** frictional unemployment
- **(b)** structural unemployment
- **(c)** cyclical unemployment
- **(d)** disguised unemployment

9. Insufficient aggregate demand results in:
- **(a)** frictional unemployment
- **(b)** structural unemployment
- **(c)** cyclical unemployment
- **(d)** disguised unemployment

10. The unemployment rate is computed by dividing the number unemployed by:
- **(a)** the labour force population
- **(b)** the civilian labour force

- **(c)** the number employed
- **(d)** total population

11. The civilian labour force in an economy is 150. If the unemployment rate is 10%, the number of employed workers in the economy is:
- **(a)** 120
- **(b)** 135
- **(c)** 125
- **(d)** 130

12. The labour force data collected by Statistics Canada have been criticized because:
- **(a)** part-time workers are not counted in the number of workers employed
- **(b)** discouraged workers are treated as a part of the civilian labour force
- **(c)** some people who are not working, and are not seeking work, are included in the civilian labour force
- **(d)** all of the above

13. The full-employment unemployment rate in the economy has been achieved when:
- **(a)** frictional unemployment is zero
- **(b)** structural unemployment is zero
- **(c)** cyclical unemployment is zero
- **(d)** the natural rate of unemployment is zero

14. Which of the following could increase the natural rate of unemployment in Canada?
- **(a)** increased participation of women and teenagers in the Canadian labour force
- **(b)** increases in employment insurance benefits in Canada
- **(c)** increases in the legal minimum wage
- **(d)** all of the above

15. The GDP gap is calculated as the value of:
- **(a)** potential output minus actual output
- **(b)** actual output minus potential output
- **(c)** output achieved if the natural rate of employment was zero minus actual output
- **(d)** nominal GDP minus nominal GNP in any one year

16. Okun's law predicts that when the actual unemployment rate exceeds the natural rate of unemployment by two percentage points the GDP gap will equal:
- **(a)** 2% of the potential GDP
- **(b)** 3% of the potential GDP

(c) 4% of the potential GDP
(d) 5% of the potential GDP

17. If the GDP gap were equal to 6% of the potential GDP, the actual unemployment rate would exceed the natural rate of unemployment by:
(a) two percentage points
(b) three percentage points
(c) four percentage points
(d) five percentage points

18. The rate of unemployment is lowest among the following groups:
(a) the uneducated
(b) teenagers
(c) workers 15-24 years of age
(d) workers 25 years of age and older

19. During periods of inflation the purchasing power of money:
(a) rises
(b) falls
(c) stays constant
(d) could rise or fall

20. If a person's nominal income increases by 8% while the price level increases by 10%, the person's real income will have:
(a) increased by 2%
(b) increased by 18%
(c) decreased by 18%
(d) decreased by 2%

21. If no inflation were anticipated, a bank would be willing to lend a business firm $10 million at an annual interest of 8%. If the rate of inflation were expected to be 6%, the bank would charge the firm an annual interest rate of:
(a) 2%
(b) 6%
(c) 8%
(d) 14%

22. Of the following, who would not be hurt by inflation?
(a) those living on company pensions that are fixed in money terms
(b) those who find prices rising more rapidly than their money incomes
(c) those who have loaned money at fixed interest rates
(d) those who took out mortgage loans prior to the inflation

23. A cost-of-living adjustment clause (COLA) in a union contract:
(a) states that the last worker hired will be the first one fired in a cyclical downturn
(b) guarantees a worker a stated percentage of regular income during layoffs
(c) adjusts worker incomes automatically to inflation
(d) provides early retirement benefits for long-term employees in case of permanent layoffs

24. Which of the following is not often associated with hyperinflation?
(a) war or its aftermath
(b) rising output in the economy
(c) the hoarding of goods and speculation
(d) a halt to the use of money as both a medium of exchange and a standard of value

■ **DISCUSSION QUESTIONS**

1. What is the historical record of the Canadian economy with respect to economic growth, full employment, and price-level stability?

2. Define the business cycle. Why do some economists prefer the term "business fluctuation" to "business cycle"? Describe the four phases of an idealized cycle.

3. What, in the opinion of most economists, is the immediate determinant or cause of most business cycles?

4. The business cycle is only one of three general causes of changes in output and employment in the economy. What are the other general causes?

5. Why do output and employment suffer more in some industries than in others when the economy goes into recession? Can you give an example of an industry in your area that would be hit particularly hard, and one that would be affected only slightly?

6. Distinguish between frictional, structural, and cyclical unemployment.

7. When is there full employment in the Canadian economy? (Answer in terms of the unemployment rate, the actual and potential output of the economy, and the markets for labour.)

8. How is the unemployment rate measured in Canada? What criticisms have been made of Statistics Canada's method of determining the unemployment rate?

9. What is the economic cost of unemployment, and how is the cost measured? What does Okun's law say is the relationship between the unemployment rate and the cost of unemployment?

10. What groups in the economy tend to bear the burdens of unemployment, and what do you think are the reasons for their relatively high rates of unemployment?

11. What is inflation and how is the rate of inflation measured?

12. What is real income and how can real income be obtained from nominal income figures?

13. What groups benefit from and what groups are hurt by inflation? How do the effects of inflation depend on whether it is anticipated or unanticipated?

14. Describe three scenarios under which inflation has effects on the level of real output.

15. How have Canada's unemployment rate and inflation rate compared with those for other industrialized nations in the 1990s?

■ **ANSWERS**

FILL-IN QUESTIONS

1. economic growth, employment, stability

2. unsteady, inflation, output, employment

3. fluctuations; recession, trough, recovery, peak; are not

4. seasonal, secular

5. durable, capital; postponed; monopoly, production, prices

6. (a) frictional unemployment (b) structural unemployment (c) cyclical unemployment

7. searching, waiting; demand, technology; recession

8. does not; (a) natural (b) frictional, structural (either order) (c) cyclical, actual, potential (either order) (d) 7 to 8

9. equal to

10. the number of persons unemployed, civilian labour force

11. output; potential, actual; increase, 2

12. (a) is, is (b) is not, is not

13. teenage, blue-collar

14. rise, prices; 1999, 1998, 1998

15. real; real, 3

16. (a) fixed; (b) unexpected, borrowers

17. anticipated; (a) cost-of-living adjustments (COLA); (b) real, nominal

18. purchasing; nominal, price; increase, decrease

PROBLEMS AND PROJECTS

1. (a) 1981, 1984, 1988, 1991, 1994, 1996, 1999; (b) 1984 to 1988; (c) 1994 to 1996; (d) 1994; (e) trend of growth in potential GDP; (f) 1995; economy was very far below potential; (g) parts of each year from 1996 to 1999; economy was temporarily operating above its normal full employment potential; (h) end of 1995 when the gap was the largest.

2. (a) The following figures complete the table:
1989: 6638, 12,395, 8.2%
1990: 6742, 1202, 8.8%
(b) The civilian labour force increased more than employment increased.
(c) Without knowing the level of the natural rate of unemployment, we cannot draw a conclusion. If the natural rate is in the 7-8% range (like Canada's), neither 1989 nor 1990 would be a year of full employment.
(d) The number of people looking for work is continually expanding, and the structure of the demand for labour is continually changing.

3. (a) (1) 100 litres; (2) $100/$1.25 per litre = 80 litres; (3) 20 litres; (b) 25%; (c) $128.75; 28.75%

4. (a) 2%; (b) $1000 + $60 interest - $27 taxes = $1033. $1033/1.04 = $993.27 in real wealth. In real terms, Chikara has lost $6.73, so his real rate of return is -0.67%.

5. (a) 0, 5% (the natural rate); (b) 590, above; (c) 4; 25.2, 604.8

6. (a) 12, 10, 5; (b) almost 6, 7, 14; (c) 3%; (d) $22,321 (in year 1 $); (e) 2%

7. His real wage in 1963 was $1.50/.25 = $6.00 (in base year $). His real wage in 1991 was $10/1.25 = $8.00 (in base year $). His real wage increased by $2.00, or 33%.

8. (a) 3%; (b) the prediction is low by 2%; the effective real interest rate falls by 2%; Ms. Theberge (the borrower) benefits.

TRUE-FALSE

1. T	**2.** F	**3.** F	**4.** T	**5.** F	**6.** T
7. F	**8.** T	**9.** F	**10.** T	**11.** T	**12.** F
13. T	**14.** T	**15.** F	**16.** T	**17.** T	**18.** F
19. F	**20.** T	**21.** F	**22.** F	**23.** T	**24.** T
25. T	**26.** T	**27.** F	**28.** F	**29.** T	

MULTIPLE-CHOICE

1. (a)	**2.** (d)	**3.** (b)	**4.** (c)	**5.** (d)	**6.** (a)
7. (b)	**8.** (a)	**9.** (c)	**10.** (b)	**11.** (b)	**12.** (c)
13. (c)	**14.** (d)	**15.** (a)	**16.** (c)	**17.** (b)	**18.** (d)
19. (b)	**20.** (d)	**21.** (d)	**22.** (d)	**23.** (c);	**24.** (b)

CHAPTER 9

Building the Aggregate Expenditures Model

In Chapter 7 we saw that GDP represents the aggregate output of the economy, and that GDP is the sum of the levels of consumption, investment, government, and net export expenditures. The Chapter 8 discussion of business cycles covered the consequences of fluctuations in output and employment, but said very little about why such fluctuations occur, and about how the level of GDP is determined in the first place. Chapter 9 begins to tackle these remaining questions with a simple model used to determine the equilibrium level of GDP for an economy.

Chapter 9 opens with an historical perspective. Before the Great Depression economists believed that the economy was inherently stable. They thought that market forces ensured that the economy would automatically reach its output potential and that it would provide employment for all those who were willing and able to work. This conclusion was based on Say's Law which held that supply creates its own demand. The tragic experience of the Great Depression provided dramatic evidence to the contrary. Many of the world's economies languished for most of a decade with very high unemployment and very large GDP gaps. The apparent failure of the market economy's self-regulating forces opened the door for new theories, such as those of John Maynard Keynes.

In the simple aggregate expenditures model of Chapter 9, the economy's output level depends only on the demand for output because the economy is assumed to have enough excess productive capacity and unemployed labour to increase real output without driving prices up. Demand has only two components: consumption and investment. (Other components of demand will be added to the aggregate expenditures model in Chapter 10.)

The main determinant of consumption spending is the level of disposable income. Since that part of disposable income which is not consumed is saved, saving also depends on disposable income. The consumption schedule and saving schedule are absolutely central to the Keynesian model. Other concepts presented include average and marginal propensities to consume and save, and the nonincome determinants of consumption and saving.

Investment expenditures — that is, purchases of capital goods — depend upon the rate of return that business firms expect from investment projects and upon the real rate of interest they have to pay for the use of money. Because firms are seeking profits, they undertake only those investments having expected rates of return at least as high as the real rate of interest. This rule implies that the lower the real rate of interest, the larger will be the level of investment expenditures. The relationship between the real interest rate and the level of investment spending, called the investment demand curve, is an inverse one. Five other determinants of investment spending influence the profit expectations of business firms, and cause investment expenditures to be a relatively unstable component of GDP.

The equilibrium level of output is that output whose production will create planned aggregate spending just sufficient to purchase that much output. The determination of the equilibrium level of real GDP is explained with both tables and graphs, first using the expenditures-output approach and then using the leakages-injections approach. These two approaches are complementary ways of reaching the same conclusions. For each approach it is important to know, given the consumption (or saving) schedule and the level of investment expenditures, what level of real GDP will tend to be produced and why.

If demand for output does not match the level of output produced, the economy is in a disequilibrium. Individual businesses will experience undesired changes in inventory levels, causing them to change their production levels, in turn leading to a change in the nation's aggregate output. Disequilibrium can also be understood as a discrepancy between actual investment and planned investment.

■ CHECKLIST

When you have studied this chapter, you should be able to:

□ State Say's Law and summarize the main ideas of classical economics.

□ Explain how the Great Depression and Keynesian ideas undermined Say's Law and classical economic theory.

□ List the four simplifying assumptions used to build the aggregate expenditures model in this chapter.

□ State the two implications of these assumptions.

□ State what determines the amount of goods and services produced and the level of employment in the aggregate expenditures model.

□ Explain how consumption and saving are related to disposable income.

□ Compute, when you are given the necessary data, the four propensities.

□ Explain how the two average propensities change as income increases, given the consumption schedule.

□ Explain the relationship that holds between the MPC and MPS in the model in this chapter.

□ Determine the MPC and MPS from consumption or savings schedules presented in tabular or graphic form.

□ From tabular data on income and consumption (saving), graph the consumption (saving) schedule.

□ List five nonincome determinants of consumption and saving; and explain how a change in each determinant will affect (shift) the consumption and saving schedules.

□ Explain the difference between a change in the amount consumed (or saved) and a change or shift in the consumption (or saving) schedule.

□ List the two basic determinants of investment; and explain when a firm will and will not invest.

□ Compute, when given the appropriate data, the investment demand curve; explain why there is an inverse relationship between investment spending and the real rate of interest.

□ Explain why the investment schedule is a horizontal line.

□ List the five noninterest determinants of investment; and explain how a change in each will shift the investment demand curve.

□ Give two reasons why investment may vary directly with income (instead of being autonomous of income as assumed in our simple model).

□ List the four factors that explain why investment spending tends to be unstable.

□ Find the equilibrium GDP, when you are given the necessary tabular or graphical data, by both the aggregate expenditures-domestic output approach and the leakages-injections approach.

□ List the conditions that are met at the equilibrium level of output using the aggregate expenditures-domestic output approach and the leakages-injections approach.

□ State the difference between planned investment and actual investment.

□ Explain why saving and actual investment can be equal when saving and planned investment are not equal.

□ Explain how the output level will adjust when GDP is either higher or lower than its equilibrium level, and explain the role of inventories in the process.

■ CHAPTER OUTLINE

1. The Great Depression led to a debate between classical economists and John Maynard Keynes and his followers, the Keynesian economists. One result was the aggregate-expenditures model.

(a) Classical economists concluded that an economy in depression would automatically return to a full-employment equilibrium, even without help from any government policy action. These conclusions were based on Say's Law which states that supply creates its own demand. If there were an oversupply of goods (and an oversupply of labour), prices (and wages) would drop until the equilibrium was restored at full employment and potential output.

(b) The Great Depression and the ideas of Keynes, in *The General Theory of Employment, Interest and Money*, led to the development of the aggregate expenditures model, and the rejection of classical economics. Keynes disputed Say's Law, arguing that while output created enough income to purchase all of the output, there was no guarantee that all of the income would be spent on the current output because savings and investment decisions are not necessarily coordinated. Secondly, wages and prices are downwardly inflexible, so recessions may be deep and prolonged. Overall, Keynes did not believe the market economy to be capable of stabilizing itself.

2. Our simple Keynesian aggregate expenditures model is based on four assumptions: (1) the economy is closed (no imports or exports); (2) there is no government sector involved in spending or taxation; (3) all saving is personal saving by households; (4) depreciation and net foreign factor income earned in Canada are zero. These assumptions imply that: (1) consumption and investment are the only expenditure components in the model, and (2) all income or output measures (GDP, NI, PI, DI) are treated as equivalent.

3. Output and employment are directly related to the level of total or aggregate expenditures. The level of total expenditures is determined by the levels of consumption and investment expenditures.

4. Consumption is the largest component of aggregate expenditures; saving is disposable income not spent on consumer goods.

(a)   Disposable income, which equals GDP in this chapter, is the main determinant of both consumption and saving; both consumption and saving increase as income increases.

(b)   The consumption schedule shows the amounts households plan to spend for consumer goods at various levels of income, given a price level.

(c)   The saving schedule indicates the amounts households plan to save at different income levels, given a price level.

(d)   The average propensities to consume and to save and the marginal propensities to consume and to save can be computed from the consumption and saving schedules.

(1) The APC and the APS are the percentages of income spent for consumption and saved; and their sum is equal to 1.

(2) The MPC and the MPS are the percentages of *additional* income spent for consumption and saved; and their sum is equal to 1.

(e)   Aside from income, several other determinants of consumption and saving can cause the consumption and saving schedules to change: wealth, expectations, household debt, and taxation.

(f)   A change in the amount consumed (or saved) refers to a move from one point to another

on a stable schedule, due to a change in income. A change in consumption (or saving) refers to a shift in the schedule, due to a change in a nonincome determinant. When these two schedules change, they normally change in opposite directions, but the schedules are normally very stable.

wealth, expectations of future prices, household debt, taxation

5. The two key determinants of the level of investment spending are the expected rate of return from the purchase of additional capital goods and the real rate of interest.

(a)   The expected rate of return is higher the more that revenues are expected to increase due to an investment, and lower the greater the cost of making an investment in capital goods.

(b)   The rate of interest is the price paid for the use of the money capital needed to buy real capital. When the expected rate of return is greater (less) than the real rate of interest, a business will (will not) invest because the investment will be profitable (unprofitable).

(c)   Therefore, the lower (higher) the real rate of interest, the greater (smaller) will be the level of investment spending in the economy; and the investment demand curve indicates this inverse relationship.

(d)   Five noninterest determinants of investment demand are: acquisition, maintenance, and operating costs; business taxes; technological change; the stock of capital goods on hand; and expectations. A change in any of these factors will shift the investment demand curve.

(e)   Investment spending may be either independent of, or directly related to, the real GDP. The model in this chapter assumes investment to be independent, so the investment schedule is horizontal when plotted against real GDP.

(f)   Because the five noninterest determinants of investment are subject to sudden changes, investment spending is unstable. Shifts in any of these variables will shift the horizontal investment schedule.

6. The chapter uses two approaches to explain what level of real GDP the economy will produce, but both approaches yield the same conclusion.

(a)   Using the aggregate expenditures-national output approach, the equilibrium real GDP is the real GDP at which:

(1) aggregate expenditures (consumption plus planned investment) equal the real GDP; or

(2) in graphical terms, the aggregate expenditures curve intersects the 45 degree line.

(b)   Using the leakages-injections approach, the equilibrium real GDP is the real GDP at which:
(1)   saving and planned investment are equal; or
(2)   in graphical terms, the saving schedule intersects the planned investment schedule.

7. If the GDP level is not at the equilibrium, market forces will tend to push the GDP back to equilibrium.
(a)   If the level of GDP is below equilibrium:
(1) $C + I_g$ will exceed GDP, so planned spending exceeds production, causing a depletion of inventories.
(2)   Planned investment will exceed saving, causing unplanned inventory decreases (so that actual investment equals saving).
(3)   The unintended disinvestment through shrinking inventories will cause firms to raise their planned production (until equilibrium GDP is reached).
(b)   If the level of GDP is above equilibrium:
(1)   GDP will exceed $C + I_g$, so production exceeds planned spending, causing an accumulation of inventories.
(2)   Saving will exceed planned investment, causing unplanned inventory increases (so that actual investment equals saving).
(3)   The unintended investment in rising inventories will cause firms to lower their planned production (until equilibrium GDP is reached).

8. Changes in planned investment (or in the consumption schedule) will cause the equilibrium real GDP to change in the same direction.

■   **TERMS AND CONCEPTS**

45-degree line	injection
actual investment	investment demand
aggregate expenditures	curve
schedule	investment schedule
aggregate expenditures-	Keynesian economics
domestic output	leakage
approach	leakages-injections
average propensity to	approach
consume	marginal propensity
average propensity to	to consume
save	marginal propensity
break-even income	to save
consumption schedule	planned investment
equilibrium GDP	saving schedule
expected rate of return	Say's Law

■   **HINTS AND TIPS**

1.   The Keynesian aggregate expenditures model is the foundation for a big part of what modern macroeconomists believe, including those who reject many Keynesian assumptions and conclusions. If you can master this chapter you will continue to benefit in future chapters.

2.   Try to practise with the concepts of this chapter from a variety of angles: drawing graphs, explaining in words, working with numerical tables.

3.   A key feature of the graphs for the aggregate expenditures model is the "45 degree line." The line is actually 45 degrees only if the measurement scale is identical on both the vertical and horizontal axes. If the scales differ, the line showing points where expenditures equal GDP will have a different angle.

4.   The distinction between actual and planned investment is key to understanding equilibrium. Actual investment includes both planned and unplanned investment. Unplanned investment refers to unplanned changes in inventories when businesses have based their production plans on faulty forecasts of what amounts their customers plan to buy.

■   **FILL-IN QUESTIONS**

1. According to classical economic theory, if the economy were in recession, prices of goods and services would tend to (rise, fall) _____ because of competition among business firms, and wage rates would tend to (rise, fall) _____ because of competition among unemployed workers. These price and wage changes will (increase, decrease) _____ employment and output until _____ employment is reached.

2. J.M. Keynes (accepted, rejected) _____ Say's Law which stated that _____ creates its own _____. In Keynes' view, economic decisions — in particular savings and investment decisions — may not be _____. Keynes also argued that the economy's power to self-adjust is limited by the (downward, upward) _____ (flexibility, inflexibility) _____ of wages and prices. For these reasons, Keynes believed that the economy is inherently (stable, unstable) _____, and (is, is not) _____ prone to long periods of recession and high unemployment.

3. The model in this chapter is based on four assumptions: a(n) (open, closed) _____ economy; no _____ or _____ by government; all saving is (personal, business) _____; depreciation and net foreign factor income earned in Canada are both _____. These assumptions imply that: the only relevant expenditure components are _____ and _____; and different measures of _____ can be treated as equivalent.

4. The level of output in the economy depends directly on the level of _____ expenditures.

5. The most important determinant of consumption and of saving in the economy is the economy's _____; and both consumption and saving are (directly, inversely) _____ related to this determinant.

6. As disposable income falls, the average propensity to consume will (rise, fall) _____ and the average propensity to save will _____.

7. The most important determinants of consumption spending, besides the level of income, are:
(a)   the wealth, or sum of _____ and _____ assets households have accumulated
(b)   household _____ about future prices, money incomes, etc.
(c)   _____
(d)   _____

8. A shift of the entire consumption schedule is referred to as a change in _____; but a movement from one point on a given consumption schedule to another point on the schedule is referred to as a change in _____.

9. Investment is defined as spending for additional _____ goods. The amount of investment spending depends on the expected rate of _____ and on the real rate of _____.

10. A firm will invest in more real capital if the expected rate of return on the investment project is (greater, less) _____ than the real rate of interest the firm must pay for the use of money capital.

11. The relation between the interest rate and the level of investment is (direct, inverse) _____, so if the interest rate rises, investment will _____.

12. The consumption schedule tends to be (stable or unstable) _____, while the investment schedule tends to be _____.

13. List five noninterest determinants of planned investment expenditures:
(a)   _____
(b)   _____
(c)   _____
(d)   _____
(e)   _____

14. The demand for new capital goods tends to be unstable because of the _____ of capital goods, the _____ of innovation, the _____ of profits, and the _____ of expectations.

15. Two complementary approaches that are employed to explain the equilibrium level of real national output are the _____ approach and the _____ approach.

16. Assuming a private and closed economy, the equilibrium level of real GDP is the real GDP at which:
(a) aggregate _____ equal real _____; (b) real GDP equals _____ plus _____; (c) the aggregate expenditures schedule or curve intersects the _____ line.

17. In this chapter, the only leakage considered is _____ and the only injection considered is _____. Equilibrium real GDP is that level of GDP at which the two are equal.

18. If:
(a)   aggregate expenditures exceed real output, saving is (greater, less) _____ than planned investment, there is unplanned (investment, disinvestment) _____ in inventories, and real GDP will (rise, fall) _____.
(b)   aggregate expenditures are less than real output, savings is _____ than planned investment, there is unplanned _____ in inventories, and real GDP will _____.
(c)   aggregate expenditures are equal to real output, saving is _____ planned investment, unplanned investment in inventories is _____, and real GDP will _____.

19. At every level of real GDP, saving is equal to (planned, actual) _____ investment.

(a) But if planned investment exceeds saving by $10, there is $10 of unplanned (investment, disinvestment) _____; and real GDP will (rise, fall) _____.

(b) And if planned investment is less than saving by $5, there is $5 of unplanned _____; and real GDP will _____.

■ **PROBLEMS AND PROJECTS**

1. Following is a consumption schedule. Assume taxes and transfers are zero and that all saving is personal saving.

GDP	C	S	APC	APS
$1500	$1540	$_____	1.027	_____
1600	1620	_____	_____	-0.013
1700	1700	_____	_____	_____
1800	_____	20	_____	_____
1900	_____	_____	_____	_____

(a) Compute saving at each of the first three levels of GDP listed.

(b) Compute consumption at GDP = $1800.

(c) The break-even level of income (GDP) is: $_____.

(d) The marginal propensity to consume (MPC) between GDP = $1500 and $1600 equals $_____ divided by $_____ = _____. Between GDP = $1600 and $1700 MPC equals $_____ divided by $_____ = _____.

(e) The marginal propensity to save (MPS) between GDP = $1500 and $1600 equals $_____ divided by $_____ = _____. Between GDP = $1600 and $1700 MPS equals $_____ divided by $_____ = _____.

(f) Since the MPC is constant, the consumption level at GDP = $1900 is $_____, and saving level is $_____.

(g) Given the value of APC at GDP = $1500, APS at this level of income is _____.

(h) Given the value of APS at GDP = $1600, APC at this level of income is _____.

(i) Compute the APC and APS values for the remaining income levels.

(j) As income rises, the APC (rises, falls) _____, and the APS _____.

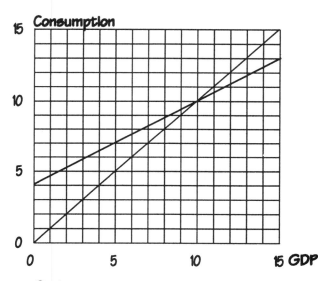

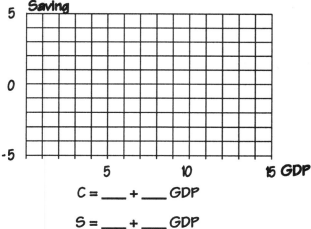

$$C = \text{\_\_\_} + \text{\_\_\_}\ GDP$$

$$S = \text{\_\_\_} + \text{\_\_\_}\ GDP$$

2. This question is based on the graphs from the previous question.

(a) When GDP = 0, the level of consumption is _____.

(b) The MPC = _____.

(c) The break-even level of income is at GDP = _____.

(d) When GDP = 0, the level of saving is _____.

(e) The MPS = _____.

(f) At the break-even level of income, the level of saving is _____.

(g) Plot the savings schedule in the lower panel of the graph.

(h) Based on your answers in (a) through (g), fill in the parameters in the consumption and saving equations shown below the graphs.

3. Indicate in the space next to each of the following events whether the event will increase (+), decrease (-), or not change (0) the consumption schedule and the saving schedule.

(a)   Consumers begin to expect that prices will be higher in the future.   **C:** ☐ **S:** ☐

(b)   Falling real estate prices reduce households' wealth.   **C:** ☐ **S:** ☐

(c)   A rise in the actual level of disposable income.   **C:** ☐ **S:** ☐

(d)   A new belief that consumer incomes will fall in the future.   **C:** ☐ **S:** ☐

(e)   The government suddenly increases income tax rates.   **C:** ☐ **S:** ☐

(f)   A rise in the level of household credit card debt.   **C:** ☐ **S:** ☐

4. A corporation has the investment opportunities shown in the following schedule. (In the economy as a whole, each firm has a similar schedule of its own.) For each project is given the dollar cost, and the expected rate of return.

Project	Investment Amount ($)	Expected Rate of Return
A: new warehouse	12 million	8%
B: new delivery vehicles	10 million	9%
C: computer upgrades	3 million	11%
D: office expansion	5 million	10%
E: retail store refurbishing	8 million	7%

(a)   From the data indicate (by letters) which projects are profitable for the firm to invest in at each possible real interest rate, and then find the total amount of investment spending that would be undertaken at each of the real interest rates given.

Real Interest Rate (%)	Profitable Projects	Investment Amount (million $)
12	_____	_____
11	_____	_____
10	_____	_____
9	_____	_____
8	_____	_____
7	_____	_____

(b)   Graph the data in the table completed in (a) as an investment demand curve in the next graph. Plot the real rate of interest on the vertical axis and the amount of planned investment on the horizontal axis.

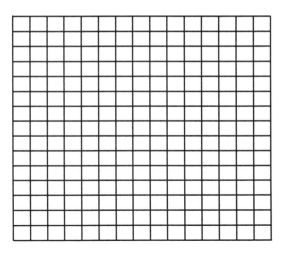

(c)   The graph and the table show that the relation between the real rate of interest and the amount of investment spending is _____. When the real rate of interest increases, investment will (increase, decrease) _____.

5. Indicate in the box to the right of the following events whether the event would tend to increase (+) or decrease (-) the investment demand curve. If the event does not shift the curve, indicate (0).

(a)   Rising stock-market prices.   ☐

(b)   A new expectation of higher business taxes.   ☐

(c)   An acceleration in the rate of new product innovations.   ☐

(d)   Business belief that wage rates will fall in the future.   ☐

(e)   A mild recession.   ☐

(f)   A belief that the economy is due for a period of "slow" consumer demand.   ☐

(g)   Rising costs in the construction industry.   ☐

(h)   A rapid population increase in the economy.   ☐

(i)   A period of a high level of investment spending that has resulted in productive capacity in excess of the current demand for goods and services.   ☐

6. (a) The table below shows consumption and saving at some levels of real GDP. The equation for the consumption schedule is: $C = 10 + .80$ GDP. Planned investment expenditures are fixed at $I_g = 20$. Complete the table that follows, indicating consumption (C), saving (S), investment (I_g), aggregate expenditure ($C+I_g$), unplanned investment (UI) with unplanned accumulation shown by + and unplanned disinvestment by -, and the tendency of GDP to rise (+) or fall (-).

Real GDP	C	S	I_g	C+I_g	UI	GDP Change (+/-)
0	___	___	___	___	___	___
50	___	___	___	___	___	___
100	___	___	___	___	___	___
150	___	___	___	___	___	___
200	___	___	___	___	___	___
250	___	___	___	___	___	___

(b) The equilibrium real GDP will be $_____, because at this income level, real GDP and _____ are equal, or savings and _____ are equal.

(c) For the given data, the value of the MPC = _____ and the value of MPS = _____.

■ TRUE-FALSE

Circle T if the statement is true, F if it is false.

1. In the model in this chapter the price level remains constant so any change in GDP is a change in real output. **T F**

2. Classical economists thought that the economy had enough wage and price flexibility to restore full employment equilibrium. **T F**

Questions 3 through 8 are based on the data in the following table. Assume that there is no government and no business saving, so GDP and disposable income (*DI*) are equal.

GDP	Consumption
160	168
200	196
240	224
280	252
320	280

3. When the GDP is 240, the average propensity to consume is 0.95. **T F**

4. At a GDP level of 320 there is dissaving. **T F**

5. The break-even level of GDP is below 240. **T F**

6. The marginal propensity to consume in the table is 0.95 at all income levels. **T F**

7. The graph of the consumption schedule above is a straight line. **T F**

8. The marginal propensity to save in the table is 0.30 at all income levels. **T F**

9. The level of saving depends primarily upon the level of disposable income. **T F**

10. Other things being equal, an increase in wealth will shift the consumption schedule upward and result in an increase in saving out of any given level of income. **T F**

11. An increase in the taxes paid by consumers will decrease both their consumption and their saving. **T F**

12. Both the consumption schedule and the saving schedule tend to be relatively stable over time. **T F**

13. The APC is relatively high in Canada and the United States, as compared to other major industrialized nations. **T F**

14. The basic determinants of investment are the expected rate of return and the wage rate. **T F**

15. A business firm will purchase additional capital goods if the real rate of interest exceeds the expected rate of return from the investment. **T F**

16. When a firm finances investment spending out of retained earnings, the interest rate will play no role in the investment decision. **T F**

17. A rapid rate of technological change will shift the investment demand curve to the left. **T F**

18. A decrease in the corporate profits tax will shift the investment demand curve to the left. **T F**

19. In this chapter it is assumed that the investment schedule is independent of the level of real income. **T F**

20. The equilibrium level of output is that output level that generates planned spending exactly equal to the value of production. **T F**

21. At the equilibrium level of income, potential and actual GDP are equal. **T F**

22. The equilibrium level of income is that GDP that corresponds to the intersection of the aggregate expenditure schedule and the 45-degree line. **T F**

23. The actual amounts saved and invested are always equal by definition, but only at the equilibrium level of GDP are planned investment and saving equal. **T F**

24. The investment schedule is a schedule of actual investment rather than a schedule of planned investment. **T F**

■ **MULTIPLE-CHOICE**

Circle the letter that corresponds to the best answer.

1. The events of what historical period undermined classical economic theory and led to the development of Keynesian economics?
 (a) World War I
 (b) World War II
 (c) Industrial Revolution
 (d) Great Depression

2. Classical economics suggests that in a market economy:
 (a) unemployment is a persistent problem
 (b) market forces will ensure full employment
 (c) a recession will cause automatic increases in prices and wages
 (d) demand creates its own supply

3. What was John Maynard Keynes' most famous book?
 (a) *The General Theory of Employment, Interest and Money*
 (b) *The Theory of Interest*
 (c) *Booms and Depressions*
 (d) *Unemployment in a Free Society*

4. Which of the following is **not** one of the assumptions made in developing the aggregate expenditure model in this chapter?
 (a) the price level is constant
 (b) business saving is zero
 (c) there is no government sector
 (d) investment spending is related to the level of income

5. In the aggregate expenditure model, output and employment depend:
 (a) directly on the level of total expenditures
 (b) inversely on the quantity of resources available
 (c) directly on the level of saving
 (d) directly on the rate of interest

6. As disposable income decreases, *ceteris paribus*:
 (a) both consumption and saving increase
 (b) consumption increases and saving decreases
 (c) consumption decreases and saving increases
 (d) both consumption and saving decrease

7. If consumption spending increases from $358 to $367 when disposable income increases from $412 to $427, then the marginal propensity to consume must be:
 (a) 0.4
 (b) 0.6
 (c) 0.8
 (d) 0.9

8. If when disposable income is $375 billion the average propensity to consume is 0.8, then:
 (a) the marginal propensity to consume is also 0.8
 (b) consumption is $325 billion
 (c) saving is $75 billion
 (d) the marginal propensity to save is 0.2

9. Suppose that the equation for the consumption schedule is given by: $C = 20 + .75 DI$ where DI is disposable income. If the level of DI is 100, consumption will be:
 (a) 75
 (b) 20
 (c) 95
 (d) 100

10. Which of the following relationships is an inverse one in the aggregate expenditure model?
 (a) the relationship between consumption spending and disposable income
 (b) the relationship between investment spending and the rate of interest
 (c) the relationship between saving and the level of income
 (d) the relationship between investment spending and GDP

Use the graph below to answer questions 11 through 15.

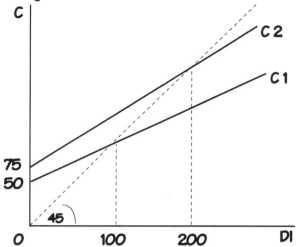

11. Which of the following could **not** cause the consumption curve to shift from C1 to C2?

(a) an expectation of a future decrease in the price level

(b) an increase in consumers' ownership of financial assets

(c) a decrease in the amount of consumers' indebtedness

(d) an increase in the income received by consumers

12. On consumption curve C1, if disposable income is at 150:

(a) saving would be greater than consumption

(b) there would be dissaving

(c) average propensity to save would be greater than 1

(d) the economy could be at an equilibrium income level

13. Which of the following is a true statement concerning the shift from C1 to C2 shown in the graph?

(a) the marginal propensity to consume has increased

(b) the marginal propensity to save has increased

(c) the break even level of income has decreased

(d) the average propensity to save has decreased

14. What is the equation of consumption curve C2?

(a) C = 75 + 0.50 DI

(b) C = 50 + 0.50 DI

(c) C = 75 + 0.625 DI

(d) C = 50 + 0.625 DI

15. What are the marginal propensities to consume for the C1 and C2 consumption curves?

(a) 0.50 for C1 and 0.625 for C2

(b) 0.50 for C1 and 0.375 for C2

(c) 0.25 for C1 and 0.75 for C2

(d) 0.25 for both C1 and C2

16. A shift to the left in the investment demand curve could be a consequence of:

(a) a decline in the rate of interest

(b) a decline in the level of wages paid

(c) a decline in business taxes

(d) a pessimistic outlook on the part of business owners

Questions 17 and 18 are based on the consumption schedule below.

Real GDP	Consumption
$350	$320
400	360
450	400
500	440
550	480
600	520

17. If planned investment is $60, what is equilibrium real GDP?

(a) $400

(b) $450

(c) $500

(d) $550

18. If planned investment is $60, and GDP is $450, unplanned investment is:

(a) $-20

(b) $-10

(c) $0

(d) $10

19. If GDP is below equilibrium:

(a) inventories will be zero

(b) inventories will be diminishing

(c) inventories will be increasing

(d) inventories will be stable

20. If the real GDP is $275 billion, consumption $250 billion, and planned gross investment $30 billion, real GDP:

(a) will tend to remain constant

(b)   will tend to increase
(c)   will tend to decrease
(d)   none of the above

The next graph is the basis for questions 21 through 25. The equation for the consumption is $C = 50 + .50$ GDP.

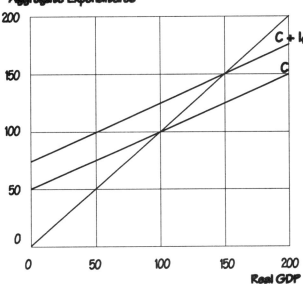

21. The level of planned investment is
  (a) $15
  (b) $25
  (c) $40
  (d) $50

22. The equilibrium level of real GDP is:
  (a) $120
  (b) $150
  (c) $175
  (d) $200

23. At a GDP level of $200, unintended investment is:
  (a) $25
  (b) $50
  (c) $75
  (d)   cannot be calculated with the information supplied

24. In the leakages-injections approach, the equilibrium GDP is characterized by:

  (a)   the equality of saving and actual investment
  (b)   the equality of saving and planned investment

(c)   the equality of planned and unplanned investment
(d)   the equality of actual investment with planned plus unplanned investment

25. Which of the following is an injection?
  (a)   investment
  (b)   saving
  (c)   consumption
  (d)   imports

Questions 26 through 28 refer to the graph below. The figures are in billion $.

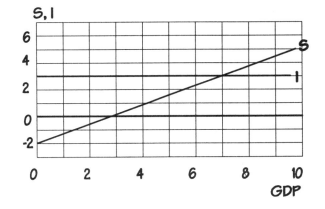

26. The equilibrium level of GDP is:
  (a) $3 billion
  (b) $4 billion
  (c) $7 billion
  (d) $10 billion

27. At equilibrium income, what is the level of consumption spending?
  (a) $3 billion
  (b) $4 billion
  (c) $5 billion
  (d) $8 billion

28. At a GDP level of $4 billion, what is the level of unintended investment?
  (a)   -$2 billion
  (b)   -$1 billion
  (c) $1 billion
  (d) $2 billion

■ DISCUSSION QUESTIONS

1. What aspects of classical macroeconomic thinking did J.M. Keynes disagree with, and why?

2. Define aggregate expenditures and explain why, in a market economy, aggregate expenditures determine the level of output and income.

3. Describe the relation between consumption and disposable income, and the relation between saving and disposable income known as the saving schedule; and then define the two average propensities and the two marginal propensities. Why does APC + APS always equal 1? Why does MPC + MPS always equal 1?

4. Determine how a change in each of the four nonincome determinants will affect the consumption schedule and the saving schedule, and for each case explain concisely why consumption and saving change as you have indicated.

5. Explain: (a) when a business firm will or will not purchase additional capital goods; (b) how changes in the five noninterest determinants of investment spending will affect the investment demand curve; (c) why investment spending tends to rise when the rate of interest falls; and (d) how changes in GDP might affect investment spending.

6. Why does the level of investment spending tend to be highly unstable?

7. Why is the equilibrium level of real GDP that level of real GDP at which national output equals aggregate expenditures and at which saving equals planned investment? What will cause real GDP to rise if it is below this level and what will cause it to fall if it is above this level?

8. Explain what is meant by a leakage and by an injection. Which leakage and which injection are considered in this chapter? Why is the output at which leakages equals injections the equilibrium level of real GDP?

9. For investment, what is the distinction between the planned level and the actual level? Is the investment schedule planned or actual investment? What adjustment causes planned and actual investment to become equal?

■ ANSWERS

FILL-IN QUESTIONS

1. fall, fall, increase; full potential

2. rejected, supply, demand; coordinated; downward, inflexibility; unstable, is

3. closed; purchases, taxes; personal; zero; consumption, investment; income

4. aggregate

5. income; directly

6. rise, fall

7. (a) real, financial (b) expectations (c) household debt (d) taxation

8. the consumption schedule; the amount consumed

9. capital, return, interest

10. greater

11. inverse, decrease

12. stable, unstable

13. (a) the cost of acquiring, maintaining, and operating the capital goods; (b) business taxes; (c) technological change; (d) the stock of capital goods on hand; (e) expectations

14. durability, irregularity, variability, variability

15. aggregate expenditure, leakages-injections

16. (a) expenditures, output (b) consumption, planned investment (c) 45-degree

17. saving, planned investment

18. (a) less, disinvestment, rise (b) greater, investment, fall (c) equal to, zero, neither rise nor fall

19. actual; (a) disinvestment, rise; (b) investment, fall

PROBLEMS AND PROJECTS

1. (a) S: -40, -20, 0; (b) 1780; (c) 1700; (d) 80, 100, 0.80; 80, 100, 0.80; (e) 20, 100, 0.20; 20, 100, 0.20; (f) 1860, 40; (g)-0.027; (h) 1.013; (i) APC: 1.000, 0.989, 0.979, APS: 0, 0.011, 0.021; (j) falls, rises

2. (a) 4; (b) 0.6; (c) 10, (d) -4; (e) 0.4; (f) 0; (h) C = 4 + 0.6 GDP; S = -4 + 0.4 GDP

3. (a) C+, S-; (b) C-, S+; (c) 0; (d) C-, S+; (e) C-,S-; (f) C-, S+

4. (a) 12% — none, 0; 11% — C, 3; 10% — C, D, 8; 9% — C, D, B, 18; 8% — C, D, B, A, 30; 7% — C, D, B, A, E, 38; (c) inverse; decrease.

5. (a) + (b) - (c) + (d) + (e) - (f) - (g) - (h) + (i) -

6. (a) C: 10, 50, 90, 130, 170, 210; S: -10, 0, 10, 20, 30, 40; I_g: 20 at all GDP values; $C+I_g$: 30, 70, 110, 150, 190, 230; UI: -30, -20, -10, 0, 10, 20; GDP Change: +, +, +, equilibrium, -, -; (b) 150; $C + I_g$, planned investment; (c) 0.80, 0.20

TRUE-FALSE

1. T	**2.** T	**3.** F	**4.** F	**5.** T	**6.** F
7. T	**8.** T	**9.** T	**10.** F	**11.** T	**12.** T
13. T	**14.** F	**15.** F	**16.** F	**17.** F	**18.** F
19. T	**20.** T	**21.** F	**22.** T	**23.** T	**24.** F

MULTIPLE-CHOICE

1. (d)	**2.** (b)	**3.** (a)	**4.** (d)	**5.** (a)	**6.** (d)
7. (b)	**8.** (c)	**9.** (c)	**10.** (b)	**11.** (d)	**12.** (d)
13. (a)	**14.** (c)	**15.** (a)	**16.** (d)	**17.** (c)	**18.** (b)
19. (b)	**20.** (b)	**21.** (b)	**22.** (b)	**23.** (a)	**24.** (b)
25. (a)	**26.** (c)	**27.** (b)	**28.** (a)		

CHAPTER 10

Aggregate Expenditures: The Multiplier, Net Exports, and Government

Chapter 9 developed the aggregate expenditures model for a private closed economy. In that model, the economy's equilibrium level of real GDP is determined by the levels of only two types of spending: consumption and investment. Chapter 10 extends this simple model in some important ways.

First, we learn that any shift in an expenditure schedule leads to a change in equilibrium GDP, and the change in GDP is larger than the initial expenditure change itself! This is the multiplier effect. When a household or firm changes their expenditure, this causes incomes to change for others in the economy; this in turn leads them to alter their expenditures, etc. The smaller is the marginal propensity to save, the larger is the multiplier, and therefore the change in GDP.

The second major extension to the Chapter 9 model involves adding exports and imports to what was previously a closed economy. Exports are an additional demand for Canada's output, so they represent an injection into the expenditures flow. Imports are a leakage from the flow of spending because they represent spending that flows out of Canada to buy products produced elsewhere. Usually we think in terms of net exports (X_n), calculated as exports minus imports. The X_n component of aggregate expenditures depends on the exchange rate between the Canadian currency and foreign currencies, and on GDP levels in both Canada and foreign economies.

In the open economy model equilibrium is found as in the closed economy model: where real GDP is equal to aggregate expenditures. The only difference is that aggregate expenditures now include net exports; so the equilibrium real GDP will equal $C + I_g + X_n$. An increase in X_n, like an increase in I_g, will increase the equilibrium real GDP — and with a multiplier effect. Because import spending is an ad-

ditional leakage from the flow of domestic income, the open economy multiplier is smaller than the simple multiplier in the closed economy model.

The final extension of the model takes us from a private economy (with no government expenditure or taxation) to a mixed economy with a public sector and a private sector. This change is made in two steps. First, government spending (G) is added as an injection into aggregate expenditures. Second, we introduce taxes (T) as a new leakage from spending. The leakage of income into taxes reduces disposable income, consumption, saving, and imports. The revised expression for equilibrium, where aggregate expenditures equal output, is: GDP = $C + I_g + X_n + G$. Similarly, the leakages equal injections expression is changed. If, as we assume in this chapter, taxes are levied as a lump sum, the open economy multiplier applies to this model also.

We now have in place the complete Keynesian aggregate expenditures model that explains the factors that determine equilibrium GDP, and that expenditure shifts change equilibrium GDP with a multiplier effect. The final theory section of Chapter 10 draws a distinction between equilibrium and full-employment. At the heart of what Keynes argued in his *General Theory* was the idea that the economy's equilibrium GDP need not coincide with the full-employment level of GDP. If the two do not equal, there will be a recessionary gap or an inflationary gap. The existence of such gaps, and what policy-makers might do about them, is addressed in future chapters.

■ CHECKLIST

When you have studied this chapter, you should be able to:

☐ Explain the multiplier effect in words, and using an equation.

☐ Cite the two facts on which the multiplier effect is based.

☐ Discuss the relationship between the size of the multiplier and the size of the marginal propensities.

☐ Calculate the multiplier when you are given the necessary data.

☐ Explain the difference between the simple multiplier and the complex multiplier.

☐ Use the concept of net exports to define aggregate expenditures in an open economy.

☐ Identify the major determinants of a nation's exports and imports.

☐ Compute, when you are given the necessary data, the marginal propensity to import and the net export schedule.

☐ Explain how equilibrium real GDP in an open economy will be affected when net exports are positive and when net exports are negative.

☐ Give examples of how incomes abroad, tariffs, and exchange rates can change equilibrium real GDP in Canada.

☐ Find the equilibrium real GDP in an open economy when you are given the necessary tabular or graphical data by employing either the aggregate expenditures-domestic output approach or the leakages-injections approach.

☐ Given the necessary data, calculate the open economy multiplier.

☐ List five simplifying assumptions made when adding the public sector to the aggregate expenditures model.

☐ Given the necessary data, find the equilibrium real GDP in a mixed open economy with a public sector, using either the aggregate expenditures-domestic output approach or the leakages-injections approach.

☐ Explain the balanced budget multiplier, and why its value is equal to one.

☐ Distinguish between the equilibrium GDP and the full-employment level of GDP.

☐ Define recessionary and inflationary gaps, and find them when you are provided with the relevant data.

☐ Apply the concepts of recessionary and inflationary gaps to historical events such as the Great Depression.

☐ Indicate some shortcomings of the aggregate expenditures model.

■ **CHAPTER OUTLINE**

1. Changes in planned gross investment (or in the consumption schedule) will cause equilibrium real GDP to change in the same direction, and by a larger amount than the initial change in investment (or consumption). This is called the multiplier effect.

(a) The multiplier is equal to the ratio of the change in real GDP to the initial change in spending.

(b) The multiplier effect occurs because a change in spending by one person causes another person's income to change by the same amount. The person whose income changes will spend a fraction, causing yet another person's income to change, and so on. $= \frac{\Delta GDP}{\text{initial change in spending}}$

(c) The value of the simple multiplier is equal to the reciprocal of the marginal propensity to save: 1/MPS. A larger propensity to save implies a smaller multiplier. $\frac{1}{MPS}$

(d) The significance of the multiplier is that relatively small changes in the spending plans of business firms or households can trigger larger changes in equilibrium real GDP. $\frac{1}{1-MPC}$

(e) If the economy has leakages other than savings, the simple multiplier is not applicable; we must use the complex multiplier which takes into account other leakages such as taxes and imports.

2. In an open economy, exports (X) add to the nation's aggregate expenditures, and imports (M) subtract from the nation's aggregate expenditures.

(a) Aggregate expenditures are equal to the sum of consumption spending, planned investment spending, and net exports (X_n) with $X_n = X - M$.

(b) Canada's imports are positively related to Canada's GDP, whereas our exports are positively related to GDP in other countries.

(c) An appreciation of the Canadian dollar will generally lead to increased imports, and to decreased exports. A depreciation of the Canadian dollar relative to foreign currencies will have the opposite effect.

(d) The net export schedule is a decreasing function of domestic GDP, with the marginal propensity to import (MPM) controlling the rate at which X_n falls as GDP rises.

3. The equilibrium real GDP in an open economy occurs where the real GDP is equal to consumption plus planned investment plus net export spending: $\text{GDP} = C + I_g + X_n$

(a)   By the leakages-injections approach, equilibrium occurs where $I_g + X = S + M$

(b)   If net exports are negative (positive), the effect of net exports is to reduce (increase) Canada's equilibrium GDP.

(c)   Any increase (decrease) in Canada's X_n will increase (decrease) our equilibrium real GDP with a multiplier effect.

(d)   Because imports are related to the level of our GDP, the open economy multiplier will be smaller than the closed economy multiplier and its value equals $1/(\text{MPS} + \text{MPM})$.

(e)   In an open economy model, the following circumstances and policies abroad can change Canada's GDP: changing prosperity levels abroad, changes in tariffs or quotas, or changes in exchange rates.

4. Adding a public sector to the aggregate expenditures model adds government expenditures as an injection and taxes as a leakage. Five simplifying assumptions are made:

(a)   Investment remains independent of GDP;

(b)   Government spending levels have no effect on private spending levels;

(c)   Government's net tax revenues are derived entirely from personal taxes, so disposable income is less than GDP;

(d)   The amount of taxes collected is fixed, regardless of GDP;

(e)   Unless otherwise noted, the price level is constant.

5. Government purchases of goods and services add to the aggregate expenditures schedule and increase equilibrium real GDP; and an increase in these purchases has a multiplier effect on GDP.

6. Taxes (*T*) reduce the aggregate expenditures schedule and decrease equilibrium real GDP; and a change in the level of lump-sum taxes has a multiplier effect on GDP. Taxes cause disposable income (*DI*) to fall short of GDP, forcing households to reduce consumption, saving, and imports below what they would be in the absence of taxes.

7. Introducing a public sector changes the expression of the equilibrium condition.

(a)   At equilibrium the real GDP is equal to the sum of consumption, planned investment, net

export spending, and government purchases. In symbols: $\text{GDP} = C + I_g + X_n + G$

(b)   By the leakages-injections approach, equilibrium is found where $I_g + X + G = S + M + T$.

8. If the amounts of government spending and taxes collected rise, and by an equal amount, equilibrium real GDP will rise by that same amount.

(a)   Therefore, changes in government spending have a more powerful effect on GDP than do changes in taxation.

(b)   Changes in government spending *directly* change aggregate expenditures by the full amount, whereas changes in taxation change aggregate expenditures only *indirectly* through the impact on disposable income. And because part of the change in *DI* is absorbed by changes in saving and imports, consumption changes by only a portion of the tax change.

(c)   The balanced budget multiplier measures the ratio of the change in equilibrium real GDP to the change (in equal amounts) to both government purchases and taxation. This multiplier equals 1.

9. The equilibrium level of real GDP can be at less than full-employment GDP, at full-employment GDP, or above full-employment GDP.

(a)   If equilibrium GDP is less than full-employment GDP, there exists a recessionary gap. The size of this gap is the amount by which the actual GDP is short of full-employment GDP.

(b)   If equilibrium GDP is greater than full-employment GDP, there exists an inflationary gap. The size of this gap is the amount by which the actual GDP exceeds full-employment GDP.

demand pull inflat

10. The concepts of recessionary and inflationary gaps can be applied to two historical episodes.

(a)   In the Great Depression of the 1930s Canada (and many other countries) experienced a drastic recessionary gap as investment spending declined 85%. This was linked to:

(1) overcapacity in industrial production, and rising business indebtedness in the 1920s;

(2) a downturn in residential construction;

(3) a crash in stock market prices;

(4) a shrinking money supply.

(b)   In the 1960s the U.S. government increased military spending to fight the Vietnam war, ultimately causing an inflationary gap. The increased aggregate expenditures spilled over into

Canada as an increase in our exports, leading Canada into an inflationary gap also.

11. The aggregate expenditures model has two main shortcomings (that will be remedied in the model presented in Chapter 11):
(a) The model is unable to measure price level changes.
(b) The model does not address cost-push in-flation.

■ TERMS AND CONCEPTS

appreciation	multiplier
depreciation	net export schedule
inflationary gap	net exports
lump-sum tax	open-economy
marginal propensity to	multiplier
import	recessionary gap

■ HINTS AND TIPS

1. Though the model we end up with in Chapter 10 has more components than the simple model of Chapter 9, the mechanics of the complete model are fundamentally the same as those of the simple model. In equilibrium, aggregate expenditures equal output, or injections equal leakages. The difference between Chapter 9 and the final model of Chapter 10 is merely the number of elements in the aggregate expenditures, or in the injections and leakages.

2. The multiplier is a crucial concept. It is simply the ratio of the change in equilibrium real GDP to the initial change in expenditures that caused the equilibrium to change. Play with numerical examples until you have a good grasp. Be sure you understand intuitively why a higher rate of leakages creates a smaller multiplier.

3. When faced with questions about the aggregate expenditure model — whether in this study guide or on an exam! — take time to assess which version of the model is indicated by the question. Is the economy open or closed? Is there a government sector? Are taxes fixed relative to income?

4. Be sure that your practice with the aggregate expenditures model covers both tabular examples and graphical examples. If your instructor favours a more algebraic approach than this text presents, then your instructor may provide you with some additional algebraic examples as well.

■ FILL-IN QUESTIONS

1. The analysis throughout this chapter assumes that the price level is (constant, variable) _____ and therefore the explanation is in terms of (real, nominal) _____ GDP.

2. The multiplier is the ratio of the change in _____ to an initial change in spending. When the initial change in spending is multiplied by the multiplier, the value equals the change in _____.

3. The multiplier effect rests on two facts:
(a) an initial increase in spending will increase the _____ of households in the economy; and
(b) this results in an increase in households' _____ spending equal to some _____ of the increase in income.

4. When planned investment spending increases, equilibrium real GDP (increases, decreases) _____, and when planned investment spending decreases, equilibrium real GDP _____.
(a) The changes in equilibrium real GDP are (greater, less) _____ than the changes in planned investment.
(b) The size of the multiplier varies (directly, inversely) _____ with the size of the MPC.

5. When a nation is able to export and import goods and services, but there is no government sector:
(a) its net exports equal its _____ minus its _____.
(b) In an open economy:
(1) aggregate expenditures are equal to consumption plus planned investment plus _____;
(2) the equilibrium real GDP is found where output equals _____.

6. Equilibrium in the open economy model, in the leakages-injections approach, is given by: _____ plus _____ equals _____ plus _____.

7. Indicate whether each of the following will increase (+) or decrease (-) an open economy's equilibrium real GDP.
(a) An increase in its imports ☐
(b) An increase in its exports ☐
(c) An increasing level of national income among trading partners ☐

(d)   An increase in trade barriers imposed by trading partners ☐
(e)   A depreciation in the value of the economy's currency ☐

8. The demand abroad for Canadian exports depends upon the GDP in (Canada, other countries) _____, whereas the demand for Canadian imports depends upon the GDP in _____.

9. An appreciation of the Canadian dollar generally causes Canada's imports to (increase, decrease) _____, and causes Canada's exports to _____.

10. The marginal propensity to import is defined as the ratio of the change in _____ over the change in _____.

11. If exports are constant and imports increase with an increasing domestic GDP, the open economy multiplier will be (greater than, less than) _____ the closed economy multiplier and is given by 1/(_____+_____).

12. In an economy with foreign trade, government purchases and taxes, the equilibrium as expressed in the leakages-injections approach is found at the GDP level where planned gross _____ plus _____, and the purchases of goods and services by _____ equals _____, plus _____, and _____.

13. Equal increases in taxes and government purchases will (increase, decrease) _____ real GDP by an amount (greater than, less than, equal to) _____ the change in taxes and government purchases. This result is called the _____ multiplier, and the value of this multiplier is _____.

14. A recessionary gap exists when equilibrium real GDP is (greater, less) _____ than the full-employment real GDP. To bring real GDP to the full-employment level, the aggregate expenditures schedule must (increase, decrease) _____.

15. The Great Depression is an historical example of a(n) (recessionary, inflationary) _____ gap, whereas the years around the Vietnam war provide an example of a(n) _____ gap.

16. The Canadian economy was pulled into the Great Depression because of a huge collapse in _____ expenditures. The factors that led to this collapse included:
(a)   _____
(b)   _____
(c)   _____
(d)   _____

17. The aggregate expenditures model does not incorporate or explain the _____ level, and it does not account for _____ inflation.

■   **PROBLEMS AND PROJECTS**

1. Assume a closed economy with no public sector. The marginal propensity to consume is 0.6. Suppose that this economy experiences an increase of $10 in planned investment because businesses become more optimistic about future profits. Work through the rounds of the multiplier effect to fill in the table below.

	Change in income	Change in C	Change in S
Increase in I_g	$10	_____	_____
2nd round	_____	_____	_____
3rd round	_____	_____	_____
4th round	_____	_____	_____
5th round	_____	_____	_____
all other rounds	_____	_____	_____
Total	_____	_____	_____

2. The table below shows consumption levels for various GDP levels in an economy that has no foreign trade or government sector. The table shows two columns of values for planned investment: (I_g and I_g^*).

GDP	C	I_g	AE	I_g^*	AE*
100	120	30	_____	55	_____
200	195	30	_____	55	_____
300	270	30	_____	55	_____
400	345	30	_____	55	_____
500	420	30	_____	55	_____
600	495	30	_____	55	

(a)   Assuming planned investment is equal to I_g, complete the aggregate expenditures column labelled AE.
(b)   Equilibrium GDP for this investment level is _____.

(c) Assuming planned investment is equal to I_g^*, complete the aggregate expenditures column labelled AE*.

(d) Equilibrium GDP for this investment level is _____.

(e) When planned investment changes by _____, equilibrium GDP changes by ___. Therefore the simple multiplier is ____/_____ = _____.

3. The graph below shows saving and planned investment for a closed economy with no public sector.

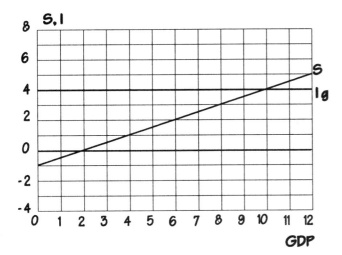

(a) The equilibrium GDP level is _____.
(b) The MPS = _____
(c) The simple multiplier = _____
(d) Given your answer for (c), a decrease of 2 in investment would (increase, decrease) _____ GDP by _____.
(e) Confirm your conclusion in (d) by showing the investment shift on your graph.

4. Suppose that households spend 80% of each dollar of disposable income on consumption goods, that imports are 10% of disposable income, and that personal taxes take 25% of each dollar of personal income.

(a) For each $100 of new personal income, $_____ goes to taxes, and the other $_____ goes to new disposable income.
(b) Of the $_____ in new disposable income, $____ goes to consumption, and the other $____ goes to saving.
(c) Of the $_____ in new consumption, $_____ is spent on imported goods.

(d) In summary, of the $100 of new income, the total new leakages is $_____ + $_____ + $_____ = $_____.

(e) The fraction of the new $100 that leaks is ____, so the complex multiplier is 1/____ = ____

(f) Given this multiplier value, a new injection of $1 would raise equilibrium GDP by $_____.

5. The tables below pertain to an open economy with a public sector. The full-employment level of GDP is $450. The consumption and import data are shown in the tables. At all GDP levels, taxes are $50, exports are $50, and government purchases are $55. Planned investment is given by the equation $I_g = 60 - i$, where i is the interest rate in percent. At present $i = 20$.

(a) Complete the blank columns in the first table.
(b) Find the equilibrium GDP by finding where GDP equals aggregate expenditures.
(c) Confirm your result in (b) by proving that leakages equal injections at this GDP level.
(d) At the equilibrium, does this economy have a recessionary gap or an inflationary gap, and what size is the gap?
(e) What is the value of the multiplier for this economy?
(f) If the interest rate falls from 20% to 14%, what is the change in I_g, and according to the multiplier effect, what is the change in GDP?
(g) If foreigners decreased by $12 their purchases from this economy, what will be the impact on equilibrium income, according to the multiplier value found in (e)?
(h) What will the new gap be after the change in interest rate, and after the drop in purchases by foreigners?
(i) How much, and in what direction, would government purchases need to change in order to close the gap calculated in (h)?
(j) Confirm your conclusion in (i) by completing the second table below. To start, remember to change Ig and X from their values in the original table.

GDP	T	DI	C	S	Ig	X	M	Xn	G	AE
$400	___	___	$340	___	___	___	$40	___	___	___
450	___	___	380	___	___	___	45	___	___	___
500	___	___	420	___	___	___	50	___	___	___
550	___	___	460	___	___	___	55	___	___	___
600	___	___	500	___	___	___	60	___	___	___

GDP	T	DI	C	S	Ig	X	M	Xn	G	AE
$400	___	___	$340	___	___	___	$40	___	___	___
450	___	___	380	___	___	___	45	___	___	___
500	___	___	420	___	___	___	50	___	___	___
550	___	___	460	___	___	___	55	___	___	___
600	___	___	500	___	___	___	60	___	___	___

■ TRUE-FALSE

Circle T if the statement is true, F if it is false.

1. The larger the marginal propensity to consume, the larger the size of the multiplier.   **T F**

2. If the multiplier is 2.5, and planned investment spending drops by 10, equilibrium real GDP will increase by 25.   **T F**

3. Because of the multiplier effect, large fluctuations in firms' investment plans, or in households' savings plans, will lead to smaller fluctuations in equilibrium real GDP.   **T F**

4. The multiplier effect ends when exactly enough new leakages have been caused to offset a new injection.   **T F**

5. If the GDP in the United States is growing, we can expect an increase in Canadian GDP, *ceteris paribus*.   **T F**

6. An increase in the imports of one nation will increase the exports of another nation.   **T F**

7. If the price of a U.S. dollar has risen from $1.40 Canadian to $1.50 Canadian, an increase in Canadian exports to the United States can be expected.   **T F**

8. A higher marginal propensity to import in Canada means that Canadian households are spending a larger percentage of their disposable income on foreign produced goods.   **T F**

9. Import spending, like investment spending, is an injection into the spending flow.   **T F**

10. The larger the marginal propensity to import, the smaller the multiplier.   **T F**

11. Net exports will be equal to zero at the economy's equilibrium level of real GDP.   **T F**

12. The complex multiplier is a multiplier that accounts for all sources of leakages from the circular flow of spending.   **T F**

13. If MPC is 0.3 and MPM is 0.2, the open-economy multiplier is 2.   **T F**

14. If the open-economy multiplier is 1.6, and the MPS is 1/4, then MPM must equal 3/8.   **T F**

15. A recessionary gap is the amount by which full-employment GDP falls short of actual GDP.   **T F**

16. The balanced budget multiplier is based on the idea that government spending causes no multiplier effects on equilibrium real GDP unless the government's budget is balanced.   **T F**

17. When the economy is in a recessionary gap, unemployment is above its natural rate.   **T F**

18. One major reason for the Great Depression was a steep decline in government spending.   **T F**

19. The Vietnam war was an example of increased government spending leading to an inflationary gap.   **T F**

20. The aggregate expenditures model provides an explanation for cost-push inflation.   **T F**

■ MULTIPLE-CHOICE

Circle the letter that corresponds to the best answer.

1. The volume of Canadian exports depends upon:
(a) the price in foreign currency of a Canadian dollar
(b) the level of Canadian prices relative to the price level abroad
(c) the level of GDP in foreign countries
(d) all of the above

2. Generally, a depreciation of the Canadian dollar will lead to:
(a) an increase in exports and an increase in imports
(b) an increase in exports and no change in imports

(c)   a decrease in exports and an increase in imports
(d)   an increase in exports and a decrease in imports

3. An increase in GDP in Canada will increase our imports and:
(a)   increase our exports
(b)   increase our net exports
(c)   decrease our exports
(d)   decrease our net exports

4. Which of the following would increase Canadian imports of fruits from California?
(a)   an increase in the price of Canadian fruit
(b)   an appreciation of the U.S. dollar relative to the Canadian dollar
(c)   an increase in the price of fruit in California
(d)   all of the above

5. A movement along Canada's net export schedule would be caused by:
(a)   an increase in export demand
(b)   an increase in our marginal propensity to import
(c)   an increase in the foreign exchange rate for our dollar
(d)   an increase in Canada's income

6. What is the correct formula for the open economy multiplier?
(a)   1/MPS
(b)   1/MPM
(c)   1/MPS + MPM
(d)   1/(MPS + MPM)

7. Suppose that a closed economy with no public sector experiences a rise of $100 in planned investment, and that this creates $100 of new income in the first round, and $75 in the second round. Then the MPC and the multiplier are, respectively:
(a)   0.75, 4.00
(b)   0.25, 1.33
(c)   0.75, 1.75
(d)   0.25, 4.00

The following table of data represents the situation of an open economy with no government sector. Use the data to answer questions 8 through 11.

GDP	S	Ig	M	X
1000	200	150	150	340
1100	220	150	165	340
1200	240	150	180	340
1300	260	150	195	340
1400	280	150	210	340

8. For the economy in this table:
(a)   MPC = 0.80 and MPM = 0.15
(b)   MPS = 0.80 and MPM = 0.15
(c)   MPC = 0.20 and MPM = 0.10
(d)   MPS = 0.20 and MPM = 0.10

9. Equilibrium GDP is:
(a)   1100
(b)   1200
(c)   1300
(d)   1400

10. The open economy multiplier is:
(a)   0.95
(b)   2.86
(c)   3.50
(d)   4.32

11. If export expenditures fall by 35, equilibrium GDP will:
(a)   decrease by 35
(b)   increase by 35
(c)   decrease by 100
(d)   increase by 100

12. Other things remaining constant, which of the following would decrease an economy's real GDP and employment?
(a)   the imposition of tariffs on goods imported from abroad
(b)   an increase in the level of national income among the trading partners for this economy
(c)   a decrease in the marginal propensity to consume
(d)   a decrease in the marginal propensity to import

13. An increase in the real GDP of an economy will, other things remaining constant:
(a)   increase its imports and decrease the real GDPs in other economies
(b)   increase its imports and increase the real GDPs in other economies

(c)   decrease its imports and increase the real GDPs in other economies
(d)   decrease its imports and the real GDPs in other economies

14. The effect of an increase in exports on GDP is similar to the effect of an increase in:
(a)   interest rates
(b)   saving
(c)   investment
(d)   business taxes

The data in this table relate to an open economy with no public sector. Use the data to answer questions 15 through 18 .

GDP	C + Ig	Xn
$900	$913	$3
920	929	3
940	945	3
960	961	3
980	977	3
1000	993	3
1020	1009	3

15. The equilibrium real GDP is:
(a) $960
(b) $980
(c) $1000
(d) $1020

16. If net exports are increased by $4 at each level of GDP, the equilibrium real GDP would be:
(a) $960
(b) $980
(c) $1000
(d) $1020

17. The multiplier in this economy is:
(a)   2
(b)   3
(c)   4
(d)   5

18. If the marginal propensity to save in this economy is .10, the marginal propensity to import must be:
(a)   .10
(b)   .20
(c)   .30
(d)   .40

19. Which of the following is not among the list of assumptions we made in adding the public sector to the aggregate expenditures model?
(a)   the price level is fixed
(b)   investment spending is independent of the GDP level
(c)   the amount of taxes collected is independent of the GDP level
(d)   the level of government spending influences the level of spending by the private sector

20. In the complete model presented in the text, what is the proper expression of where equilibrium output is found?
(a) $GDP = C + I_g + G + X$
(b) $GDP = C + I_g + G + X_n$
(c) $GDP = C + I_g + G + X + M$
(d) $GDP = C + I_g + G + X_n - M$

Questions 21 through 24 are based on this graph.

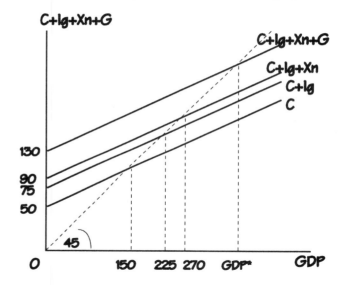

21. The multiplier in this economy is:
(a)   2
(b)   2.5
(c)   3
(d)   3.5

22. In this diagram it is assumed that government purchases, net exports, and planned investment add up to:
(a)   130 and are constant at all levels of GDP
(b)   80 and are constant at all levels of GDP
(c)   130 and increase as GDP increases
(d)   80 and increase as GDP increases

23. What is the equilibrium level labelled GDP*?
- **(a)** 300
- **(b)** 390
- **(c)** 420
- **(d)** 450

24. If full-employment GDP happens to be 400, then what is the gap at GDP*?
- **(a)** recessionary gap of 10
- **(b)** inflationary gap of 10
- **(c)** recessionary gap of 30
- **(d)** none of the above

25. A change in which variable would change the slope of the $C+Ig+Xn+G$ curve?
- **(a)** the level of planned investment
- **(b)** the level of lump-sum taxes
- **(c)** the level of government purchases
- **(d)** the marginal propensity to import

26. In the open economy model with a public sector, which of the following does not affect the vertical intercept of the aggregate expenditures function?
- **(a)** the marginal propensity to save
- **(b)** planned investment
- **(c)** lump-sum taxes
- **(d)** government purchases

27. An inflationary gap is:
- **(a)** the amount by which actual GDP falls short of full-employment GDP
- **(b)** the amount by which actual GDP exceeds full-employment GDP
- **(c)** the number of workers that would be employed at full employment minus the number actually employed
- **(d)** the increase in investment spending needed to reach full-employment GDP from present GDP

28. Which of the following contributed to the decline of investment spending during the Great Depression?
- **(a)** a decrease in business production capacity during the 1920s
- **(b)** an increase in net exports during the 1930s
- **(c)** a rapid money supply expansion during the 1930s
- **(d)** an increase in business indebtedness during the 1920s

29. If the American economy moves towards an inflationary gap, this automatically affects Canada's situation because:

- **(a)** Canada would begin importing more from the U.S.
- **(b)** the U.S. would begin importing more from Canada
- **(c)** the Canadian government must follow the same policies that the U.S. government does
- **(d)** our price level follows the same path as the U.S. price level

30. A nation that enters a free trade agreement can expect that:
- **(a)** their multiplier will decrease because their MPM will rise
- **(b)** their multiplier will increase because their MPM will decrease
- **(c)** their multiplier will increase because their exports will increase
- **(d)** their multiplier will be unaffected

■ **DISCUSSION QUESTIONS**

1. What is the multiplier effect? Why is there such an effect, and what determines how large it will be?

2. How do exports and imports affect aggregate expenditure within a nation? In terms of injections and leakages, what condition is met at the equilibrium level of output for the open economy?

3. If imports rise as GDP rises, why is the open economy multiplier smaller than the closed economy multiplier?

4. How does a change in the volume of exports and the volume of imports affect real GDP and the level of employment in an economy?

5. What are some examples of international economic linkages affecting the level of Canada's GDP?

6. How would Canada's economy be affected by increased spending undertaken by the United States government to combat an American recession?

7. Explain the five simplifying assumptions made when the public sector is included in the aggregate expenditures model in this chapter.

8. Explain what the injections are, and what the leakages are, in the complete model that includes both foreign trade and the public sector.

9. If taxes and government expenditures increase by equal amounts, what will happen to real GDP? Why?

10. Explain what is meant by a recessionary gap and an inflationary gap. What economic conditions are present in the economy when each of these gaps exist? How is the size of each of these gaps measured?

11. What factors influenced investment spending during the 1920s and early 1930s? How did these factors contribute to the Great Depression? Explain using an aggregate expenditures graph.

12. How did an inflationary gap arise during the Vietnam war period? How can this event be characterized using an aggregate expenditures graph?

13. What are the limitations of the aggregate expenditures model?

■ **ANSWERS**

FILL-IN QUESTIONS

1. constant, real

2. equilibrium real GDP; equilibrium real GDP

3. (a) income (b) consumption, fraction

4. increases, decreases (a) greater (b) directly

5. (a) exports, imports (b) (1) net exports (2) aggregate expenditures

6. saving, imports, planned investment, exports

7. (a) -; (b) +; (c) +; (d) -; (e) +

8. other countries; Canada

9. increase, decrease

10. imports, GDP

11. less than; MPS + MPM

12. investment, exports, government, saving, imports, taxes.

13. increase, equal to; balanced budget, 1.

14. less, increase

15. recessionary, inflationary

16. investment; (a) overcapacity and business indebtedness; (b) declining housing construction; (c) stock market crash; (d) shrinking money supply

17. price, cost-push

PROBLEMS AND PROJECTS

1. Changes in income: $10, 6.00, 3.60, 2.16, 1.30, 1.94, 25.00; changes in C: $6.00, 3.60, 2.16, 1.30, 0.78, 1.16, 15.00; changes in S: $4.00, 2.40, 1.44, 0.86, 0.52, 0.77, 10.00

2. (a) 150, 225, 300, 375, 450, 525; (b) 300; (c) 175, 250, 325, 400, 475, 550; (d) 400; (e) 25, 100, 100, 25, 4

3. (a) 10 (b) 0.50 (c) 2 (d) decrease, 4

4. (a) 25, 75; (b) 75, 60, 15; (c) 60, 7.5; (d) 25, 15, 7.5, 47.5; (e) .475, .475, 2.11; (f) 2.11

5. (a) T: $50 at all GDP levels; DI: $350, 400, 450, 500, 550; S: $10, 20, 30, 40, 50; Ig: $40 at all levels; X: $50 at all levels; Xn: $10, 5, 0, -5, -10; G: $55 at all levels; AE: $445, 480, 515, 550, 585; (b) $550 (c) $145=145 (d) inflationary gap of $100 (e) 3.33 (f) $6 $20 (g) decrease of $40 (h) inflationary gap of $80 (i) decrease by $24 (j) T: $50 at all GDP levels; DI: $350, 400, 450, 500, 550; S: $10, 20, 30, 40, 50; Ig: $46 at all levels; X: $38 at all levels; Xn: $-2, -7, -12, -17, -22; G: $31 at all levels; AE: $415, 450, 485, 520, 555

TRUE-FALSE

1. T	2. F	3. F	4. T	5. T	6. T
7. T	8. T	9. F	10. T	11. F	12. T
13. F	14. T	15. F	16. F	17. T	18. F
19. T	20. F				

MULTIPLE-CHOICE

1. (d)	2. (d)	3. (d)	4. (a)	5. (d)	6. (d)
7. (a)	8. (a)	9. (d)	10. (b)	11. (c)	12. (c)
13. (b)	14. (c)	15. (b)	16. (c)	17. (d)	18. (a)
19. (d)	20. (b)	21. (c)	22. (b)	23. (b)	24. (a)
25. (d)	26. (a)	27. (b)	28. (d)	29. (b)	30. (a)

CHAPTER 11

Aggregate Demand and Aggregate Supply

The aggregate expenditures model of Chapters 9 and 10 has an important limitation: it holds the price level fixed. Therefore, that model cannot explain how macroeconomic events affect the price level. Chapter 11 introduces the aggregate demand-aggregate supply model which overcomes this problem, and allows us to explain simultaneously the determination of both real GDP and the price level.

The aggregate demand curve (AD) shows the total amounts of goods and services demanded in the economy at each possible price level. Plotted on the price level vs. real output axes, AD is downsloping because less is demanded at higher price levels. Movements along a given AD curve are caused by three consequences of price changes: the wealth effect, the interest-rate effect, and the foreign-trade effect.

Although the aggregate expenditures model uses fixed prices, and the AD-AS model allows prices to vary, the two are closely related. The key is that the price level can be fixed at any particular level. The AD curve is derived from the aggregate expenditures model by finding the position of the aggregate expenditures curve, and the equilibrium level of GDP, at various different price levels. The resulting price-level-real-GDP combinations yield a downsloping AD curve. Therefore, price level changes cause movements along a given AD curve. The determinants of aggregate demand that can shift the entire AD curve are outlined in Figure 11-3 in the textbook. A vertical shift in the aggregate expenditures schedule causes AD to shift horizontally by a multiple of the amount that aggregate expenditures shifted.

The short-run aggregate supply (AS) curve shows the level of real domestic output which will be produced at each price level *if input prices remain fixed*. A rising price level implies greater profits for producers, and an incentive to produce and sell more output. But as output expands and full capacity is approached, increasing shortages of inputs and various inefficiencies in production raise the per unit costs of production and the selling prices. When the economy is far below capacity output, these problems are minor, so the AS curve is quite flat. But as output rises these problems become more severe, so the curve eventually becomes steeper, until it becomes nearly vertical as the economy nears its short-run full capacity output. In most instances the short-run AS curve will be upward sloping (meaning that the economy is neither in deep recession, nor at full-capacity production). Figure 11-6 lists the factors that affect the per-unit production costs, and therefore shift the entire AS curve.

The intersection of the AD and AS curves determines equilibrium real domestic output and price level. If the determinants of these curves do not change, competitive pressures will tend to keep the economy at this equilibrium. If the determinants of AD or AS change, one of the curves will shift, and typically both equilibrium real GDP and the equilibrium price level will be affected. An increase in the AD curve will increase real GDP, as in the aggregate expenditures model, but with a smaller multiplier effect because some of the impact is absorbed in rising prices. The steeper the AS curve, the smaller the multiplier effect on real GDP.

We define the short run as a period when nominal wages are fixed, and the long run as a period when nominal wages are fully responsive to changes in the price level. Starting from a full-employment equilibrium, an increase in AD will raise prices, employment and production. Because nominal wages are fixed, firms' profit margins rise and they gain from hiring more labour and producing more output. But given enough time, nominal wages will eventually catch up to the price increases, eliminating the improvement in profit margins and the impetus for higher than normal employment and output. So the short-run AS curve is upsloping, but the long-run AS curve is vertical. After long-run adjustments in nominal wages, real GDP is equal to potential GDP, regardless of the specific price level.

If the short-run equilibrium in the AD-AS model is not at full-employment GDP, there will be an inflationary or recessionary gap. Adjustments in nominal wages will eventually shift the short-run AS until it intersects AD and the long-run AS at the full-employment equilibrium. Because this adjustment may be unacceptably slow, fiscal and monetary policies may be used to keep the economy at or near a noninflationary, full-employment equilibrium. These policies are examined in the next few chapters.

■ CHECKLIST

When you have studied this chapter, you should be able to:
□ Identify the crucial limitation of the aggregate expenditures model that leads us to the aggregate demand-aggregate supply (AD-AS) model.
□ Define aggregate demand.
□ Explain the three reasons why the AD curve is downsloping.
□ Derive the AD curve from the aggregate expenditures model when you are supplied with the necessary price level data.
□ List the major determinants of AD and explain how they shift the AD curve.
□ Explain the relationship between shifts in the aggregate expenditures curve, the AD curve, and the multiplier.
□ Define aggregate supply.
□ Explain the shape of the short-run AS curve.
□ List the major determinants of AS in the short run and describe how they shift the AS curve.
□ Explain how the equilibrium price level and real domestic output level are determined in the AD-AS model.
□ Predict the effects of a change in AD on the price level and the equilibrium real GDP.
□ Demonstrate how the multiplier effect of a shift in AD depends on the slope of the short-run AS curve.
□ Predict the effects of a change in short-run AS on the price level and the equilibrium real GDP.

□ Define the short run and the long run as they relate to macroeconomics.
□ Explain the adjustments in the labour market that make the long-run AS curve vertical.
□ Distinguish between the equilibrium GDP and the full-employment, noninflationary level of GDP.
□ Find the recessionary and the inflationary gaps when you are provided with the relevant data.
□ Explain why recessionary and inflationary gaps will automatically resolve themselves, given time.

■ CHAPTER OUTLINE

1. The aggregate expenditures model is a fixed-price-level model in which real GDP is determined by demand side factors. The aggregate demand and aggregate supply model is more satisfactory because it includes the supply side of the economy, and it explains the determination of both real GDP and the price level.

2. Aggregate demand (AD) is a curve which shows an inverse relationship between the total quantity of goods and services that will be purchased by households, firms, foreigners, and government and the price level. There are three reasons why the AD curve is downward sloping:
   (a) A higher price level reduces the purchasing power of financial assets, making assetholders feel less wealthy and causing them to reduce their spending. This is the wealth effect.
   (b) A higher price level causes people to demand more money to hold. With a fixed supply of money, the interest rate will rise, reducing interest-sensitive expenditures (by consumers and businesses). This is the interest-rate effect.
   (c) A higher price level, when foreign prices are unchanged, will increase the relative price of goods produced in the domestic economy, reducing purchases of domestic output and increasing purchases of foreign output. This change in net export demand is the foreign-trade effect.

3. Price level increases shift the aggregate expenditures curve down.
   (a) consumption decreases due to the wealth effect;
   (b) investment decreases due to the interest-rate effect; and
   (c) net exports decrease due to the foreign-trade effect.

4. The inverse relationship between the price level and the equilibrium real GDP known as the AD curve is derived from the intersections of a series of aggregate expenditures curves (one for each price level) and the 45-degree line. As the price level rises, the aggregate expenditures curve shifts downwards, and the equilibrium real GDP decreases.

5. When changes in spending are caused by factors other than price level changes, the AD curve will shift. The determinants of AD discussed below are also summarized in Figure 11-3 in the textbook. Note that an increase in AD is a rightward shift; a decrease in AD is a leftward shift.

(a) Consumption spending will increase if domestic consumers experience: increases in wealth, improved expectations, reductions in indebtedness, or lower taxes.

(b) Investment spending — purchases of capital goods — will increase if businesses experience: lower interest rates, improved expected returns, lower taxes, improved technology, or less excess capacity.

(c) Government spending will increase if government purchases more goods and services, assuming that tax collections and interest rates do not change as a result.

(d) Net export spending will increase if the national incomes of our trading partners rise, or if our dollar depreciates and makes our goods relatively less expensive.

6. The short-run aggregate supply (AS) is a curve that shows the level of real domestic output that will be produced at each price level. Higher price levels create incentives for firms to produce more output, so the curve is upsloping. The steepness of AS depends on capacity utilization.

(a) When there is enough slack in the economy that output can expand without creating input shortages or production bottlenecks, there is no reason to raise prices when more is produced, so AS is flat.

(b) When the economy is already at its short-run capacity output, as firms try to produce more output they will simply bid resources away from one another without producing any more. Prices rise, but output does not, so AS is vertical.

(c) In most instances, the AS is upsloping because the economy is neither in severe recession nor at full-capacity, so more can be produced, but not profitably at the same price level. As bottle-necks and inefficiencies begin to occur as output expands, per unit production costs rise, so the extra output will be produced only if prices are higher.

7. When per-unit production costs change for reasons other than a change in real output, firms collectively alter the amount of output they produce at each price level, so the AS curve shifts. The determinants of AS discussed below are also summarized in Figure 11-6 in the textbook. An increase (a decrease) in AS is a rightward (leftward) shift.

(a) Higher input prices increase per-unit production costs and decrease AS. Input prices could rise because of reductions in the supply of resources (land, labour, capital, and entrepreneurial ability), because of depreciation of the domestic currency that raises the price of imported resources, or because of an increased market power of resource suppliers.

(b) An increase in the amount of output per unit of input means that productivity increases, and that AS increases. Note that productivity increase is the same as decrease in per-unit production costs.

(c) Increases in taxes, reductions in subsidies, or increased regulation of business will tend to raise per-unit costs of output and decrease the AS curve.

8. The equilibrium real GDP and the equilibrium price level occur at the intersection of the AD and AS curves.

(a) If the price level were above the equilibrium level, the amount of output produced would exceed the amount demanded, so competition among sellers would drive the price level down to equilibrium.

(b) If the price level were below the equilibrium level, the amount of output demanded would exceed the amount supplied, so competition among buyers would drive the price level up to equilibrium.

9. In the aggregate expenditures model any increase in aggregate demand simply increases equilibrium real output, because the price level is fixed. In the AD-AS model, an increase in AD usually leads to both inflation and increased output. To the extent that inflation results, the multiplier impact on real output is reduced. If AD increases:

(a) Equilibrium real output and price level both rise in the normal case where AS is upsloping. The multiplier effect is reduced.

(b) Equilibrium real output rises and the price level is unchanged if AS is perfectly horizontal. The multiplier effect is maximum.

(c) The equilibrium price level rises and real output is unchanged if the AS is vertical. There is no multiplier effect.

10. The aggregate supply has a different shape in the long run. If the price level rises, workers will eventually recognize that their real wages have fallen, and they will demand and obtain nominal wage increases to restore their real wage rates. Therefore, long-run aggregate supply must take into account the changes in nominal wages that occur in response to price level changes. Exactly what is the difference between the short run and the long run in macroeconomics?

(a) The short run is a period in which nominal wages (and other input prices) remain fixed as the price level changes. Nominal wages may remain fixed temporarily either because workers are not immediately aware of the change in their real wages, or because contracts have fixed nominal wages for a certain period of time.

(b) The long run is a period in which nominal wages are fully responsive to changes in the price level. Given enough time, nominal wage changes will match price level changes so that real wages are unchanged.

11. Given these definitions of the short run and long run, we can be specific about the shape of the AS curve over these two periods.

(a) In the short run a price increase pushes real wages down because nominal wages are fixed. This raises profit margins for producers, giving them incentive to hire more labour (and other inputs) and produce more real output. AS in the short run is upsloping.

(b) In the long run, assuming full flexibility of nominal wages, a price increase is matched by a nominal wage increase, so real wages are constant. Therefore there is no incentive to produce more than usual. The price level increase has no effect on real output, so the aggregate supply in the long run (AS_{LR}) is vertical.

12. Long-run equilibrium in the AD-AS model must be at the intersection of AD and AS (where demand for output and supply of output are equal), but it must also be on the vertical AS_{LR} curve (where nominal wages have adjusted to accomodate the price level and maintain the real wage). The AS_{LR} is vertical at the economy's full employment or potential GDP, and is consistent with the natural rate of unemployment.

13. The equilibrium level of real GDP in the short run need not be at full employment; it could be at a point with higher than natural unemployment, or at a point with inflation.

(a) A recessionary gap is the amount by which equilibrium GDP falls short of full-employment GDP. In the absence of any policy action to combat the problem, prices and nominal wages will eventually fall until the economy returns to full-employment GDP, but this is likely to take an unacceptably long time.

(b) An inflationary gap is the amount by which equilibrium GDP exceeds full-employment GDP. In the absence of any policy action, prices and nominal wages will rise far enough to reduce output until it returns to full-employment GDP. This will add to the inflation, and will also take some time.

■ **TERMS AND CONCEPTS**

aggregate demand	interest-rate effect
determinants of	long-run aggregate
aggregate demand	supply curve
determinants of	productivity
aggregate supply	recessionary and
equilibrium price level	inflationary gaps
equilibrium real	short-run aggregate
domestic output	supply
foreign-trade effect	wealth effect

■ **HINTS AND TIPS**

1. You must recognize a key difference between the AD-AS model and the supply and demand model of Chapter 3. In the aggregate model the price level measures the average of prices overall, and the aggregate quantity of all goods, rather than the price and quantity of any particular good.

2. A price level change shifts the aggregate expenditures curve, but causes a movement along a given aggregate demand curve.

3. Figures 11-3 and 11-6 list the determinants that cause shifts in the AD and AS curves, respectively. Study these tables carefully.

4. A common mistake when working with AS curves is to shift the curve in the wrong direction. If supply is increasing, the curve shifts rightward. It is easy to see how this leads to **more** output and **lower** prices.

■   **FILL-IN QUESTIONS**

1. In the AD-AS model the price level is _____, whereas in the aggregate expenditures model it is _____.

2. The graph for the AD-AS model plots _____ on the vertical axis, and _____ on the horizontal axis.

3. The AD curve shows the quantity of goods and services that will be _____ at various price _____. It slopes (upward, downward) _____ because of the _____, the _____, and the _____ effects.

4. In the aggregate expenditure model, a price increase will shift the aggregate expenditure curve (up, down) _____, and the equilibrium level of real GDP will (increase, decrease) _____. This (direct, inverse) _____ relationship between the price level and the amount of output demanded can be used to derive the _____ curve (or schedule).

5. (a) A change in one of the determinants of AD will cause a (movement along, shift of) _____ the AD curve.
   (b) A change in the price will cause a (movement along, shift of) _____ the AD curve.

6. List the determinants of AD that affect consumption spending:
   (a) _____
   (b) _____
   (c) _____
   (d) _____

7. List the determinants of AD that affect investment spending:
   (a) _____
   (b) _____
   (c) _____

   (d) _____
   (e) _____

8. List the determinants of AD that affect net export spending:
   (a) _____
   (b) _____

9. An event that shifts the aggregate expenditures curve upward will cause the (AD, AS) _____ curve to shift to the (left, right) _____ by (the same, a larger, a smaller) _____ amount. This is the _____ effect.

10. The AS curve shows the quantity of goods and services that will be _____ at various _____ levels. At all points along a given AS curve we assume that (input, output) _____ prices are constant.

11. The AS curve is _____ sloping because of the (increase, decrease) _____ in the per-unit costs of producing goods and services as output expands.

12. List the determinants of short-run aggregate supply:
   (a)   From a change in input prices due to a change in:
      (1) _____
      (2) _____
      (3) _____
   (b)   From a change in _____
   (c)   From a change in the legal-institutional environment due to a change in:
      (1) _____
      (2) _____

13. Were AD to increase,
   (a)   the flatter the AS curve, the (greater, smaller) _____ is the multiplier effect on the real equilibrium GDP and the _____ is the effect on the equilibrium price level; and
   (b)   the steeper the AS curve, the _____ is the multiplier effect on the equilibrium real GDP and the _____ is the effect on the equilibrium price level.

14. Along the long-run aggregate supply curve, prices and (real, nominal) _____ wages change, but _____ wages are constant, and therefore so are producers' _____ margins, the level of _____ of labour, and the level of real output.

15. The economy can come to a (short, long) _____ run equilibrium at an output level below potential GDP. Such a situation is termed a(n) _____ gap. Eventually the gap would be resolved automatically by (rising, falling) _____ prices and nominal wages.

■ **PROBLEMS AND PROJECTS**

1. This question involves the derivation of a downsloping AD curve from the aggregate expenditure model. Suppose the equation for aggregate expenditures is given by: C+Ig+Xn+G = 4 + 0.5 GDP when the price level is 100. If the price level falls to 50, the intercept of this function rises by 2, whereas if the price level increases to 150 the intercept falls by 2.
(a)   In the upper panel of the graph plot the aggregate expenditure functions pertaining to three price levels: 50, 100, 150, and determine the equilibrium level of GDP that would correspond to each.
(b)   Use your findings in (a) to plot three combinations of price level and equilibrium GDP. Join these points to form the AD curve.

2. This question continues with the data used in question 1. Assume that potential GDP is $7.
(a)   Plot on the lower panel of the graph the AS data shown in the next table.
(b)   The short-run equilibrium price level is $_____, and the short-run equilibrium real GDP is $_____.
(c)   Draw in the long-run aggregate supply curve (AS$_{LR}$) on the graph.
(d)   At the short-run equilibrium in (b), there is a _____ gap of $_____.

Price level	Real domestic output
50	2
50	4
75	6
100	8
125	9
150	9

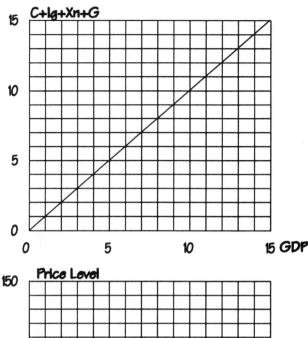

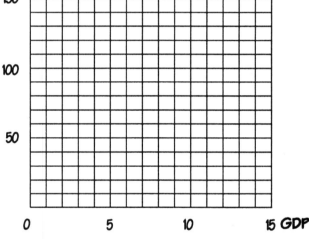

3. This question continues with the data from questions 1 and 2.
(a)   Plot a new aggregate demand curve, AD', that results from a $1 increase in investment spending. (Hint: the increase in investment will shift all three aggregate expenditures curves in the top panel upward by 1.)
(b)   Given the horizontal shift from AD to AD', the size of the multiplier for this economy is equal to _____.
(c)   The new short-run equilibrium price level is approximately $_____, and the short-run equilibrium real GDP is approximately $_____.
(d)   The multiplier with price level changes is equal to the change in real output divided by the change in spending. This is $_____/$_____ = _____. (Hint: this should be a smaller value than found in (b), showing that inflation weakens the multiplier.)

4. The data below shows relationships between the real domestic output and the quantity of input resources needed to produce each level of output.

GDP	Input	Productivity		Per-unit cost		
		(1)	(2)	(3)	(4)	(5)
2500	500	___	___	___	___	___
2400	400	___	___	___	___	___
2100	300	___	___	___	___	___
1600	200	___	___	___	___	___

(a)   In column (1) compute the level of productivity at each level of GDP.

(b)   In column (2) compute the level of productivity if now there is a doubling in the quantity of inputs required to produce each level of output.

(c)   In column (3) compute the per-unit production cost at each level of output, if each unit of input costs $3, given the productivity in column (1).

(d)   In column (4) compute the new per-unit production cost at each level of output given that input price is $3, given that there has been a doubling in the required quantity of inputs required to produce each level of output as shown in column (2). What happens to the AS curve if this situation occurs?

(e)   In column (5), compute the new per-unit production cost at each level of output, given that input price is now $2 instead of $3, but the level of productivity stays as it was originally, as in column (1). What will happen to the AS curve if this situation occurs?

5. For each event listed below, what is the most likely effect on Canada's: (1) aggregate demand; (2) aggregate supply; (3) the equilibrium price level, and; (4) equilibrium real domestic output? Assume that all other things are equal, and that the AS curve is upsloping. Use the following symbols to indicate the expected effects: I = increase; D = decrease; S = remains the same; and U = uncertain. (You are also encouraged to sketch out these situations on your own graphs).

(a)   A decrease in labour productivity:
AD _____ AS _____ P _____ Q _____

(b)   A fall in interest rates:
AD _____ AS _____ P _____ Q _____

(c)   Consumers' indebtedness increases to record high levels:
AD _____ AS _____ P _____ Q _____

(d)   The price of oil on the world market falls to a low level:
AD _____ AS _____ P _____ Q _____

(e)   An appreciation of the Canadian dollar:
AD _____ AS _____ P _____ Q _____

(f)   An increase in personal income tax rates:
AD _____ AS _____ P _____ Q _____

(g)   The United States recovers from a recession:
AD _____ AS _____ P _____ Q _____

6. Wimpyland produces nothing but hamburgers. The price level is therefore in $ per burger, nominal wages are in $, and real wages are in burgers. The initial nominal wage rate is $12. The current situation in Wimpyland is depicted by AS, AD_1, and AS_{LR} on the following graph.

(a)   The short-run equilibrium price level is $_____ per burger, and the equilibrium output level is _____ burgers.

(b)   Why is this equilibrium both a short-run equilibrium and a long-run equilibrium?

(c)   In this equilibrium, the real wage rate is $_____ ÷ $_____ per burger = _____ burgers.

(d)   If AD_1 shifts up to AD_2, the new short-run equilibrium price level is $_____ per burger, and the output level is _____ burgers. There is a(n) _____ gap of 100 burgers.

(e)   At this new short-run equilibrium, the real wage is $_____ ÷ $_____ per burger = _____ burgers. Therefore, the real wage is now (above, below) _____ the long-run equilibrium real wage.

(f)   This disequilibrium will cause the AS curve to shift (rightward, leftward) _____ until a new long-run equilibrium is reached where the price level is $_____ per burger, and the equilibrium output level is _____ burgers.

(g)   At this new equilibrium, the real wage will have returned to _____ burgers. Given the new price level, this implies that the nominal wage must have risen to $_____.

Price level ($ / burger)

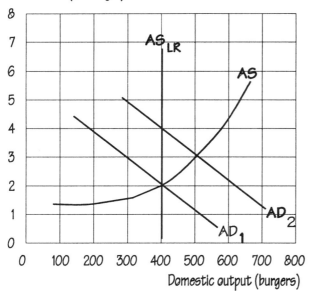

Domestic output (burgers)

■   **TRUE-FALSE**

Circle T if the statement is true, F if it is false.

1. An aggregate demand schedule shows the net amounts of goods and services that consumers, businesses, governments, and foreigners collectively wish to purchase at different price levels.   **T** F

2. The AD curve slopes downward.   **T** F

3. A change in aggregate demand is caused by a change in the price level, other things equal.   T **F**

4. A fall in the price level increases the real value of financial assets with fixed money value and, as a result, increases spending by the holders of these assets.   **T** F

5. A fall in the price level reduces the demand for money in the economy, pushes interest rates upward, and decreases investment spending.   T **F**

6. A rise in the price level of an economy (relative to foreign price levels) tends to increase that economy's net exports.   T **F**

7. According to the wealth effect, when the price level rises, households feel more wealthy, and increase their spending.   T **F**

8. A decrease in the degree of excess capacity in the economy will retard the demand for new capital goods and therefore reduce AD.   T **F**

9. A high level of consumer indebtedness will tend to increase consumption spending and AD.   T **F**

10. An increase in government purchases will shift the aggregate expenditures curve upwards, and shift AD leftward.   T **F**

11. A depreciation in the Canadian dollar would shift the AD curve for Canada to the right.   **T** F

12. If the aggregate expenditures curve shifts up by $1 million, the AD curve will shift right by $1 million.   **T** F

13. The steepness of the AS curve depends on the degree of capacity utilization.   **T** F

14. Lower prices for land, labour or capital will tend to shift the AS to the left.   T **F**

15. Productivity can be defined as the ratio of input divided by real output. $\frac{out}{in}$ T **F**

16. Increased government regulation tends to decrease the AS curve.   **T** F

17. An increase in the short-run aggregate supply increases both the equilibrium real GDP and the potential output of the economy.   T **F**

18. A decrease in AS is "doubly good" because it increases the real domestic output and prevents inflation.   T **F**

19. When the determinants of AS change, they alter the per-unit production cost and thereby shift AS.   **T** F

20. An increase in productivity will shift the aggregate supply curve rightward.   **T** F

21. A recessionary gap is the amount by which full-employment GDP falls short of actual GDP.   T **F**
equilibrium GDP falls short of full employmen GDP

22. When the AS curve is upsloping, the multiplier effect of a change in a spending flow on real output is less than in the aggregate expenditure model of Chapter 10.   **T** F

■ MULTIPLE-CHOICE

Circle the letter that corresponds to the best answer.

1. The AD curve is the relationship between the:
(a) price level and the real domestic output purchased
(b) price level and the equilibrium real gross domestic product
(c) price level producers are willing to accept and the price level purchasers are willing to pay
(d) real domestic output purchased and the real domestic output produced

2. When the price level rises:
(a) holders of financial assets with fixed money values increase their spending
(b) the demand for money falls
(c) interest rates rise and investment expenditures fall
(d) exports increase and imports fall

3. The downward slope of the AD curve is the result of:
(a) the wealth effect
(b) the interest-rate effect
(c) the foreign-trade effect
(d) all of the above effects

4. In the aggregate expenditures model, a drop in the price level will lead to:
(a) a lower aggregate expenditures curve and a lower multiplier
(b) a higher aggregate expenditures curve and a higher multiplier
(c) a lower aggregate expenditures curve and a lower equilibrium real output
(d) a higher aggregate expenditures curve and a higher equilibrium real output

5. Which of the following does not increase as a result of a decrease in the price level?
(a) consumption
(b) planned investment
(c) net exports
(d) government spending

6. The AS curve is the relationship between the:
(a) price level and the real domestic output purchased
(b) price level and the real domestic output produced

(c) price level producers are willing to accept and the price level purchasers are willing to pay
(d) real domestic output purchased and the real domestic output produced

7. The AS curve is upsloping in the short run due to:
(a) increased input prices as output rises
(b) decreased input prices as output rises
(c) rising per-unit production costs as output rises
(d) a shortage of domestic resources

8. Which of the following is held constant when moving from one point on an AS curve to another point on the same curve?
(a) the price level
(b) the prices of inputs
(c) the per unit cost of production
(d) none of these are held constant

9. The AD curve will tend to be increased (shifted to the right) by:
(a) a decrease in the price level
(b) an increase in the price level
(c) an increase in the excess capacity of factories
(d) a depreciation in the value of the Canadian dollar

10. An increase in business taxes will tend to:
(a) decrease AD but not change AS
(b) decrease AS but not change AD
(c) decrease AD and AS
(d) decrease AS and increase AD

11. An increase in AS will:
(a) reduce the price level and real domestic output
(b) reduce the price level and increase the real domestic output
(c) increase the price level and real domestic output
(d) reduce the price level and decrease the real domestic output

12. Which of the following is not one of the reasons that nominal wages are fixed in the short run, even when prices rise?
(a) workers may not immediately be aware of the price increases
(b) workers' wages may be fixed by contracts
(c) both of the above
(d) none of the above

13. If Parliament passed much stricter laws to control the air pollution from business, then this action would tend to:
  (a) increase per-unit production costs and shift the AS curve to the right
  (b) increase per-unit production costs and shift the AS curve to the left
  (c) increase per-unit production costs and shift the AD curve to the left
  (d) decrease per-unit production costs and shift the AS curve to the left

14. An increase in aggregate expenditures in the aggregate expenditure model shifts the AD curve to the:
  (a) right by the amount of the increase in aggregate expenditure
  (b) right by the amount of the increase in aggregate expenditure times the multiplier
  (c) left by the amount of the increase in aggregate expenditure
  (d) left by the amount of the increase in aggregate expenditure times the multiplier

15. A decrease in the price level will shift the:
  (a) consumption, investment, and net exports curves downward
  (b) consumption, investment, and net exports curves upward
  (c) consumption and investment curves downward and the net exports curve upward
  (d) consumption and net exports curves upward, but the investment curve downward

Suppose that real domestic output in an economy is 50, the quantity of inputs is 10, and the price of each input is $2. Answer questions 16 through 19 on the basis of this information.

16. The level of productivity in this economy is:
  (a) 5
  (b) 4
  (c) 3
  (d) 2

17. The per unit cost of production is:
  (a) $0.40
  (b) $0.50
  (c) $0.75
  (d) $1.00

18. If real domestic output in the economy rose to 60 units, then per-unit production costs would:

(a) remain unchanged and AS would remain unchanged
(b) increase and AS would decrease
(c) decrease and AS would increase
(d) decrease and AS would decrease

19. All else equal, if the price of each input increases from $2 to $4, productivity would:
  (a) decrease from $4 to $2 and AS would decrease
  (b) decrease from $5 to $3 and AS would decrease
  (c) increase from $4 to $2 and AS would increase
  (d) remain unchanged and AS would decrease

20. In the AD-AS model, an increase in the price level will:
  (a) shift the AD curve
  (b) shift the AS curve
  (c) shift both AD and AS curves
  (d) shift neither AD nor AS curve

21. When the economy is in deep recession, an increase in AD will:
  (a) increase the price level without affecting real output much
  (b) increase real output without affecting the price level much
  (c) substantially increase input prices
  (d) lead to widespread shortages of labour and raw materials

22. Which of the following statements is true in the aggregate demand-aggregate supply model?
  (a) there is no multiplier effect in this model
  (b) the effective multiplier is lower the steeper the aggregate supply curve
  (c) the multiplier effect is strengthened by price level changes
  (d) none of the statements is true

23. A decrease in the price of imported productive resources will:
  (a) expand output and lower the price level
  (b) expand output and raise the price level
  (c) contract output and lower the price level
  (d) contract output and raise the price level

■ DISCUSSION QUESTIONS

1. Define the AD and AS curves.

2. How is the AD curve derived from the aggregate expenditure model?

3. Explain why (a) the interest-rate effect, (b) the wealth effect, and (c) the foreign-trade effect cause the AD curve to be downsloping.

4. What factors that affect investment spending would cause the AD curve to shift to the left? What factors affecting consumption spending would move the AD curve to the left?

5. Why does the AS curve slope upward in the short run? What happens to per-unit costs of production as we move along the curve?

6. Explain how a change in input prices affects the AS curve. Define productivity and explain the effect on AS of an improvement in productivity.

7. What is the long-run aggregate supply curve? Why is it vertical?

8. How is the equilibrium real domestic output determined? Why will domestic producers reduce or expand their production when they find themselves producing more or less than the equilibrium output?

9. How are real domestic output and the price level affected when AD increases, and how do these effects depend on the slope of the AS curve? How are real domestic output and the price level affected when the AS decreases?

10. What are the characteristics of long-run equilibrium? What roles do the adjustments in nominal wages and real wages play in restoring the economy to a long-run equilibrium?

11. What is a recessionary gap, and an inflationary gap? What economic conditions are present in the economy when each of these gaps exist? How is the size of each of these gaps measured? What changes in the economy would be needed to resolve an inflationary gap, or a recessionary gap?

■ ANSWERS

FILL-IN QUESTIONS

1. variable, fixed

2. price level, real GDP

3. demanded (purchased), levels; downward, wealth, interest-rate, foreign-trade

4. down, decrease; inverse, AD

5. (a) shift of; (b) movement along

6. consumer wealth, consumer expectations, consumer indebtedness, personal taxes

7. interest rates, profit expectations, business taxes, technology, degree of excess capacity

8. domestic income of other nations; exchange rates

9. AD, right, a larger; multiplier

10. produced, price; input

11. upward, increase

12. (a) domestic resource availability, prices of imported resources, market power; (b) productivity; (c) business taxes and subsidies, government regulation

13. (a) greater, smaller; (b) smaller, greater

14. nominal, real, profit, employment

15. short, recessionary; falling

PROBLEMS AND PROJECTS

1.   (b) three points: P = 150, GDP = 4, P = 100, GDP = 8, P = 50, GDP = 12

2.   (b) 100, 8; (d) inflationary, 1

3.   (b) 2; (c) 115, 8.5; (d) 0.5, 1, 0.5

4.   (a) 5, 6, 7, 8; (b) 2.5, 3, 3.5, 4; (c) 0.60, 0.50, 0.43, 0.38; (d) 1.20, 1.00, 0.86, 0.75; AS shifts leftward; (e) 0.40, 0.33, 0.29, 0.25; AS shifts rightward

5.   (a) S, D, I, D; (b) I, S, I, I; (c) D, S, D, D; (d) I, I, U, I (e) I, I, U, I; (f) D, S, D, D; (g) I, S, I, I

6.   (a) 2, 400; (b) AS = AD = AS_{LR}; (c) 12, 2, 6; (d) 3, 500; inflationary; (e) 12, 3, 4; below; (f) leftward, 4, 400; (g) 6; 24

TRUE-FALSE

1. T	**2.** T	**3.** F	**4.** T	**5.** F	**6.** F
7. F	**8.** F	**9.** F	**10.** F	**11.** T	**12.** F
13. T	**14.** F	**15.** F	**16.** T	**17.** F	**18.** F
19. T	**20.** T	**21.** F	**22.** T		

MULTIPLE-CHOICE

1. (a)	**2.** (c)	**3.** (d)	**4.** (d)	**5.** (d)	**6.** (b)
7. (c)	**8.** (b)	**9.** (d)	**10.** (c)	**11.** (b)	**12.** (c)
13. (b)	**14.** (b)	**15.** (b)	**16.** (a)	**17.** (a)	**18.** (c)
19. (d)	**20.** (d)	**21.** (b)	**22.** (b)	**23.** (a)	

CHAPTER 12

Fiscal Policy

Chapter 12 is concerned with fiscal policy, which is the federal government's use of its spending and taxation powers to help achieve full-employment GDP, price level stability, and a high rate of economic growth. The business cycle is one of the major problems for our economy, and since 1945 Canadian governments have used fiscal policy to avoid or smooth out macroeconomic fluctuations.

Fiscal policy can be discretionary or nondiscretionary. Discretionary fiscal policy occurs when Parliament decides to make deliberate changes in taxes and/or government spending with the goal of shifting the aggregate demand curve (AD). In a recession, expansionary fiscal policy is called for because AD is insufficient to produce an equilibrium at full-employment GDP. To expand AD, the appropriate policy is to: (1) increase government spending; (2) reduce taxes (so that households have more disposable income and will consume more); or (3) implement a combination of the two. An expansionary fiscal policy pushes the government's budget towards a deficit. An inflationary gap calls for a contractionary policy (which requires a cut in AD, and therefore opposite changes in government spending and taxation from an expansionary policy). A contractionary policy pushes the government's budget towards surplus. Whether the gap is recessionary or inflationary, the government could wait for full employment equilibrium to be restored through wage and price adjustments stemming from the supply side, but these automatic changes are bound to be slow and painful.

The effects of fiscal policy depend on the method of financing the policy. For example, an expansionary policy that causes a deficit financed by government borrowing will be less expansionary than a similar policy financed by creating new money. The debt-financed initiative causes government to compete with firms and households for available funds, therefore tending to raise interest rates and "crowd out" some consumption and investment spending in the private sector. In contrast, if the government creates new money, consumption and investment spending are not adversely affected, but the inflation rate might be! (This point will be more clear after Chapter 15 on monetary policy.)

Nondiscretionary fiscal policy does not require deliberate government action to change tax laws or government spending plans. Instead, nondiscretionary fiscal policy relies on built-in stabilizers which automatically increase government deficits during recessions and increase government surpluses during inflation. These changes occur automatically because most taxes vary directly with GDP, and many transfer payments are inversely related to GDP. The strength of built-in stabilizers is that they do not have to wait for Parliament's decisions. Unfortunately, nondiscretionary fiscal policy alone is not enough to eliminate all recessions and inflations that occur in Canada, so full-employment GDP and price stability cannot be restored quickly without discretionary fiscal policy.

How do we determine whether the government's stance on fiscal policy is contractionary or expansionary? We cannot tell simply from the government's actual budget. Built-in stabilizers cause the actual budget to fluctuate whenever GDP does, even when the government has made no decision to change fiscal policy. Such illusions created by the built-in stabilizers forced economists to develop the "cyclically adjusted budget" to measure the budget balance at a standardized point: the full-employment level of real GDP. This measure of the budget changes only if there are discretionary policy changes.

As well as the crowding-out effect, the use of fiscal policy faces several other complications. Time lags prevent the policy from working immediately when it is needed, and political constraints often make it impossible or unpalatable for the government to take the necessary policy actions. When the economy is in the upsloping section of the aggregate supply curve, some of the impact of expansionary fiscal policy will be dissipated in inflation instead of raising real GDP and employment. Canada's growing trade with foreign countries makes it more difficult to know what fiscal policy to use because unpredictable AD disturbances abroad can be transmitted to Canada, and because the net export effect weakens the impact of fiscal policy.

■ CHECKLIST

When you have studied this chapter, you should be able to:

□ Describe the history behind the Canadian government acquiring a mandate to use stabilization policies.

□ Distinguish between discretionary and nondiscretionary fiscal policy.

□ Explain expansionary fiscal policy and the effect of three main policy options on AD.

□ Explain contractionary fiscal policy and the effect of three main policy options on AD.

□ Identify the fiscal policy options appropriate for a recessionary gap, and for an inflationary gap.

□ Explain how the economy will adjust from a recessionary gap, and from an inflationary gap, if fiscal policy is not applied.

□ Explain the two options the government has for financing a deficit, the two options for dealing with a surplus, and the effects of each.

□ Summarize the different views on fiscal policy held by "liberal" economists and "conservative" economists.

□ Explain how built-in stabilizers work.

□ Describe how a more progressive tax system creates a greater degree of built-in stability for the economy.

□ Define the actual budget and the cyclically adjusted budget, and explain which one indicates the government's fiscal policy stance.

□ Given the necessary data, calculate the cyclically adjusted (structural) deficit and the cyclical deficit.

□ Summarize Canada's recent history on actual and cyclically adjusted deficits.

□ Outline three types of time lags and four types of political problems encountered in applying fiscal policy.

□ Describe the crowding-out effect and how it may weaken the intended stimulus of an expansionary fiscal policy.

□ Illustrate how an upsloping aggregate supply curve can weaken the intended stimulus of an expansionary fiscal policy.

□ Explain how shocks originating from abroad can render domestic fiscal policies inappropriate.

□ Describe the net export effect and how it may weaken the intended stimulus of an expansionary fiscal policy.

■ CHAPTER OUTLINE

1. Since World War II, when unemployment insurance was introduced, the Canadian government has held a legislative mandate to use stabilization policy to counter the unemployment and inflation consequences of the different phases of the business cycle.

2. Fiscal policy can be either discretionary or nondiscretionary. Discretionary fiscal policy is the deliberate manipulation of taxes and government spending to offset cyclical fluctuations. Its goals are: full employment, price stability, and steady growth.

(a) Two assumptions simplify our analysis of the effects of fiscal policy: that government purchases do not affect private spending, and that fiscal policy does not shift the aggregate supply curve.

(b) Government purchases of goods and services increase the AD curve and increase equilibrium real GDP and employment.

(c) Taxes decrease disposable income, and therefore decrease consumption and the AD curve.

3. The elimination of an inflationary (recessionary) gap is accomplished by contractionary (expansionary) fiscal policy, which is composed of an increase (decrease) in taxes, a decrease (increase) in government purchases, or a combination of both. Contractionary (expansionary) fiscal policy moves the government's budget towards a surplus (deficit). If a discretionary policy is not adopted, the market forces will eventually shift the AS curve enough to restore full employment, but that could take too long.

4. The effects of an expansionary fiscal policy that causes a deficit depend on how the deficit is financed.

(a)   Government may finance a deficit by borrowing, or by issuing new money.

(b)   New money creation has the larger impact on AD, but may become inflationary.

(c)   Borrowing may lead to the crowding-out effect (discussed below) which offsets some of the expansionary effect of the fiscal stimulus.

5. The effects of a contractionary fiscal policy that creates a surplus depend on how the surplus is disposed of.

(a)   Government may spend the surplus retiring debt, or may impound the surplus (and thereby withdraw purchasing power from the economy).

(b)   Impounding the surplus has a more powerful contractionary effect, because when debt is retired there is a return of purchasing power to the economy which will provoke some increase in private spending.

6. Whether government spending or taxes should be altered to reduce recession and inflation depends to a large extent upon whether an expansion or a contraction of the public sector is desired.

(a)   In a recession, "liberal" economists would favour an increase in government spending (tending to make the public sector grow); in an inflationary period, they would prefer a tax increase (tending again to make the public sector grow).

(b)   In a recession, "conservative" economists would favour a cut in taxes (making the public sector shrink); in an inflationary period, they would favour a cut in government spending (tending again to shrink the public sector).

7. Nondiscretionary fiscal policy is in place at all times because of built-in stabilizers inherent in our tax system (and our transfer payments and subsidies).

(a)   Net tax revenues (tax receipts minus government transfers and subsidies) increase as the GDP rises and decrease as the GDP falls.

(b)   This net tax system serves as a built-in stabilizer of the economy because it reduces purchasing power when there is an inflationary gap and expands purchasing power when there is a recessionary gap.

(c)   As GDP increases, the average tax rates will increase in progressive systems, remain constant in proportional systems, and decrease in

regressive tax systems, so there is more built-in stability with a more progressive tax system.

(d)   Built-in stabilizers can reduce, but cannot fully eliminate, economic fluctuations.

8. Built-in stabilizers cause the actual budget deficit or surplus to automatically fluctuate as GDP fluctuates. Therefore, movements in the actual budget do not reflect changes in fiscal policy.

(a)   The cyclically adjusted budget is a better fiscal policy indicator than the actual budget because it measures what the federal budget deficit or surplus would be if the economy were to be at full employment.

(b)   If the cyclically adjusted budget deficit (also called the structural deficit) increases, then the stance of fiscal policy has become more expansionary.

9. Canada's consistently large cyclically adjusted deficits that began in the mid-1970s caused the federal government to all but abandon the use of fiscal policy for macroeconomic stabilization. The priority throughout most of the 1990s was on reducing deficits. This situation is common to most major industrial nations. In 1997-98 Canada had a federal budget surplus for the first time since the 1970s.

10. Certain problems and complications arise in the use of fiscal policy.

(a)   Problems of timing create three lags: a recognition lag, an administrative lag, and an operational lag.

(b)   Political problems arise because: the economy has goals other than economic stability; provincial and municipal government policies don't coordinate easily with federal policies; governments' desires for popularity may create an expansionary bias in fiscal policy; and there may be a political business cycle (if taxes fall and spending rises just before an election).

(c)   An expansionary fiscal policy may raise the interest rate and crowd out private spending, weakening the effect of the fiscal policy stimulus on real GDP. The increased demand from the government is offset by decreased demand from the private sector. But this crowding-out effect may be small, especially when there is a large recessionary gap.

(d)   The effect of an expansionary fiscal policy on real GDP will also be weakened when it results in a rise in the price level (inflation). The steeper the AS curve the greater is this concern.

(e)   Canada's connection to the world economy means that we could be surprised by demand shocks from abroad that affect our exports in a way that renders our domestic fiscal policy inappropriate.

(f)   When an expansionary fiscal policy raises our interest rates, the Canadian dollar will appreciate against other currencies, causing a drop in the demand for our net exports, and cancelling some of the fiscal stimulus. This net export effect is very similar to the crowding-out effect.

11. One tool available to help policy-makers forecast fluctuations in real GDP is a set of "leading indicators." These are variables that have historically changed prior to GDP fluctuations, so provide some advance warning.

■   TERMS AND CONCEPTS

actual budgets	**net export effect**
budget deficit	**political business**
budget surplus	**cycle**
built-in stabilizers	**progressive,**
crowding-out effect	**proportional, and**
cyclical deficit	**regressive tax**
cyclically adjusted	**systems**
budget	**structural deficit**
discretionary fiscal	
policy	
expansionary and	
contractionary fiscal	
policy	

■   HINTS AND TIPS

1.   Discretionary fiscal policy occurs when government deliberately chooses to change taxes or spending. Nondiscretionary fiscal policy occurs when automatic stabilizers are at work. Using the analogy of your car, discretionary fiscal policy operates like brakes: you must deliberately decide to apply them or they cannot reduce your speed. Nondiscretionary fiscal policy operates like shock absorbers: they work automatically when you go over a bump, whether or not you noticed the bump, and without you deciding how to respond to it.

2.   The most difficult concept in this chapter is the cyclically adjusted deficit. This measure was designed because the government budget can fluctuate either because government makes deliberate policy changes or because of GDP fluctuations that

lead automatically to fluctuations in net tax revenues. The cyclically adjusted deficit is calculated at a constant real GDP (the full employment level). If this number changes we are certain that the government has changed its fiscal policy.

3.   If you have studied Chapter 10 you should recognize that multiplier effects are at work when the government changes its fiscal policy by raising or lowering its expenditures on goods and services, or its tax collections.

■   FILL-IN QUESTIONS

1. In order to increase real GDP during a recession, taxes should be (increased, decreased) _____ and government spending should be _____. If such a fiscal policy is not employed, the (AD, AS) _____ curve will (soon, eventually) _____ shift to the right to close the gap.

2. If fiscal policy is to help offset business cycles, it will probably be necessary for the government to incur a budget (surplus, deficit) _____ during a recession and a budget _____ during inflation.

3. A contractionary fiscal policy is composed of (1) decreased _____, or (2) increased _____, or (3) a combination of both.

4. When the Parliament votes to increase tax revenues by raising income tax rates, this is an example of (discretionary, nondiscretionary) _____ fiscal policy, whereas when income tax revenues increase because the GDP rises, this is an example of _____ fiscal policy.

5. Government can finance a deficit either by _____ from the public, or by issuing new _____ to its creditors.

6. Government can use a budget surplus to _____ existing debt, or it can _____ the surplus funds.

7. A leading indicator is an economic variable that has traditionally reached its peak or trough (after, before) _____ the corresponding turns in the business cycle.

8. Those who favour growth in the public sector would, during a period of inflation, advocate a(n) (increase, decrease) _____ in government (spending, taxes) _____; and those who wish to contract the public sector during a recession would advocate a(n) _____ in _____.

9. Net taxes equal _____ minus _____ and _____.

10. When net tax revenues are directly related to the GDP the economy has some _____ stability because:
(a) when the GDP rises, tax revenues (increase, decrease) _____, helping to curb spending.
(b) when the GDP falls, tax revenues _____, helping to cushion the drop in spending.

11. As GDP increases, the average tax rate will increase in (progressive, proportional, regressive) _____ systems, remain constant in _____ systems, and decrease in _____ systems. Economies with more progressivity of taxes have (more, less) _____ built-in stability.

12. The cyclically adjusted budget balance:
(a) indicates what the federal _____ would have been if the economy had operated at _____ during the year; and (b) tells us whether the fiscal policy was _____ or _____.

13. A timing problem in the use of discretionary fiscal policy stems from the _____, _____, and _____ lags.

14. Political problems arise in the use of discretionary fiscal policy to stabilize the economy because government also has _____ goals; because voters have a bias in favour of budget (surpluses, deficits) _____; and because politicians use fiscal policies in a way that creates a _____ business cycle.

15. When the federal government employs an expansionary fiscal policy, it usually has a budget (surplus, deficit) _____ and normally (lends, borrows) _____ funds in the money market.
(a) This will (raise, lower) _____ interest rates in the economy and (contract, expand) _____ investment spending.
(b) This change in investment spending is the _____ effect of the expansionary fiscal policy, and it tends to (weaken, strengthen) _____ the impact of the expansionary fiscal policy on real GDP and employment.

16. In an economy with an upsloping AS curve, an expansionary fiscal policy will raise the real GDP and (raise, lower) _____ the price level. This change in the price level will (weaken, strengthen) _____ the impact of the expansionary fiscal policy on output and employment.

17. Fiscal policy is subject to further complications from mutual _____ with the world economy. The economy can be influenced by _____ shocks that might reinforce or offset fiscal policy actions.

18. A contractionary fiscal policy will tend to (raise, lower) _____ the interest rate. In an open economy this will create capital (inflows, outflows) _____ that will lead to (appreciation, depreciation) _____ of the domestic currency. This currency value change will cause net exports to (increase, decrease) _____, which will (reinforce, offset) _____ part of the intended contraction in AD. This phenomenon is known as the _____ effect.

■ **PROBLEMS AND PROJECTS**

1. In the table that follows, columns A, B and C show levels of taxes corresponding to different income levels, under three tax systems.

Income	A:_____	B:_____	C:_____
1000	200	200	100
2000	375	400	300
3000	525	600	600
4000	625	800	1000

(a) Indicate in the blanks whether each system is progressive, regressive, or proportional.
(b) In which system is there the greatest degree of built-in stability? _____ The least? _____

2. The next table shows a nation's fiscal situation in each of five different years. The budget amounts shown are measured in billions of $.

Year	1	2	3	4	5
Actual budget (surplus +, deficit -)	-10	+10	-20	-120	-150
Cyclically adjusted budget (surplus +, deficit -)	+10	-20	0	-120	-130
Direction of fiscal policy	___	___	___	___	___

(a)   For each year, determine whether the fiscal policy stance of the government was expansionary (E), contractionary (C), or neutral (N).

(b)   The best gauge of the direction of fiscal policy is the (actual, full-employment) _____ budget deficit or surplus because it removes the (cyclical, structural) _____ component from the discussion of the budget situation.

(c)   In which years was there a cyclical deficit, and what was the size of the cyclical deficit in each of those years?_____

3. The nation whose situation is illustrated in the following graph would reach full employment at GDP_f.

(a)   The full-employment deficit is $_____.

(b)   At which of the GDP levels labelled on the graph would this nation have a recessionary gap? _____

(c)   In this recessionary gap situation, the actual budget deficit is $_____, of which $_____ is the cyclical deficit, and $_____ is the full-employment deficit.

(d)   At which of the GDP levels labelled on the graph would this nation have an inflationary gap?

_____

(e)   In this inflationary gap situation, the actual budget deficit is $_____, of which $_____ is the cyclical deficit, and $_____ is the full-employment deficit.

(f)   If the GDP in this economy fell from GDP_1 to GDP_2, the (structural, actual) _____ deficit would increase, which might make it seem as though fiscal policy has become more expansionary. In fact, because the (structural, actual) _____ deficit has remained unchanged, there would have been no discretionary policy change.

(g)   Given that the tax curve has a constant slope, the taxation system in this nation is (progressive, proportional, regressive) _____.

(h)   If the G curve shifts upwards, there has been a decision to make fiscal policy more (expansionary, contractionary) _____, and the full-employment deficit will (decrease, increase) _____.

(i)   If the T curve shifts upwards, there has been a decision to make fiscal policy more (expansionary, contractionary) _____, and the full-employment deficit will (decrease, increase) _____.

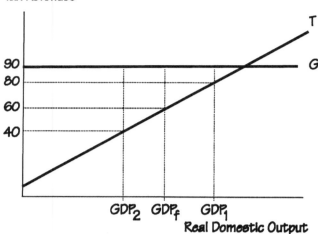

Government Expenditures, Tax Revenues

Real Domestic Output

4. This question is based on the analysis of Chapters 9 and 10, and shows that an economy with a proportional tax system is more stable than an economy without taxes that vary with income. Assume the economy is closed. Initially assume no taxes or government spending. The consumption schedule is given by the equation: $C = 80 + 0.8$ GDP, and planned investment is constant at $I = 40$.

(a)   Fill in the C and AE columns in the table below.

(b)   The equilibrium GDP is _____.

GDP	C	I	I'	C+I = AE	C+I' = AE'
500	___	40	30	_____	_____
550	___	40	30	_____	_____
600	___	40	30	_____	_____
650	___	40	30	_____	_____
700	___	40	30	_____	_____

(c)   Column I' shows a drop of 10 in investment spending. Fill in column AE' accordingly.

(d)   After the drop in investment, the new equilibrium GDP is _____.

(e)   The multiplier in this model is = change in GDP / initial change in spending = _____/_____ = _____.

Now we introduce a public sector. Taxes (T) are 10% of GDP. The consumption function is as before, except the relevant income measure is disposable (after-tax) income (DI): $C = 80 + 0.80\ DI$. Government purchases are constant at 48. Again, investment is initially 40.

GDP	T	DI	C	I	G	C+I+G = AE
500	___	___	___	40	48	___
550	___	___	___	40	48	___
600	___	___	___	40	48	___
650	___	___	___	40	48	___
700	___	___	___	40	48	___

(f)   Fill in the table above.

(g)   The equilibrium income is _____.

(h)   Suppose that planned investment drops by 14. Fill in the table below.

GDP	T	DI	C	I'	G	C+I+G = AE'
500	___	___	___	26	48	___
550	___	___	___	26	48	___
600	___	___	___	26	48	___
650	___	___	___	26	48	___
700	___	___	___	26	48	___

(i)   After investment falls, equilibrium GDP becomes _____.

(j)   The multiplier in this model is = change in GDP / initial change in spending = _____/_____ = _____.

(k)   Because the multiplier is (larger, smaller) _____ in the economy with taxes that depend on income, this economy is (less, more) _____ stable in the face of shifts in expenditures.

5. The equation representing the economy's taxes (net of transfers) is $T = 20 + 0.25$ GDP. The level of government purchases is constant: $G = 100$. Full employment real GDP is 300.

(a)   What would GDP have to be for the government's budget to be in balance?

(b)   What is the structural deficit?

(c)   If GDP increases from 270 to 290, what happens to the actual deficit?

(d)   If GDP increases from 270 to 290, what happens to the cyclically adjusted deficit?

■   **TRUE-FALSE**

Circle T if the statement is true, F if it is false.

1. A major goal of fiscal policy is to stabilize economic activity at some desired level of employment.   **T** F

2. Fiscal policy is carried out by manipulating government spending, taxation, and the money supply.   **T F**

3. A decrease in taxes will cause an upward shift in the consumption schedule and an increase in equilibrium GDP.   **T** F

4. Fiscal policy is contractionary whenever it results in an actual deficit on the government's budget.   **T F**

5. Fiscal policy should move toward a surplus in the government's budget during the recession phase of the business cycle.   **T F**

6. Built-in stabilizers are not sufficiently strong to prevent recession or inflation, but they can reduce the severity of a recession or of inflation.   **T** F

7. Built-in stabilizers operate automatically to increase the government's deficit during inflation and increase its surplus during recessions.   **T F**

8. A look at the historical record of budgetary deficits and surpluses provides an accurate picture of the government's fiscal stance.   **T F**

9. The cyclically adjusted budget balance compares government spending to the tax revenue that would be forthcoming at full employment.   **T** F

10. Recognition, administrative, and operational time lags in fiscal policy make the policies more effective in reducing the rate of inflation and decreasing unemployment in the economy.   **T F**

11. Macroeconomic stabilization is the sole goal of the federal government's spending and taxing policies.   **T F**

12. Economists who see evidence of a political business cycle argue that the government tends to increase taxes and reduce expenditures before elections and to reduce taxes and increase expenditures after elections.   **T F**

13. If financing a deficit results in increased interest rates, investment spending will be reduced and the stimulative effect of the deficit on aggregate expenditure reduced.   **T F**

adjusted budget

14. The structural deficit and the cyclical deficit are one and the same.　　　　　　　　　　**T　(F)**

15. If the extra revenues from a budget surplus are impounded, rather than used to retire debt, the surplus will be more contractionary.　　　　**(T) F**

16. When a given increase in government spending is applied, the ultimate effect on real GDP is less if the AS curve is steeper.　　　　　　**(T) F**

17. The greater the percentage of demand for Canadian goods that comes from foreign countries, the more vulnerable Canada is to AD fluctuations that arise from events abroad.　　　　　　**(T) F**

■　**MULTIPLE-CHOICE**

Circle the letter that corresponds to the best answer.

1. Fiscal policy influences the level of economic activity by manipulating:
　(a)　the interest rate
　(b)　the money supply
　(c)　the foreign exchange rate
　(d)　the level of government spending and taxes

2. Contractionary fiscal policy is composed of:
　(a)　a reduction in government expenditure and the money supply or some combination of both
　(b)　an increase in government expenditure and taxes or some combination of both
　(c)　a reduction in government expenditure and increase in taxes or some combination of both
　(d)　a reduction in taxes and the money supply or some combination of both

3. In the aggregate expenditure model, taxes:
　(a)　are paid out of savings and have no effect on equilibrium output
　(b)　reduce consumption at each level of GDP by an amount equal to the amount of the tax
　(c)　reduce both consumption and saving at each level of GDP
　(d)　are an injection into the spending flow

4. During which Prime Minister's term was unemployment insurance introduced in Canada?
　(a)　Louis St. Laurent
　(b)　Mackenzie King

　(c)　Pierre Trudeau
　(d)　John Diefenbaker

5. If the government wishes to increase the level of real GDP, it might:
　(a)　reduce taxes
　(b)　reduce its purchases of goods and services
　(c)　reduce transfer payments
　(d)　reduce the size of the budget deficit

6. If the economy is to have built-in stability, when real GDP falls:
　(a)　tax receipts and government transfer payments should fall
　(b)　tax receipts and government transfer payments should rise
　(c)　tax receipts should fall and government transfer payments should rise
　(d)　tax receipts should rise and government transfer payments should fall

7. A direct relation between net taxes and real GDP:
　(a)　automatically produces budget surpluses during a recession
　(b)　makes it easier for discretionary fiscal policy to move the economy out of a recession and toward full employment
　(c)　makes it easier to maintain full employment in a growing economy
　(d)　reduces the effect of a change in planned investment spending upon the national output and employment

8. Why is Canada's employment insurance system considered a type of automatic stabilizer?
　(a)　approximately the same amount of employment insurance benefits are paid out each year
　(b)　the employment insurance system has the effect of stabilizing the unemployment rate
　(c)　employment insurance benefits paid out increase every year
　(d)　employment insurance benefits paid out increase when the economy is in recession

9. Which of the following is not an automatic stabilizer in the Canadian economy?
　(a)　GST
　(b)　CPP deductions
　(c)　income taxes
　(d)　all of these are automatic stabilizers

10. The crowding-out effect of an expansionary (deficit) fiscal policy is the result of government borrowing in the money market, which: *b*
  (a) increases interest rates and net investment spending
  (b) increases interest rates and decreases net investment spending
  (c) decreases interest rates and increases net investment spending
  (d) decreases interest rates and net investment spending

11. An expansionary fiscal policy will be most powerful if: *b*
  (a) the resulting deficit is financed by borrowing
  (b) the resulting deficit is financed by creating new money
  (c) the resulting surplus is impounded
  (d) the resulting surplus is used to retire existing debt

12. Which of the following is not an example of a discretionary fiscal policy action? *b*
  (a) a new plan to spend $100 million on childbirth centres
  (b) an increase in expenditures on employment insurance benefits because of rising unemployment
  (c) a 10% cut in the rate of income tax
  (d) a change in the maximum number of weeks of benefits available under employment insurance

Answer questions 13 through 16 on the basis of the following diagram:

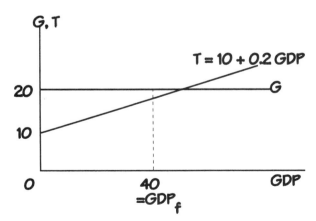

13. If GDP_f signifies full-employment real GDP, then the cyclically adjusted deficit is:
  (a) 0
  (b) 2

b

  (c) 4
  (d) 6

14. If actual GDP is at 35, then the actual budget deficit or surplus will be:
  (a) a surplus of 1
  (b) a deficit of 1
  (c) a deficit of 3 *c*
  (d) a deficit of 5

15. If the government employs an expansionary fiscal policy by increasing government purchases by 2, and this moves equilibrium real GDP from 35 to 39, then:
  (a) the cyclically adjusted deficit rises by 2, and the actual deficit rises by 1.2 *a*
  (b) the cyclically adjusted deficit rises by 1.2, and the actual deficit drops by 0.8
  (c) the cyclically adjusted deficit falls by 2, and the actual deficit rises by 1.2
  (d) the cyclically adjusted deficit does not change, and the actual deficit rises by 1.2

16. If the slope of the line T was steeper, there would be:
  (a) more built-in stability for the economy *a*
  (b) less built-in stability for the economy
  (c) no change in the built-in stability in the economy
  (d) a need for more emphasis on discretionary fiscal policy

Questions 17 through 19 pertain to the next graph.

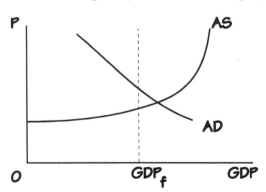

17. Given the current position of AD and AS, what is the situation in this economy? *a*
  (a) there is an inflationary gap and fiscal policy should be contractionary
  (b) there is an inflationary gap and fiscal policy should be expansionary

(c) there is a recessionary gap and fiscal policy should be contractionary

(d) there is a recessionary gap and fiscal policy should be expansionary

18. In the neighbourhood of the current equilibrium, an expansionary fiscal policy will lead to changes in:

(a) the price level, but not output

(b) output, but not the price level

(c) both output and the price level

(d) neither output nor the price level

c

19. If the government does not take any fiscal policy action, how will the economy shown in the graph adjust?

(a) wages and input prices will eventually rise enough to shift the AS upward until it intersects AD at GDP$_f$

(b) wages and input prices will eventually fall enough to shift the AS upward until it intersects AD at GDP$_f$

(c) expenditures will eventually fall enough that AD will shift left until it intersects AS at GDP$_f$

(d) none of the above

a

20. The length of time it takes for the fiscal action taken by the federal government to affect output, employment, or the price level is referred to as the:

(a) administrative lag

(b) operational lag

(c) recognition lag

(d) fiscal lag

b

21. The length of time it takes for government to decide what policy to adopt to address a recessionary or inflationary gap is referred to as the:

(a) administrative lag

(b) operational lag

(c) recognition lag

(d) fiscal lag

a

22. If there is an inflationary gap, those who favour smaller government would advocate that fiscal policy take the form of:

(a) increased taxes and government spending

(b) decreased taxes and government spending

(c) decreased government spending

(d) increased taxes

c

23. Suppose that the economies of Canada's trading partners improved substantially and at the same time Canada had adopted an expansionary fiscal policy. What would most likely happen in Canada?

a

(a) there would be a rise in net exports, a rise in aggregate demand, and the potential for inflation

(b) there would be a fall in interest rates, a rise in aggregate demand, and the potential for a recession

(c) there would be a rise in the incomes of trading partners, less demand for Canadian goods, and the potential for a recession

(d) there would be a rise in the employment in other nations, a fall in net exports, and the potential for inflation

24. The effect of an expansionary (deficit) fiscal policy on the real GDP of an economy with an upward sloping aggregate supply curve is lessened by:

(a) increases in aggregate supply

(b) the crowding-out effect

(c) increases in the price level

(d) both (b) and (c)

d

25. A change in the government's fiscal policy stance is best measured by changes in:

(a) equilibrium real GDP

(b) the actual deficit or surplus

(c) the cyclical deficit or surplus

(d) the cyclically adjusted deficit or surplus

d

26. If expansionary fiscal policy is adopted in an open economy, the resulting increase in interest rates will tend to raise demand for the nation's currency, causing currency appreciation and reduction in the demand for the nation's exports. This is termed the:

(a) net export effect

(b) crowding-out effect

(c) exchange rate effect

(d) interest rate effect

a

■ **DISCUSSION QUESTIONS**

1. What is meant by fiscal policy? When would expansionary (contractionary) fiscal policy be used?

2. What options are open to the government when it applies expansionary (contractionary) fiscal policy?

3. What are the effects of different policy options on the federal budget? What are the implications of how the government finances additional deficits, or disposes of additional surpluses?

4. Explain, for both a recession and an inflation, what kind of fiscal policy would be advocated (a) by those who wish to expand the public sector and (b) by those who wish to contract the public sector.

5. What is the difference between discretionary and nondiscretionary fiscal policy? How do the built-in stabilizers work to reduce fluctuations in the level of nominal GDP?

6. Explain why a tax system in which net tax receipts vary directly with the level of nominal GDP makes it difficult to achieve and sustain full employment.

7. Define progressive, proportional, and regressive tax systems. Explain which system leads to the most built-in stability for the economy.

8. How is the cyclically adjusted budget defined? For what purpose did economists define this measure? Under what circumstances will the cyclically adjusted deficit change, and under what circumstances will the actual deficit change?

9. Explain the three kinds of time lags that make it difficult to use fiscal policy to stabilize the economy.

10. What are four political problems that complicate the use of fiscal policy to stabilize the economy?

11. Explain how the following reduce the effectiveness of fiscal policy: (a) crowding-out effect, (b) inflation, and (c) net export effect.

12. Why does Canada's close trading relationship with the United States complicate the job of fiscal policy-makers in Canada?

■ **ANSWERS**

FILL-IN QUESTIONS

1. decreased, increased; AS, eventually

2. deficit, surplus

3. (1) government spending, (2) taxes

4. discretionary, nondiscretionary

5. borrowing, money

6. retire, impound

7. before

8. increase, taxes; decrease, taxes

9. taxes, transfers, subsidies

10. built-in; (a) increase; (b) decrease

11. progressive, proportional, regressive; more

12. (a) budget surplus or deficit, full employment GDP; (b) expansionary, contractionary

13. recognition, administrative, operational

14. other, deficits, political

15. deficit, borrows; (a) raise, contract; (b) crowding-out, weaken

16. raise; weaken

17. interdependency; AD

18. lower; outflows, depreciation; increase, offset; net export

PROBLEMS AND PROJECTS

1. (a) A regressive; B proportional; C progressive; (b) C; A

2. (a) C, E, N, E, E (b) full-employment, cyclical (c) Yr 1: $20 billion, Yr 3: $20 billion, Yr 5: $20 billion

3. (a) 30; (b) GDP_2; (c) 50, 20, 30; (d) GDP_1; (e) 10, -20, 30; (f) actual; structural; (g) proportional; (h) expansionary, increase; (i) contractionary, decrease

4. (a) C: 480, 520, 560, 600, 640; AE: 520, 560, 600, 640, 680; (b) 600; (c) AE': 510, 550, 590, 630, 670: (d) 550; (e) -50, -10, 5; (f) T: 50, 55, 60, 65, 70; DI: 450, 495, 540, 585, 630; C: 440, 476, 512, 548, 584; AE: 528, 564, 600, 636, 672; (g) 600; (h) T: 50, 55, 60, 65, 70; DI: 450, 495, 540, 585, 630; C: 440, 476, 512, 548, 584; AE': 514, 550, 586, 622, 658; (i) 550; (j) -50, -14, 3.57; (k) smaller; more

5. (a) 320; (b) 5; (c) decreases by 5; (d) no change if there is no policy change

TRUE-FALSE

1. T	2. F	3. T	4. F	5. F	6. T
7. F	8. F	9. T	10. F	11. F	12. F
13. T	14. F	15. T	16. T	17. T	

MULTIPLE-CHOICE

1. (d)   **2.** (c)   **3.** (c)   **4.** (b)   **5.** (a)   **6.** (c)
7. (d)   **8.** (d)   **9.** (d)   **10.** (b)   **11.** (b)   **12.** (b)
13. (b)   **14.** (c)   **15.** (a)   **16.** (a)   **17.** (a)   **18.** (c)
19. (a)   **20.** (b)   **21.** (a)   **22.** (c)   **23.** (a)   **24.** (d)
25. (d)   **26.** (a)

CHAPTER 13

Money and Banking

Chapter 13 explains the nature and functions of money and identifies the basic institutions in Canada's banking system. This information will prepare you for Chapter 14, which explains how banks can change the money supply, and Chapter 15, which explains how the Bank of Canada uses monetary policy to promote macroeconomic stability.

Anything that performs the functions of money is considered to be money. The most important function of money is to serve as a medium of exchange. Money also serves as a unit of account and a store of value. In Canada, the assets that clearly meet these criteria are currency (coins and paper money) outside chartered banks, and demand deposits (funds held in chequing accounts at chartered banks). These assets make up the money supply measure known as M1. Certain assets excluded from M1 are called near-monies (e.g., savings deposits, or deposits in credit unions and trust companies). Some economists prefer to work with broader measures of the money supply that include M1 plus some or all of these near-monies (e.g., M2, M2+). Although our emphasis will be on M1, any particular definition of money is somewhat arbitrary, and for some purposes it is useful to refer to more than one measure.

What "backs" the money supply? Currency is the debt of the Bank of Canada, and deposits are the debts of chartered banks. Ultimately, the Bank of Canada has nothing with which to redeem the paper money that it is responsible for. When depositors write cheques, chartered banks are obligated to surrender currency to honour the cheques. But currency is not backed by anything tangible! So why does money have value? First, by social convention, money is acceptable in exchange for goods and services (so these goods and services back the money, in a sense). Second, government buttresses the acceptability of money by declaring currency to be legal tender. Third, the value of money depends on its relative scarcity. Many historical cases have shown that when money suddenly becomes much more plentiful, prices rise and money loses its value. In cases of hyperinflation, people may cease to accept currency as a medium of exchange and revert to transacting business by barter, or substitute a more stable foreign currency.

The final section of the chapter outlines the Canadian banking system. Chartered banks are business firms that seek to maximize profits for their shareholders, mainly by lending at interest rates higher than the rates they pay to depositors. They try to create as many interest-earning loans of their deposits as possible, while still retaining enough currency to meet the needs of depositors who wish to withdraw funds from their accounts. From a macroeconomic perspective, the most important aspect of banks' activities is their ability to create money by creating new loans and deposits. This is studied in depth in Chapter 14.

Other financial intermediaries such as trust companies, loan companies, credit unions, and *caisses populaires* also hold deposits and compete with chartered banks. Like banks, these institutions have access to the cheque clearing system of the Canadian Payments Association. Canadian financial institutions are under pressure to restructure in order to become more competitive in Canada and in world markets. In 1998 the government ultimately rejected two controversial merger proposals between four of Canada's largest banks, but we likely have not seen the end of the issue.

■ CHECKLIST

When you have studied this chapter, you should be able to:

☐ List and explain the three functions of money.

☐ Define the money supply, M1.

☐ Explain the meaning of near-money, identify some principal near-monies, and define M2 and M2+.

☐ Present three reasons why near-monies are important.

☐ Explain why Canadian money is debt, and reveal whose debts paper money and deposits are.

☐ Explain why credit cards are not money.

☐ Explain why currency and demand deposit money have value even though they have no intrinsic value and are not backed by anything tangible.

☐ Indicate the precise relationship between the value of money and the price level.

☐ Explain why hyperinflation affects the acceptability of money.

☐ Explain what actions are entailed if the government wishes to stabilize the value of money.

☐ Describe the structure of the Canadian banking system.

☐ Outline how banks operate to maximize their profits.

☐ Give examples of nonbank financial intermediaries.

☐ Identify the role played by the Canadian Payments Association.

☐ Explain why beer came to be a medium of exchange in Angola.

☐ Give reasons for and against the proposed mergers of leading Canadian banks.

■ CHAPTER OUTLINE

1. Money is whatever performs the three basic functions of money: a medium of exchange, a standard of value, and a store of value. Historically, many different items have been used in different societies.

2. In Canada, currency (coins and paper money) outside the chartered banks, and demand deposits (chequing account funds in chartered banks) are accepted media of exchange and constitute M1, which is the narrowest measure of the money supply.

(a)   Coins are token money because their intrinsic value is below their face value.

(b)   Paper currency is in the form of Bank of Canada notes.

(c)   Demand deposits, which are bank-created money, account for over 60% of M1.

(Currency and deposits owned by the federal government and the banks are not included in the money supply.)

3. Other highly liquid financial assets (such as savings account funds) are so easily converted into media of exchange that they are called near-monies, and are included in broader measures of the money supply.

(a)   M2 adds personal savings deposits and business notice deposits to M1.

(b)   M2+ adds deposits at nonbank depository institutions to M2.

4. The amount of these near-monies held by the public is important for at least three reasons:

(a)   Household spending depends on balances of near-monies as well as on M1 holdings;

(b)   Substitution of near-monies for money (and vice versa) can threaten the stability of the money supply;

(c)   Monetary authorities must decide which is the appropriate monetary total to attempt to control with their policies.

5. Credit cards are not money, but rather a device for getting short-term loans. The credit card user must eventually pay money to the bank issuing the credit card. However, use of credit cards allows people to carry less money, and to hold less money in their accounts.

6. What "backs" the money supply in Canada?

(a)   In Canada, money is debt owed by chartered banks or the Bank of Canada.

(b)   Currency has no significant intrinsic value, and cannot be redeemed for anything of tangible value.

(c)   Money has value only because people can exchange it for desirable goods and services. This occurs because of:

(1) a general social consensus to accept money as payment;

(2) the government's declaration that currency is legal tender (which makes currency fiat money);

(3) the relative scarcity of money.

7. The value of money is determined by its purchasing power in terms of real goods and services.

    (a)   The value of a dollar is inversely related to the price level.

    (b)   In a hyperinflation money can lose value so quickly that people become unwilling to hold money or to accept it as a medium of exchange. Then society reverts to barter or switches to a more stable money such as some foreign currency.

    (c)   Money is "backed" by the public's confidence that the value of money will remain stable. (The federal government can use monetary and fiscal policy to stabilize the value of money.)

8. In Canada, chartered banks are privately-owned firms with Parliamentary-granted charters to operate as banks.

    (a)   There are numerous banks in Canada, but about 90% of deposits are held by the largest five chartered banks.

    (b)   All of the largest banks in Canada are Canadian-owned. Many foreign banks operate here, but their market shares will always remain small because the Bank Act places legal restrictions on their growth.

    (c)   The banks perform the two essential functions of holding deposits and making loans. They strive to make profits for shareholders by making as many loans as they prudently can, and by charging higher interest rates on loans than they pay on deposits.

9. In addition to chartered banks, financial intermediaries include trust companies, loan companies, credit unions, *caisses populaires*, and insurance companies.

    (a)   All of these institutions act as intermediaries by accepting deposits from savers and lending to investors.

    (b)   Deposits at the nonbank institutions are included in broader money supply measures, but not in M1.

    (c)   The Canadian Payments Association provides a cheque clearing system between the chartered banks and other deposit-taking institutions.

10. Greater integration of world financial markets is being facilitated by rapid technological progress. Technological innovation has also created electronic money (e-cash) that can be accessed by "smart cards."

■ TERMS AND CONCEPTS

Bank of Canada notes	**M1, M2, and M2+**
Canadian Payments	**medium of exchange**
Association	**near-monies**
chartered banks	**nonchequable savings**
credit unions	**accounts**
demand deposits	**prime rate**
e-cash	**smart cards**
fiat money	**store of value**
financial intermediaries	**term deposits**
intrinsic value	**token money**
legal tender	**unit of account**

■ HINTS AND TIPS

1. Money is not defined by its physical attributes; nor does something become money solely because the government declares that it is. The public must accept it as a medium of exchange.

2. Rapid inflation causes money to become a poor store of value (because the value of monetary assets erodes), and a poor unit of account (because the prices of goods and services are constantly changing). These problems can be so severe as to cause people to look for alternative forms of money, or even to resort to barter. In either case, the original money loses its status as the unquestioned medium of exchange.

■ FILL-IN QUESTIONS

1. Three functions of money are

    (a) _____

    (b) _____

    (c) _____

2. The supply of money, M1, in Canada consists of currency (_____ and _____) outside chartered banks and _____ in chartered banks.

3. Financial intermediaries channel funds from _____ to _____.

4. Near-monies are highly _____ financial assets that do not directly function as a medium of _____ but can be readily converted in _____ or _____ deposits. Near-monies (are, are not) _____ counted in the M1 measure of the money supply.

5. Paper money is the debt of the _____, and demand deposits are the debts of the _____.

6. In Canada currency and chequable deposits:
(a)   (are, are not) _____ "backed" by gold and silver;
(b)   are money because they are used as a medium of _____, they are (in the case of currency) _____ tender, and they are relatively (abundant, scarce)_____.

7. Money has value because it can be exchanged for _____ and its value varies (directly, inversely) _____ with changes in the _____ level.

8. In post-World War I Germany a rapid expansion in the _____ led to rapidly rising _____. In recent times, some nations with similar experiences have found their own currency being replaced by a more _____ currency such as the American dollar.

9. In order to operate as a bank in Canada, a financial institution requires a _____ granted by the (federal, provincial) _____ government.

10. In Canada, there are (fewer, more) _____ Canadian-owned banks than there are foreign-owned banks, but the market is dominated by _____ banks.

■   **PROBLEMS AND PROJECTS**

1.   With the information given below, obtain M1, M2 and M2+.

Currency outside financial institutions:	$ 39
Currency at chartered banks:	17
Demand deposits at chartered banks:	60
Nonpersonal notice deposits at chartered banks:	205
Personal savings deposits at chartered banks:	112
Deposits at trust and mortgage companies, credit unions, and *caisses populaires:*	240

Calculate:
M1 = $_____
M2 = $_____
M2+ = $_____

2. Complete the following table showing the relationship between the percentage change in the price level and the percentage change in the value of money. Calculate to one decimal place.

Change in the Price Level	Change in the Value of Money
(a) Rise by:	
5%	- _____%
10%	- _____%
20%	- _____%
(b) Fall by:	
5%	+ _____%
10%	+ _____%
20%	+ _____%

3. Indicate which money supply measure(s) include each of the following items. Check off as many as apply. If an item is not included in any of the money supply measures, indicate "none."

	M1	M2	M2+	None
(a) Currency in your pocket	☐	☐	☐	☐
(b) A savings deposit in a credit union	☐	☐	☐	☐
(c) Currency in the vault of a bank	☐	☐	☐	☐
(d) A savings account in a bank	☐	☐	☐	☐
(e) Money market mutual funds	☐	☐	☐	☐
(f) A Canada Savings Bond	☐	☐	☐	☐

4. Match the term on the left with the appropriate description on the right.

(a) fiat money

(b) token money

(c) near money

(d) chequebook money

(1) demand deposits

(2) declared by government to be legal tender

(3) readily convertible into medium of exchange

(4) intrinsic value is less than face value

■ TRUE-FALSE

Circle T if the statement is true, F if it is false.

1. Anything that is convertible into gold is money. **T F**

2. Money, by providing a convenient way to exchange goods and services, promotes specialization. **T F**

3. What we employ as money in Canada are actually debts of the chartered banks and the Bank of Canada. **T F**

4. Money serves as a store of value when it is used for measuring the worth of goods. **T F**

5. When a person writes a cheque on a deposit in a chartered bank to pay for groceries, money is being used as a medium of exchange. **T F**

6. Currency includes both coins and paper money. **T F**

7. If a coin is "token money," its face value is less than its intrinsic value. *intrisè below face* **T F**

8. Canadian paper money can be converted into gold at a rate fixed by the Bank of Canada. **T F**

9. The demand deposits of the federal government in the chartered banks are a component of M1. **T F**

10. The most inclusive measure of money discussed in the chapter is M2+. **T F**

11. Economists are in general agreement that M1 is the best definition of the money supply. **T F**

12. A near-money is a medium of exchange. **T F**

13. The larger the volume of near-monies owned by consumers, the higher their consumption expenditures will be. **T F**

14. The fastest growing part of the Canadian money supply is credit card money. **T F**

15. Currency and chequable deposits are money because they are acceptable to sellers in exchange for goods and services. **T F**

16. If money is to have a fairly stable value, its supply must be limited relative to the demand for it. **T F**

17. If the price level triples, the value of one unit of currency will be only one-third of what it was previously. **T F**

18. Hyperinflation can cause money to fall out of use. **T F**

19. Appropriate fiscal policy is one way for the government to maintain stability in the value of money. **T F**

20. The Royal Bank of Canada is one of the ten largest banks in the world. **T F**

21. There have been many bank mergers in Canada's history. **T F**

22. When a person makes a purchase by e-cash, he or she is charging the transaction on a credit card. **T F**

■ MULTIPLE-CHOICE

Circle the letter that corresponds to the best answer.

1. Which of the following is not one of the functions of money?
  (a) a factor of production
  (b) a medium of exchange
  (c) a store of value
  (d) a unit of account

2. Which of the following best expresses how the use of money benefits our society?
  (a) money is intrinsically valuable
  (b) money creates wealth by generating interest income
  (c) money creates wealth by facilitating specialization
  (d) the larger the money supply the larger the economy's output

3. Which of the following makes up the biggest share of Canada's M1 money supply?
  (a) coins
  (b) paper money
  (c) term and notice deposits
  (d) demand deposits

4. Demand deposits are money because they are:
(a) legal tender
(b) fiat money
(c) accepted as a medium of exchange
(d) fully guaranteed by the chartered banks

5. The supply of money, M1, consists of the debts of:
(a) the federal government
(b) the Bank of Canada
(c) chartered banks
(d) the Bank of Canada and chartered banks

6. Which of the following best describes the "backing" of money in Canada?
(a) the gold bullion stored in the Bank of Canada's vaults
(b) the belief of holders of money that it can be exchanged for desirable goods and services
(c) the willingness of banks and the government to surrender something of value in exchange for money
(d) the faith and confidence of the public in the ability of government to pay its debts

7. Bank of Canada notes are:
(a) "backed" by gold
(b) count as part of the money supply when held by the chartered banks
(c) legal tender in Canada
(d) circulating assets of the Bank of Canada

8. Whenever a person withdraws cash from a demand deposit at a chartered bank, the M1 money supply has:
(a) increased
(b) decreased
(c) stayed the same
(d) not enough information provided to tell

9. If a person closes her personal chequing account at the Bank of Montreal and deposits the balance in her personal chequing account at Canada Trust, then:
(a) M1 falls, M2 falls, and M2+ rises
(b) M1 is unchanged, M2 rises, and M2+ rises
(c) M1 falls, M2 is unchanged, and M2+ rises
(d) M1 falls, M2 falls, M2+ is unchanged

10. Pre-1967 dimes and quarters with high silver content have virtually disappeared from circulation, whereas pre-1967 pennies and nickels still circulate. Why?

(a) the quarters and dimes wore out
(b) the token value of quarters and dimes exceeds the intrinsic value
(c) more pennies and nickels were issued in the first instance
(d) the intrinsic value of quarters and dimes exceeds the token value

11. The purchasing power of money would decrease whenever:
(a) the unemployment rate rises
(b) the GDP price index falls
(c) the Consumer Price Index rises
(d) the interest rate falls

12. Which of the following is **not** an example of a financial intermediary?
(a) a credit union
(b) a *caisse populaire*
(c) a trust company
(d) the Bank of Canada

13. The Canadian Payments Association:
(a) represents the Canadian chartered banks in discussions with the government
(b) helps restructure loans for individuals and institutions who are unable to repay borrowings from the banks
(c) operates the inter-bank cheque clearing system
(d) determines the prices to be charged for different banking services

14. The prime rate of interest is:
(a) the interest rate paid on Canada Savings Bonds
(b) the interest rate on Government of Canada Bonds
(c) the interest rate charged by the chartered banks to their best corporate customers
(d) the interest rate charged by the chartered banks for home mortgages

15. One reason that the government in 1998 disallowed proposed mergers between the Royal Bank and Bank of Montreal, and between the TD Bank and the CIBC, was that they feared:
(a) Canadian banks would become too powerful in world markets
(b) retaliation from American trade officials

(c) the public would lose faith in the safety of the banking system

(d) banking would become more concentrated and less competitive

16. One argument in favour of the bank mergers that were disallowed by the government in 1998 was that:

(a) bigger banks could better afford to invest in new technologies to improve service and efficiency

(b) the mergers would increase the amount of competition in the Canadian banking market

(c) the mergers would increase the number of jobs in the Canadian banking industry

(d) all of the above

17. Hyperinflation has occurred:

(a) several times in Canada in the 20th century

(b) in Germany in the 1920s

(c) in some Latin American countries in the 1950s

(d) all of the above

18. Many transactions in Russia now occur in American dollars rather than in rubles because:

(a) Russian people are beginning to support capitalism

(b) there is a severe shortage of rubles

(c) there is an oversupply of dollars

(d) the value of the dollar is much more stable than the ruble

■ DISCUSSION QUESTIONS

1. How would you define money?

2. At the University of B.C., plastic tokens redeemable for beer at the student pub were routinely accepted instead of currency in card games in the student residences. To what extent were these tokens considered to be money, and why did they function as such?

3. What are the components of M1? What are some examples of near-monies? What is the argument for defining the money supply to include these? What is the argument against including near-monies?

4. Suppose that you work on a grain farm to earn money for school. Why would you rather be paid with money instead of with grain of equivalent market value? In responding, consider the three functions of money.

5. What "backs" the money used in Canada? What determines the value of money?

6. Why did cigarettes emerge as money in World War II prisoner-of-war camps?

7. Explain the relationship between the value of money and the price level.

8. What roles do financial intermediaries play in a modern economy? What is the difference between chartered banks and other financial intermediaries?

9. Should the government permit mergers between chartered banks that already have large market shares in the Canadian banking industry? Give arguments on both sides.

10. How is the growing use of e-cash affecting the public's use of currency and cheques? How are e-cash and debit cards different from credit cards?

■ ANSWERS

FILL-IN QUESTIONS

1. (a) medium of exchange; (b) unit of account; (c) store of value

2. coins, paper money, demand deposits

3. savers, borrowers (or investors)

4. liquid, exchange, currency, demand; are not

5. Bank of Canada, chartered banks

6. (a) are not; (b) exchange, legal, scarce

7. goods and services, inversely, price

8. money supply, prices; stable

9. charter, federal

10. fewer, Canadian

PROBLEMS AND PROJECTS

1. M1 = 99; M2 = 416; M2+ = 656

2. (a) 4.8, 9.1, 16.7; (b) 5.3, 11.1, 25.0

3. (a) M1, M2, M2+; (b) M2+; (c) none; (d) M2, M2+; (e) M2+; (f) none

4. (a)(2); (b)(4); (c)(3); (d)(1)

TRUE-FALSE

1. F	**2.** T	**3.** T	**4.** F	**5.** T	**6.** T
7. F	**8.** F	**9.** F	**10.** T	**11.** F	**12.** F
13. T	**14.** F	**15.** T	**16.** T	**17.** T	**18.** T
19. T	**20.** F	**21.** T	**22.** F		

MULTIPLE-CHOICE

1. (a)	**2.** (c)	**3.** (d)	**4.** (c)	**5.** (d)	**6.** (b)
7. (c)	**8.** (c)	**9.** (d)	**10.** (d)	**11.** (c)	**12.** (d)
13. (c)	**14.** (c)	**15.** (d)	**16.** (a)	**17.** (b)	**18.** (d)

CHAPTER 14

How Banks Create Money

Chapter 14 shows how the chartered banks can create deposits. Since chequing deposits are a form of money (as explained in Chapter 13), banks are literally able to create money! We need to understand how they accomplish this, and also what limits the amount of money they can create. The fundamental principles of this process are laid bare by the brief history of goldsmiths.

To explain banking operations we use the very simple and convenient device of the balance sheet. On the left side of a balance sheet are listed the firm's assets, and on the right side are listed the claims on those assets: liabilities and net worth. Based on accounting principles, the assets must equal liabilities plus net worth. The balance sheet for the Canadian chartered banks was presented in Table 13-2. There we can see that (aside from foreign-currency assets and liabilities) loans represent the majority of bank assets, and various kinds of deposits represent the majority of bank liabilities. As illustrated in this chapter, all banking transactions cause balance sheet changes.

In reading this chapter, you must analyze the effect upon the balance sheet of each and every banking transaction discussed. The most important items in the balance sheet are deposits and reserves, because deposits are money, and the ability of a bank to create new deposits is determined by the amount of its reserves. Chartered banks can expand the money supply only when they have excess reserves. Excess reserves are not listed separately in the balance sheet, but can be inferred because excess reserves equal actual reserves less desired reserves.

The money creation process is explained in two scenarios: a single chartered bank, and the banking system. It is important to understand that the money-creating ability of the banking system as a whole is subject to a multiplier effect because the system as a whole does not lose reserves, whereas the money-creating ability of a single bank is not, because the bank must account for loss of reserves to other banks in the system.

The equilibrium level of deposits in the banking system is achieved through banks balancing the conflicting goals of profit and liquidity. Banks wish to create loans (and buy securities) in order to earn interest, but they also want to have enough liquidity (e.g., cash reserves) to be able to meet obligations to depositors.

■ **CHECKLIST**

When you have studied this chapter, you should be able to:

□ Define the basic items in a bank's balance sheet.

□ Recount the story of how goldsmiths came to issue paper money and operate as fractional reserve bankers.

□ Explain the parallels between the operations of goldsmiths and modern banks.

□ Compute a bank's desired and excess reserves when you are given the balance-sheet data.

□ Explain the implications of fractional reserve banking for: (a) money creation, and (b) depositor risk.

□ Explain the fundamental conflict between the two basic goals held by banks.

□ Indicate how the deposit of a cheque drawn on one bank in a second bank will affect the reserves and excess reserves of the two banks.

□ Show what happens to the money supply when a bank makes a loan (or buys securities); and what happens to the money supply when a loan is repaid (or a bank sells securities).

☐   Explain what happens to a bank's reserves and deposits after it has made a loan, a cheque has been written on the newly created deposit, deposited in another bank, and cleared; and what happens to the reserves and deposits of the bank in which the cheque was deposited.

☐   Describe what would happen to a bank's reserves if it made loans (or bought securities) in an amount that exceeded its excess reserves.

☐   State the money-creating potential of a single bank.

☐   State the money-creating potential of the banking system; and contrast this potential with that of a single bank.

☐   Compute the size of the monetary multiplier and the money-creating potential of the banking system when you are provided with the necessary data.

☐   List the two leakages that reduce the money-creating potential of the banking system.

☐   Explain why the size of the money supply needs to be controlled.

■   CHAPTER OUTLINE

1. The balance sheet of the chartered bank is a statement of the assets, liabilities, and net worth of the bank at a specific time. In any balance sheet, assets must equal liabilities plus net worth. Chartered banks can create demand deposit money, and the process of money creation is easily followed using a bank's balance sheet.

2. Medieval goldsmiths operated like modern banks.

(a)   Traders deposited gold with a goldsmith in exchange for receipts which began to circulate in place of gold; in effect, the receipts became paper money.

(b)   Eventually goldsmiths realized that little of the gold deposited with them was ever withdrawn, so they began to create interest-earning loans by creating additional gold receipts.

(c)   Once loans were created, even though the receipts (paper money) remained redeemable for gold, these receipts were only fractionally backed by gold. Thus, there was always some risk of a bank panic.

(d)   Goldsmiths' receipts (and gold in their vaults) are analogous to chartered banks' demand deposits (and cash reserves).

3. By examining how the balance sheet of the chartered bank is affected by various transactions,

one can understand how a single chartered bank in a multibank system can create money.

(a)   The initial transactions that are shown include: the founding and capitalization by sale of shares; the acquisition of property and equipment; and the acceptance of deposits from customers.

(b)   The chartered bank intends to keep some cash reserves for depositor withdrawals (usually as vault cash), and for cheque clearing (usually as deposits at the Bank of Canada). These reserves are referred to as desired reserves.

(c)   When a cheque is drawn against an account in one bank and deposited to an account at a second bank, the first bank loses reserves and deposits, and the second bank gains reserves and deposits.

4. There are several important points regarding reserves.

(a)   Desired reserves are usually some percentage of deposits; this can be expressed as the desired reserve ratio.

(b)   Actual reserves of vault cash and deposits at the Bank of Canada may not equal desired reserves.

(c)   Excess reserves equal actual reserves less desired reserves.

(d)   Money creation depends upon the presence of excess reserves.

5. The next transactions are crucial for understanding money creation and destruction.

(a)   When a single bank extends loans or buys securities, it increases its own deposit liabilities (and, therefore, the supply of money) by the amount of the loan or security purchase. But the bank only lends or buys securities in an amount equal to its excess reserves because it anticipates a loss of reserves to other banks.

(b)   When a single bank receives loan payments or sells securities, its deposit liabilities decrease (and the money supply shrinks) by the same amount.

(c)   A bank balances its desire for profits (from interest earned on loans and securities) with its desire for liquidity or safety (which it achieves by having reserves).

6. The banking system taken as a whole can create new loans and deposit money in an amount beyond its excess reserves. The maximum amount is equal to the excess reserves in the system multiplied by the monetary multiplier.

(a) The banking system as a whole can do this — even though no single bank ever lends an amount greater than its excess reserves — because the banking system, unlike a single chartered bank, does not lose reserves.

(b) The monetary multiplier is equal to the reciprocal of the desired reserve ratio; the maximum expansion of demand deposits is equal to the excess reserves in the system times the monetary multiplier.

(c) The banking system reaches an equilibrium when it is "loaned up" such that actual reserves equal desired reserves.

(d) The multiplier process applies to money destruction as well as money creation.

(e) The money multiplier process will not create the maximum amount of new money if there are leakages because borrowers choose to have additional currency or if bankers choose to have excess reserves.

(f) If bankers lend the maximum during periods of prosperity and less than the maximum during recessions, they add to the instability of the economy. To reduce the instability, the Bank of Canada must control the money supply.

■ TERMS AND CONCEPTS

actual, desired, and
   excess cash reserves
balance sheet
cash reserves
desired reserve ratio

fractional reserve
   system of banking
money multiplier
vault cash

■ HINTS AND TIPS

1. The story of the goldsmith is superbly instructive because the scenario is easily understood, yet parallels very closely our current system of banking which is more difficult to understand.

2. A balance sheet must balance. A bank's assets are either claimed by owners (net worth) or by non-owners (liabilities). Assets = liabilities + net worth. Use this principle to check both your calculations and your intuition when you work with balance sheets.

3. Chartered banks can be considered to be in equilibrium when they have zero excess reserves, because at this point they have precisely balanced their conflicting goals of profit and liquidity. A bank is

said to be "loaned up" when it has no excess reserves. If we know a bank's desired reserve ratio, we can determine how many reserves a bank will desire for a given level of deposits, *or* we can determine how many deposits a bank can support with a given level of actual reserves.

4. When first using bank balance sheets, it is common to confuse two very different concepts of "balance." Since assets must *always* equal liabilities + net worth, the accounts will always balance, but this does not imply that the bank is satisfied with its present balance between demand deposits and its reserves.

5. Even though other depository institutions also create chequable deposits, this chapter deals only with the chartered banks. But where the term chartered bank (or bank) appears, it is legitimate to substitute depository institution.

■ FILL-IN QUESTIONS

1. The balance sheet of a chartered bank is a statement of the bank's _____, _____, and _____ at some specific point in time.

2. Medieval goldsmiths issued gold receipts that could be redeemed for _____ but were also used as a medium of exchange. Therefore these receipts served as _____.

3. Like modern banks, the medieval goldsmiths operated on a _____ reserve system. Under such a system, banks (or medieval goldsmiths) are able to _____ money.

4. A bank _____ can occur when many depositors lose confidence in banks and decide to _____ large amounts of deposits.

5. When a person deposits cash in a chartered bank and receives a deposit account in return, the size of the money supply has (increased, decreased, not changed) _____.

6. When a person gets a loan at a bank and takes it in the form of a demand deposit, the money supply has (increased, decreased, not changed) _____.

7. The reserves of chartered banks can be held as _____ cash, or as deposits at the _____.

8. Prior to 1995 chartered banks in Canada were required by law to keep reserves equal to a specified _____ of their deposit liabilities. Today these banks still choose to hold enough reserves to meet _____ in excess of _____ from day to day. Banks are reluctant to hold more reserves than this because reserves earn _____ interest.

9. The excess reserves of a chartered bank equal its _____ reserves less its _____ reserves.

10. When a cheque is drawn upon bank X, deposited in bank Y, and cleared, the reserves of bank X are (increased, decreased, not changed) _____ and the reserves of bank Y are _____; deposits in bank X are _____, and deposits in bank Y are _____.

11. A single bank in a multibank system can safely make loans or buy securities equal in amount to their own _____.

12. When a chartered bank sells a $2,000 government bond to a securities dealer, the supply of money (increases, decreases) _____ by $_____.

13. A bank ordinarily pursues two conflicting goals; they are _____ and _____.

14. The banking system can make loans (or buy securities) and create money in an amount equal to its excess reserves multiplied by the _____. Its lending potential per dollar of excess reserves is greater than the lending potential of a single bank because it does not lose _____ to other banks.

15. The greater the desired reserve ratio is, the (larger, smaller) _____ is the monetary multiplier.

16. If the desired cash reserve ratio is 5%, the banking system is $6 million short of reserves, and the banking system is unable to increase its reserves, the banking system must _____ the money supply by $_____. This can be accomplished by customers making _____ payments totalling this amount, or by banks selling this amount of _____ to the public. In either case, we assume that payments would be made by writing _____ that would result in an (increase, reduction) _____ in the banks' _____ liabilities.

17. The money-creating potential of the chartered banking system is lessened by the withdrawal of _____ from banks and by the decision of bankers to keep _____ reserves.

18. Chartered banks, in the past, (a) have kept considerable excess reserves during periods of (prosperity, recession) _____ and have kept few or no excess reserves during periods of _____; (b) and by behaving in this way have made the economy (more, less) _____ unstable.

■ **PROBLEMS AND PROJECTS**

1. Indicate whether each item following would be listed under the assets (A) or under the liabilities + net worth (L) of a bank's balance sheet.
- (a)   A government bond held by the bank   ___
- (b)   A mortgage loan to a homeowner   ___
- (c)   The computer owned by the bank   ___
- (d)   Demand deposits   ___
- (e)   Cash held in a bank vault   ___
- (f)   A government deposit held in the bank   ___
- (g)   Reserves held at the Bank of Canada   ___
- (h)   Common stock issued by the bank   ___

2. Following is the simplified balance sheet of a chartered bank. Assume that the figures given show the bank's situation prior to each of the following four transactions. Fill in the blanks in each column to show the balance sheet effects of the corresponding transaction. For each transaction, start from the "initial" figures. Cash is included in the Reserves.

	Initial	(a)	(b)	(c)	(d)
Assets					
Reserves	$100	$___	$___	$___	$___
Loans	700	___	___	___	___
Securities	200	___	___	___	___
Liabilities					
& net worth					
Deposits	900	___	___	___	___
Capital	100	100	100	100	100

(a)   A cheque for $50 is written by one of the bank's depositors, given to a person who deposits it in another bank, and then cleared.
(b)   The bank loans $40 to a customer, and deposits the $40 into the customer's account.
(c)   A cheque for $60 drawn on another bank is deposited in this bank and cleared.
(d)   The bank sells $100 of government bonds to the Bank of Canada.

3. In the table below are four balance sheets for a single chartered bank [columns (1)-(4)]. The desired reserve ratio is 20%.

(a) In the opening situation shown in column (1), compute the following amounts:

Desired reserves = $_____, Excess reserves = $_____, and New loans that can be extended = $_____

(b) Fill in column (2) showing the bank's new balance sheet after the bank has extended the maximum amount of new loans, and has deposited the funds in borrowers' deposit accounts.

(c) Fill in column (3) showing the bank's new balance sheet after the borrowers have spent the funds just borrowed, assuming that they do so by writing cheques to people who are customers of other banks.

(d) Given the situation shown in column (3), confirm that the bank is "loaned up" and incapable of further expansion deposits and loans.

	(1)	(2)	(3)
Assets			
Reserves	$50	$_____	$_____
Loans	100	_____	_____
Securities	50	_____	_____
Liabilities & net worth			
Deposits	175	_____	_____
Capital	25	_____	_____

4. Suppose that banks desire a 4% reserve ratio.

(a) What is the value of the monetary multiplier? _____

(b) What is the maximum amount of new loans and deposits that a single bank could create if they had $1 of excess reserves? $_____

(c) What is the maximum amount of new loans and deposits that the whole banking system could create if one bank had $1 of excess reserves? $_____

(d) How many excess reserves would have to exist in the banking system to make possible the creation of $75 of new loans and deposit money? $_____

5. Following is the simplified consolidated balance sheet for all chartered banks in the economy. Assume that the figures given show the bank's assets and liabilities prior to each of the following three transactions, and that the desired reserve ratio is 5%. For each of the three transactions ((a), (b), and (c)), start with the figures in the "initial" column.

(a) The public deposits $5 in cash in the banks, and the banks keep the cash in their vaults. Fill in column 1. Fill in column 2 on the assumption that the banking system extends the maximum amount of new loans.

(b) The banking system sells $8 worth of securities to the Bank of Canada in exchange for new reserves. Complete column 3. Assuming the system extends the maximum amount of loans that it can, fill in column 4.

(c) The Bank of Canada sells $1 worth of securities to the chartered banks. Complete column 5. Complete column 6 showing the condition of the banks after they have contracted their loans by the amount necessary to meet the desired reserve ratio.

	initial	(1)	(2)	(3)	(4)	(5)	(6)
Assets:							
Reserves	$25	$__	$__	$__	$__	$__	$__
Loans	425	__	__	__	__	__	__
Securities	100	__	__	__	__	__	__
Liabilities & net worth							
Deposits	500	__	__	__	__	__	__
Capital	50	50	50	50	50	50	50

6. Imagine a banking system with only three chartered banks: the Bank of Charlottetown, Newfoundland Marine Bank, and the Moncton Commercial Bank. At the end of the day agents of the three meet at the "clearinghouse" to settle claims against one another as follows:

Charlottetown depositors wrote cheques to Newfoundland depositors = $20

Charlottetown depositors wrote cheques to Moncton depositors = $80

Newfoundland depositors wrote cheques to Charlottetown depositors = $50

Newfoundland depositors wrote cheques to Moncton depositors = $60

Moncton depositors wrote cheques to Charlottetown depositors = $30

Moncton depositors wrote cheques to Newfoundland depositors = $70.

(a) How much do the inter-bank clearing settlements increase or decrease each bank's reserves:

Bank of Charlottetown: _____

Newfoundland Marine Bank: _____

Moncton Commercial Bank: _____

(b)   How much will each bank expand or contract their deposits (and loan or security holdings), assuming the maximum effects?

Bank of Charlottetown: $_____
Newfoundland Marine Bank: $_____
Moncton Commercial Bank: $_____

(c)   Ultimately, what is the net effect on the money supply of this shuffling of reserves among the three banks? $_____

■ TRUE-FALSE

Circle T if the statement is true, F if it is false.

1. The balance sheet of a chartered bank shows the transactions which the bank has undertaken over a given period.   **T F**

2. A chartered bank's assets plus its net worth equal the bank's liabilities.   **T F**

3. Banks, operating under a fractional reserve system, can create money.   **T F**

4. Some of a bank's income is obtained from the interest earned on loans extended out of deposits created by the bank.   **T F**

5. Goldsmiths increased the money supply when they made loans and issued paper receipts that were not fully backed by gold in their vaults.   **T F**

6. Chartered banks hold their reserves either as deposits in the Bank of Canada or as government bonds in their own vaults.   **T F**

7. If the office owned by a bank increases in value, this will increase the bank's assets and owner's net worth.   **T F**

8. A goldsmith might experience a bank panic if customers began to doubt whether the goldsmith would be able to redeem gold receipts.   **T F**

9. An increase in a bank's deposit liabilities will increase the bank's desired reserve ratio.   **T F**

10. The actual reserves of a chartered bank equal excess reserves plus desired reserves.   **T F**

11. Chartered banks are required by law to hold a certain percentage of their deposits in reserves. **T F**

12. A cheque for $1,000 drawn on bank X by a depositor and deposited in bank Y will increase the excess reserves of bank Y by $1,000.   **T F**

13. A single chartered bank can safely loan an amount equal to its excess reserves multiplied by the desired reserve ratio.   **T F**

14. If the banking system has $10 million in excess reserves and if the reserve ratio is 5%, it can increase its loans by $200 million.   **T F**

15. When a borrower repays a loan of $500, either in cash or by cheque, the supply of money is reduced by $500. ↓ loan ↑ cash   **T F**

16. The granting of a $5,000 loan and the purchase of a $5,000 government bond from a securities dealer by a chartered bank have the same effect on the money supply.   **T F**

17. The monetary multiplier effect is reduced if the public wishes to hold more currency when their deposit balances increase.   **T F**

18. The monetary multiplier is increased if banks are content to hold excess reserves.   **T F**

19. Profit-seeking banks will tend to create more new money when the economy is booming, and this adds to macroeconomic instability.   **T F**

20. A chartered bank seeks both profits and liquidity, but these are conflicting goals.   **T F**

■ MULTIPLE-CHOICE

Circle the letter that corresponds to the best answer.

1. The fundamental balance identity is:
(a)   assets = liabilities - net worth
(b)   assets = liabilities + net worth
(c)   assets = liabilities
(d)   assets + liabilities = net worth

2. On a bank's balance sheet, loans are recorded as:
(a)   part of net worth
(b)   an asset
(c)   a liability
(d)   none of the above since loans are recorded on the income statement and not the balance sheet

3. The entry on the balance sheet of a bank that counts as part of the money supply is:
- (a) cash held by the bank
- (b) bank loans
- (c) reserves held at the central bank
- (d) demand deposits

4. The goldsmiths became bankers when:
- (a) they accepted deposits of gold for safe storage
- (b) they issued receipts for the gold stored with them
- (c) their receipts for deposited gold were used as paper money
- (d) they issued paper money in excess of the amount of gold stored with them

5. The immediate effect when cash is deposited in a deposit account in a chartered bank is:
- (a) a decrease in the money supply
- (b) an increase in the money supply
- (c) no change in the composition of the money supply
- (d) a change in the composition of the money supply

6. A chartered bank has actual reserves of $2,000 and deposit liabilities of $30,000; the desired reserve ratio is 5%. The excess reserves of the bank are:
- (a) $500
- (b) $0
- (c) minus $1,000
- (d) $1,500

7. A chartered bank chooses to hold reserves in order:
- (a) to protect the deposits in the chartered bank against losses
- (b) to maximize the bank's interest income
- (c) to meet the Bank of Canada's regulations
- (d) to add to the liquidity of the chartered bank and protect it against a "run" on the bank

8. A depositor places $1,000 in cash in a chartered bank, and the reserve ratio is 5%. As a result, the reserves and the excess reserves of the bank have been increased, respectively, by:
- (a) $1,000 and $50
- (b) $1,000 and $950
- (c) $1,000 and $1,000
- (d) $500 and $500

9. A chartered bank has no excess reserves, but then a depositor places $600 in cash in the bank, and the bank adds the $600 to its reserves. The bank then loans $300 to a borrower. The net effect is that the money supply has:
- (a) not been affected
- (b) increased by $300
- (c) increased by $600
- (d) increased by $900

10. A chartered bank has excess reserves of $500 and desires a reserve ratio of 10%; it grants a loan of $1,000 to a borrower. If the borrower writes a cheque for $1,000, which is deposited in another chartered bank, the first bank will be short of reserves, after the cheque has been cleared, in the amount of:
- (a) $100
- (b) $700
- (c) $500
- (d) $1,000

11. A chartered bank sells a $1,000 government security to a securities dealer. The dealer pays for the bond in cash, which the bank adds to its vault cash. The money supply has:
- (a) not been affected
- (b) decreased by $1,000
- (c) increased by $1,000
- (d) increased by $1,000 multiplied by the reciprocal of the desired reserve ratio

12. A chartered bank has deposit liabilities of $100,000, reserves of $37,000, and a desired reserve ratio of 25%. The amount by which a single chartered bank and the amount by which the banking system can increase loans are, respectively:
- (a) $12,000 and $48,000
- (b) $17,000 and $68,000
- (c) $12,000 and $60,000
- (d) $17,000 and $85,000

13. If the desired reserve ratio were 4%, the value of the monetary multiplier would be:
- (a) 16
- (b) 20
- (c) 24
- (d) 25

14. By making new loans of $7,000 the banking system eliminates its excess reserves of $700, and becomes "loaned up." The desired reserve ratio for this banking system must be:

(a)   5%
(b)   6.25%
(c)   8%
(d)   10%

15. The chartered banking system finds that its desired reserve ratio has risen from 5% to 6.25%, with the result that it is $100 million short of reserves. If it is unable to obtain any additional reserves, it must decrease its money supply by:
(a) $100 million
(b) $125 million
(c) $1,600 million
(d) $2,000 million

16. The money-creating potential of the banking system is reduced when:
(a)   bankers choose to have excess reserves
(b)   borrowers choose to hold none of the funds they have borrowed in currency
(c)   bankers borrow reserves from the Bank of Canada
(d)   banks reduce the interest rates they charge on loans

17. The excess reserves held by banks tend to:
(a)   rise during periods of prosperity
(b)   fall during periods of recession
(c)   rise during periods of recession
(d)   fall when interest rates in the economy fall

18. Unless controlled, the money supply will:
(a)   fall during periods of prosperity
(b)   rise during periods of recession
(c)   change in a fashion that reinforces cyclical fluctuations in the economy
(d)   change in a fashion that counters cyclical fluctuations in the economy

Use the following balance sheet for the First National Bank for questions 19 through 22. Assume the desired reserve ratio is 20%.

Assets		Liabilities and Net Worth	
Reserves	$50,000	Demand deposits	$150,000
Loans	70,000	Capital	100,000
Securities	30,000		
Property	100,000		

19. This chartered bank has excess reserves of:
(a) $10,000
(b) $20,000

(c) $30,000
(d)   -$20,000

20. This bank can safely expand its loans by a maximum of:
(a) $50,000
(b) $40,000
(c) $30,000
(d) $20,000

21. If the original bank balance sheet was for the chartered banking system, rather than a single bank, loans and deposits could have been expanded by a maximum of:
(a) $50,000
(b) $100,000
(c) $150,000
(d) $200,000

22. The claims of the owners of the bank against the bank assets is the bank's:
(a)   net worth
(b)   liabilities
(c)   balance sheet
(d)   fractional reserves

Answer questions 23 and 24 on the basis of the following consolidated balance sheet for the banking system. All figures are in billions. Assume that the desired reserve ratio is 12.5%.

Assets		Liabilities and Net Worth	
Reserves	$40	Demand deposits	$200
Loans	80	Capital	120
Securities	100		
Property	200		

23. The maximum amount by which this chartered banking system can expand the supply of money by lending is:
(a) $120 billion
(b) $240 billion
(c) $350 billion
(d) $440 billion

24. If there is a deposit of $20 billion of new currency into chequing accounts in the banking system, excess reserves will increase by:
(a) $16.5 billion
(b) $17.0 billion
(c) $17.5 billion
(d) $18.5 billion

25. The formula for the monetary multiplier is given by $m = 1/R$, where R stands for:

  (a) excess reserves

  (b) the desired reserve ratio

  (c) the marginal propensity to save

  (d) the interest rate

26. The maximum deposit expansion for the whole banking system is found by multiplying the volume of excess reserves by:

  (a) the desired reserve ratio

  (b) 1 minus the desired reserve ratio

  (c) the monetary multiplier

  (d) the reciprocal of the interest rate

■ DISCUSSION QUESTIONS

1. List and explain each category of assets and liabilities in the simplified balance sheet of a bank.

2. How did the early goldsmiths come to issue paper money and then become bankers? Explain the difference between 100% and a fractional reserve system of banking, and why the latter system is subject to "runs" and may require public regulation.

3. Chartered banks seek both profits and liquidity. Why are the two objectives in conflict?

4. Do the reserves held by chartered banks satisfactorily protect the bank's depositors? Are the reserves of banks needed? Explain your answers.

5. Explain why the granting of a loan by a chartered bank increases the supply of money. Why does the repayment of a loan decrease the supply of money?

6. The owner of a ski shop writes a cheque on his account in a Banff bank and sends it to one of his suppliers, who deposits it in a different bank in Calgary. How does the Calgary bank obtain payment from the Banff bank? How are the reserves of the two banks affected?

7. Why is a single bank able to loan safely an amount equal to only its excess reserves? But why can the banking system as a whole extend loans and expand the money supply by an amount that is a multiple of the system's excess reserves? How does such a multiple expansion of deposits (that is, money) take place?

8. On the basis of a given amount of excess reserves and a given reserve ratio, a certain expansion of the money supply may be possible. What are two reasons the potential expansion of the money supply may not be fully achieved?

9. Why is there a "need for monetary control" in the Canadian economy?

■ ANSWERS

FILL-IN QUESTIONS

  1. assets, liabilities, net worth

  2. gold; money

  3. fractional; create

  4. panic (failure), withdraw

  5. not changed

  6. increased

  7. vault, Bank of Canada

  8. percentage; withdrawals, deposits; zero

  9. actual, desired

  10. decreased, increased, decreased, increased

  11. excess reserves

  12. decreases, 2,000

  13. profits, liquidity (safety)

  14. monetary multiplier (reciprocal of the reserve ratio); reserves

  15. smaller

  16. decrease, 120 million; loan, securities; cheques, reduction, deposit

  17. currency, excess

  18. (a) recession, prosperity; (b) more

PROBLEMS AND PROJECTS

1. (a) A; (b) A; (c) A; (d) L; (e) A; (f) L; (g) A; (h) L

2.	(a)	(b)	(c)	(d)
Assets:				
Reserves	50	100	160	200
Loans	700	740	700	700
Securities	200	200	200	100
Liabilities and net worth:				
Deposits	850	940	960	900

3. (a) 35, 15, 15; (b) entries down column (2): 50, 115, 50, 190, 25; (c) entries down column (3): 35, 115, 50, 175, 25; (d) Deposits = 175, and Reserves = 35 = 20% of 175.

4. (a) 25; (b) 1; (c) 25; (d) 3

5.	(1)	(2)	(3)	(4)	(5)	(6)
Assets:						
Reserves	$30	$30	$33	$33	$24	$24
Loans	425	520	425	585	425	405
Securities	100	100	92	92	101	101
Liabilities and net worth:						
Deposits	505	600	500	660	500	480

6. (a) Charlottetown pays $50 to Moncton, and receives $30 from Newfoundland = net reserve decrease of $20; Newfoundland pays $30 to Charlottetown, and receives $10 from Moncton = net reserve decrease of $20; Moncton: receives $50 from Charlottetown, and pays $10 to Newfoundland = net reserve increase of $40;
(b) Charlottetown: contract by $20; Newfoundland: contract by $20; Moncton: expand by $40;
(c) No change, since the banking system as a whole experiences neither loss nor gain of reserves.

TRUE-FALSE

1. F	**2.** F	**3.** T	**4.** T	**5.** T	**6.** F
7. T	**8.** T	**9.** F	**10.** T	**11.** F	**12.** F
13. F	**14.** T	**15.** T	**16.** T	**17.** T	**18.** F
19. T	**20.** T				

MULTIPLE-CHOICE

1. (b)	**2.** (b)	**3.** (d)	**4.** (d)	**5.** (d)	**6.** (a)
7. (d)	**8.** (b)	**9.** (b)	**10.** (c)	**11.** (b)	**12.** (a)
13. (d)	**14.** (d)	**15.** (c)	**16.** (a)	**17.** (c)	**18.** (c)
19. (b)	**20.** (d)	**21.** (b)	**22.** (a)	**23.** (a)	**24.** (c)
25. (b)	**26.** (c)				

CHAPTER 15

The Bank of Canada and Monetary Policy

Chapter 15, the last of three chapters on money and banking, explains how the Bank of Canada uses monetary policy — the control of the money supply — to fight macroeconomic fluctuations. The goals of monetary policy are broadly the same as the goals of fiscal policy: to achieve full employment without inflation.

The five functions of the Bank of Canada are to: (1) serve as a "bankers' bank" when chartered banks need to borrow extra reserves; (2) to issue paper currency; (3) to act as fiscal agent for the federal government; (4) to supervise the chartered banks; and (5) to regulate the supply of money. The last of these functions is the most important from a macroeconomic standpoint, and is the focus of the chapter.

Because monetary policy entails transactions involving items listed on the Bank of Canada's balance sheet, one must be familiar with these items. Over 80% of the Bank of Canada's assets are held in various forms of Government of Canada securities, such as Treasury bills and bonds. Another important asset is advances to chartered banks (IOUs for reserves that chartered banks have borrowed temporarily). The Bank of Canada's liabilities consist of notes in circulation (such as the $5 bill in your pocket), chartered bank deposits held at the Bank of Canada, and Government of Canada deposits held at the Bank of Canada.

In Chapter 14 we learned how chartered banks can create new deposit money, as long as they have excess reserves. The main tools of monetary policy work by changing the level of chartered bank reserves. These tools are open-market operations, and switching government deposits. In open-market operations the Bank of Canada buys or sells securities in the open market (from the chartered banks, or the public). For example, if the goal is to expand the money supply, the Bank of Canada will buy securities, paying for these securities by creating deposits at the Bank of Canada. These newly created deposits are new reserves, and enable chartered banks to make new loans and deposits that expand the money supply. If the Bank of Canada switches some of the government's deposits from itself to chartered banks, the result will be the same. A third method of influencing the money supply is to change the bank rate — the interest rate that the Bank of Canada charges chartered banks for advances of reserves.

The next section turns to the demand for money. The role of money as a medium of exchange creates the transactions demand for holding money, and its role as a store of value creates the asset demand for holding money. Because the transactions demand varies with nominal GDP, and the asset demand varies with the rate of interest, the total demand for money is an inverse function of the interest rate, and a direct function of nominal GDP. At the interest rate where the demand for money is equal to the supply of money, the money market is in equilibrium. A shift in the money supply will throw the money market out of equilibrium. For example, if the Bank of Canada decreases the money supply, there will be a shortage of money which people will try to make up by selling financial assets (bonds). This causes the price of bonds to fall, and the interest rate on bonds to rise. Money market equilibrium is restored when the interest rate has risen enough to make people satisfied with their money balances relative to their holdings of bonds.

The cause-effect chain from money supply changes to changes in the key macroeconomic variables of employment, output, and inflation, is known as the transmission mechanism. Consider the case of an expansionary monetary policy. The creation of excess reserves for chartered banks will stimulate deposit creation, leading to a surplus of money and shortage of bonds. As people try to buy more bonds, bond prices rise and interest rates fall. Lower interest rates stimulate investment spending, causing AD to expand, increasing the equilibrium levels of employment, output, and prices. In the case of a contractionary monetary policy, the effects are opposite, but the transmission mechanism is otherwise similar.

As is true of fiscal policy, the effectiveness of monetary policy in expanding real GDP depends on a number of factors, or potential complications. As we saw for fiscal policy, how the effects of an expansionary policy are divided between real GDP growth and price increases depend on where the economy is along the short-run aggregate supply curve. There are time lags and political constraints on the use of monetary policy, but probably less so than for fiscal policy. Some complications are specific to monetary policy. First, the effect of a money supply shift depends upon the steepness of the money-demand and investment-demand curves. Second, an expansionary monetary policy leads to feedback effects that partially offset the interest rate decreases that drive the expansion. Five more concerns about the effectiveness of monetary policy in certain situations are discussed under the heading of shortcomings and problems.

Linkages between Canada and foreign economies also pose complications for monetary policy. An expansionary monetary policy will lower domestic interest rates, and thereby reduce capital inflows. Less financial investment from abroad means less demand for the Canadian dollar, so the dollar will depreciate. The depreciation will raise net exports (our exports increase and our imports fall). This net export effect reinforces the demand stimulus intended by the expansionary monetary policy. Another consideration is that we may desire a balance between our exports and imports. If so, the effects of an expansionary monetary policy intended to boost our domestic economy could either help or hinder the achievement of our goal of balance in our foreign trade.

The final element of Chapter 15 is a schematic diagram (Figure 15-6) that summarizes the theories presented in Chapters 9 through 15. This very important diagram provides a compact overview of many important models, and highlights how the principles from the previous chapters are connected parts of an overall theory; and that the policies discussed in these chapters are alternative means of achieving the goals of economic stabilization and growth.

■   CHECKLIST

When you have studied this chapter, you should be able to:

☑   Identify the goals of monetary policy.

☑   Explain the five functions of the Bank of Canada.

☑   List the principal assets and liabilities of the Bank of Canada.

☐   Explain how the two main tools of monetary policy (open-market operations and switching government deposits) can be used to expand or contract the money supply.

☐   Work out examples of monetary policy actions using balance sheets for the Bank of Canada and chartered banks.

☐   Identify when expansionary (easy) monetary policy and contractionary (tight) monetary policy is appropriate.

☐   Explain how changing the bank rate works as a tool of monetary policy.

☐   Explain two reasons for holding money, and explain what variables determine the total demand for money.

☐   Draw a graph showing how the equilibrium level of the interest rate is determined.

☐   Explain the adjustments that will take place if there is a surplus or shortage of money.

☐   Indicate the relationship that exists between the price of bonds and the interest rate.

☐   Explain and illustrate, using a set of three graphs, the transmission mechanism from money supply changes to changes in real GDP and the price level.

☐   Show how the shape of the aggregate supply curve influences the effectiveness of monetary policy.

☐   Explain the feedback effect inherent in the use of monetary policy.

☐   Analyze the effect of the steepness of the money-demand and investment-demand curves on the effectiveness of monetary policy.

☐   List three strengths and five shortcomings of monetary policy.

☐   Explain how the Bank of Canada now links the bank rate to the overnight loans rate, and how changes in the bank rate indicate changes in monetary policy.

☐   Explain how monetary policy creates a net export effect, and why the goals of domestic stabilization and trade balance could be either complementary or conflicting.

□ Work through Figure 15-6 which integrates the various components of macroeconomic theory and stabilization policy.

■ **CHAPTER OUTLINE**

1. The objective of monetary policy is full employment without inflation. The Bank of Canada can achieve this objective by controlling the level of excess reserves held by the chartered banks, thereby influencing the size of the money supply, the interest rate, and the level of aggregate expenditures and demand.

2. The Bank of Canada has five functions:
  (a) to serve as the "bankers' bank";
  (b) to supply paper currency to the economy;
  (c) to act as fiscal agent for the federal government;
  (d) to supervise chartered banks;
  (e) to regulate the supply of money.

3. To understand how monetary policy tools operate, it is necessary to understand the assets and liabilities on the balance sheet of the Bank of Canada.
  (a) The relevant assets are Government of Canada securities (bonds and Treasury bills), and advances (normally very short-term loans) to chartered banks.
  (b) The relevant liabilities are bank notes in circulation, the reserve deposits of chartered banks, and Government of Canada deposits.

4. The Bank of Canada employs two principal tools to control the reserves of banks and the size of the money supply: open-market operations and switching Government of Canada deposits between itself and chartered banks.
  (a) In order to increase bank reserves and the money supply, the Bank of Canada could:
    (1) Buy bonds or other government securities from banks or the public in the open market.
    (2) Switch government deposits from the Bank of Canada to chartered banks.
  (b) In order to decrease bank reserves and the money supply, the Bank of Canada could:
    (1) Sell bonds or other government securities to banks or the public in the open market.
    (2) Switch government deposits from chartered banks to the Bank of Canada.

5. A less important technique of monetary policy is to change the bank rate, which is the interest rate charged by the Bank of Canada for short-term advances of reserves.
  (a) Since 1996 the bank rate has been set at 1/4% above the prevailing overnight loans rate in the money market. The Bank of Canada publicizes a target range for the overnight loans rate.
  (b) When the Bank of Canada lends and borrows in the overnight loans market, it affects the availability of reserves, and the opportunity cost of these reserves, for the chartered banks.

6. The public holds money for two reasons:
  (a) The transactions demand stems from money's use as a medium of exchange. The higher nominal GDP is, the more transactions are made, and the greater the transactions demand for money.
  (b) The asset demand stems from money's function as a liquid and riskless store of value. The higher is the interest rate on bonds and other interest-bearing assets, the greater the opportunity cost of holding money, and the less the asset demand for money.
  (c) The total demand for money is found by adding the asset demand horizontally to the transactions demand. There is an inverse relation between the quantity of money the public wants to hold and the interest rate. Increases in nominal GDP shift the money-demand curve to the right.
  (d) The supply of money can be determined by the Bank of Canada, and does not vary with the interest rate.
  (e) Equilibrium in the money market occurs at the interest rate where the downsloping money-demand curve and the vertical money-supply curve intersect.
  (f) If there is a shortage of money, people will attempt to sell bonds and financial assets to restore their desired money balances. These transactions will decrease the prices of existing bonds and increase the interest rate. This interest rate adjustment continues until the amount of money demanded falls enough to match the fixed supply of money.
  (g) If there is a surplus of money, people will attempt to purchase bonds and other interest-bearing financial assets. This will drive up the prices of bonds, and drive down the interest rate. This continues until the interest rate is low enough to induce the public to willingly hold the amount of money that exists.

7. The cause-effect chain from monetary policy changes to changes in equilibrium GDP and price level is known as the transmission mechanism, and is summarized as follows:

(a)   In the money market the money-demand curve and the money-supply curve determine the equilibrium interest rate; the investment-demand curve and the equilibrium rate of interest determine planned investment; and planned investment helps determine the level of the aggregate demand curve (and the aggregate expenditures curve, for those who studied Chapters 9 and 10); the intersection of aggregate supply and aggregate demand determines the equilibrium GDP and price level.

(b)   If recession is the problem, the Bank of Canada moves to increase the money supply, causing the interest rate to fall and investment spending to increase, thereby increasing real GDP by a multiple of the increase in investment.

(c)   If inflation is the problem, the Bank of Canada moves to decrease the money supply, causing the interest rate to rise and investment spending to decrease, thereby reducing inflation.

8. A full explanation of the transmission mechanism requires that refinements and feedback effects be considered.

(a)   The extent to which a given change in the money supply will change investment depends on two factors: the shape of the money-demand curve and the shape of the investment-demand curve. Monetary policy is most powerful when the money-demand curve is steep (so a given change in money supply creates a large interest rate change), and when the investment-demand curve is flat (so a given interest rate change creates a large investment spending change).

(b)   A change in the money supply leads to change in equilibrium GDP, but there is a feedback effect because money demand depends on nominal GDP. This feedback effect offsets some of the interest rate impact of the money supply change, and therefore weakens monetary policy.

(c)   In terms of the AD-AS model, the flatter the aggregate supply curve is, the greater is the effect of a change in the money supply on real GDP and the smaller is the effect on the price level.

(d)   If the Bank of Canada takes no monetary policy (or fiscal policy) action when there is a recessionary or inflationary gap, the short-run aggregate supply curve will eventually shift to close the gap.

9. In practice, the effectiveness of monetary policy depends on certain strengths and shortcomings.

(a)   Its strengths are that:

(1)   it can be more quickly changed than fiscal policy;

(2)   it is more isolated from political pressure than fiscal policy;

(3)   it has been successful in recent years in reducing inflation and in pulling the economy out of recession.

(b)   Its five shortcomings or problems are that:

(1)   it may be subject to less control by the Bank of Canada because of recent innovations in banking practices;

(2)   it is subject to the cyclical asymmetry of being more effective in fighting inflation than in curbing recession;

(3)   it can be offset by changes in the velocity of money;

(4)   it may not have a significant impact on investment spending;

(5)   it may produce changes in interest income and expenses that have offsetting impacts.

10. The Bank of Canada has, since 1996, set the bank rate based on the upper level of its operating band for the overnight loans rate. When the Bank of Canada sells bonds or switches government deposits out of the chartered banks, the increased scarcity of reserves will drive up the overnight loans rate. The increase in this rate, and thus the bank rate, signals a tighter monetary policy.

11. Linkages with foreign economies complicate the effects of monetary policy.

(a)   Expansionary monetary policy will decrease Canadian interest rates, thereby decreasing the amount of capital inflows from abroad. Demand for the Canadian dollar will fall, and the dollar will depreciate, causing increased demand for Canada's exports, and decreased demand for imports. In sum, expansionary monetary policy will cause net exports to increase, thus reinforcing the expansionary effect on AD.

(b)   A widely held economic goal is that Canada should balance its exports and imports. A monetary policy that is appropriate for alleviating a domestic stabilization problem may assist in achieving balanced trade, or may exacerbate a trade imbalance.

12. The equilibrium levels of real GDP, employment, and prices are determined by aggregate supply and aggregate demand.

(a)   There are four expenditure components of AD: consumption, planned investment, government, and net exports.

(b)   The three major components of AS are: input prices, productivity, and legal-institutional environment.

(c)   Fiscal, monetary, or other government policies may effect either AD or AS, and thereby influence the level of real GDP, employment and prices.

■ TERMS AND CONCEPTS

asset demand	overnight loans rate
bank rate	prime interest rate
contractionary (tight) monetary policy	switching government deposits
expansionary (easy) monetary policy	total demand for money
money market	transactions demand
open-market operations	velocity of money

■ HINTS AND TIPS

1.   To understand how open-market operations and switching of government deposits works, it is important to have mastery of the balance sheets of the Bank of Canada (presented in this chapter) and the chartered banks (presented in Chapter 14).

2.   If you find counterintuitive the concept of a "surplus" of money, you may be confusing money and assets. A person with a surplus of money does not have too many assets; they are simply holding too large a portion of their assets in the form of money. They prefer less money and more bonds (or other interest-bearing financial assets).

3.   The transmission mechanism is crucial. Be sure that you can explain it thoroughly, and that you can draw the set of graphs to illustrate all of the linkages: the money market graph, the investment-demand graph, and the aggregate supply and aggregate demand graph.

4.   Figure 15-6 is an excellent tool for preparing for the final exam. It is a comprehensive diagram of all of the macroeconomic models and theories from previous chapters.

■ FILL-IN QUESTIONS

1. The objective of monetary policy in Canada is to help achieve and maintain a _____, _____ level of total output. The institution responsible for these monetary policies is the _____.

2. The five major functions of the Bank of Canada are to:

(a)   _____

(b)   _____

(c)   _____

(d)   _____

(e)   _____

3. When the Bank of Canada acts as fiscal agent, it holds part of the federal government's _____, helps the government collect _____, and administers the sale and redemption of government _____.

4. In open-market operations, the Bank of Canada buys and sells _____ in the open market in order to change the level of chartered banks' _____, and therefore influence the amount of new _____ that chartered banks can create.

5. The total demand for money is the sum of:

(a) the _____ demand, which relates to money's function as a medium of exchange, and which depends (directly, inversely) _____ upon the _____;

(b) and the _____ demand, which relates to money's function as a store of value, and which depends _____ upon the _____.

6. The equilibrium real interest rate is determined by the money _____ and money _____ curves. This equilibrium interest rate and the _____ curve determine the level of planned investment. The level of investment helps to determine the level of aggregate _____.

7. There is a(n) (direct, inverse) _____ relation between interest rates and the price of existing bonds.

8. If the Bank of Canada sells $10 million in government bonds to the public, who pays for them by cheque, and the desired reserve ratio is 5%, the supply of money is immediately reduced by $_____, the reserves of the chartered banks are immediately reduced by $_____, and the excess reserves of the banks are immediately reduced by $_____. But if these bonds are sold to the chartered banks instead, the supply of money is immediately reduced by $_____, the reserves of the banks are immediately reduced by $_____, and the excess reserves of the banks are immediately reduced by $_____. In either case, the final net effect on the money supply will be a reduction of $_____ if the maximum money multiplier effects take place.

9. Suppose that the Bank of Canada buys government securities in the open market. Complete the chain of effects by indicating increase (+) or decrease (-) in each case:

(a)   chartered bank reserves ☐
(b)   chartered bank deposit liabilities ☐
(c)   money supply ☐
(d)   interest rate ☐
(e)   planned investment ☐
(f)   aggregate demand ☐
(g)   price level and real GDP level ☐

10. Beginning from an equilibrium in the money market, a decrease in the supply of money will cause a (surplus, shortage) _____ of money, and a _____ of bonds and other interest-bearing assets. This causes the prices of bonds to be bid (down, up) _____, and interest rates to (fall, rise) _____. The change in interest rates causes the public to adjust its (transactions, asset) _____ demand for money until money demand and supply are once again _____.

11. To eliminate inflationary pressures in the economy, the Bank of Canada should (increase, decrease) _____ the reserves of chartered banks; this would tend to _____ the money supply and to _____ the rate of interest; and this, in turn, would cause investment spending, aggregate demand, and output to _____. This action by the Bank of Canada would be considered a(n) _____ monetary policy.

12. Compared to fiscal policy, monetary policy has the advantages of working more (quickly, slowly) _____, and being (less, more) _____ isolated from political pressure. The weaknesses of monetary policy are that it is more effective in curbing (recession, inflation) _____ than _____, can be ineffective if the _____ of money changes in the (same, opposite) _____ direc-

tion as the money supply, and will not be effective if changes in the interest rate have little or no effect on _____ spending in the economy.

13. Expansionary monetary policy will tend to push interest rates (down, up) _____, which in turn (increases, decreases) _____ the demand for the domestic currency. Therefore the currency will (appreciate, depreciate) _____, leading net exports to (increase, decrease) _____. This net export effect (reinforces, counteracts) _____ the intended expansionary effect of the monetary policy.

■   **PROBLEMS AND PROJECTS**

1. The consolidated balance sheet of the chartered banks and the balance sheet of the Bank of Canada are shown below. The chartered banks have a desired reserve ratio of 10%.

(a)   Initially, the money supply is $_____.
(b)   Suppose that the Bank of Canada conducts open-market operations by purchasing $10 in government securities directly from chartered banks. In the (b) columns of the two balance sheets show the immediate results — prior to the chartered banks making any adjustments to restore their desired reserve ratio.

CHARTERED BANKS		(b)	(d)
Assets			
Reserves	$50	_____	_____
Government Securities	100	_____	_____
Loans	350	_____	_____
Liabilities			
Demand deposits	500	_____	_____

BANK OF CANADA		(b)	(d)
Assets			
Government Securities	$300	_____	_____
Liabilities			
Reserves of banks	50	_____	_____
Government deposits	100	_____	_____
Bank of Canada Notes	150	_____	_____

(c)   The money supply immediately after the open-market operation is $_____.
(d)   In the (d) columns, show the balance sheet entries after the chartered banks create as many new loans and deposits as they can, consistent with their desired reserve ratio.

(e)   The money supply after these adjustments is $_____.

(f)   Because an increase of $____ in chartered bank reserves led to a money supply increase of $___, the money multiplier in this example is ___.

2. Below are balance sheets for the Bank of Canada and the chartered banks. Suppose that the Bank of Canada wants to decrease chartered bank reserves by $5.

(a)   In the (a) columns show how this could be accomplished by an open-market operation.

(b)   In the (b) columns show how this could be accomplished by switching government deposits. Start this part of the question from the original data.

CHARTERED BANKS		(a)	(b)
Assets			
Reserves	$25	____	____
Government Securities	50	____	____
Loans	250	____	____
Liabilities			
Demand deposits	325	____	____

BANK OF CANADA		(a)	(b)
Assets			
Government Securities	$80	____	____
Liabilities			
Reserves of banks	25	____	____
Government deposits	15	____	____
Bank of Canada Notes	40	____	____

3. Below are graphs of the money market and the demand for investment. The money demand curve is given by the equation: $D_m = 400 - 50\ i$ where D_m is the quantity of money demanded in billion $, and i is the interest rate in percent. The amount of planned investment spending is given by $I_g = 80 - 10\ i$ where I_g is investment spending in billion $.

(a)   Graph the D_m function and the I_g function.

(b)   The current money supply is $200 billion. Graph this, labelling the line S_{m0}.

(c)   The equilibrium interest rate is _____%.

(d)   The level of planned investment at the equilibrium interest rate is $_____ billion.

(e)   If the Bank of Canada increases the money supply by $100 billion, will there be a surplus or a shortage of money?

(f)   The new equilibrium interest rate is ____%.

(g)   The new level of investment demand is $_____ billion.

(h)   If the expenditures multiplier in this situation is 3, the money supply increase will shift the AD curve (leftward, rightward) _____ by $___ billion.

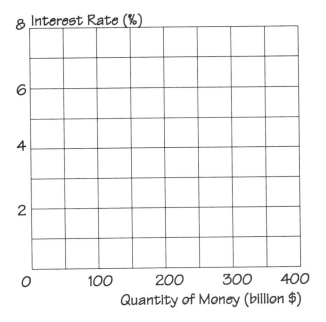

Interest Rate (%) vs Quantity of Money (billion $)

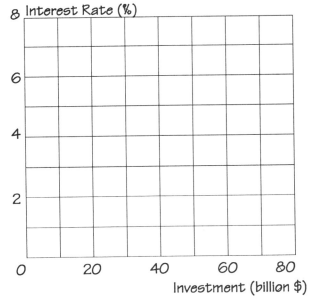

Interest Rate (%) vs Investment (billion $)

4. This question uses the two graphs from question 3.

(a)   Suppose the money-demand curve is $D_{m^*} = 600 - 100\ i$ instead of the initial curve given in question 3. Plot this curve.

(b)   Money demand D_{m^*} is (less, more) _____ responsive to interest rate changes than the initial D_m. As a result, when the money supply increases from $200 billion to $300 billion, the equilibrium interest rate drops by only _____%, as compared to a drop of _____% in the initial case. The rise in investment created by the money supply increase is $_____ billion, as compared to $_____ billion in the initial case. Consequently, monetary policy is less effective when the money-demand curve is (less, more) _____ responsive to interest rate changes.

5. This question also uses the two graphs from question 3.

(a)   Suppose the investment-demand curve is $Ig^* = 60 - 5\,Ig$ instead of the initial curve given in question 3 above. The money-demand curve is the initial one used in question 3. Plot the Ig^* curve.

(b)   Investment demand Ig^* is (less, more) _____ responsive to interest rate changes than the initial Ig. As a result, the same interest rate decrease that occurs when the money supply increases from $200 billion to $300 billion, will generate $_____ billion in new investment, as compared with $_____ billion in new investment in the original case. Consequently, monetary policy is less effective when the investment-demand curve is (less, more) _____ responsive to interest rate changes.

■   **TRUE-FALSE**

Circle T if the statement is true, F if it is false.

1. The stated objective of monetary policy is to stabilize interest rates. **T F**

2. Paper currency is among the main assets of the Bank of Canada. **T F**

3. Evidence shows that countries whose central banks are more independent tend to have lower inflation rates. **T F**

4. The Bank of Canada supplies the economy with needed paper currency. **T F**

5. The Bank of Canada holds all of the government's chequing accounts. **T F**

6. Chartered banks' deposits held at the Bank of Canada are counted as assets by the chartered banks and as liabilities by the Bank of Canada. **T F**

7. The Bank of Canada's policies are determined by the federal government. **T F**

8. When the Bank of Canada sells bonds in the open market, the price of these bonds falls. **T F**

9. As the "lender of last resort," the Bank of Canada makes short-term loans of cash reserves to chartered banks. **T F**

10. If the Bank of Canada wished to follow a contractionary monetary policy, it would seek to reduce the reserves of the chartered banks. **T F**

11. The major tool of monetary policy is changes in the prime rate of interest. **T F**

12. When the Bank of Canada switches government deposits from itself to the chartered banks, the reserves of the chartered banks will be decreased. **T F**

13. The asset demand for money varies inversely with the rate of interest. **T F**

14. An increase in the equilibrium GDP will shift the money demand curve to the left and increase the equilibrium interest rate. **T F**

15. Monetary policy is more effective in fighting recession than it is in curbing inflation. **T F**

16. An expansionary monetary policy shifts the aggregate demand curve to the right. **T F**

17. A surplus of money will cause bond prices to rise. **T F**

18. It is generally agreed that fiscal policy is more effective than monetary policy in controlling the business cycle because fiscal policy is more flexible. **T F**

19. If no monetary policy or fiscal policy is initiated to close an inflationary gap, the AS curve will eventually shift leftward to close the gap. **T F**

20. There is concern that changes in banking practices may eventually make monetary policy less effective. **T F**

21. When the AS curve is very steep, expansionary monetary policy has more impact on real GDP than on prices. **T F**

22. If the economy has a trade surplus and a recessionary gap, an expansionary monetary policy is compatible with both the domestic stabilization goal and the balance of trade goal.   **T F**

23. In the 1990s monetary policy became the primary stabilization tool in Canada because fiscal policy was focused on deficit reduction rather than on macroeconomic stabilization.   (T) F

■ **MULTIPLE-CHOICE**

Circle the letter that corresponds to the best answer.

1. The agency directly responsible for monetary policy in Canada is:
   (a)   the Canadian Bankers' Association
   (b)   the Bank of Canada
   (c)   the Parliament of Canada
   (d)   the Department of Finance

2. The largest single asset on the Bank of Canada's balance sheet is:
   (a)   government securities
   (b)   loans
   (c)   notes in circulation
   (d)   chartered banks' deposits

3. All of the following are functions of the Bank of Canada with the exception of:
   (a)   acting as fiscal agent of the government
   (b)   holding deposits of the chartered banks
   (c)   regulating the supply of money
   (d)   determining the prime rate of interest

4. Open-market operations refer to:
   (a)   the buying and selling of government bonds by the Bank of Canada
   (b)   the buying and selling of government bonds by the chartered banks
   (c)   the buying and selling of stocks and bonds by the Bank of Canada
   (d)   the shifting of government deposits to and from the commercial banks by the Bank of Canada.

5. Which of the following is not one of the tools of monetary policy used by the Bank of Canada?
   (a)   switching of government deposits
   (b)   open-market operations
   (c)   setting the bank rate
   (d)   setting the required reserve ratio

6. Which of the following acts would not have the same general effect upon the money supply as the other three?
   (a)   the Bank of Canada sells bonds to chartered banks
   (b)   the Bank of Canada raises the bank rate
   (c)   the Bank of Canada shifts government deposits to the chartered banks
   (d)   the Bank of Canada sells bonds to the public

7. In the last decade, which has been the main method used by the Bank of Canada to control the money supply?
   (a)   open-market operations
   (b)   changing the bank rate
   (c)   switching of government deposits
   (d)   changing required reserve ratio

8. If the Bank of Canada sells $20 million in government securities to chartered banks who have a desired reserve ratio of 10%, then the potential change on the money supply is:
   (a)   an increase of $20 million
   (b)   an increase of $200 million
   (c)   a decrease of $20 million
   (d)   a decrease of $200 million

9. In the chain of cause and effect between changes in the excess reserves of chartered banks and the resulting changes in output and employment in the economy:
   (a)   an increase in excess reserves will decrease the money supply
   (b)   a decrease in the money supply will increase the rate of interest
   (c)   an increase in the rate of interest will increase aggregate demand
   (d)   an increase in aggregate expenditures will decrease output and employment

10. To contract the money supply, the Bank of Canada could:
   (a)   buy bonds or switch government deposits away from chartered banks
   (b)   sell bonds or switch government deposits away from chartered banks
   (c)   buy bonds or switch government deposits into chartered banks
   (d)   sell bonds or switch government deposits into chartered banks

d

11. There is an asset demand for money because money is:
(a)   a medium of exchange
(b)   a standard of value
(c)   a store of value
(d)   a standard of deferred payment

c

12. The transactions demand for money:
(a)   varies directly with nominal GDP
(b)   varies inversely with nominal GDP
(c)   varies directly with the interest rate
(d)   varies inversely with the interest rate

a

13. The total demand for money would shift to the left as a result of:
(a)   an increase in the interest rate
(b)   a decline in nominal GDP
(c)   a decrease in the interest rate
(d)   an increase in nominal GDP

b

14. The equilibrium rate of interest is determined by:
(a)   the demand for money and the level of nominal GDP
(b)   the transactions demand for money and the supply of money
(c)   the total demand for money and the supply of money
(d)   the demand for money and the demand for bonds

c

15. An increase in the rate of interest would increase:
(a)   the opportunity cost of holding money
(b)   the transactions demand for money
(c)   the asset demand for money
(d)   the price of bonds

a

16. Suppose the transactions demand for money is equal to 10% of the nominal GDP, the supply of money is $45 billion, and the asset demand for money is that shown in the following table. If the nominal GDP is $300 billion, the equilibrium interest rate is:
(a)   14%
(b)   13%
(c)   12%
(d)   11%

b

Interest Rate (%)	Asset Demand (billions)
14	$10
13	15
12	20
11	25

17. Which one of the following statements is true?
(a)   bond prices and the interest rates are directly related
(b)   a lower interest rate shifts the aggregate demand curve to the left
(c)   the supply of money is directly related to the interest rate
(d)   bond prices and interest rates are inversely related

18. A bond that pays fixed interest payment of $100 per year falls in price from $1,000 to $800. What happens to the interest rate on the bond?
(a)   increase by 1.25 percent per year
(b)   decrease by 1.25 percent per year
(c)   increase by 2.50 percent per year
(d)   decrease by 2.50 percent per year

c   *2.50*

19. When the Bank of Canada decides to buy government bonds, the demand for government bonds will:
(a)   decrease, bond prices will decrease, and the interest rate will decrease
(b)   increase, bond prices will increase, and the interest rate will decrease
(c)   increase, bond prices will increase, and the interest rate will increase
(d)   decrease, bond prices will increase, and the interest rate will decrease

b

20. A change in the money supply has the least effect on the equilibrium GDP when:
(a)   both the money-demand and investment-demand curves are steep
(b)   both the money-demand and investment-demand curves are flat
(c)   the money-demand curve is flat and the investment-demand curve is steep
(d)   the money-demand curve is steep and the investment-demand curve is flat

c

21. An expansionary monetary policy:
(a)   reduces the supply of money, increases the interest rate, reduces investment, and reduces the equilibrium GDP
(b)   increases the money supply, reduces the rate of interest, increases investment, and reduces the equilibrium GDP
(c)   reduces the money supply, reduces the rate of interest, increases investment, and increases the equilibrium GDP
(d)   increases the money supply, reduces the interest rate, increases investment, and increases the equilibrium GDP

d

22. An increase in the money supply is least effective in stimulating aggregate demand when the velocity of money:

- **(a)** falls as the money supply increases
- **(b)** remains constant
- **(c)** rises as the money supply increases
- **(d)** is equal to 5

a

23. The transmission mechanism through which monetary policy affects aggregate demand is primarily through:

- **(a)** consumption spending
- **(b)** investment spending
- **(c)** government spending
- **(d)** net exports

b

24. In which situation would a contractionary monetary policy help to resolve both the domestic stabilization problem and the balance of trade problem?

- **(a)** inflationary gap and trade surplus
- **(b)** inflationary gap and trade deficit
- **(c)** recessionary gap and trade surplus
- **(d)** recessionary gap and trade deficit

a

■ DISCUSSION QUESTIONS

1. Define monetary policy and state its basic objective.

2. Describe the five main functions of the Bank of Canada.

3. What are the principal assets and liabilities of the Bank of Canada?

4. List the instruments of monetary control available to the Bank of Canada. Which is currently the main one?

5. Using open-market operations, what would the Bank of Canada do to contract the money supply? Or to expand it?

6. Use a simplified balance sheet of the chartered banking system to explain the effect on reserves of switching government deposits between the Bank of Canada and the commercial banks.

7. Why does a change in the bank rate end up affecting interest rates and the money supply?

8. For what two reasons do people wish to hold money? How are these two reasons related to the functions of money?

9. Explain the determinants of the two demands for money. Explain how changes in these determinants will affect the amount of money people want to hold.

10. Explain how the demand for money and the supply of money determine the interest rate. Explain how the money market adjusts if there is a shortage or a surplus of money.

11. Describe the relationship between the changes in the interest rate and changes in the price of existing bonds.

12. Use a set of three graphs to explain what determines: (a) the equilibrium interest rate; (b) planned investment; and (c) the equilibrium GDP. Now employ these graphs to show the effects of a cut in the money supply on equilibrium GDP.

13. What are the strengths and shortcomings of monetary policy?

14. Why is monetary policy more effective in controlling inflation than in reducing unemployment?

15. Explain the net export effect caused by monetary policy.

16. Distinguish between fiscal and monetary policy and explain how each may be used to achieve reasonably full employment and relatively stable prices.

■ ANSWERS

FILL-IN QUESTIONS

1. full-employment, noninflationary; Bank of Canada

2. (a) serve as a bank for the chartered banks (b) supply the economy with paper currency (c) act as fiscal agent for the government (d) supervise the chartered banks (e) regulate the supply of money

3. deposits, taxes, bonds

4. bonds, reserves, money (or deposits)

5. (a) transactions, directly, nominal GDP; (b) asset, inversely, rate of interest

6. supply, demand, investment-demand; demand

7. inverse

8. 10 million, 10 million, 9.5 million; 0, 10 million, 10 million; 200 million

9. (a) +, (b) +, (c) +, (d) -, (e) +, (f) +, (g) +

10. shortage, surplus; down, rise; asset, equal

11. decrease, decrease, increase, decrease; contractionary

12. quickly, more; inflation, recession, velocity, opposite, investment

13. down, decreases; depreciate, increase; reinforces

PROBLEMS AND PROJECTS

1. (a) $650; (b) Chartered banks: $60, 90, 350, 500; Bank of Canada: $310, 60, 100, 150; (c) $650; (d) Chartered banks: $60, 90, 450, 600; Bank of Canada: $310, 60, 100, 150; (e) $750; (f) 10, 100, 10

2. (a) Chartered banks: $20, 55, 250, 325; Bank of Canada: $75, 20, 15, 40; (b) Chartered banks: $20, 50, 250, 320; Bank of Canada: $80, 20, 20, 40

3. (c) 4; (d) 40; (e) surplus of $100 billion; (f) 2; (g) 60; (h) rightward, 60

4. (b) more; 1, 2; 10, 20; more

5. (b) less; 10, 20; less

TRUE-FALSE

1. F	**2.** F	**3.** T	**4.** T	**5.** F	**6.** T
7. F	**8.** T	**9.** T	**10.** T	**11.** F	**12.** F
13. T	**14.** F	**15.** F	**16.** T	**17.** T	**18.** F
19. T	**20.** T	**21.** F	**22.** F	**23.** T	

MULTIPLE-CHOICE

1. (b)	**2.** (a)	**3.** (d)	**4.** (a)	**5.** (d)	**6.** (c)
7. (c)	**8.** (d)	**9.** (b)	**10.** (b)	**11.** (c)	**12.** (a)
13. (b)	**14.** (c)	**15.** (a)	**16.** (b)	**17.** (d)	**18.** (c)
19. (b)	**20.** (c)	**21.** (d)	**22.** (a)	**23.** (b)	**24.** (a)

CHAPTER 16

Long-Run Macroeconomic Adjustments

The aggregate expenditures models of Chapters 9 and 10 provided an explanation of macroeconomic equilibrium that failed to explain price level fluctuations. The aggregate demand-aggregate supply model of Chapter 11 was an improvement because it could explain rising prices. This chapter examines new perspectives on aggregate supply, and applies the AD-AS model to analyze demand-pull inflation, cost-push inflation, and recession. We examine the relationship between inflation and unemployment, and the role of expectations in that relationship. Finally, we consider the ideas of supply-side economics.

In a situation of demand-pull inflation the economy can temporarily exceed its potential real GDP, but labour market adjustments will eventually restore real wages and return the economy to its long-run equilibrium at potential GDP. When the economy experiences cost-push inflation the real output drops below the potential level, causing policymakers to face a dilemma. They can wait for market forces to close the recessionary gap, but this will take a very long time. The alternative is to use expansionary fiscal or monetary policy, but this approach will push prices yet higher, running the risk of setting off an inflationary spiral of nominal wage increases followed by price increases. In a recession stemming from falling demand, output drops below potential but will eventually recover when prices and nominal wages fall far enough. Here the key question is how long the process will take.

In the 1960s economists accepted the Phillips Curve model which showed a trade-off between inflation and unemployment that fit the evidence from many countries during the 1950s and 1960s. Using the AD-AS model, when AD shifts up against a fixed AS curve the level of output (and employment) will increase, while prices will rise. Thus infla-

tion has risen and unemployment has fallen. Policymakers came to think that they could choose any inflation and unemployment combination on the Phillips Curve. For example, a lower rate of unemployment could be achieved, but only if the country was willing to tolerate the corresponding higher rate of inflation. By the 1970s and early 1980s the data no longer supported a stable Phillips Curve. Many economies, including Canada, had stagflation (simultaneously rising inflation rate and unemployment rate). The inflation during this period began as cost-push inflation. Since macroeconomic models of the time ignored the supply side, economists had work to do.

The explanation most favourable to the Phillips Curve hypothesis was that cost-push inflation had shifted the AS curve to the left, and thus shifted the Phillips Curve outward, to combinations of higher unemployment and inflation. Under this interpretation there was still a Phillips Curve showing a trade-off, but it had shifted. A competing explanation was the natural-rate hypothesis which rejected the idea of a stable inflation-unemployment trade-off, claiming instead that the economy tends towards a natural rate of unemployment (at the full-employment GDP), and that this natural rate could exist at any level of inflation. There are two versions of that theory: one based on adaptive expectations, and the other based on rational expectations. Both draw the conclusion that when market participants react to their expectations about inflation, there is no lasting Phillips Curve trade-off. This theory casts doubt on whether governments should try to use stabilization policies.

These questions about the Phillips Curve have led economists to build the supply side into their models. A group known as supply-side economists recommend policies to deal with stagflation by directly affecting the supply side. They blame high tax rates and government regulations for slumping productivity and sluggish economic growth. Their main policy advice is to cut marginal tax rates on personal and corporate incomes in order to increase incentives to work, save and invest. According to the Laffer Curve theory, lower tax rates would stimulate economic activity, and will therefore generate at least as much total tax revenue. This is a logical possibility, but it need not be the case.

■ **CHECKLIST**

When you have studied this chapter, you should be able to:

□ Apply the AD-AS model to analyze demand-pull inflation, and how the economy adjusts from this problem in the long run.

□ Apply the AD-AS model to analyze cost-push inflation, and how the economy adjusts from this problem in the long run.

□ Explain the policy dilemma created by cost-push inflation.

□ Apply the AD-AS model to analyze recession due to falling AD, and how the economy adjusts from this problem in the long run.

□ Draw a traditional Phillips Curve and use the AD-AS model to develop a justification for the trade-off between inflation and unemployment.

□ Explain the policy choice implied by the traditional Phillips Curve.

□ Describe the supply-side shocks that hit Canada in the 1970s and early 1980s, and use the AD-AS model to explain why these shocks led to stagflation.

□ Describe the supply-side shocks of 1983-1988, and use the AD-AS model to show how they ended stagflation.

□ Describe the changes to Canada's Phillips Curve from the 1960s to the present using the AD-AS model.

□ Explain the natural-rate hypothesis.

□ Explain what adaptive expectations are, and what rational expectations are.

□ Use the adaptive expectations model to explain the process of inflation and disinflation in the economy.

□ Compare and contrast how adaptive expectations and rational expectations theorists view the Phillips Curve.

□ Explain what supply-side economists consider to be the causes of stagflation and the policies that they recommend.

□ Explain the hypothesized relationship between tax rates and tax revenues known as the Laffer curve.

□ State three criticisms of the Laffer curve and supply-side economics.

■ **CHAPTER OUTLINE**

1. Demand-pull inflation occurs when, beginning from a full-employment equilibrium, AD increases.

(a) The short-run impact is an expansion in output and an increase in the price level. Because nominal wages are fixed over this period, real wages drop.

(b) The long-run equilibrium is achieved once real wages are restored. When workers' contracts expire, and when they realize that their real wages have fallen, workers demand and get higher nominal wages. This shifts the AS curve leftward until the inflationary gap is closed and the economy is back at full-employment equilibrium.

(c) In summary, demand-pull inflation produces a lasting price level increase and a temporary real output increase.

2. Cost-push inflation occurs when, beginning from a full-employment equilibrium, per-unit production costs rise, and AS decreases.

(a) The short-run impact is a drop in output and an increase in the price level.

(b) If no government stabilization policy is used, input prices will eventually fall, shifting the AS back to the right until a long-run equilibrium is restored at full-employment output. This will be a very slow process, leaving the economy in a prolonged recession.

(c) If government uses an expansionary monetary or fiscal policy, the AD curve could be increased to meet the new AS curve at full-employment. However, this would drive prices even higher, and might ignite an inflationary spiral of further increases in wages and prices.

3. A recession that stems from falling expenditures will decrease the AD curve.

(a) The short-run impact is a drop in output and a decrease in the price level. Because nominal wages are fixed, real wages rise, leading to employment losses.

(b) Eventually nominal wages will fall to restore the previous real wage, employment and output levels. This process will not be complete before the economy has endured a lengthy recession.

4. If AS is upsloping, the greater the rate of increase in AD the greater is the rate of increase in the price level and in real output, and the lower is the rate of unemployment (and vice versa).

(a)   This inverse relationship between the inflation rate and the unemployment rate is called the Phillips Curve.

(b)   According to the Phillips Curve theory, fiscal and monetary policy can be used to manage AD and to affect unemployment and the rate of inflation, but there is a serious policy dilemma: full employment with price stability is impossible, so the nation must choose one of the combinations of inflation and unemployment that lies on the Phillips Curve.

(c)   Data from the late 1950s and 1960s showed this inverse relationship between unemployment and inflation rates for many countries, including Canada.

5. Events of the 1970s and 1980s called into question the stability of the Phillips Curve. During this time Canada experienced higher rates of inflation **and** unemployment: a problem that came to be called "stagflation." Either there is no dependable relationship between the inflation and unemployment rates, or the Phillips Curve had shifted to the right. This latter result could be explained by a leftward shift of the AS curve.

(a)   During these years a series of adverse supply shocks (especially a quadrupling of oil prices) decreased AS, and increased both inflation and unemployment in Canada. This experience suggests that the Phillips Curve is not a stable relationship and cannot be used as the basis for economic policy.

(b)   Stagflation ended in the 1983-88 period because of various factors. Unemployment and inflation both decreased, rather than moving in opposite directions as predicted by the Phillips Curve theory.

(c)   Some economists who use the AD-AS model believe that a trade-off between unemployment and inflation does exist. The data problems were explained by the supply shocks that shifted the Phillips Curve rightward between 1971 and 1982, and other events that shifted it leftward between 1983 and 1988.

6. The natural-rate hypothesis questions the existence of the Phillips Curve trade-off and views the economy as stable in the long run at the natural rate of unemployment. There are two variants to this hypothesis: the adaptive expectations theory and the rational expectations theory.

7. The adaptive expectations theory assumes people form their expectations of future inflation on the basis of previous and present inflation rates and only gradually change their expectations as their experience changes.

(a)   An increase in AD created by government policy may temporarily reduce unemployment as the price level increases and profits expand; but the additional employment and output is temporary.

(b)   The rising prices are gradually factored into inflation expectations and nominal wage demands. Once nominal wages are rising at the same rate as prices, unemployment returns to its natural rate.

(c)   Now back at the original unemployment level, the economy now has a higher actual and expected rate of inflation, so the short-run Phillips Curve has shifted upward.

(d)   The process is repeated if government tries again to reduce unemployment, and the inflation rate accelerates as the short-run Phillips Curve shifts upward. Expansionary policies generate accelerating inflation rather than lower unemployment.

(e)   In the long run, the Phillips Curve is stable only as a vertical line at the natural rate of unemployment. There is no trade-off between unemployment and inflation.

8. Rational expectations theory assumes that workers understand how government policies will affect the economy, so they anticipate the impacts. Therefore, they can anticipate inflation and will demand nominal wage increases to coincide with inflation in order to avoid real wage cuts.

(a)   Inflation produces no increases in output and employment, either in the short run or in the long run.

(b)   The Phillips Curve is vertical in the short run and the long run, so expansionary government policies can produce more inflation but will not budge the economy's unemployment rate, so there is no trade-off.

(c)   Most economists do not accept this extreme model, believing instead that there is at least a temporary trade-off between inflation and unemployment, but many accept the idea of a vertical long-run Phillips Curve.

9. Supply-side economists argue that mainstream models overemphasize the AD side and neglect the AS side.

(a) They argue that the tax-transfer system has negatively affected incentives to work, save, invest, innovate, and take entrepreneurial risks. They call for lower marginal tax rates and reduced social programs (such as employment insurance and welfare programs).

(b) The Laffer Curve suggests that lower tax rates are compatible with constant or even larger tax revenues. If tax rates are cut, enough taxable economic activity would be generated to increase the total tax revenue. Reduced tax evasion and transfer payments would also result.

(c) Supply-siders argue for less regulation of businesses in order to improve productivity and shift the long-run AS curve to the right.

10. Critics of supply-side economics and the Laffer Curve suggest that the policy of tax cuts will not work because:

(a) The effects on incentives are small or uncertain.

(b) The policy will cause AD to increase, and inflation to be reinforced.

(c) Tax revenues will only increase if the economy is on the right section of the Laffer Curve, and there is no evidence that it is.

■ TERMS AND CONCEPTS

adaptive expectations theory	**natural-rate hypothesis**
aggregate supply shocks	**Phillips Curve**
	rational expectations theory
disinflation	**stagflation**
Laffer Curve	**supply-side economics**

■ HINTS AND TIPS

1. This chapter provides one of the best examples of how real world experience has caused changes in the prevailing economic theories. Actual experience with inflation and unemployment during the period from the late 1960s through the early 1980s had great influence on theories of the Phillips Curve. At the beginning of the period, the orthodox position was one of a stable unemployment-inflation trade-off, whereas by the end of the period, many economists believed that there is no stable or long-run trade-off.

2. Several different theories of the Phillips Curve are given in this chapter. Be sure that you can summarize the arguments that the Phillips Curve trade-off is stable, the arguments that the Phillips Curve poses a trade-off in the short-run only, and the arguments that the Phillips Curve is vertical even in the short run and that there is no trade-off.

■ FILL-IN QUESTIONS

1. Demand-pull inflation is initiated by a shift to the (right, left) _____ of the (AD, AS) _____ curve. This will (decrease, increase) _____ the price level and temporarily _____ real output. As a consequence, the (short-run, long-run) _____ aggregate supply curve will shift left because of a rise in (real, nominal) _____ wages, producing a (lower, higher) _____ price level at the original level of real output. Eventually equilibrium is restored at the _____ level of output.

2. Cost-push inflation starts with a shift to the (right, left) _____ of the (AD, AS) _____ curve. Thus the price level will (increase, decrease) _____ and real output will temporarily _____. If government takes no actions to counter the cost-push inflation, the resulting recession will _____ nominal wages, and shift the _____ curve back to its original position. Yet, if the government tries to counter the cost-push inflation and recession with an expansionary monetary or fiscal policy, the price level will move (back down, even higher) _____.

3. If the AS curve is upward sloping (and stable), the greater the increase in AD, the (greater, smaller) _____ will be the increase in the price level, the _____ will be the increase in real output, and the _____ will be the unemployment rate; and there will be a(n) (direct, inverse) _____ relationship between the inflation rate and the unemployment rate. This relationship is known as the _____ Curve.

4. According to the Phillips Curve theory, the policy dilemma faced by government policy-makers is that:

(a) to have full employment we must also have _____, and to have stable prices we must tolerate _____;

(b) to reduce the unemployment rate, the rate of inflation must (increase, decrease) _____; and to reduce the rate of inflation the unemployment rate must _____.

5. In the 1970s and early 1980s the economy experienced several (adverse, favourable) _____ supply shocks. Five factors that shifted AS were:

(a) _____

(b) _____

(c) _____

(d) _____

(e) _____

6. According to those who defended the original Phillips Curve theory of a trade-off between inflation and unemployment, the supply shocks in the 1970s and early 1980s caused a (shift of, movement along) _____ the Phillips Curve.

7. List four factors that contributed to stagflation's demise during the 1983-88 period:

(a) _____

(b) _____

(c) _____

(d) _____

8. The expectation of inflation by workers and employers leads to (higher, lower) _____ nominal wage rates and in turn to a (rise, fall) _____ in per-unit production costs, to a(n) (increase, decrease) _____ in AS, to a (higher, lower) _____ price level, and to a _____ rate of unemployment in the economy.

9. Economists continue to debate the Phillips Curve. Some economists conclude that the downsloping Phillips Curve does not exist in the long run, and they subscribe to the _____ hypothesis, for which there are two variants: _____ and _____ expectations.

10. The theory of adaptive expectations suggests that:

(a) People form their expectations of _____ based on experience and (immediately, gradually) _____ change expectations over time.

(b) The (short-run, long-run) _____ Phillips Curve may be downsloping, but the _____ Phillips Curve is vertical at the _____ level of output;

(c) Attempts by government to reduce the unemployment rate (will be, will not be) _____ successful in the short run, but (will be, will not be) _____ successful in the long run.

11. The rational expectations theory suggests that:

(a) attempts by government to reduce the unemployment rate lead workers to anticipate perfectly the amount of _____ this will cause, and to keep their (real, nominal) _____ wages constant to obtain a(n) (increase, decrease) _____ in their _____ wages; and

(b) this brings about (a rise, a fall, no change) _____ in the price level and _____ in the unemployment rate.

12. Supply-side economists believe that inflation has increased and growth slowed down because governments have: (1) set excessively high marginal tax rates that reduce _____ to work, save, invest, and take risks; (2) created too many and overly generous _____ payment programs; and (3) decreased productivity because of increased _____ of industry. These economists argue that the main remedy for stagflation is a substantial (increase, decrease) _____ in taxes, transfers and regulation.

13. The Laffer curve depicts the relationship between tax rates and tax _____. In theory, as the tax rates increase from 0%, tax revenues will (increase, decrease) _____ to some maximum level, after which tax revenues will _____ as the tax rates increase.

■ **PROBLEMS AND PROJECTS**

1. Following is a traditional Phillips Curve.

(a) At full employment (an 8% unemployment rate), the price level would rise by _____ % each year.

(b) If the price level were stable (increasing by 0% a year), the unemployment rate would be _____%.

(c) Which of the combinations along the Phillips Curve would you choose for the economy? Why would you select this combination?

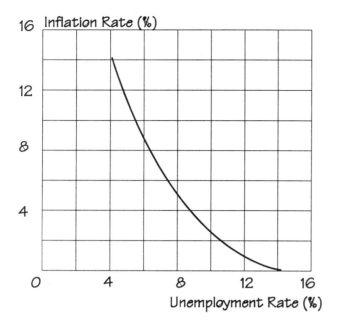

Inflation Rate (%)

Unemployment Rate (%)

2. The next graph is an adaptive expectations model of the short-and long-run Phillips Curve.

(a) The economy is initially at point X_1, with nominal wages currently being set on the expectation that a 3% rate of inflation will continue.

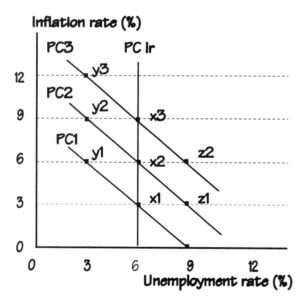

Inflation rate (%)

Unemployment rate (%)

(1) If government invokes expansionary monetary or fiscal policy to reduce unemployment from 6% to 3%, then the actual rate of inflation will move to _____%. The higher product prices will lift profits of firms and they will hire more workers; thus the economy will temporarily move to point _____.

(2) If workers now demand and receive higher wages to compensate for the loss of purchasing power from higher than expected inflation, then business profits will fall from previous levels and firms will reduce employment. Therefore, employment will move from point _____ to point _____ on the graph. The short-run Phillips Curve has shifted from _____ to _____ on the graph.

(3) If the government again tries to stimulate AD with monetary or fiscal policy to reduce the unemployment rate from 6% to 3%, then prices will rise before nominal wages, and output and employment will increase, so there will be a move from point _____ to point _____ on the graph.

(4) But when workers get nominal wage increases, profits fall, and unemployment moves from point _____ at _____% to point _____ at _____ %. The short-run Phillips Curve has now shifted from _____ to _____ on the graph.

(5) The long-run Phillips Curve is the line _____.

(b) Suppose this time the economy begins at point X_3, with an expected and actual rate of inflation of 9% and an unemployment rate of 6%.

(1) If AD decreases because of a recession and if the actual rate of inflation should fall to 6%, well below the expected rate of 9%, then business profits will fall and the unemployment rate will increase to 9% as shown by the movement from point X_3 to point _____

(2) If firms and workers adjust their expectation to the 6% rate of inflation, then nominal wages will fall, profits will rise, and the economy will move from point _____ to point _____. The short-run Phillips Curve has shifted from _____ to _____.

(3) If this process is repeated, the long-run Phillips Curve will be traced as line _____.

3. Following is a graph of the AD-AS model. Assume that the economy is initially in equilibrium at AD_1 and AS_1. The price level will be _____ and the real domestic output will be _____.

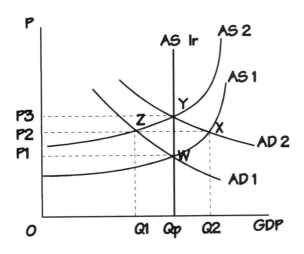

(a) If there is demand-pull inflation, then:

(1) in the short run, the new equilibrium is at point _____, with the price level at _____ and real output at _____;

(2) in the long run, nominal wages will rise so the aggregate supply curve will shift from _____ to _____. The equilibrium will be at point _____ with the price level at _____ and real output at _____; and so the increase in aggregate demand has only moved the economy along its _____ curve.

(b) Now assume that the economy is initially in equilibrium at point W, where AD_1 and AS_1 intersect. If there is cost-push inflation, then:

(1) in the short run, the new equilibrium is at point _____, with the price level at _____ and real output at _____.

(2) if the government tries to counter the cost-push inflation with expansionary monetary and fiscal policy, then AD shifts from _____ to _____, with the price level becoming _____ and real output _____. But this policy has a trap because the price level has shifted from _____ to _____ and the new level of inflation might shift _____ leftward.

(3) if government does not counter the cost-push inflation, the price level will eventually move to _____ and real output to _____ as the recession reduces nominal wages and shifts the AS curve from _____ to _____.

4. The following table shows the level of real output the economy would achieve at various different levels for the marginal tax rate on household and business incomes.

Tax Rate	Level of GDP ($ billions)	Tax Revenue ($ billions)
20%	4,500	_____
30%	4,000	_____
40%	3,500	_____
50%	3,100	_____
60%	2,500	_____
70%	2,000	_____

(a) Fill in the blank column for tax revenues at each tax rate.

(b) The data in this example supports the supply-siders' policy advice only for tax rates above _____%. At any tax rates lower than this, tax revenue will (fall, rise) _____ if the tax rate is cut.

■ TRUE-FALSE

Circle T if the statement is true, F if it is false.

1. The aggregate expenditures model provided a fairly satisfactory explanation of the macroeconomic behaviour of the Canadian economy between 1930 and 1970, but could not explain the stagflation of the 1970s and early 1980s. **T F**

2. When aggregate supply is constant, higher rates of inflation are accompanied by higher rates of unemployment. **T F**

3. According to the conventional Phillips Curve, the rate of inflation increases as the level of unemployment decreases. **T F**

4. Stagflation refers to a situation in which both the price level and the unemployment rate are falling. **T F**

5. The stagflation of the 1970s and early 1980s was due to a series of demand shocks. **T F**

6. Both inflationary expectations and increasing labour productivity shift the aggregate supply curve leftward and cause stagflation. **T F**

7. Expectations of inflation induce workers to demand a higher nominal wage and their employers to pay them higher nominal wages. **T F**

8. When the nominal wage rate increases at a rate greater than the rate at which the productivity of labour increases, unit labour costs will rise. **T F**

9. A change in the level of expected inflation will cause the economy to move to a different point on the same short-run Phillips Curve. **T F**

10. The natural-rate hypothesis suggests that there is a natural rate of inflation for the economy. **T F**

11. According to the natural-rate hypothesis, the economy's natural rate of unemployment can be achieved only if the rate of unemployment is zero. **T F**

12. The theory of adaptive expectations indicates that there may be a short-run trade-off between inflation and unemployment, but no long-run trade-off. **T F**

13. From the adaptive expectations perspective, when the actual rate of inflation is higher than expected, the unemployment rate will rise. **T F**

14. According to rational expectations theory, economic agents understand how government policies affect the economy and anticipate these impacts in their decision making. **T F**

15. The long-run Phillips Curve is, according to rational expectations theory, upsloping. **T F**

16. The natural-rate hypothesis concludes that, in the long run, demand-management policies cannot influence the price level but can influence the level of real output and employment. **T F**

17. The short-run AS curve is upward sloping because nominal wages are considered variable and rise as prices rise. **T F**

18. The long-run supply curve is vertical at that level of output corresponding to the natural rate of unemployment. **T F**

19. Demand-pull inflation will increase the price level and real output in the short run; but, in the long run, only the price level will increase. **T F**

20. An inflationary spiral is likely to result from the use of stabilization policies to maintain full employment when the economy is experiencing cost-push inflation. **T F**

21. Wage and price controls have been used as anti-inflation policies in many different countries and centuries. **T F**

■   **MULTIPLE-CHOICE**

Circle the letter that corresponds to the best answer.

1. As long as AS remains constant and the economy operates along the upward sloping portion of AS, the greater the increase in AD:
 (a)   the greater is the increase in the price level
 (b)   the greater is the increase in the unemployment rate
 (c)   the smaller is the increase in real output
 (d)   the smaller is the increase in employment

2. The conventional Phillips Curve:
 (a)   shows the inverse relation between the rate of increase in the price level and the unemployment rate
 (b)   indicates that it is possible for the economy to achieve full employment and stable prices
 (c)   indicates that prices do not rise until full employment has been achieved
 (d)   slopes upward from left to right

3. The stabilization policy dilemma illustrated by a Phillips Curve is the mutual inconsistency of:
 (a)   more employment and price stability
 (b)   a higher unemployment rate and price stability
 (c)   inflation and more employment
 (d)   inflation and a lower unemployment rate

4. Stagflation is characterized by:
 (a)   rising inflation and rising government deficits
 (b)   rising unemployment and rising government deficits
 (c)   rising taxes and rising government deficits
 (d)   rising inflation and rising unemployment

5. Which of the following was a supply-side shock that affected Canada during the 1970s and early 1980s?
 (a)   the imposition of wage and price controls
 (b)   the appreciation of the dollar
 (c)   the fall in the price charged by OPEC nations for oil
 (d)   worldwide agricultural shortfalls

6. If productivity of labour rises by 2% and nominal wage rates rise 5%, the percentage change in unit labour costs is:
 (a)   1%
 (b)   3%

(c) 7%
(d) 10%

7. Which of the following was a factor contributing to the demise of stagflation during the 1983-1988 period?
(a) a lessening of foreign competition
(b) a strengthening of the monopoly power of OPEC
(c) a recession brought on by a tight monetary policy
(d) an increase in regulation of transportation industries

8. According to the AD-AS supply model, the collapse of the traditional inflation rate-unemployment rate trade-off and the likely shift in the Phillips Curve during the later 1980s was the consequence of a:
(a) rightward shift in AD
(b) rightward shift in AS
(c) leftward shift in AD
(d) leftward shift in AS

9. The natural-rate hypothesis suggests that the economy is stable only in the:
(a) short run at the natural rate of unemployment
(b) short run at the natural rate of inflation
(c) long run at the natural rate of unemployment
(d) long run at the natural rate of inflation

10. According to the natural-rate hypothesis:
(a) the inflation rate is 0 at the natural rate of unemployment
(b) any rate of inflation is compatible with the natural rate of unemployment
(c) a stable Phillips Curve does exist, which indicates the long-run trade-off between inflation and unemployment
(d) the long-run Phillips Curve is horizontal

11. The theory of adaptive expectations suggests that if increases in nominal wages lag behind increases in the prices, and government attempts to reduce unemployment by using fiscal policies, then employment:
(a) and the price level increase in the long run
(b) remains constant and the price level increases in the short run
(c) increases and the price level remains constant in the short run
(d) remains constant and the price level increases in the long run

12. Rational expectations theorists contend that when government attempts to reduce unemployment by using monetary or fiscal policies, unemployment decreases:
(a) temporarily and the price level rises
(b) permanently and the price level rises
(c) both temporarily and permanently and the price level rises
(d) neither temporarily nor permanently and the price level rises

13. In the view of natural-rate theorists, the long-run Phillips Curve is:
(a) horizontal
(b) vertical
(c) upsloping
(d) downsloping

14. Disinflation, or reductions in the rate of inflation, can be explained based on the natural-rate conclusion that when the:
(a) actual rate of inflation is lower than the expected rate, the unemployment rate will rise to bring the expected and actual rates into balance
(b) expected rate of inflation is lower than the actual rate, the unemployment rate will rise to bring the expected and actual rates into balance
(c) actual rate of inflation is higher than the expected rate, the unemployment rate will fall to bring the expected and actual rates into balance
(d) expected rate of inflation is higher than the actual rate, the unemployment rate will fall to bring the expected and actual rates into balance

15. According to the rational expectations theory, fully anticipated changes in the price level do not change:
(a) the level of real output
(b) the level of prices
(c) the inflexibility of wages and prices
(d) the effectiveness of stabilization policy

16. In the short run, demand-pull inflation:
(a) is caused by a downward shift in the Phillips Curve
(b) is the result of a decrease in AD
(c) produces an increase in real output
(d) is caused by rising wage rates

17. In the long run, demand-pull inflation will:
(a) decrease the unemployment rate
(b) decrease the level of nominal wages
(c) increase the level of prices
(d) increase real national output

18. A likely result of treating cost-push inflation by stimulating AD with monetary and fiscal policies is:
  (a)   an inflationary spiral
  (b)   a price level surprise
  (c)   disinflation
  (d)   a recession

19. An economist who argues that the long-run Phillips Curve is vertical is likely a follower of which theory?
  (a)   conventional AD-AS model
  (b)   adaptive expectations
  (c)   rational expectations
  (d)   adaptive or rational expectations

20. From the viewpoint of supply-side economists, stagflation is the result of:
  (a)   excessive taxation
  (b)   government deregulation
  (c)   a shifting Phillips Curve
  (d)   unanticipated inflation

21. Supply-side economists believe that our tax-transfer system reduces:
  (a)   unemployment, but increases inflation
  (b)   incentives to work, save, and invest
  (c)   transfer payments to the poor and homeless
  (d)   interest rates

22. The Laffer Curve shows the relationship between:
  (a)   the rate of inflation and the rate of unemployment
  (b)   the rate of inflation and the rate of employment
  (c)   the tax rate and the budget deficit
  (d)   the tax rate and tax revenue

23. Which of the following is a criticism of the argument for tax cuts based on the Laffer Curve?
  (a)   tax cuts have large effects on incentives to work, save and invest
  (b)   tax cuts reinforce inflation
  (c)   tax cuts will generate more tax revenue
  (d)   none of the above

24. Which of the following is **not** one of the difficulties with wage and price controls?
  (a)   controls address the symptoms, not the causes
  (b)   controls are difficult and costly to enforce
  (c)   controls prevent black market transactions
  (d)   controls lead to allocative inefficiency

■ **DISCUSSION QUESTIONS**

1. Describe the process of demand-pull inflation in the short run and in the long run. How does demand-pull inflation influence the AS curve?

2. Define cost-push inflation and describe how it comes about. How does the economy adjust to cost-push inflation in the short run? In the long run? What dilemma does cost-push inflation pose for macroeconomic policy-makers?

3. How does the economy recover in the long-run from a recession if: (a) the government uses no expansionary policy, and (b) the government uses expansionary policy when the recession is diagnosed?

4. What is a Phillips Curve? Explain how a Phillips Curve with a negative slope may be derived by holding AS constant and increasing AD.

5. What is the stabilization policy dilemma illustrated by the traditional Phillips Curve? Does the manipulation of AD through monetary and fiscal policy shift the Phillips Curve or cause a movement along the Phillips Curve?

6. Over what period(s) of Canada's history was our experience consistent with the conventional Phillips Curve explanation?

7. What supply-side shocks brought stagflation to the Canadian economy during the 1970s and early 1980s? How did these shocks affect aggregate supply and the Phillips Curve? What factors contributed to stagflation's demise during the 1983-88 period?

8. What are the two different models of how expectations are formed, and what are the assumptions in each? In each case, how do expectations of inflation affect aggregate supply and the Phillips Curve? In which case does expansionary policy affect real output? Is the effect temporary or permanent?

9. Explain the natural-rate hypothesis and what it implies for the long-run Phillips Curve.

10. Supply-side economists believe that there are significant tax and transfer payment disincentives in the economy. What are they, and what policies are suggested?

11. Draw a Laffer Curve. Explain the economic implications of the curve according to supply-side economists. Outline three criticisms of the ideas expressed by the Laffer Curve.

■ ANSWERS

FILL-IN QUESTIONS

1. right, AD; increase, increase; short-run, nominal, higher, full-employment

2. left, AS; increase, decrease; decrease, AS; even higher

3. greater, greater, smaller, inverse; Phillips

4. (a) inflation, unemployment; (b) increase, increase

5. adverse; (a) dramatic rise in oil prices (OPEC); (b) agricultural shortfalls around the world (higher agricultural prices); (c) devaluation of the dollar; (d) fall in the rate of growth of labour productivity; (e) inflationary expectations

6. shift of

7. (a) recession of 1981-82 with tight monetary policy; (b) intensive foreign competition suppressed some wages and prices; (c) deregulation in some industries depressed wages; (d) a decline in OPEC's monopoly power

8. higher, rise, decrease, higher, higher

9. natural-rate, adaptive, rational

10. (a) inflation, gradually; (b) short-run, long-run, full-employment (potential); (c) will be, will not be

11. (a) inflation, real, increase, nominal; (b) a rise, no change

12. incentives, transfer, regulation, decrease

13. revenues; increase, decrease

PROBLEMS AND PROJECTS

1. (a) 5 (b) 14 (c) (it's your choice)

2. (a) (1) 6, Y_1 (2) Y_1, X_2; PC_1, PC_2, (3) X_2, Y_2 (4) Y_2, 3, X_3, 6, PC_2, PC_3 (5) PC_{lr}; (b) (1) Z_2 (2) Z_2, X_2, PC_3, PC_2, (3) PC_{lr}

3. P_1, Q_p (a) (1) X, P_2, Q_2 (2) AS_1, AS_2; Y, P_3, Q_p, AS_{lr}; (b) (1) Z, P_2, Q_1 (2) AD_1, AD_2, P_3, Q_p; P_2, P_3, AS (3) P_1, Q_p, AS_2, AS_1

4. (a) 900, 1200, 1400, 1550, 1500, 1400; (b) 50; fall

TRUE-FALSE

1.T	2. F	3. T	4. F	5. F	6. F
7. T	8. T	9. F	10. F	11. F	12. T
13. F	14. T	15. F	16. F	17. F	18. T
19. T	20. T	21. T			

MULTIPLE-CHOICE

1. (a)	2. (a)	3. (a)	4. (d)	5. (d)	6. (b)
7. (c)	8. (d)	9. (c)	10. (b)	11. (d)	12. (d)
13. (b)	14. (a)	15. (a)	16. (c)	17. (c)	18. (a)
19. (d)	20. (a)	21. (b)	22. (d)	23. (b)	24. (c)

CHAPTER 17

Disputes in Macro Theory and Policy

A good majority of economists accept most of the macroeconomic theories developed in the previous chapters, but some important points are in dispute. In fact, throughout the history of economics there have always been ongoing battles over points of theory and policy. This chapter deals mainly with current disputes, but opens with a contrast between the views of classical economists and the views of Keynes. Some of the issues on which they disagreed are still grounds over which today's economists disagree.

Classical economists of the 19th century believed in a vertical AS curve, a stable AD curve, and highly flexible wages and prices. These conditions meant that equilibrium would always occur at full-employment output. Developing his theories during the Great Depression, Keynes disputed each of these assumptions, and concluded that the economy was unstable, and incapable of pulling itself back to full-employment. Today there is still no consensus on how unstable the economy is, or on what the main sources of instability are. The mainstream view, which is Keynesian-based, holds that instability comes from fluctuations in AD, particularly investment, and from adverse AS shocks. Monetarists, adopting more classically-based views, hold that market forces are stabilizing, and that our economy would be quite stable except for interventions by government — with erratic and inappropriate monetary policy being the biggest culprit. Other modern schools of thought include the real-business-cycle view which blames instability mainly on real supply side factors like irregular changes in technology, and in resource supplies. Yet other economists stress coordination failures at the aggregate level.

Whether or not the economy is self-correcting is enormously important and vigorously debated. Followers of monetarism and rational expectations take the "new classical" view that if the economy moves away from full-employment output, market forces pull it back. They do not quite agree on the usual speed of such adjustments, but they are more optimistic than Keynesians. The nature of how expectations are formed determines within these models whether AD or AS disturbances will disturb the economy away from full-employment output for a brief time, or not at all. Mainstream economists reject the idea of such rapid and efficient adjustment. They point to downward inflexibility of wages, based on various institutional features of labour markets.

Dealing squarely with policy, there is argument over whether government should adhere to policy rules (that would put economic policies on "automatic pilot") or exercise discretionary policies as called for by individual situations. Monetarists argue for a monetary rule to prevent monetary disturbances, and rational expectations economists support such a rule because they believe discretionary policy simply has no real effects. Both groups also oppose discretionary fiscal policy. Mainstream economists, with more Keynesian views, defend discretionary monetary and fiscal policies. Both sides can point to episodes in recent Canadian experience that support their perspective.

Economic theory has been changed profoundly by ideas from each of these schools of thought. Macroeconomic theory is a continually evolving body of thought. The evolution is shaped by the theoretical debates and real world economic events.

■ CHECKLIST

When you have studied this chapter, you should be able to:

□ Compare and contrast the classical and Keynesian views of AD and AS, and the stability of the economy.

□ Compare and contrast the mainstream and monetarist views on the sources of economic instability.

□ Write the equation of exchange, and define each of the four terms in the equation.

□ Explain what velocity is, and what importance monetarists place on the stability of velocity.

□ Explain why monetarists believe nominal GDP is directly and predictably linked to the money supply.

□ Explain the real-business-cycle theory.

□ Explain how business cycles can stem from coordination failures.

□ Explain the new classical school's reasoning for why the economy is self-correcting.

□ Using rational expectations theory, show how the effect of a price-level change depends on whether or not it is anticipated.

□ Explain the mainstream view of why the economy is not self-correcting.

□ Present arguments for and against the use of macroeconomic policy rules.

□ Present arguments for and against the use of discretionary macroeconomic policies.

□ Give examples of episodes when discretionary policy was successful in Canada.

■ **CHAPTER OUTLINE**

1. Classical and Keynesian economics can be compared by examining their views of the AD, AS and the stability of the economy.

   (a)   In the classical model the AS curve is vertical at the economy's full-employment output; a drop in AD will lower the price level, but not the real output level. This result depends on high flexibility of wages and prices.

   (b)   In the Keynesian model the AS curve is horizontal at the current price level; a drop in AD will lower real output, but not the price level. This result depends on downward rigidity of wages and prices.

   (c)   In both models the AD curve is downsloping. The classical view is that AD is quite stable if the money supply is kept stable, whereas the Keynesian view is that AD fluctuates unpredictably due to instability in expenditure components such as investment and export demand.

   (d)   Believing that the market economy would automatically ensure a full-employment level of

output, classical economists saw no need for government interference with stabilization policies; whereas Keynes recommended an active stabilization role for fiscal policy, especially to close recessionary gaps.

2. There are different schools of thought concerning what causes macroeconomic instability.

   (a)   The mainstream view, heavily influenced by Keynesian ideas, is that investment volatility and adverse AS shocks create instability. The economy is considered to be inherently unstable, and requiring government intervention.

   (b)   Monetarism is a modern form of classical economics that: (1) focuses on the money supply, (2) holds that markets are highly competitive, and (3) says that competition makes the economy highly stable.

3. Both mainstream and monetarist models rely on a central equation.

   (a)   In the mainstream view the central equation is: $C_a + I_g + G + X_n = \text{GDP}$

   (b)   In the monetarist model the basic equation is the equation of exchange: $MV = PQ$

   (c)   Because MV (total spending) $= C_a + I_g + G + X_n$, and $PQ = \text{GDP}$, the two equations are different ways of stating the same relationship.

   (d)   Monetarists, believing that velocity (V) is stable, argue that though a change in M may affect Q in the short run, only P will be affected in the long run. They believe inappropriate monetary policy is the primary source of macroeconomic instability; particularly inflation.

4. The real-business-cycle view of instability is that business cycles are caused by real factors shifting the long-run aggregate supply. Changes in technology or resource availability will shift the AS_{LR}. As output changes, so does the demand for money, which is accommodated by a change in the money supply. Ultimately, AD shifts as much as AS_{LR}, so the end results are on real output, not on prices.

5. Some economists characterize macroeconomic instability as a consequence of coordination failures. For example, a recession can occur simply because many individuals anticipate a recession and behave accordingly. Business cycles can become self-fulfilling prophecies.

6. Monetarists and rational expectations economists take the new classical view that if the economy moves away from full employment, market forces quickly move it back to full employment.

(a)   The speed of this adjustment depends on how expectations are formed. Monetarists tend to favour the adaptive expectations theory, which predicts a gradual adjustment. Other new classical economists who favour the rational expectations theory (RET), predict that when price-level changes are fully anticipated the adjustment back to full-employment output will be very quick, or even instantaneous.

(b)   RET is based on two assumptions: that people behave rationally, and in their own interests, in collecting and analyzing information to form expectations about relevant future events; and that all markets are highly competitive and have ultimate flexibility of prices.

(c)   From these assumptions the proponents of the RET conclude that anticipated price-level changes will have no real effects. Unanticipated price-level changes will have temporary real output effects.

7. The mainstream view of self-correction now accepts some of the insights of RET, but continues to stress downward inflexibility of wages and prices that prevent or delay the economy's adjustment back to a full-employment equilibrium. Several reasons are given for downward wage inflexibility.

(a)   Contracts and minimum wage laws may pose legal barriers to cutting wages.

(b)   Some firms pay efficiency wages (above market wages) to elicit greater work effort, reduce job turnover, and reduce supervision costs.

(c)   Many labour markets have both "insiders" and "outsiders," and in recessions the jobs and wages of insiders are protected, so their wages will not fall.

8. The divergence of views on the sources of instability and the economy's ability to self-correct lead to dispute over whether the government should use discretionary fiscal and monetary policies, or it would be better to adhere to policy rules that involve no discretion.

(a)   Monetarists have long argued for a monetary rule whereby the money supply would grow steadily at a predetermined rate in order to prevent erratic money supply changes that cause erratic AD shifts.

(b)   RET economists mainly support the monetary rule because only surprise or random money

supply changes would have any real effect under their theory.

(c)   Monetarists and RET economists also oppose discretionary fiscal policy, albeit for different reasons. The arguments range from concern over the crowding-out effect to the view that anticipated fiscal policy has no real effects.

9. Mainstream economists argue for the use of discretionary monetary and fiscal policies.

(a)   They reject the monetary rule proposal because they do not agree that there is a stable relation in the short run between the quantity of money and the level of GDP. In other words, they reject the monetarist claim that the velocity of money is stable.

(b)   They dispute the significance of the crowding-out effect, so they favour discretionary fiscal policy during deep recessions.

(c)   They are more optimistic than monetarists and new classical economists about the competence of monetary and fiscal policy-makers to typically implement the right sort of policy at the right time.

(d)   Mainstream economists can also point to several major policy successes in Canada during the 1980s and 1990s. Tight monetary policy reduced inflation in the early 1980s, expansionary fiscal policy reduced unemployment in the mid-1980s, and easy money helped to pull us out of recession in the early 1990s.

10. None of these new theories has completely supplanted previous views. However, the ongoing controversies and debates, along with actual macroeconomic experiences, have led to the incorporation of several ideas from monetarism and RET into contemporary mainstream thinking about macroeconomics.

■   **TERMS AND CONCEPTS**

classical economics
coordination failures
efficiency wage
equation of exchange
insider-outsider theory
Keynesianism
monetarism
monetary rule

new classical
   economics
new Keynesian
   economics
price-level surprises
real-business-cycle
   theory
velocity

■ HINTS AND TIPS

1. You may want to review the discussion of the AD-AS model in Chapter 11 and the discussion of money demand, interest rates, and the transmission mechanism in Chapter 15.

2. In the equation of exchange, PQ is the same as nominal GDP because P can be thought of as the average price of goods, and Q is the quantity of goods and services being produced, so PQ is just the dollar value of output.

■ FILL-IN QUESTIONS

1. The classical economists believed that a _____ economic policy was desirable.

2. The AS curve of the classical economists is (horizontal, vertical) _____, and the AS curve of the Keynesian economists is _____ up to the full-employment level of output. For this reason, a decrease in AD will have no effect on the price level and will decrease output in the (classical, Keynesian) _____ model; but a decrease in AD will decrease the price level and have no effect on output and employment in the _____ model.

3. The views of the classical and Keynesian economists also differ on the nature of the AD curve.

(a) In classical theory, the money supply set the basis for AD. If the price level falls and the money supply is constant, the purchasing power of money will (rise, fall) _____ and consumers and business firms will (expand, contract) _____ their expenditures for goods and services; AD will be reasonably stable if the nation's monetary authorities maintain a _____.

(b) From the Keynesian perspective, AD is (stable, unstable) _____, even if there are no changes in the supply of money, in part because business investment tends to be _____. Keynesians then believe that the market system is inherently (stable, unstable) _____.

4. Monetarists argue that capitalism is inherently (stable, unstable) _____ because most of its markets are _____.

5. The basic equation of the monetarists is _____ = _____.

(a) This equation is called the _____.

(b) Indicate below what each of the four letters in this equation represents.

(1) M: _____
(2) V: _____
(3) P: _____
(4) Q: _____

6. The basic equation of the Keynesians is: $C + I_g + G + X_n = GDP$.

(a) $C + I_g + G + X_n$ is _____ and in the equation of exchange is equal to _____.

(b) Nominal GDP is equal to _____ in the equation of exchange.

7. Monetarists argue that:

(a) any increase in M will (increase, decrease) _____ PQ;

(b) in the short run any increase in M may (increase, decrease) _____ both P and Q; but

(c) in the long run any increase in M will (increase, decrease) _____ only (P, Q) _____.

(d) the velocity is (stable, volatile) _____.

8. If the macroeconomy does not reach a mutually beneficial equilibrium because households have not chosen jointly compatible actions, this is an example of _____.

9. In the debate on the use of fiscal policy, the monetarists argue that government borrowing to finance a budget deficit will (raise, lower) _____ the rate of interest and have a _____ effect on investment spending.

10. Monetarists would have the supply of money increase at the same annual rate as the potential rate of growth of _____ and this is a rate from _____ to _____%.

11. The rational expectations theory assumes that:

(a) individuals correctly _____ the effects of any economic event or a change in public policy on the economy and make decisions based on their anticipations to maximize their own _____;

(b) the markets in the economy are (not competitive, purely competitive) _____, and prices in these markets are perfectly (inflexible, flexible) _____; and that as a result,

(c)   an expansionary monetary or fiscal policy will lead the public to expect (inflation, a recession) _____, and they will react in a way that results in (an increase, a decrease, no change) _____ in the real output of the economy and _____ in the price level.

12. Proponents of the RET:
(a)   contend that discretionary monetary and fiscal policies can reinforce economic (cycles, stability) _____ and,
(b)   like the monetarists, favour (policy rules, discretionary policy) _____.

■   **PROBLEMS AND PROJECTS**

1. Suppose that the monetarists are correct, that V is stable, and in this problem is equal to 4. In the table below is the short-run aggregate supply schedule: the real output Q that producers will offer to sell at different price levels P.

P	Q	PQ	MV
$1	100	$_____	$_____
2	110	_____	_____
3	120	_____	_____
4	130	_____	_____
5	140	_____	_____
6	150	_____	_____

(a)   Compute and enter in the table above the six values of PQ.
(b)   Assume M is $90. Enter the values of MV on each of the six lines in the table. The equilibrium:
(1) nominal GDP is $_____
(2) price level is $_____
(3) real output is   _____
(c)   Assume M is $175. MV at each P level is $_____. The equilibrium:
(1) nominal GDP is $_____
(2) price level is $_____
(3) real output is   _____

2. This problem makes Keynesian assumptions. The left half of the table below shows the amounts of money firms and households wish to have for transactions at different levels of nominal GDP. The right half shows the amounts of money they want to have as assets at different rates of interest.

(a)   Suppose the nominal GDP is $500, the interest rate is 7%, and the supply of money is $125.
(1) The amount of money demanded for transactions is $_____.
(2) The amount of money demanded as an asset is $_____.
(3) The total amount of money demanded for both purposes is $_____.
(4) The amount of money firms and households wish to have is (greater than, less than, equal to) _____ the amount of money they actually have.
(5) The velocity of money (equal to nominal GDP divided by the supply of money) is _____.

Nominal GDP	Transactions demand	Interest Rate	Asset demand
$500	50	7.0%	$75
600	60	6.8	80
700	70	6.6	85
800	80	6.4	90
900	90	6.2	95
1000	100	6.0	100

(b)   Assume the Bank of Canada expands the supply of money to $160 by purchasing securities in the open market; and that as a result the rate of interest falls to 6% and the nominal GDP rises to $600.
(1) The amount of money demanded for transactions is now $_____, and the amount demanded as an asset is now $_____.
(2) The total amount of money demanded is $_____, and the amount of money the public wishes to have is _____ the amount of money they actually have.
(3) The velocity of money is _____.
(c)   Suppose the federal government pursues an expansionary fiscal policy that raises the nominal GDP from $600 to $800 and the interest rate from 6% to 6.8%; and the money supply remains at $160.
(1) The transactions demand for money is $_____, the asset demand is $_____, and the total demand is $_____.
(2) The velocity of money is _____.
(d)   The effect of the easy money policy was to (increase, decrease) _____ the velocity of money, and the effect of the expansionary fiscal policy was to _____ it.

3. Suppose that the economy is presently operating at full employment. The potential real output is growing at an average of 3% per year.

(a) According to monetarist analysis, what will be the average annual percentage change in real output and in the price level if the money supply grows by 8% per year? Output growth = _____% Inflation = _____%

(b) Under the same assumptions, what money supply growth rate would allow for full-employment and zero inflation? M growth = _____%

■ **TRUE-FALSE**

Circle T if the statement is true, F if it is false.

1. The classical economists believed that discretionary policies were required to overcome economic instability.   **T F**

2. In the classical model, macroeconomic equilibrium occurs at full-employment.   **T F**

3. Keynes doubted the ability of price and wage flexibility to pull the economy out of a depression. **T F**

4. A less than full-employment equilibrium is possible in the Keynesian model.   **T F**

5. The classical model used a horizontal AD curve and a vertical AS curve.   **T F**

6. Keynes believed that volatility of investment spending means that the AD curve may not always be downsloping.   **T F**

7. Monetarists hold that competitive markets, free from government interference, provide substantial economic stability.   **T F**

8. The monetarists favour discretionary monetary policy and a balanced budget as weapons to fight business cycles.   **T F**

9. The basic equations of the Keynesians and the monetarists are two different ways of stating the same relationship.   **T F**

10. The fundamental equation of monetarism is termed the equation of exchange.   **T F**

11. Most monetarists believe that an increase in the money supply will have no effect on real output and employment in either the short run or the long run. **T F**

12. In the monetarist model, a stable velocity of money means a constant velocity of money.   **T F**

13. If the velocity of money is stable, the monetarist model predicts a direct relationship exists between the money supply and nominal GDP.   **T F**

14. According to the Keynesians, the velocity of money is unstable so there is no stable relationship between changes in the money supply and nominal GDP.   **T F**

15. Monetarists believe that fiscal policy is weak because of a severe crowding-out effect.   **T F**

16. Monetarists conclude that discretionary monetary policy has resulted in macroeconomic instability.   **T F**

17. Rational expectations theory assumes that both product and resource markets are uncompetitive and that wages and prices are inflexible.   **T F**

18. Rational expectations macroeconomists argue that economic agents understand the workings of the economy and make decisions that further their own self-interests.   **T F**

19. According to the RET, an expansionary policy that the public fully expects will have no effects on real output.   **T F**

20. According to the RET, an expansionary policy that the public fully expects will have no effects on the price level.   **T F**

21. Some new classical economists advocate a constitutional amendment that would require government to balance its budget annually.   **T F**

22. A legacy of new classical economics is that economists and policy-makers are more sensitive about how expectations might affect the outcome of a policy change.   **T F**

■ **MULTIPLE-CHOICE**

Circle the letter that corresponds to the best answer.

1. The Keynesian AS curve:
   (a)   is horizontal up to full employment
   (b)   slopes upward
   (c)   is vertical
   (d)   slopes downward

2. The AS curve of the classical model:
   (a)   is horizontal at the prevailing price level
   (b)   slopes upward
   (c)   is vertical at the full-employment level
   (d)   slopes downward

3. According to the classical model:
   (a)   AD will determine the level of real domestic output, while AS determines the price level
   (b)   the money supply determines the interest rate, which in turn determines the level of investment, which in turn determines the level of real output
   (c)   AS will determine the full employment level of output, while AD will determine the price level
   (d)   the key to price stability was to control the interest rate in order to prevent changes in investment spending shifting the AD curve

4. In the classical theory of employment, a decrease in AD results in:
   (a)   a decrease in the price level and no change in output
   (b)   a decrease in both the price level and output
   (c)   no change in the price level and a decrease in output
   (d)   no change in either the price level or output

5. A decrease in AD in the Keynesian model results in:
   (a)   a decrease in both the price level and in output
   (b)   a decrease in the price level and no change in output
   (c)   no change in the price level and a decrease in output
   (d)   no change in either the price level or output

6. Classical theory concludes that the production behaviour of firms will not change when the price level:

(a)   decreases because input costs would rise along with product prices to leave real profits and output unchanged
(b)   decreases because input costs would fall but product prices would rise, offsetting any change in real profits or output
(c)   increases because input costs would fall along with product prices to leave real profits and output unchanged
(d)   increases because input costs would rise along with product prices to leave real profits and output unchanged

7. Monetarists:
   (a)   argue for the use of discretionary monetary policy
   (b)   contend that government policies have reduced the stability of the economy
   (c)   believe a capitalistic economy is inherently unstable
   (d)   believe the markets in a capitalistic economy are largely noncompetitive

8. According to the real-business-cycle theory, a recession could occur because of:
   (a)   a decrease in the money supply
   (b)   a decrease in AD
   (c)   an increase in the price level
   (d)   a decrease in the supply of real resources

9. Keynesians believe that:
   (a)   the market economy is inherently stable
   (b)   markets are highly competitive
   (c)   discretionary monetary policy is inadvisable
   (d)   government intervention is useful

10. Which of the following is not true?
    (a) MV is total spending
    (b) PQ is the real GDP
    (c) MV is nominal GDP
    (d) $MV = C_a + I_g + G + X_n$

11. Monetarists argue that velocity is stable and that the amount of money that the public will want to hold depends primarily on the level of:
    (a)   nominal GDP
    (b)   investment
    (c)   consumption
    (d)   prices

12. From the monetarist viewpoint, an increase in the supply of money will:

(a)   raise the rate of interest
(b)   increase spending for consumer and capital goods
(c)   increase the asset demand for money
(d)   decrease the demand for government securities

13. Which is not one of the reasons for downward wage inflexibility?
(a)   insider-outsider relationships
(b)   crowding-out effect
(c)   contracts
(d)   efficiency wages

14. From the Keynesian viewpoint, an increase in the supply of money will:
(a)   raise the rate of interest
(b)   decrease spending for consumer and capital goods
(c)   increase the asset demand for money
(d)   decrease the demand for government securities

15. Which of the following is not among the reasons that firms pay efficiency wages?
(a)   to get greater work effort from employees
(b)   to reduce supervision costs
(c)   to reduce turnover among employees
(d)   to reduce wage rates

16. The rule suggested by the monetarists is that the money supply should be increased at the same rate as:
(a)   the price level
(b)   the inverse of the price level
(c)   the velocity of money
(d)   the growth rate in potential real GDP

17. Which perspective would be most closely associated with the view that discretionary monetary policy is ineffective because of policy errors and timing problems?
(a)   monetarism
(b)   Keynesianism
(c)   rational expectations
(d)   new classical economics

18. In which theory would a decrease in AD not reduce output, even in the short run?
(a)   rational expectations theory
(b)   insider-outsider theory
(c)   efficiency wages theory
(d)   real-business-cycle theory

19. What is the monetarists' view on the velocity of money?
(a)   it never changes
(b)   it changes frequently and predictably
(c)   it changes gradually and unpredictably
(d)   it changes gradually and predictably

20. In the rational expectations theory:
(a)   individuals understand how the economy works and can correctly anticipate the effects of an event or a change in public policy on the economy
(b)   the markets in the economy are purely competitive
(c)   to maximize their own self-interests, individuals respond to any expansionary fiscal or monetary policy in a way that prevents an increase in real output and fosters an increase in the price level
(d)   all of the above are true

21. In the rational expectations theory, an increase in AD will:
(a)   increase the price level and have no real effect on real domestic output
(b)   increase real domestic output and have no effect on the price level
(c)   increase both the price level and the real domestic output
(d)   have none of the above effects

22. To stabilize the economy, rational expectation theorists favour the use of:
(a)   price controls
(b)   discretionary fiscal policy
(c)   discretionary monetary policy
(d)   policy rules

23. The contention that changes in the money supply cause direct changes in AD and therefore changes in nominal GDP is most closely associated with the view of:
(a)   Keynesians
(b)   monetarists
(c)   new classical economists
(d)   rational expectations economists

24. Proponents of rational expectations argue that people:
(a)   are not as rational as they are assumed to be by monetarists
(b)   tend to forecast the consequences of economic change, which frustrates policy-makers

(c) consistently make forecasting errors, which can be exploited by policy-makers

(d) do not respond quickly to changes in wages and prices, causing a misallocation of resources in the economy

25. The idea that the Bank of Canada should follow a monetary rule would find the most support from which combination?

(a) Keynesians and monetarists

(b) RET economists and Keynesians

(c) RET economists and monetarists

(d) neoclassical economists and Keynesians

26. Which of the following is an idea from monetarism or rational expectations that has been absorbed into mainstream macroeconomics?

(a) the importance of government spending, taxation, and fiscal policy

(b) the importance of the money supply and monetary policy

(c) the building of macroeconomic foundations for microeconomics

(d) the emphasis on discretion rather than rules for guiding economic policy

■ DISCUSSION QUESTIONS

1. According to the classical economists, what level of employment would tend to prevail in an economy? What two assumptions formed the basis for their analysis of the level of employment?

2. How do Keynesian and classical views on the AS curve differ? How do their views on AD differ?

3. What is the basic equation of the mainstream view and the basic equation of the monetarist view? Define all terms in both equations and explain how the mainstream equation can be converted to the monetarist equation.

4. Explain how a change in M in the equation of exchange will, to the monetarist way of thinking, affect nominal GDP, real GDP, and the price level.

5. Explain why a critical issue in the mainstream-monetarist debate centres on the question of whether the velocity of money is stable.

6. Why do mainstream economists advocate (and monetarists reject) discretionary fiscal policy to stabilize the economy?

7. What is the role of the insider-outsider theory, and of the efficiency wages theory, in the mainstream view of self-correction?

8. Why do monetarists suggest the monetary rule to replace discretionary monetary policy?

9. Explain how and why rational expectations theorists believe firms, workers, and consumers will respond to an expansionary monetary or fiscal policy; and how these responses make the policy ineffective and promote economic instability.

10. What is the basic hypothesis of real-business-cycle theory? What is the basic hypothesis of the coordination failures theory?

11. What influence have monetarism and rational expectations had on mainstream macroeconomic theory and policy? Give three examples of ideas that have changed contemporary thinking.

■ ANSWERS

FILL-IN QUESTIONS

1. *laissez-faire*

2. vertical, horizontal; Keynesian, classical

3. (a) rise, expand, constant supply of money (b) unstable, unstable; unstable.

4. stable, competitive

5. $MV = PQ$; (a) equation of exchange; (b) (1) money supply, (2) velocity of money, (3) average price of each unit of physical output, (4) physical volume of goods and services produced

6. (a) total spending, MV; (b) PQ

7. (a) increase; (b) increase; (c) increase, P; (d) stable

8. coordination failures

9. raise, crowding-out

10. real GDP, 3, 5

11. (a) anticipate, self interest; (b) purely competitive, flexible; (c) inflation, no change, an increase

12. (a) cycles; (b) policy rules

PROBLEMS AND PROJECTS

1.   (a) 100, 220, 360, 520, 700, 900; (b) 360 at all levels, (1) 360, (2) 3, (3) 120; (c) 700, (1) 700, (2) 5, (3) 140

2.   (a) (1) 50, (2) 75, (3) 125, (4) equal to, (5) 4; (b) (1) 60, 100, (2) 160, equal to, (3) 3.75; (c) (1) 80, 80, 160, (2) 5; (d) decrease, increase

3.   (a) 3, 5; (b) 3

TRUE-FALSE

1. F	**2.** T	**3.** T	**4.** T	**5.** F	**6.** F
7. T	**8.** F	**9.** T	**10.** T	**11.** F	**12.** F
13. T	**14.** T	**15.** T	**16.** T	**17.** F	**18.** T
19. T	**20.** F	**21.** T	**22.** T		

MULTIPLE-CHOICE

1. (a)	**2.** (c)	**3.** (c)	**4.** (a)	**5.** (c)	**6.** (d)
7. (b)	**8.** (d)	**9.** (d)	**10.** (b)	**11.** (a)	**12.** (b)
13. (b)	**14.** (c)	**15.** (d)	**16.** (d)	**17.** (a)	**18.** (a)
19. (d)	**20.** (d)	**21.** (a)	**22.** (d)	**23.** (b)	**24.** (b)
25. (c)	**26.** (b)				

CHAPTER 18

Economic Growth

Throughout this century economic growth has been the source of tremendous increases in the standard of living for Canadians. While our economy is still growing, the rate of growth in Canada has slowed in the last thirty years, particularly in comparison to other industrial nations. Given this worrisome trend, it is very important to understand what economic growth is (and what it is not), how it affects our society, what its ingredients are, and how these factors come into play to determine Canada's particular experience with growth.

After briefly defining and pointing out the significance of growth, the text analyzes six factors that make growth possible. Four supply factors determine the output potential of the economy. Whether the full potential is reached depends upon two other factors: the demand factor, and the efficiency factor. To illustrate how the six factors determine growth we can use two familiar models: the production possibilities model (first seen in Chapter 2) and the aggregate demand-aggregate supply model (introduced in Chapter 11). Economic growth requires that the production possibilities curve shift outward, but there must also be enough demand, and efficient use of the resources, in order for the expanded potential to be realized. Similarly, in the aggregate demand-aggregate supply model, growth requires shifts in both the long-run aggregate supply and aggregate demand curves.

What accounts for Canada's economic growth that has seen our real GDP grow at an average of about 4% per year since World War II, and our per capita GDP grow about 2% per year? The amounts of labour and capital inputs have increased, and so has the productivity of these inputs. These factors can be traced back to such things as: population growth and increased participation in the labour force, investment in capital goods, technological advances, improvements in education and training, economies of scale and reallocation of resources, a large endowment of natural resources, and a favourable social, cultural, and political environment. Complementing this, aggregate demand has expanded sufficiently to bring to fruition most of the potential output growth stemming from these factors on the supply side.

In about 1975 the rate of growth in Canadian factor productivity, and labour productivity in particular, began falling significantly below earlier levels. This slowdown was experienced in many industrialized countries, but Canada's was relatively severe. A continuation of such a trend would cause our historical productivity advantage to continually dwindle, eventually slowing down the rate of improvement in Canadian living standards, especially in today's more globally competitive economy. The chapter explores possible reasons for the productivity slowdown, and also considers whether the trend may be turning around in recent years. Finally, the chapter discusses the policy options for stimulating increased growth.

■ CHECKLIST

When you have studied this chapter, you should be able to:

□ Define economic growth in two different ways.

□ Explain why economic growth is important to any economy.

□ Use the "rule of 70" to demonstrate how different growth rates affect real GDP over time.

□ Identify the four supply factors that determine the rate of economic growth.

□ Explain the demand and efficiency factors that affect economic growth.

□ Show graphically how economic growth shifts the production possibilities curve.

□ Show graphically how economic growth shifts the aggregate demand and aggregate supply curves.

□ Describe Canada's growth record in the twentieth century, in terms of the two definitions of economic growth.

□ List three qualifications to keep in mind when interpreting data on long-run economic growth.

□ Explain the difference between the productivity of labour and total factor productivity (TFP).

□ State the two fundamental means by which an economy can increase its real GDP, and the relative importance of these two means of increasing the real GDP in Canada since 1961.

□ Enumerate the several sources of the growth of the productivity of labour in Canada.

□ Enumerate some factors that have been detrimental to growth in Canada.

□ Explain why Canada's actual growth rate has been less than its potential growth rate and why it has been unstable.

□ Enumerate five principal causes and three principal implications of the productivity slowdown in Canada since 1975.

□ Comment on whether there has been a productivity resurgence in the so-called "new economy."

□ Outline some economic policies that might be utilized to stimulate growth in Canada.

□ Present the case against, and the case for, economic growth.

■ **CHAPTER OUTLINE**

1. Growth economics deals with the changes in the economy's productive capacity over the long run.

(a) Economic growth means an increase in either the total or the per capita real GDP of an economy, and is often measured in terms of the annual percentage rate of growth in each of these two variables.

(b) Economic growth is important because it lessens the burden of scarcity by providing the means of satisfying existing wants more fully and of fulfilling new wants.

(c) One or two percentage point differences in the rate of growth result in substantial differences in annual increases in the economy's output.

2. The potential for economic growth is created by increasing the quantity of inputs, or by using inputs more efficiently, or a combination of both. Whether the potential growth will be realized depends upon demand factors and the efficient allocation of existing resources.

(a) Supply factors include the quantity and quality of resources (human, natural, capital) and technology.

(b) Aggregate demand growth must be adequate to provide employment for all resources in the economy.

(c) Productive efficiency requires that goods be produced in the least costly way, and allocative efficiency requires that resources be used to produce goods that maximize society's well-being.

3. Two economic models used in earlier chapters can be used to analyze economic growth.

(a) In the production possibilities model:

(1) Economic growth shifts the production possibilities curve outward because of improvement in supply factors that increase real output by increasing labour inputs or by increasing the productivity of labour (in equation terms: Total output = worker-hours × labour productivity).

(2) However, whether the economy operates on the curve depends on demand considerations as well as the efficient allocation of the inputs.

(b) In the aggregate demand-aggregate supply model:

(1) Supply factors that contribute to economic growth shift the long-run aggregate supply curve to the right.

(2) Assuming downward price and wage inflexibility, for growth to be realized the aggregate demand curve must also increase.

4. The growth record of the Canadian economy has been impressive, with real GDP increases averaging about 4% per year since 1948. On a per capita basis the growth rate has been about 2%.

(a) Our performance has been about average among the advanced industrialized countries over that time.

(b) Growth rates must be qualified by noting that they do not reflect improvements in products and services, they overlook increased amounts of leisure time, and they fail to account for changes in the quality of our environment.

(c) Macroeconomic instability has cut into our growth rates, particularly because accumulation of human and physical capital and R&D activity decrease during recessions.

5. Output can increase due to an increase in resource inputs and/or an improvement in the output per unit of input. Between 1961 and 1996, growth in labour accounted for 29% of GDP growth, growth in capital accounted for 45%, leaving a residual of about 27% of growth attributed to gains in total factor productivity.

6. The following factors have contributed to real growth in the Canadian economy:

(a)   labour force growth driven by immigration and increased labour force participation by women;

(b)   technological advances as new knowledge is applied to production activities;

(c)   capital accumulation through investment in plant and equipment;

(d)   human capital accumulation through investment in education and training of workers;

(e)   improved resource allocation through industrial restructuring, lessening of labour market discrimination, freer international trade;

(f)   economies of scale from growing size of markets and firms;

(g)   an abundant and varied endowment of natural resources; and

(h)   a very favourable social-cultural-political environment.

7. Some developments have been detrimental to growth of the Canadian economy; for example, increases in regulations regarding environmental pollution, worker health and safety, etc. Of course, these obstacles to growth may be justified given that society may choose to trade some economic growth for other goals that contribute to our well-being.

8. From the mid 1970s through the early 1980s, the annual rates of increase in total factor productivity (TFP) slowed down, and at a faster rate in Canada than in other industrialized nations, causing our productivity advantage to diminish. The productivity slowdown is significant because it:

(a) decreases the rates at which real wage rates and the standard of living can rise;

(b) contributes to rising unit labour costs and to inflation; and

(c) this price inflation for Canadian goods causes Canadian producers to lose competitive advantage in world markets.

9. There are several theories of the causes of the slowdown:

(a)   low saving rates, threats from import competition and regulations deterred investment spending

(b)   increased energy prices led to the use of less productive labour-intensive techniques and, because they caused inflation, provoked government to use restrictive macroeconomic policies

(c)   a slowing of technological progress

(d)   slower improvements in labour quality due to increased participation of women with little work experience, and declining worker capabilities as measured by student test scores

(e)   dismal productivity growth in the services sector

10. There has been some recovery of TFP since 1982. Some economists argue that Canada is establishing a "new economy" based on innovations in communications and computers, and increased international trade. There is a hope that we can now maintain higher growth rates, while remaining free of inflation, than were achieved in the 1970s and 1980s. The jury is still out on this hypothesis.

11. Various policies have been discussed for achieving more economic growth in Canada:

(a)   Demand-side policies focus on monetary and fiscal policies to generate enough demand to keep the economy functioning at or near its potential. A key is to achieve low interest rates through relatively easy monetary policy and tight enough fiscal policy to avoid budget deficits and growing government debt.

(b)   Supply-side policies call for expansion of the economy's output potential and often involve changes in tax policy to increase saving, investment in physical and human capital, work effort, and risk taking.

12. Some Canadians debate whether economic growth is or is not desirable.

(a)   Opponents of economic growth contend that it pollutes the environment, creates poor-quality, alienating jobs, does little or nothing to solve social problems such as poverty or crime, and while providing more goods and services, it does not provide a better life.

(b)   Advocates of growth argue that it results in a higher standard of living and lessens the burden of scarcity, thereby giving us the resources to fight social problems, pollution, etc. They argue that many problems are falsely blamed on growth.

■ **TERMS AND CONCEPTS**

demand factor economic growth efficiency factor labour force participation rate

labour productivity supply factors total factor productivity (TFP)

■ **HINTS AND TIPS**

1. The rate of economic growth depends on the rate of increase in the quantity and the quality of inputs, and on changes in technology (which represent our "know how" for turning inputs into outputs). However, these factors merely increase the potential output of the economy. For growth to occur, actual output must increase. That takes growth in demand as well as growth in supply.

■ **FILL-IN QUESTIONS**

1. Growth economics is concerned with an economy whose productive capacity (increases, remains constant) _____ over time.

2. Economic growth can mean an increase in either the _____ or the _____ of an economy.

3. A rise in output per capita (increases, decreases) _____ the standard of living and _____ the burden of scarcity in the economy.

4. Assume that an economy has a GDP of $800 billion. If the growth rate is 4%, GDP will increase by $_____ billion in one year; but if the rate of growth is only 2%, the year's increase in GDP will be $_____ billion. A two percentage point difference in the growth rate results in a $_____ billion difference in the year's increase in GDP. At a constant annual growth rate of 4%, real GDP will double in _____ years, whereas at a growth rate of 2%, it will take _____ years for real GDP to double.

5. Graphically, economic growth can be shown as a _____ shift of the production possibilities curve or as a combined shift to the right of the _____ and _____ curves.

6. In the production possibilities model, economic growth increases primarily because of (demand, supply) _____ factors, but the economy may not reach its full potential because there may be less than full _____ or full _____.

7. The four supply factors in economic growth are:
(a) increases in _____
(b) increases in _____
(c) increases in _____
(d) improvements in _____
The other two factors are the _____ factor and the _____ factor.

8. The real GDP of any economy in any year is equal to the _____ of labour employed multiplied by the _____ of labour.
(a) The former is measured by the number of _____.
(b) The latter is measured as the real GDP per _____ per _____.

9. In recent decades a (rising, falling) _____ price level has accompanied economic growth. This suggests that the aggregate _____ has increased somewhat more rapidly than the aggregate _____.

10. Data on growth in output may understate the improvement in living standards since improvements in _____ of products and services and increases in _____ are not reflected in the figures. On the other hand, the same data may overstate improvement in living standards because _____ effects are not reflected.

11. Any tendency towards slowdown in the rate of growth in productivity can be lessened or overcome by increasing the productivity of workers. The three principal means of doing this are to increase the stock of _____, to improve _____, and to improve the _____ and _____ of the work force.

12. Since 1961 Canadian real GDP has increased on average about _____% per year, while per capita real output has increased at a rate of about _____% per year.

13. Technological progress means that we learn how to employ given quantities of resources to obtain greater _____; and, more often than not, this progress requires _____ in new machinery and equipment.

14. In the 1961-1996 period about 27% of the increase in real output was due to total _____ or getting more output per unit of _____ and _____.

15. Beginning around 1975, the rate of growth in labour productivity (increased, decreased) _____ .
(a)   This resulted in a (rise, fall) _____ in the rates at which the standard of _____ and the (money, real) _____ wages of labour have increased, in a (rise, fall) _____ in unit labour costs and (inflation, deflation) _____ in Canada, and a (gain, loss) _____ of competitiveness for Canadian producers selling in international markets.
(b)   Its causes probably included (falling, rising) _____ levels of investment, (increased, decreased) _____ energy prices, a slow-down in _____ progress, slower improvements in the quality of _____, and particularly weak productivity performance in the _____ sector of the economy.

16. To stimulate economic growth in Canada:
(a)   demand-side policies would focus on ensuring that there is enough _____ to avoid having the economy slip into _____.
(b)   supply-side policies would include changes in the _____ system designed to create incentives to work, save, invest, and bear risks, so as to expand (aggregate expenditures, capacity output) _____.

■   **PROBLEMS AND PROJECTS**

1. Suppose the real GDP and the population of an economy in six different years were those shown in the following table.

Year	Population (millions)	Real GDP (billions $)	Per Capita Real GDP
1	30	$9	$300
2	60	24	$_____
3	90	45	_____
4	120	66	_____

(a)   Calculate and fill in the remaining values for real per capita GDP.
(b)   Between year 1 and year 2, real GDP grew by $_____.
(c)   Between year 3 and year 4, the rate of growth in real GDP was _____%.

2. The next table shows the quantity of labour (measured in hours) and the productivity of labour (measured in real GDP per hour) in a hypothetical economy in three different years.
(a)   Compute the economy's real GDP in each of the three years and enter them in the table.
(b)   Between years 1 and 2, the quantity of labour remained constant; but
(1)   the productivity of labour increased by _____%; and
(2) as a consequence, real GDP increased by _____%.
(c)   Between years 2 and 3, the productivity of labour remained constant; but
1) the quantity of labour increased by _____%; and
(2) as a consequence, real GDP increased by _____%.

Year	Quantity of Labour	Productivity of Labour	Real GDP
1	1000	$100	$_____
2	1000	105	_____
3	1100	105	_____

(d)   Between years 1 and 3,
(1) real GDP increased by _____%; and
(2) this rate of increase is approximately equal to the sum of the rates of increase in the _____ and the _____ of labour.

■   **TRUE-FALSE**

Circle T if the statement is true, F if it is false.

1. Growth economics is concerned with an economy in which productive capacity is not fixed.   **T** F

2. The better of the two definitions of economic growth is an increase in the per capita real output of the economy.   **T** F

3. An economy that expands its productive capacity will not realize its potential economic growth unless there is full employment of resources and full production in the economy.   **T** F

4. Growth will increase the long-run aggregate supply curve and the short-run aggregate supply curve, but decrease the aggregate demand curve.   **T** F

5. The demand factor means that creating more demand for goods is a sufficient condition for growth to occur. **T F**

6. The efficiency factor in economic growth incorporates issues of productive efficiency and allocative efficiency. **T F**

7. The rate of increase in TFP measures the increase in the productivity of labour. *eff. factors used together* **T F**

8. Real GDP has tended to increase more rapidly than per capita GDP in Canada. **T F**

9. Estimates of an economy's growth rate generally attempt to take account of changes in the quality of goods produced and in the amount of leisure that members of the economy enjoy. **T F**

10. The real GDP of an economy in any year is equal to its input of labour divided by the productivity of labour. **T F**

11. The growth rate in Canada's real GDP continues to fall steadily. **T F**

12. A decline in the rate of increase of population may cause a decline in the rate of growth of real GDP, but may also raise the growth rate of real GDP per capita if a larger percentage of the population is able to find employment. **T F**

13. Total factor productivity measures the change in output not accounted for by changes in the quantity of inputs. **T F**

14. More often than not, technological progress requires the economy to invest in new machinery and equipment. **T F**

15. The Canadian social, cultural, and political environment has, in general, worked to slow Canadian economic growth. **T F**

16. Increased total factor productivity was more important than increased labour and capital inputs in the growth of the Canadian economy between 1961 and 1996. **T F**

17. The productivity of the nation's labour is affected by both the amount of education and quality of education received by workers. **T F**

18. Since 1961, increased inputs of capital have accounted for close to half of real GDP growth in Canada. **T F**

19. Among major industrialized countries, only Canada suffered a decrease in productivity growth in the 1970s. **T F**

20. Increases in labour productivity can, at least in the Canadian economy, be taken largely for granted, because the rate of increase has been nearly constant for much more than half a century. **T F**

21. The availability of natural resources in Canada has been a significant factor in the growth of the Canadian economy. **T F**

22. Supply-side policies to stimulate growth would tend to favour tax cuts to create incentives for increased production. **T F**

23. Critics of economic growth point to the negative consequences for the nature of work and the number of meaningful jobs in the economy. **T F**

24. Economic growth lessens the problem of scarcity, therefore making more resources available for addressing social problems, if we so decide. **T F**

■ **MULTIPLE-CHOICE**

Circle the letter that corresponds to the best answer.

1. Which of the following is not one of the benefits of economic growth?
  (a) everyone enjoys a greater real income
  (b) the standard of living in that society increases
  (c) the burden of scarcity decreases
  (d) the society is better able to satisfy new wants

2. If the real GDP of a nation increases from $2,000 billion to $2,100 billion in one year, the rate of growth of real GDP during that year would be:
  (a) 0.5%
  (b) 5%
  (c) 10%
  (d) 50%

3. Suppose an economy has a GDP of $700 billion and a steady annual growth rate of 5%. Over a two-year period, GDP will increase by:
- **(a)** $14 billion
- **(b)** $35 billion
- **(c)** $70 billion
- **(d)** $71.75 billion

The labour input in hours worked and the real GDP for a hypothetical economy are given in the table below. Answer questions 4 and 5 on the basis of the data.

Year	Hours Worked (Millions)	Real GDP (Billion $)
1990	150	30.0
1995	156	31.2
2000	160	32.4

4. From 1990 to 2000 the total growth in GDP was:
- **(a)** 8%
- **(b)** 2.4%
- **(c)** 4%
- **(d)** none of the above

5. Labour productivity was highest in:
- **(a)** 1990
- **(b)** 1995
- **(c)** 2000
- **(d)** labour productivity was constant

6. An outward shift of the entire production possibilities curve of an economy is most likely caused by:
- **(a)** supply factors
- **(b)** demand factors
- **(c)** allocative factors
- **(d)** efficiency factors

7. If a nation is presently operating at a point that lies inside its current production possibilities curve, the most likely reason is:
- **(a)** supply and environmental factors
- **(b)** demand and efficiency factors
- **(c)** increased labour productivity
- **(d)** increased total factor productivity

8. Which of the following is not a supply factor in economic growth?
- **(a)** an expansion in purchasing power
- **(b)** an increase in the economy's stock of capital goods

- **(c)** more natural resources
- **(d)** technological improvements

9. That Canada's real GDP growth has been accompanied by inflation is a sign that:
- **(a)** the AD and AS_{LR} curves have grown at the same rate
- **(b)** the AD curve has grown more than the AS_{LR}
- **(c)** the AD curve has grown less than the AS_{LR}
- **(d)** the AD curve has grown but the AS_{LR} curve has remained fixed

10. Which of the following is an accurate statement about the relationship between technological advance and investment spending?
- **(a)** technological advances usually spur spending on new capital goods
- **(b)** technological advances are not related to investment spending
- **(c)** technological advances reduce the need for spending on new capital goods
- **(d)** spending on technology and on capital goods are usually substitutes

11. Concerns about the quality of Canadian education arise from:
- **(a)** the fact that a smaller percentage of our population is attending college or university
- **(b)** the fact that more students are attending college instead of university
- **(c)** decreases in government expenditures on post-secondary education
- **(d)** deterioration in the performance of Canadian students on standardized achievement tests

12. Total factor productivity measures the increase in real GDP attributable to:
- **(a)** increases in the quantities of labour and capital
- **(b)** increases in the quantity of labour
- **(c)** increases in the quantity of capital
- **(d)** increases in everything but the quantities of labour and capital

13. Which of the following has contributed to improved resource allocation in the Canadian economy?
- **(a)** decline of discrimination against women in labour markets
- **(b)** freer international trade
- **(c)** the shift of labour out of the agricultural sector
- **(d)** all of the above

14. Canada enjoys a social-cultural-political environment that is on the whole very favourable for growth. Which of the following does not contribute to this favourable environment?
(a) few taboos against work, production, and material progress
(b) strong personal and corporate incentives encouraging growth
(c) a stable rule of law and enforcement of contracts
(d) some social programs give incentives not to work

15. The decline in the growth rate of labour productivity that began in the mid-1970s in Canada can be attributed to a number of factors. Which of the following is not one of these factors?
(a) an increase in the relative prices of Canadian goods in world markets
(b) increased energy prices
(c) slower improvements in labour quality
(d) the decline in R&D expenditures as a percentage of GDP

16. A continuing decline in the growth rate of Canadian labour productivity, as compared to other nations, would result in:
(a) a rise in the international value of the Canadian dollar
(b) a decline in the standard of living in Canada
(c) falling prices in Canada
(d) all of the above

17. Productivity in the service sector has been relatively stagnant because:
(a) it is difficult to replace labour with capital in this sector
(b) competition is very strong in the services sector
(c) as consumers are becoming wealthier they demand less services
(d) the service sector is a shrinking sector of our GDP

18. Proponents of the "new economy" hypothesis believe that in the upcoming years Canada will be able to:
(a) achieve high growth rates without experiencing inflationary pressures
(b) avoid pressures for growth and stabilize real GDP per capita
(c) find ways to cope with high inflation while achieving high growth rates
(d) none of the above

19. In order to stimulate growth through investment spending, which policy combination would be most effective?
(a) relatively easy fiscal and monetary policy
(b) relatively easy money and fiscal policy tight enough to avoid budget deficits
(c) relatively tight fiscal and monetary policy
(d) relatively tight money and relatively easy fiscal policy

20. Which of the following is not among the consequences when aggregate expenditures increase by less than the productive capacity of the economy?
(a) inflation
(b) a recessionary gap
(c) a slower rate of economic growth
(d) unemployed labour

21. Which of the following is not a part of the case against economic growth?
(a) growth produces pollution
(b) growth impedes the increased production of consumer goods
(c) growth prevents the attainment of a better life
(d) growth is not needed to provide us with the means of solving domestic social problems

22. Which of the following is not a part of the case in favour of economic growth?
(a) growth lessens the scarcity problem
(b) growth lessens the extent of anxiety and insecurity
(c) growth need not be accompanied by the pollution of the environment
(d) growth is the only practical way to reduce poverty

■ **DISCUSSION QUESTIONS**

1. What is meant by economic growth? Why should Canadians be concerned with economic growth?

2. How does economic growth affect the production possibilities curve? What demand and efficiency assumptions are necessary to achieve maximum productive potential?

3. Describe how economic growth can be illustrated in an aggregate demand-aggregate supply model. What evidence is there to indicate whether aggregate demand or long-run aggregate supply has historically grown more rapidly in Canada?

4. What are the six basic ingredients of economic growth? What is the essential difference between the supply factors and the other two factors?

5. What is Canada's record on economic growth? How well have we done compared to other nations?

6. What is the relationship between the annual real GDP, the quantity of labour employed, and the productivity of labour? What factors affect the productivity of labour?

7. What is the relationship between investment and the stock of capital? What is the connection between increases in the capital stock and the rate of economic growth?

8. If the quantity of the labour and capital inputs stayed constant from year to year what productivity measure would indicate how quickly production is growing? How much has this source of productivity contributed to Canada's economic growth since 1961?

9. What reasons are given for the productivity slowdown experienced in Canada that began in 1975? What reasons are given for the apparent increase in productivity more recently?

10. What are the arguments for and against economic growth in Canada?

11. How might demand-side and supply-side policies work to stimulate economic growth? Give some examples of policies recently adopted by the Canadian government in order to generate growth.

12. What relationship exists between international competitiveness of Canadian firms and the relative rates of productivity growth in Canada and abroad?

13. The former Soviet Union is struggling to maintain GDP levels, let alone create growth. What social-cultural-political differences in the former Soviet Union (as compared to Canada) are contributing to their economic woes?

■ **ANSWERS**

FILL-IN QUESTIONS

1. increases

2. total real output (GDP), real output (GDP) per capita

3. increases, decreases

4. 32, 16; 16; approx. 18, 35

5. rightward, AD, AS_{LR}

6. supply, employment, production

7. (a) quantity and quality of natural resources (b) quantity and quality of human resources (c) the supply or stock of capital goods (d) technology; demand, efficiency

8. quantity, productivity; (a) worker hours; (b) worker, hour

9. rising; demand, supply

10. quality, leisure time; environment

11. capital, technology, education, training

12. 4, 2

13. output (production), investment

14. factor productivity, capital, labour

15. decreased, (a) fall, living, real, rise, inflation, loss; (b) falling, increased, technological, labour, services

16. (a) demand, recession; (b) taxation, capacity output

PROBLEMS AND PROJECTS

1. (a) 400, 500, 550; (b) $100 billion; (c) 10%

2. (a) 100,000, 105,000, 115,500; (b) (1) 5, (2) 5; (c) (1) 10, (2) 10; (d) (1) 15.5, (2) quantity, productivity

TRUE-FALSE

1. T	**2.** T	**3.** T	**4.** F	**5.** F	**6.** T
7. F	**8.** T	**9.** F	**10.** F	**11.** F	**12.** T
13. T	**14.** T	**15.** F	**16.** F	**17.** T	**18.** T
19. F	**20.** F	**21.** T	**22.** T	**23.** T	**24.** T

MULTIPLE-CHOICE

1. (a)	**2.** (b)	**3.** (d)	**4.** (d)	**5.** (c)	**6.** (a)
7. (b)	**8.** (a)	**9.** (b)	**10.** (a)	**11.** (d)	**12.** (d)
13. (d)	**14.** (d)	**15.** (a)	**16.** (b)	**17.** (a)	**18.** (a)
19. (b)	**20.** (a)	**21.** (b)	**22.** (b)		

CHAPTER 19

Budget Deficits and the Public Debt

The federal government can operate with a budget deficit, budget surplus, or balanced budget. Canada had a budget surplus in 1974, and again in 1998, but a deficit in every year in between! In the early 1980s, budget deficits grew rapidly, causing regular problems for the Canadian economy. Chapter 19 looks at the issues surrounding budget deficits and the related growth of the public debt. Any time there is a deficit this adds to the total stock of the government's debt (public debt), whereas a surplus decreases the debt. As a consequence of persistent deficits from World War II on, Canada has a hefty public debt. The federal government finances the public debt by selling securities (bonds). Government pays interest on these bonds, so the levels of debt and of interest rates have consequences for how much flexibility government has in spending its tax revenues. These facts are the background for this chapter.

There are three fundamental budget philosophies. Until the Great Depression people believed in annually balanced budgets. More liberal is a cyclically balanced budget approach (under which the budget is balanced on average over the whole business cycle). Finally, a functional finance approach requires that fiscal policy be used to balance the macroeconomy, but not necessarily the budget.

The next section gives three main reasons for increases in the public debt, and examines the absolute and relative sizes of Canada's debt and interest payments on our debt. Although there has been some improvement recently, Canada's debt to GDP ratio is high, and a large part of government revenue goes to interest payments. Most of our debt is held within Canada, but the fraction held outside Canada is growing.

What are the economic implications of the debt? To be sure, the debt creates serious problems for the economy, but contrary to popular belief, these problems do not include bankrupting the federal government or shifting a huge burden onto future generations. Five problems which the debt contribute to are: (1) increased inequality of incomes; (2) reduced incentives for work and production (because of higher taxes); (3) decreased standard of living when repayments must be made on external debt; (4) curbs on fiscal policy; and (5) crowding out of capital investment.

The crowding-out effect is likely the most serious of these problems, and may arise when increased government spending is financed by selling bonds. By competing with private firms for loanable funds, the government drives up the interest rate and reduces private sector investment in capital goods. This imposes a burden on future generations by reducing the growth of the nation's capital stock, and the future output potential of the economy. If deficit financing is obtained abroad, interest rates in Canada will not be driven up, so investment will not be crowded out. However, because external bond sales will cause the Canadian dollar to appreciate, this will reduce net exports. It is also important to note that the problem of crowding out is cancelled out to the extent that the government's spending is being used to acquire public capital, or is creating employment for unemployed workers.

Recent deficits are of concern because of their enormous size, rising interest costs, balance of trade problems, and the government's difficulty in eliminating large deficits even when we are operating near full-employment. Finally, government debt can also have a positive role in ensuring that the economy's savings are borrowed and spent, rather than sitting idle. Recall that if savings are not reinjected as spending, there will be insufficient demand to purchase all of the economy's output.

■ CHECKLIST

When you have studied this chapter, you should be able to:

☐ Define a budget deficit (and surplus) and the public debt; and explain their relationship.

☐ Explain each of the three budget philosophies, and evaluate the merits of each.

☐ Identify three principal causes of the public debt.

☐ Describe the absolute and relative size of Canada's public debt, the annual interest on the debt, and the fraction of the debt held externally.

☐ Give some examples of how accounting methods make the data on deficit and debt difficult to interpret.

☐ Give three reasons why a large public debt will not bankrupt the government.

☐ Discuss whether the public debt imposes a burden on future generations; and why the public debt is for the most part also a public credit.

☐ Enumerate the five real issues related to the public debt.

☐ Explain the effects of a large debt on income distribution and incentives.

☐ Explain why it matters whether debt is held externally or internally.

☐ Explain how debt can curb the government's ability to use fiscal policy for stabilization purposes.

☐ Describe how the crowding-out effect places a burden on future generations.

☐ Compare the future consequences of borrowing to finance government expenditures with raising taxes to finance government expenditures.

☐ Explain how the burden for future generations depends on whether government spends on public investment goods, and whether unemployed workers become employed.

☐ Discuss the four concerns with the deficits and growing public debt during the 1980s and 1990s.

☐ Trace how deficits that lead to foreign borrowing also lead to Canadian dollar appreciation and falling net exports.

☐ Explain how public debt can play a positive role in helping a growing economy stay near full employment.

■ CHAPTER OUTLINE

1. The budget deficit of the federal government is the amount by which its expenditures exceed its revenues in any year. The public debt is the total accumulation at a given point of past deficits and surpluses.

2. If the government utilizes fiscal policy to combat recession and inflation, its budget is not likely to be balanced in any particular year. Three budgetary philosophies may be adopted by government; and the adoption of any of these philosophies will affect employment, real output, and the price level.

(a)   The "annually balanced budget" philosophy requires government to balance its expenditures and tax revenues each year. Such a budget is pro-cyclical, meaning that the government's actions will amplify the business cycle. This philosophy is favoured by conservatives who see it as a way to control the expansion of the public sector.

(b)   The "cyclically balanced budget" philosophy requires government to run surpluses in years of prosperity, and deficits in recession years. The effect is counter-cyclical because the output swings in the business cycle are dampened by the government's actions. Ideally, surpluses will equal the deficits over the years, so that the budget is balanced on average, but this is not assured.

(c)   The "functional finance" philosophy means to choose fiscal policies that will achieve the goal of noninflationary full employment, regardless of the effects of these policies upon the deficit and the public debt.

3. The three principal reasons for Canada's debt are: wars (World War I and World War II); recessions (including major recessions in 1981-82 and 1990-91); and a lack of political will to cut spending or to raise taxes as needed to eliminate deficits. At the end of 1996, the total federal public debt was about $465 billion. Adding provincial and local government debt increases the total substantially.

4. To assess Canada's debt situation it is useful to evaluate the amount of debt and its interest charges in proportion to other variables, and to compare Canada with other nations.

(a)   The debt as a percentage of GDP fell from the end of World War II until 1975. It then rose until the mid-1990s, and has fallen somewhat since. By 1997 the debt was 54.3% of our GDP.

(b)   In terms of total public sector debt as a percentage of GDP in 1997, Canada was third highest among OECD countries, with only Italy and Belgium higher.

(c)   Since the late 1970s, an increasing debt and higher interest rates combined to push up the ratio of interest payments to GDP. This trend has subsided in the 1990s as lower inflation has allowed for lower interest rates.

(d)   About 6% of the public debt is held by the Bank of Canada and 94% by private households, companies, and financial institutions. More importantly, about 25% is held by foreigners.

(e)   Because the accounting system used by the federal government records public debts but not public assets, the debt does not give a true picture of the government's financial position. Also, because the debt is expressed in nominal terms, the effects of inflation exaggerate the growth of the debt.

5. Claims that a large debt will bankrupt the government and pass the cost onto future generations are largely false.

(a)   The debt cannot bankrupt the government:

(1) because the government has the option of refinancing debt rather that retiring it;

(2) because the government has the constitutional authority to levy and collect taxes; and

(3) because the government can always print (or create) money to pay its debts

(b)   Deficit financing does not necessarily shift the burden of the debt to future generations.

(1) The debt is largely internally held and the repayment of any portion of the principal or interest causes a transfer of wealth between Canadians, not a reduction of wealth for Canadians collectively.

(2) If the increase in government spending is financed by increased personal taxes, the burden of the increased spending is on the present generation whose consumption is reduced; but if it is financed by an increased public debt, the increased government borrowing will raise interest rates, crowd out investment spending, and future generations will inherit a smaller stock of capital goods.

(3) The burden imposed on future generations is lessened if the increase in government expenditures is for real or human capital or if the economy were initially operating at less than full employment (and it stimulates an increase in investment demand).

(4) Debt held in foreign countries is a burden because both interest and debt repayment require a transfer of real output to other nations.

6. The debt creates several other real and potential problems in the economy.

(a)   The payment of interest on the debt probably increases the extent of income inequality.

(b)   The taxes levied to finance the debt reduce incentives to bear risks, to innovate, to invest, and to work, so economic growth is reduced.

(c)   Public concern over a growing debt makes it politically difficult for government to use fiscal policy to pull the economy out of recession.

7. In the 1980s and most of the 1990s the federal deficits grew enormously, hitting a high of $40 billion in 1993. This of course produced massive growth in the accumulated debt. The government had a small surplus in 1998, producing hope that the trend has been broken.

(a)   The huge debt overhang has produced such large interest charges that a significant share of tax revenues must be dedicated to this purpose and cannot be spent on new programs.

(b)   Another concern is that large deficits have been incurred in years when the economy is nearly at full employment. This is inappropriate from a stabilization perspective, and has forced the Bank of Canada to use tighter monetary policy than would have been ideal.

(c)   These large deficits have also put pressure on our balance of trade. As deficits push up interest rates, they also cause more demand for Canadian dollars with which to purchase Canadian securities. This results in dollar appreciation which causes exports to fall and imports to rise, contracting aggregate demand and Canada's GDP.

(d)   Despite these problems, public debt (and private debt) has an important role to play. In a growing economy, saving rises along with income. If the extra saving is not borrowed and invested there may be insufficient aggregate demand to maintain the economy at full employment. If consumers and firms do not borrow sufficient amounts, the public debt must be increased to maintain full employment and economic growth.

■   **TERMS AND CONCEPTS**

annually balanced budget	**functional finance**
budget deficit	**public debt**
cyclically balanced budget	**public investments**
external debt	

■ HINTS AND TIPS

1. Media reports often use the terms debt and deficit interchangeably. Don't make the same mistake. A deficit is a flow variable: so many dollars *per year*. A debt is a stock variable: so many dollars. The two are related: the larger the deficit flows the larger the stock of debt.

2. The most meaningful measure of how the debt problem is changing over time is the debt to GDP ratio. Inflation affects both the numerator and denominator, so it washes out of the ratio. The ratio also incorporates real output growth in the economy which improves our ability to "carry" the debt.

■ FILL-IN QUESTIONS

1. The budget deficit of the federal government in any year is equal to its (expenditures, revenues) _____ less its _____ in that year; and the public debt is equal to the sum of the federal government's past budget _____ less its budget _____.

2. An annually balanced budget is (pro-, counter-) _____ cyclical because when a recession sets in, tax revenues tend to (fall, rise) _____ so government must (cut, increase) _____ its spending to keep the budget balanced. This ends up (increasing, reducing) _____ AD at a time when the opposite is needed to stabilize the economy at full-employment output.

3. A cyclically balanced budget suggests that, to ensure full employment without inflation, the government incur deficits during periods of _____ and surpluses during periods of _____, with the deficits and surpluses balancing out over the business cycle.

4. Functional finance has as its main goal the achievement of _____, and would regard budget _____ and increases in the _____ as being of secondary importance.

5. The principal causes of Canada's public debt are _____, _____, and lack of _____.

6. At the end of 1997 Canada's public debt was:
(a) about $____ billion and about ____% of the GDP, and the annual interest charges on this debt are about $____ billion and about ____% of GDP;
(b) for the most part an (internal, external) _____ debt.

7. (a) About 75% of the public debt is owed to the _____ and to the Bank of _____; and
(b) _____% of the public debt is owed to foreigners.

8. The accounting procedures used by the federal government reflect its (assets, debts) _____ but do not reflect its _____.

9. The possibility that the federal government will go bankrupt is a false issue because the government can retire maturing securities by _____ them, or by creating _____; and it has the constitutional authority to _____ and _____ taxes.

10. As long as the government expenditures that lead to the increase in the public debt are not financed by foreign borrowing, Canada's public debt is also an _____ of Canadians who own our government's bonds.

11. The public debt is a burden on an economy if it is (internally, externally) _____ held. The debt and the payment of interest on it may, however, (increase, decrease) _____ income inequality in the economy; dampen the _____ to work, take risks, save, and invest; and have a _____ effect on investment.

12. A public debt that is internally held will burden future generations if the borrowing done to finance an increase in government expenditures (increases, decreases) _____ interest rates, _____ investment spending, and leaves future generations with a smaller stock of _____ goods.
(a) But if the increased government expenditures are financed by an increase in the taxes on personal income, the present generation will have fewer _____ goods and the burden of the increased government expenditures will be on the _____ generation.
(b) There are two qualifications to these generalizations: the burden on future generations of increased government expenditures financed by borrowing is reduced if the government expenditures pay for increases in physical or human _____ or if the economy had been operating at (full, less than full) _____ employment.

13. A government deficit results in a(n) (increased, decreased) _____ interest rate, which causes an (inflow, outflow) _____ of foreign capital. The increased (demand for, supply of) _____ Canadian dollars results in a(n) (appreciation, depreciation) _____ of the Canadian dollar, which in turn causes a(n) (increase, decrease) _____ in Canadian exports and a(n) _____ in Canadian imports. The change in net exports has a(n) (expansionary, contractionary) _____ effect on GDP in Canada.

14. Growing concerns over the budget deficits of the last decade are due to:
   (a) _____
   (b) _____
   (c) _____
   (d) _____

15. Public and private debts play a positive role if they absorb a sufficient amount of _____ to enable an economy that is (stationary, growing) _____ to remain at _____.

■ **PROBLEMS AND PROJECTS**

1. Suppose that a nation's full-employment level of output is $500 billion per year. Over the course of a business cycle the nation's average output would be $450 billion per year. Government spending has already been determined, and is $100 billion for the current year.
   (a) If the nation pursues a cyclically balanced budget, how much tax revenue should be collected per year, and what tax rate would generate this much revenue? Revenue = $_____ billion, Tax rate = _____%
   (b) In order to have an annually balanced budget, how would taxes have to change from your result in (a) — assuming that the level of government spending is held constant at $100 billion per year?
   (c) If the government follows the functional finance philosophy, how would taxes have to change from your result in (a) — again assuming government spending is set at $100 billion?

2. The table below shows data for four years for some country.
   (a) Fill in the table assuming that: (1) all income is taxed at a 20% rate; (2) the government annually pays 6% interest on the debt owing at the beginning of the year. Round numbers to the nearest integer.

(b) Because there is a deficit every year, the debt _____ each year.
(c) In years 1 and 2 there would be no deficit were it not for the _____ on debt from previous years.
(d) Though the debt increases each year, the country's debt situation improves in year _____ as measured by the _____.

Years	1	2	3	4
GDP ($)	1000	1100	1200	1300
Government purchases ($)	200	220	250	300
Tax revenues ($)	____	____	____	____
Interest on debt ($)	____	____	____	____
Debt at Jan 1 ($)	300	____	____	____
Deficit ($)	____	____	____	____
Debt at Dec 31 ($)	____	____	____	____
Debt at Dec 31 / GDP (%)	____	____	____	____

3. Two years of data for a hypothetical nation is shown in the table below.
   (a) Inflation reduces the real value of the government debt and some economists argue that the "real" deficit for a year should be calculated by subtracting this decline in purchasing power from the nominal deficit. Find the approximate "real" deficit for 1996 and 1997 by subtracting the loss in purchasing power of the public debt from the nominal budget deficit.
   (b) In which year is this nation's debt situation worse, based on the information given, and what criterion have you used to draw this conclusion?

	1996	1997
GDP ($)	600	675
Debt ($)	200	225
Nominal Deficit ($)	25	30
Inflation Rate	2%	10%
Debt to GDP Ratio	_____	_____
Real Deficit ($)	_____	_____

■ **TRUE-FALSE**

Circle T if the statement is true, F if it is false.

1. The budget deficit in any year is equal to the amount by which the government's revenues exceed its expenditures.   **T F**

2. The public debt includes debt of federal, provincial, and local governments.   **T F**

3. There is no assurance that a nation can use fiscal policy both to promote full employment and balance its budget cyclically.   **T** **F**

4. Proponents of functional finance argue that a balanced budget, whether it is balanced annually or over the business cycle, is less important than the objective of full employment without inflation.   **T** **F**

5. According to the aggregate expenditure model an annually balanced budget would promote economic stability.   **T** **F**

6. The main reason for the large increase in Canada's public debt is the growth in social programs spending.   **T** **F**

7. About half of Canada's public debt is currently held by foreigners.   **T** **F**

8. Inflation increases the real value of the nominal public debt.   **T** **F**

9. Selling government securities to foreigners to finance increased expenditures by the federal government imposes a burden on future generations.   **T** **F**

10. The crowding-out effect of borrowing in the money market to finance an increase in government expenditures results from a rise in interest rates.   **T** **F**

11. Crowding out shifts the investment demand curve to the left.   **T** **F**

12. Financing increased government expenditures by increasing personal taxes imposes a burden on future generations.   **T** **F**

13. Higher interest rates in Canada make it more attractive for foreigners to buy Canadian financial securities.   **T** **F**

14. The higher interest rates due to a budget deficit cause a depreciation of the Canadian dollar.   **T** **F**

15. The federal government could finance a deficit by selling bonds to the Bank of Canada and, through this method, effectively print money to cover its revenue shortfall.   **T** **F**

16. A government deficit tends to push the balance of trade toward a deficit.   **T** **F**

■   **MULTIPLE-CHOICE**

Circle the letter that corresponds to the best answer.

1. The Canadian public debt is the sum of all previous:
   (a)   expenditures of the federal government
   (b)   budget deficits of the federal government
   (c)   budget deficits less the budget surpluses of the federal government
   (d)   budget deficits less the budget surpluses of the federal and provincial governments

2. Which of the following would involve cutting government expenditures and raising tax rates during a depression?
   (a)   an annually balanced budget policy
   (b)   functional finance
   (c)   a cyclically balanced budget policy
   (d)   a policy employing built-in stability

3. Since 1980:
   (a)   both the public debt relative to the GDP and the per capita debt have increased
   (b)   the public debt relative to the GDP has decreased, and the per capita debt has increased
   (c)   the public debt relative to the GDP has increased, and the per capita debt has decreased
   (d)   both the public debt relative to the GDP and the per capita debt have decreased

4. Which nation has the largest public sector debt relative to its GDP in 1997?
   (a)   Canada
   (b)   United States
   (c)   Germany
   (d)   Italy

5. The accounting procedures used by the federal government record:
   (a)   only its assets
   (b)   only its debts
   (c)   both its assets and debts
   (d)   its net worth

6. Inflation is a tax on:
   (a)   the holders of the public debt and reduces the real size of a budget deficit
   (b)   the holders of the public debt and expands the real size of a budget deficit

(c) the federal government and reduces the real size of a budget deficit
(d) the federal government and expands the real size of a budget deficit

7. The public debt cannot bankrupt the federal government because the federal government:
(a) need not reduce the size of the debt
(b) is able to refinance the debt
(c) can create money to repay the debt and pay the interest on it
(d) all of the above

8. Which one of the following is not a way for the government to finance its budget deficit?
(a) sale of bonds to the Canadian public
(b) sale of bonds to the Canadian central bank
(c) sale of bonds to foreign investors
(d) sale of common stock to Canadian investors

9. Canada's public debt is mainly held by:
(a) the Bank of Canada
(b) the Government of Canada
(c) private households and financial institutions
(d) foreign investors

10. Incurring internal debts to finance a war does not pass the cost of war on to future generations because:
(a) the opportunity cost of the war is borne by the generation that fights it
(b) the government need not pay interest on internally held debts
(c) there is never a need for government to refinance the debt
(d) war-time inflation reduces the relative size of the debt

11. Which of the following would be a consequence of the retirement of the internally held portion of public debt?
(a) a reduction in the nation's productive capacity
(b) a reduction in the nation's standard of living
(c) a redistribution of the nation's wealth among its citizens
(d) an increase in aggregate expenditures in the economy

12. Which of the following is a consequence of the public debt of Canada?
(a) it increases incentives to work and invest
(b) it transfers a portion of the Canadian output of goods and services to foreign nations

(c) it reduces income inequality in Canada
(d) it leads to greater saving at every level of disposable income

13. The crowding-out effect of borrowing in the money market to finance an increase in government expenditures:
(a) increases the interest rate and reduces current private investment expenditures
(b) decreases the interest rate and increases private investment expenditures
(c) allows an increase in government and private borrowing
(d) places the burden of the debt on today's generation

14. The crowding-out effect of government borrowing to finance its increased expenditures is reduced:
(a) when the economy is operating at less than full employment
(b) when the expenditures expand human capital in the economy
(c) when the government's deficit financing improves the profit expectations of business firms
(d) when any one or more of the above are true

15. Which of the following is not one of the sources of the recent concern over government deficits and the growth of the public debt?
(a) the large increases in the sizes of the deficits and in the public debt
(b) the fact that deficits have helped move the economy to full employment
(c) the mounting interest costs of the debt
(d) the fact that large deficits were being incurred during all four phases of the business cycle

16. The increased demand by foreigners for Canadian bonds that result from higher Canadian interest rates:
(a) increase the external debt of Canada and cause the Canadian dollar to depreciate
(b) lower the external debt of Canada and cause the Canadian dollar to appreciate
(c) increase the external debt of Canada and cause the Canadian dollar to appreciate
(d) lower the external debt of Canada and cause the Canadian dollar to depreciate

17. When the Canadian dollar appreciates:
(a) Canadian exports tend to increase
(b) Canadian imports tend to increase

(c) Canadian net exports tend to increase

(d) none of the above tend to occur

18. If the government uses a surplus to retire some existing bonds, this will tend to: *b*

(a) lower interest rates and produce appreciation of the nation's currency

(b) lower interest rates and produce depreciation of the nation's currency

(c) raise interest rates and produce appreciation of the nation's currency

(d) raise interest rates and produce depreciation of the nation's currency

■ DISCUSSION QUESTIONS

1. What is the difference between the government's budget deficit and the public debt?

2. Explain the three different budget philosophies, and explain whether each one tends to intensify or reduce the fluctuations of GDP during the business cycle.

3. How big is the public debt of Canada, absolutely and relatively? How large are the interest charges on the debt, absolutely and relatively? What has happened to the size of the debt and interest charges since 1926, and since 1975? Why have these changes occurred?

4. How could the accounting procedures of the federal government be changed to better represent the government's actual financial position (its net worth)? How does inflation affect the real size of the public debt and the real size of the federal government's budget deficits?

5. Why can't the public debt bankrupt the federal government? Are the same arguments true for provincial government debts?

6. Explain the difference between an internally held and an externally held public debt. If the debt is internally held, government borrowing to finance a war does not pass all the cost of the war on to future generations. Why? Why does the portion of the public debt externally held impose a burden on the economy?

7. How does the public debt and the payment of interest on the debt affect the income distribution and incentives?

8. Under what conditions will deficits impose a burden on future generations? Why don't increases in government expenditures financed by increased personal taxes impose the same burden on future generations? What will lessen the burden of deficit financing on future generations?

9. What tends to happen to the amount of saving done at full employment as the full-employment GDP grows? How, in a growing economy, does debt — public and private — help to maintain full employment and growth?

10. Trace through the cause-effect chain from increases in deficits and public debt to changes in: (a) interest rates; (b) domestic investment in real capital and financial investment by foreigners in Canadian bonds; (c) the external debts of Canada and the international value of the dollar; (d) Canadian exports and imports; and (e) employment and real output in the Canadian economy.

11. If Canada is able to avoid deficits, as we did in 1998, what will the consequences be for our economy? Will there be any consequences for you?

■ ANSWERS

FILL-IN QUESTIONS

1. expenditures, revenues, deficits, surpluses

2. pro-, fall, cut, reducing

3. recession, inflation

4. full employment without inflation, deficits, public debt

5. wars, recessions, political will

6. (a) 465, 54, 44, 5; (b) internal

7. (a) Canadian public, Canada; (b) 25

8. debts, assets

9. refinancing, money, levy, collect

10. asset

11. externally; increase, incentives, crowding-out

12. increases, decreases, capital; (a) consumer, present; (b) capital, less than full

13. increased, inflow; demand for, appreciation, decrease, increase; contractionary

14. (a) enormous size (b) rising interest costs (c) inappropriate cyclical policy (d) balance of trade problems

15. saving, growing, full employment

PROBLEMS AND PROJECTS

1. (a) 100, 22; (b) higher some years, lower other years; (c) lower taxes to expand AD to move GDP to full-employment

2. (a) Tax revenues: 200, 220, 240, 260; Interest on debt: 18, 19, 20, 22; Debt at Jan 1: 300, 318, 337, 367; Deficit: 18, 19, 30, 62; Debt at Dec 31: 318, 337, 367, 429; Debt/GDP: 32, 31, 31, 33
(b) increased; (c) interest; (d) 2, Debt/GDP.

3. (a) 1996: 21, 1997: 7.5; (b) both years have same debt to GDP ratio.

TRUE-FALSE

1. F	**2.** F	**3.** T	**4.** T	**5.** F	**6.** F
7. F	**8.** F	**9.** T	**10.** T	**11.** F	**12.** F
13. T	**14.** F	**15.** T	**16.** T		

MULTIPLE-CHOICE

1. (c)	**2.** (a)	**3.** (a)	**4.** (d)	**5.** (b)	**6.** (a)
7. (d)	**8.** (d)	**9.** (c)	**10.** (a)	**11.** (c)	**12.** (b)
13. (a)	**14.** (d)	**15.** (b)	**16.** (c)	**17.** (b)	**18.** (b)

CHAPTER 20

International Trade

Chapter 20 builds on Chapter 6 which introduced you to Canada's connections with the global economy. After a review of the key facts about world trade, the chapter examines the theory of comparative advantage. This theory provides the basis for international specialization and trade, by demonstrating that both nations in an export-import relationship can gain. Though free trade agreements with the United States and Mexico have gained much attention in recent years, the Canadian economy has always been heavily dependent on international trade. We export and import with many different nations, and over an astonishing range of goods and services.

We trade because trade benefits us; so what is the source of these benefits? Economic resources (natural, human, and capital) are distributed unevenly between nations. Efficient production of various goods requires different technologies or combinations of resources. Therefore, some nations are well-suited to producing labour-intensive goods while others are well-suited to capital-intensive goods. The theory of comparative advantage predicts that each nation will specialize in producing those products for which they have the lower opportunity cost. Production according to this principle will maximize the total output of goods, and through exports and imports, each nation will end up able to consume larger quantities than they could without free trade.

The standard supply and demand model can be adapted to find export supply and import demand curves. If the Canadian domestic price is above (below) the world price, Canada will supply exports (demand imports) equal to our domestic surplus (shortage). In a two-country model, the world price for a product is found where one country's export supply curve intersects the other country's import demand curve.

The second half of the chapter analyzes impacts of trade barriers, and the general arguments for protectionism versus free trade. Despite the strong case for specialization and free trade according to comparative advantage, virtually all nations have erected various barriers to free trade: tariffs, quotas, and other restrictions on imports. Thus, the chapter looks at: (1) what techniques nations use to limit imports; (2) the economic impacts of trade barriers; and (3) the arguments in favour of protectionism. Even if protectionism is beneficial on balance — which most economists seriously doubt! — the costs of protectionism are significant, and must be understood.

The final section of the chapter reviews the history of Canadian trade policy, starting with the National Policy, and emphasizing more recent initiatives including GATT, the Canada-U.S. Free Trade Agreement (FTA), and the North American Free Trade Agreement (NAFTA).

■ CHECKLIST

When you have studied this chapter, you should be able to:

☐ Explain the importance of international trade to Canada's economy and list our major exports and imports.

☐ State the two economic circumstances that make it desirable for nations to specialize and trade.

☐ Explain the basic concept of comparative advantage.

☐ Compute, when you are given the necessary figures, the opportunity cost of producing two commodities in two countries and determine which nation has the comparative advantage in the production of each commodity.

□ Calculate the range in which the terms of trade will be found in examples using two goods, and calculate the gains to each nation and to the world from specialization and trade.

□ Assuming constant opportunity costs, work out comparative advantage examples using data for two nations on their production possibilities diagrams.

□ Explain how the model's predictions on trade and production patterns will change if the constant cost assumption is changed to increasing opportunity costs.

□ Given data on two countries' supply and demand curves for a good, derive export supply and import demand curves, and determine the world equilibrium price, and quantity of exports and imports of the good.

□ Identify the four principal types of artificial barriers to international trade and the motives for erecting these barriers.

□ Explain the economic effects of a protective tariff on resource allocation, the price of the commodity, the total production of the commodity, and the outputs of foreign and domestic producers of the commodity.

□ Identify the gainers and losers from trade restrictions.

□ Analyze the economic effects of an import quota and compare them with the economic effects of a tariff.

□ Enumerate six arguments used to support the case for protection and find the weakness in each of these arguments.

□ Discuss the costs of protectionism for society.

□ Describe the National Policy and its effects.

□ Outline the nature of trade liberalization through multilateral and bilateral trade agreements such as GATT, EU, FTA and NAFTA.

□ Discuss some of the benefits and the problems associated with Canada's involvement in free trade agreements.

■ **CHAPTER OUTLINE**

1. International trade is vital to the Canadian economy.

(a) Canada is more trade dependent than most nations; exports are more than one-third of Canadian GDP, and rising.

(b) This trade provides both important capital goods and markets for raw materials.

(c) Canada's principal commodity exports are automotive products, machinery and equipment, and forestry products. Its main imports are machinery and equipment and automotive products.

(d) Most of Canada's trade is with other industrialized nations, particularly the United States, Japan and Western European nations.

2. Specialization and trade between nations are advantageous because the world's resources are not evenly distributed and the efficient production of different commodities necessitates different methods and combinations of resources.

3. The basis for trade is the principle of comparative advantage, which states that total output will be greatest when each good is produced in the country where its opportunity cost is lowest. A simple hypothetical example illustrates comparative advantage and the gains from trade.

(a) Suppose the world is composed of only two nations, each capable of producing two different commodities and having straight-line production possibilities curves with different slopes. That is, the opportunity cost of producing each good is constant but differs between the two countries.

(b) With different opportunity costs, each nation has a comparative (cost) advantage in the production of one of the two goods; and if the world is to use its resources economically, each nation must specialize according to their comparative advantage.

(c) The ratio at which one product is traded for another is called the "terms of trade" and lies between the opportunity cost ratios of the two nations.

(d) Each nation can share in the gains from trade because specialization permits a greater total output from the same resources and a better allocation of the world's resources.

(e) If cost ratios in the two nations are not constant, specialization may not be complete.

(f) If opportunity cost ratios do not differ, there is no basis for mutually beneficial trade.

(g) The basic argument for free trade among nations is that it leads to a better allocation of resources and a higher standard of living in the world; but it also increases competition and deters monopoly in these nations.

4. Supply and demand analysis can be used to explain how the equilibrium price and quantity of exports and imports for a product are determined in trade between two nations.

   (a)   For each of the two nations there is a domestic demand and a domestic supply. In the absence of international trade, the intersections of these curves establish the price in each nation.

   (b)   In a world with trade, the export supply curve shows how much the domestic producers are willing to sell abroad at each world price above the domestic (no-trade) equilibrium price. The import demand curve shows how much consumers are willing to buy from abroad at each world price below the domestic equilibrium price.

   (c)   The equilibrium world price and world levels of exports and imports are determined where one nation's import demand curve intersects the other nation's export supply curve.

5. Nations restrict international trade by imposing tariffs, import quotas, a variety of nontariff barriers, and voluntary export restrictions. Special-interest groups within nations benefit from protection and persuade their governments to erect trade barriers. The costs to consumers of this protection exceed the benefits to workers and shareholders, so the economy experiences a net cost. Demand and supply diagrams can be used to show the effects of trade barriers.

6. The imposition of a tariff on a good imported from abroad has both direct and indirect effects on an economy.

   (a)   The tariff increases the domestic price of the good, reduces its domestic consumption, expands its domestic production, decreases foreign production, and transfers income from domestic consumers to producers and the government.

   (b)   It also reduces the income of foreign producers and the ability of foreign nations to purchase goods and services in the nation imposing the tariff, causes the contraction of relatively efficient industries in that nation, decreases world trade, and lowers the real output of goods and services.

7. The imposition of a quota on an imported product has the same direct and indirect effects as that of a tariff on that product, except that what would otherwise be tariff revenue for the government ends up as revenue for foreign producers.

8. The military self-sufficiency argument for protectionism is questionable because it is difficult to say which industry is "vital" to national defence and must be protected. It would be more efficient economically to provide a direct subsidy to military producers rather than impose a tariff.

9. Trade barriers are often implemented to protect jobs at home, but this strategy often fails because:

   (a) imports may eliminate some jobs, but they create others; therefore, imports may only change the composition of employment, not the overall level of employment;

   (b) the exports of one nation become the imports of another; tariff barriers can be viewed as "beggar thy neighbour" policies;

   (c) other nations are likely to retaliate with their own tariffs, leading to reduced national output and employment; and,

   (d) they reduce the efficiency of resource allocation by shielding domestic industries from competition.

10. Tariffs are sometimes supported as devices to help diversify, and thereby stabilize, the economy. The Canadian economy is already quite diversified, so the strategy is not necessary. In less-developed nations this strategy could have huge economic costs because it pushes nations to produce contrary to comparative advantage.

11. It is alleged that infant industries need protection until they are strong enough to compete. But the argument may not apply to developed economies: it is difficult to select which industries will prosper; protectionism tends to persist long after it is needed; and direct subsidies may be more economically efficient.

12. As instruments of strategic trade policy, tariffs may give domestic producers an advantage over foreign competitors, allowing them to grow more rapidly and achieve greater economies of scale than foreign competitors. The protected firms can then dominate world markets because of lower costs. In other words, the goal is to acquire comparative advantage by strategic economic policies rather than depending solely on a country's resource allocation. Such strategies, however, tend to provoke retaliatory strategies by nations whose industries have lost due to such strategies.

13. Sometimes protection is sought against the "dumping" of foreign goods on Canadian markets. Dumping is a legitimate concern and is restricted under Canadian trade law; but to use dumping as an excuse for widespread tariff protection is unjustified, because there are few proven cases of dumping. If foreign companies are more efficient than our firms, what may appear to be dumping may actually be the result of comparative advantage.

14. Protection is sometimes sought to shield Canadian workers from cheap foreign labour. In fact these differences in labour costs are the very basis for mutually beneficial trade. If countries with low wages cannot export labour-intensive goods to high-wage nations, their living standards, and our living standards, will be lower.

15. In summary, there are many arguments for protectionism, but most are fallacious or based on half-truths. The only points that have some validity, under certain conditions, are the infant-industry and military-sufficiency arguments, but both are subject to abuse. The historical evidence suggests that free trade promotes prosperity and growth in the world.

16. For Canadian society trade protectionism has costs.
(a)   Consumers pay higher prices for imported goods.
(b)   The higher prices induce some consumers to switch to buying less desired goods instead of the imports.
(c)   Prices of domestically produced goods will rise because import competition is lessened.

17. Trade policies in Canada have undergone major shifts in the last century or so.
(a)   The National Policy of 1879 made Canada a highly protected market for our manufacturers.
(b)   Canada has slowly reduced tariffs, with the 1947 General Agreement on Trade and Tariffs (signed by Canada and 22 other nations) being a significant vehicle for eliminating trade barriers. The GATT has been renegotiated and revised eight times (including the Uruguay Round in 1994).
(c)   In 1989 Canada signed the Free Trade Agreement (FTA) with the United States. In 1994, Canada, the United States and Mexico signed the North American Free Trade Agreement (NAFTA). These agreements have eliminated a wide range of tariffs and other trade restrictions.
(d)   The European Union, or Common Market, has sought the economic integration of Western Europe, and its member nations have achieved

considerable integration and have increased their growth rates; but their success has created problems for nonmember nations.

■   **TERMS AND CONCEPTS**

absolute advantage
Canada-U.S. Free
   Trade Agreement
   (FTA)
capital-intensive
   goods
comparative
   advantage
cost ratios
domestic price
dumping
economic integration
European Union (EU or
   Common Market)
export supply curve
gains from trade
General Agreement on
   Tariffs and Trade
   (GATT)
import demand curve
import quotas

labour-intensive goods
land-intensive goods
most-favoured-nation
   clause
National Policy
nontariff barriers
   (NTBs)
North American Free
   Trade Agreement
   (NAFTA)
revenue and protective
   tariffs
strategic trade policy
terms of trade
trade bloc
trading possibilities
   line
voluntary export
   restrictions (VERs)
world price

■   **HINTS AND TIPS**

1.   Spend time working numerical examples of the comparative advantage model because this is a very important model, but its insights can be elusive.

2.   To understand why tariffs exist, even if the costs to consumers exceed the benefits to domestic producers, consider the following questions. Do you know whether or not Canada has a tariff on shoelaces, and if so, what is it? If you were a Canadian manufacturer of shoelaces, do you think that you would know more about the tariff? Why?

■   **FILL-IN QUESTIONS**

1. In recent years, Canada's imports and exports have (grown, declined) _____ as a % of the economy's GDP.

2. Ranked in order of their importance, the principal exports of Canada are _____, _____, and _____; and Canada's most important imports are _____, _____, and _____.

3. Nations tend to trade among themselves because the distribution of economic resources among them is (even, uneven) _____ and because the efficient production of various goods and services necessitates (the same, different) _____ technologies or combinations of resources.

4. The nations of the world tend to specialize in and export those goods in the production of which they have a _____, and to import those goods in the production of which they do not have a _____.

5. Given two nations that can each produce the same two goods, the principle of comparative advantage states that total output can be increased if each country produces that good with the _____ and trades with the second country for the other good.

6. If the opportunity cost of 1 banana in country X is 4 hats, while in country Y, the opportunity cost of 1 banana is 3 hats:
   (a)   hats are relatively (more, less) _____ expensive in country X and bananas relatively _____ expensive;
   (b)   hats are relatively _____ expensive in country Y and bananas relatively _____ expensive;
   (c)   X has a comparative advantage and should specialize in the production of _____ and Y has a comparative advantage and should specialize in the production of _____.
   (d)   When X and Y specialize and trade, the terms of trade will be somewhere between _____ and _____ hats for each banana; and will depend upon world _____ and _____ for hats and bananas.
   (e)   If the terms of trade turn out to be 3.5 hats for 1 banana, the cost of obtaining 1 hat has been decreased from _____ to _____ bananas in Y, and the cost of 1 banana has been decreased from _____ to _____ hats in X.
   (f)   This international specialization will not be complete if the cost of producing either good (increases, decreases, remains constant) _____ as a nation produces more of it.

7. The basic argument for free trade is that it results in a better _____ of resources and a higher _____ of living.

8. The barriers to international trade include _____, _____ quotas, _____ barriers, and _____ restrictions.

9. A trade war can result if one nation's imposition of a tariff causes its trading partners to _____.

10. When Canada imposes a tariff on a good that is imported from abroad,
   (a)   the price of that good in Canada will (increase, decrease) _____;
   (b)   the total purchases of the good in Canada will _____;
   (c)   the output of:
      (1)   Canadian producers of the good will _____;
      (2)   foreign producers of the good will _____;
   (d)   the ability of foreigners to buy goods and services from Canada will _____, and, as a result, output and employment in Canadian industries that sell goods and services abroad will _____.

11. While a tariff generates revenue for the Canadian _____, an import quota transfers that revenue to _____.

12. List the six main arguments that protectionists use to justify trade barriers.
   (a) _____
   (b) _____
   (c) _____
   (d) _____
   (e) _____
   (f) _____

13. The only two arguments containing any reasonable justification for protection are the _____ and the _____ arguments.

14. Canada became a high-tariff country in 1879 as a result of the _____. Since 1988 Canada has promoted free trade by taking an active role in _____ negotiations, by completing the _____ with the United States, and by completing the _____ with Mexico and the United States.

15. The best example of economic _____ is the European Common Market, or European

_____. The original goals of the EU were the abolition of _____ among member nations, the establishment of common tariffs on goods imported from _____ nations, the free movement of _____ and _____ among member nations, and common policies with respect to other matters.

16. Under terms of the Free Trade Agreement all trade restrictions will be eliminated by the year ____.

17. NAFTA has strengthened rules of _____ to ensure that there is a minimum amount of North American content in what is traded between Canada, the United States and Mexico.

■ PROBLEMS AND PROJECTS

1. Assume there is only one input: labour hours. In England it takes 6 hours to produce 1 unit of cloth and 4 hours to produce 1 unit of wine. There are a total of 60 hours of labour available in the English economy.

In Canada it takes 2.5 hours to produce 1 unit of cloth and 2 hours to produce 1 unit of wine. There are a total of 30 labour hours available in Canada.

(a) Construct the production possibilities graphs for cloth and wine in England and Canada.

(b) What does Canada have a comparative advantage in producing?

(c) If trade takes place, what should Canada produce, export, and import?

(d) Suppose that the number of labour hours available in England increases to 120. What does Canada now have a comparative advantage in producing?

(e) If trade takes place, what should Canada produce, export, and import?

2. Below are the production possibilities curves for Canada and Chile. Suppose these two nations do not currently engage in international trade or specialization, and suppose that points *A* and *a* show the combinations of wheat and copper they now produce and consume.

(a) The fact that the curves are straight indicates that the cost ratios in the two nations are (changing, constant) _____.

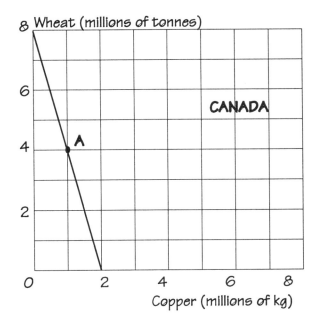

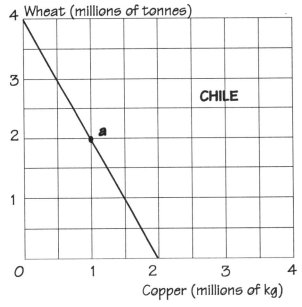

(b) Examination of the two curves reveals that the cost ratio in

(1) Canada is _____ million tonnes of wheat for 1 million kilograms of copper.

(2) Chile is _____ million tonnes of wheat for 1 million kilograms of copper.

(c) If these two nations were to specialize and trade wheat for copper,

(1) Canada would specialize in the production of _____ (Why?);

(2) Chile would specialize in the production of _____.

(d)   The terms of trade, if specialization and trade occur, will be greater than 2 and less than 4 million tonnes of wheat for 1 million kilograms of copper. Why?

(e)   Assume the terms of trade turn out to be 3 million tonnes of wheat for 1 million kilograms of copper. Draw in the trading possibilities lines for Canada and Chile.

(f)   With these trading possibilities lines, suppose Canada decides to consume 5 million tonnes of wheat and 1 million kilograms of copper, while Chile decides to consume 3 million tonnes of wheat and 1 million kilograms of copper. The gains from trade to

(1) Canada are _____ million tonnes of wheat and _____ million kilograms of copper.

(2) Chile are _____ million tonnes of wheat and _____ million kilograms of copper.

3. Suppose that the Canadian demand for woven blankets is given in the table.

Price	Canadian Qd	Canadian Qs
21	62,000	42,000
22	59,000	44,000
23	56,000	46,000
24	53,000	48,000
25	50,000	50,000
26	47,000	52,000

(a)   The domestic equilibrium price is $_____, and quantity is _____.

(b)   Suppose that Canada can now import blankets. Foreign suppliers are willing to sell at a price of $22 as many blankets as Canada will buy. The new price in Canada will be $_____, and quantity consumed with be _____. Canadian producers will supply _____ and the remaining quantity of _____ will be imported.

(c)   If the Canadian government imposes an import tariff of $1 per blanket, the new price in Canada will be $_____, and quantity consumed with be _____. Canadian producers will supply _____ and the remaining quantity of _____ will be imported. The government will collect tariff revenue of $_____.

4. The following table shows demand and supply in two nations for some product.

(a)   In the absence of trade, the price in Nation 1 would be $_____, and the price in Nation 2 would be $_____.

(b)   Use the data to generate export supply and import demand curves for each nation, and plot these curves in the graph below.

Price	Nation 1 Qd	Nation 1 Qs	Nation 2 Qd	Nation 2 Qs
$8	2	10	4	8
7	3	9	5	7
6	4	8	6	6
5	5	7	7	5
4	6	6	8	4
3	7	5	9	3

(c)   When trade occurs between the two nations, the equilibrium price in both nations will be $_____.

(d)   In equilibrium:
Nation 1 produces _____ units, consumes _____ units, and (exports, imports) _____ the difference.
Nation 2 produces _____ units, consumes _____ units, and (exports, imports) _____ the difference.

■   **TRUE-FALSE**

Circle T if the statement is true, F if it is false.

1. Exports account for more than one-third of Canada's GDP.   **T F**

2. Canada exports mainly raw materials, and imports mainly manufactured and other finished goods.   **T F**

3. The United States is Canada's main trading partner. **T F**

4. International trade is a substitute for the international mobility of resources. **T F**

5. A nation that is experiencing rising wages will become less likely to export labour-intensive goods. **T F**

Use the following production possibilities tables to answer true-false questions 6 through 11 and multiple-choice questions 4 and 5.

ADANAC		
Butter	0	20
Cloth	40	0

ZATELBA		
Butter	0	60
Cloth	60	0

6. In Adanac the opportunity cost of 1 unit of cloth is 1/4 unit of butter. **T F**

7. In Adanac the opportunity cost of butter is constant. **T F**

8. In Zatelba the opportunity cost of one unit of cloth is 1 unit of butter. **T F**

9. Adanac has the comparative advantage in the production of cloth. **T F**

10. Zatelba has the comparative advantage in the production of both goods. **T F**

11. With specialization and trade, the trading possibilities line of both nations would move to the right of their production possibilities curve. **T F**

12. Increasing production costs lead to incomplete specialization in production in trading nations. **T F**

13. Trade among nations tends to bring about a more efficient use of the world's resources and a greater world output of goods and services. **T F**

14. A tariff on coffee in Canada is an example of a protective tariff. **T F**

15. When a tariff is placed on a Canadian import, there are groups in Canada who gain and other groups in Canada who lose. **T F**

16. The use of tariffs to achieve goals of military self-sufficiency has economic costs because resources are allocated inefficiently. **T F**

17. An import quota specifies the minimum price that can be charged for an imported good. **T F**

18. Most of the economic consequences of tariffs and import quotas are similar. **T F**

19. One significant difference between a tariff and an import quota is that the quota generates revenue for the government, whereas the tariff does not. **T F**

20. One-crop economies may be able to make themselves more stable and diversified by imposing tariffs on goods imported from abroad; but these tariffs are apt also to lower the standard of living in these economies. **T F**

21. The only argument for tariffs that has, in the appropriate circumstances, any economic justification is the argument of increasing domestic employment. **T F**

22. Canada is a world leader in the use of strategic trade policy. **T F**

23. The economic integration of nations creates larger markets for firms within the nations that integrate, and makes it possible for these firms and their customers to benefit from the economies of large-scale (mass) production. **T F**

24. The cost of protecting Canadian firms and employees from foreign competition is the rise in the prices of products produced in Canada, and this cost almost always exceeds its benefits. **T F**

25. Tariffs can be a legitimate strategy for combatting dumping, whereby foreign producers may try to establish market power in this country. **T F**

26. One reason Canada joined the NAFTA was to gain leverage in future negotiations to join other trade blocs, perhaps with Japan and the EU. **T F**

27. The NAFTA will be beneficial to almost all Canadian manufacturing industries. **T F**

28. A major concern with NAFTA is whether Canada's own environmental and labour standards will be threatened by the fact that Mexico's lower standards give them a competitive advantage.   **T F**

■ **MULTIPLE-CHOICE**

Circle the letter that corresponds to the best answer.

1. Nations would not need to engage in trade if:
(a) all products were produced from the same combinations of resources
(b) world resources were evenly distributed among nations
(c) world resources were perfectly mobile
(d) all of the above

2. Country A has a comparative advantage over country B in the production of good G:
(a) when good G is produced in both countries and wages are lower in country A
(b) when country A has an absolute advantage in the production of good G
(c) when the opportunity cost of good G is lower in country A than in country B
(d) when the opportunity cost of good G is lower in country B than in country A

3. If country B has a comparative advantage over country A in the production of good G, then:
(a) country B has an absolute advantage in the production of good G
(b) the production of good G in country B uses less resources than in country A
(c) the opportunity cost of producing good G is less in country B than in country A
(d) inputs are more efficient in country B than in country A

Use the tables preceding true-false question 6 to answer the following three questions.

4. If Adanac and Zatelba engage in trade, the terms of trade will be:
(a) between 1 and 2 units of butter for 1 unit of cloth
(b) between 1/2 and 1 unit of butter for 1 unit of cloth
(c) between 3 and 4 units of butter for 1 unit of cloth
(d) between 1/8 and 1/4 unit of butter for 1 unit of cloth.

5. If, after trade commenced, the exchange ratio was 1 cloth for 1/2 butter, the gains from trade would:
(a) all go to Adanac
(b) all go to Zatelba
(c) be equally distributed between Adanac and Zatelba
(d) be captured by the larger of the two countries

6. The terms of trade:
(a) are given by the reciprocal of the foreign exchange rate
(b) measure the number of units of imports obtained per unit of export
(c) are given by the reciprocal of the foreign trade multiplier
(d) improve whenever the exchange rate depreciates

7. If two countries produce and trade two goods according to the principle of comparative advantage:
(a) both countries can produce at a point to the right of their production possibilities curves
(b) at least one country will produce at a point to the right of its production possibilities curve
(c) at least one country will consume a combination of the two goods to the right of its production possibilities curve
(d) all of the above

8. Changing the assumption of constant costs to one of increasing costs in the trade model results in:
(a) the principle of comparative advantage no longer holding
(b) only one of two trading partners gaining from trade
(c) a tendency towards incomplete specialization
(d) trade flows being greater than in the constant cost model

9. Which one of the following is characteristic of tariffs?
(a) they legally prohibit the importation of goods from abroad
(b) they specify the maximum amounts of specific commodities that may be imported during a given period of time
(c) they often protect domestic producers from foreign competition

(d) they enable nations to reduce their exports and increase their imports during periods of depression

10. The motive for a nation to erect barriers to the importation of goods and services is to:
(a) improve economic efficiency in that nation
(b) protect and benefit special-interest groups in that nation
(c) reduce the prices of the goods and services produced in that nation
(d) expand the export of goods and services to foreign nations

11. Which of the following is the likely result of Canada employing tariffs to protect its high wages and standard of living from cheap foreign labour?
(a) a decrease in the productivity of Canadian workers
(b) an increase in Canadian exports
(c) a rise in the Canadian real GDP
(d) a decrease in the quantities of resources employed by industries producing the goods on which tariffs have been levied

12. Which of the following is a likely result of imposing tariffs to increase domestic employment?
(a) a short-run increase in domestic employment
(b) retaliatory increases in the tariffs of foreign nations
(c) a long-run decline in exports
(d) all of the above

13. Which of the following is not true of tariffs established to support an infant industry?
(a) such tariffs tend to remain in place long after the industry has matured
(b) it is difficult for government to determine which infant industries have potential to benefit from such a tariff
(c) such tariffs may not be the best way to achieve the goal: direct subsidies might be more effective
(d) all of the above are true

Answer the next four questions (14 through 17) on the basis of the following diagram, where *Sd* and *Dd* are the domestic supply and demand for a product and *Pw* is the world price of that product.

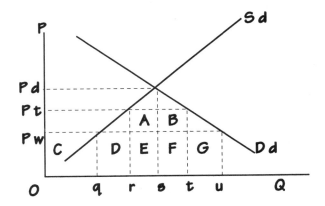

14. In a closed economy (without international trade), the equilibrium price would be:
(a) *OPd*; but in an open economy, the equilibrium price will be *OPt*
(b) *OPd*; but in an open economy, the equilibrium price will be *OPw*
(c) *OPd*; but in an open economy, the equilibrium price will be *OPd*
(d) *OPd*; but in an open economy, the equilibrium price will be *OPt*

15. If there were free trade in this economy and no tariffs, the total revenue going to the foreign producers is represented by:
(a) area *C*
(b) areas *A* and *B* combined
(c) areas *A, B, E,* and *F* combined
(d) areas *D, E, F,* and *G* combined

16. If a per unit tariff was imposed in the amount of *PwPt,* then domestic producers would supply:
(a) *Oq* units and foreign producers would supply *qu* units
(b) *Os* units and foreign producers would supply *su* units
(c) *Or* units and foreign producers would supply *rt* units
(d) *Ot* units and foreign producers would supply *tu* units

17. Given a per unit tariff in the amount of P_wP_t, the amount of the tariff revenue paid by consumers of this product is represented by:
(a) area *A*
(b) area *B*
(c) areas *A* and *B* combined
(d) areas *D, E, F,* and *G* combined

18. A tariff introduced to protect the Canadian furniture industry would create:

(a) benefits for shareholders, workers and consumers of the Canadian furniture industry

(b) benefits for shareholders and workers that exceed the costs to consumers

(c) costs to consumers that exceed the benefits for shareholders and workers

(d) costs to shareholders, workers and consumers

19. An example of a nontariff barrier is:

(a) unreasonable labelling standards for imported products

(b) a quota on imports

(c) voluntary export restriction

(d) an export subsidy

20. Under the National Policy introduced in 1879:

(a) Canada entered into a free trade agreement with the United States

(b) Canada became a member of GATT

(c) Canada declared free trade in natural resource products

(d) Canada imposed high tariffs to protect the manufacturing sector

21. Which of the following is not characteristic of the General Agreement on Tariffs and Trade? Nations signing the agreement were committed to:

(a) the elimination of import quotas

(b) the reciprocal reduction of tariffs by negotiation

(c) the nondiscriminatory treatment of all trading nations

(d) the establishment of a world customs union

22. The European Common Market:

(a) is designed to eliminate tariffs and import quotas among its members

(b) aims to allow the free movement of capital and labour within the member nations

(c) imposes common tariffs on goods imported into the member nations from outside the Common Market area

(d) does all of the above

23. The Canada-U.S. Free Trade Agreement is resulting in:

(a) complete free trade

(b) freer trade

(c) less trade between Canada and the U.S.

(d) none of the above

24. If Japanese manufacturers dump VCRs in Canada, they are:

(a) selling VCRs in Canada at a price less than the cost of production

(b) selling VCRs in Canada at a price less than the price in Japan

(c) selling VCRs in Canada at a price that is less than the price in Japan plus the cost of shipping to Canada

(d) selling VCRs in Canada that were produced in a foreign government-owned establishment

■ **DISCUSSION QUESTIONS**

1. In relative and absolute terms, how important is international trade to Canada? What are the principal exports and imports of the Canadian economy? What are the trends in Canada's trade patterns?

2. Why do nations specialize in certain products and export their surplus production of these goods at the same time that they are importing other goods? Why not reallocate their resources to producing on their own the goods and services that they wish to consume?

3. What two facts — one dealing with the distribution of the world's resources and the other related to the technology of producing different products — are the basis for trade among nations?

4. Explain: (a) the theory or principle of comparative advantage; (b) what is meant by and what determines the terms of trade; (c) the gains from the trade.

5. What motivates nations to erect barriers to the importation of goods from abroad, and what types of barriers do they erect?

6. Suppose Canada were to increase the tariff on wines imported from Europe (and elsewhere). What would be the effect of this tariff-rate increase on

(a) the price of wines in Canada;

(b) the total number of wines sold in Canada during a year;

(c) the number of wines produced by and employment in the European wine industry;

(d) production and employment in the Canadian wine industry;

(e) European incomes obtained by selling wines in Canada;

(f) the European demand for goods produced in Canada;

(g) the production and employment in those Canadian industries that now export goods to Europe;

(h) the standards of living in Canada and in Europe;

(i) the allocation of resources in the Canadian economy;

(j) the allocation of Europe's resources?

7. What is the "case for protection"? How valid and pertinent to Canada is each of the six basic arguments for protection?

8. If economists are correct that trade barriers impose greater costs on consumers than the benefits conferred on businesses and workers, why have tariffs and other protective measures been so prevalent throughout our history?

9. What were the three cardinal principles contained in the General Agreement on Tariffs and Trade (GATT)?

10. What economic factors led Canada to seek a greater integration of its economy with the economies of the United States and Mexico?

■ **ANSWERS**

FILL-IN QUESTIONS

1. grown

2. automotive goods, machinery and equipment, forest products; machinery, equipment, automotive products

3. uneven, different

4. comparative advantage, comparative advantage

5. lowest opportunity cost

6. (a) less, more; (b) more, less; (c) hats, bananas; (d) 3, 4, demand, supply; (e) 1/3, 2/7; 4, 3; (f) increases

7. allocation, standard

8. tariffs, import, nontariff, voluntary export

9. retaliate

10. (a) increase; (b) decrease; (c) (1) increase, (2) decrease; (d) decrease, decrease

11. government, foreign producers

12. (a) military self-sufficiency; (b) infant industry; (c) increase domestic employment; (d) diversification for stability; (e) cheap foreign labour; (f) protection against dumping

13. military self-sufficiency, infant-industry

14. National Policy: GATT, Free Trade Agreement, North American Free Trade Agreement

15. integration, Union; tariffs and import quotas, non-member, capital, labour

16. 1999

17. origin

PROBLEMS AND PROJECTS

1. (a) endpoints: England: 10 cloth and 0 wine, 0 cloth and 15 wine; Canada: 12 cloth and 0 wine, 0 cloth and 15 wine; (b) cloth; (c) cloth, cloth, wine; (d) cloth; (e) cloth, cloth, wine

2. (a) constant; (b) (1) 4, (2) 2; (c) (1) wheat; because its cost of producing wheat is less than Chile's, (2) copper; (d) one of the two nations would be unwilling to trade if the terms of trade were outside this range; (f) (1) 1, 0, (2) 1, 0

3. (a) 25, 50,000; (b) 22, 59,000, 44,000, 15,000; (c) 23, 56,000, 46,000, 10,000, 10,000

4. (a) 4, 6; (c) 5; (d) Nation 1 produces 7, consumes 5, exports 2; Nation 2 produces 5, consumes 7, imports 2

TRUE-FALSE

1. T	2. F	3. T	4. T	5. T	6. F
7. T	8. T	9. T	10. F	11. T	12. T
13. T	14. F	15. T	16. T	17. F	18. T
19. F	20. T	21. F	22. F	23. T	24. T
25. T	26. T	27. F	28. T		

MULTIPLE-CHOICE

1. (d)	2. (c)	3. (c)	4. (b)	5. (b)	6. (b)
7. (c)	8. (c)	9. (c)	10. (b)	11. (a)	12. (d)
13. (d)	14. (b)	15. (d)	16. (c)	17. (c)	18. (c)
19. (a)	20. (d)	21. (d)	22. (d)	23. (b)	24. (a)

CHAPTER 21

Exchange Rates and the Balance of Payments

Chapter 21 is about the financial or monetary side of the international trade discussed in Chapter 20. The key topics include: (1) how nations using different currencies are able to trade with each other; (2) how transactions with non-residents are recorded in the balance of payments accounts; (3) how to interpret various balance of payments accounts and terminology; (4) how foreign exchange rates are determined in flexible rate and fixed rate systems; and (5) a brief outline of different exchange rate systems that trading nations have used in the present century.

Countries use different currencies, so when they trade there must be a way to exchange their currencies. When a Canadian resident (e.g., a consumer or a firm) wishes to make a payment to a resident of, say, Mexico, they buy pesos. They pay for the Mexican pesos with Canadian dollars. And when, for example, a French resident sells goods and receives a payment from a Canadian resident, and obtains Canadian dollars, they sell this foreign money — often called foreign exchange — in return for some of their own francs. The markets in which one money is sold and is paid for with another money are called foreign exchange markets. The price that is paid (in one money) for a unit of another money is called the foreign exchange rate (or the rate of exchange). Under the system in use in Canada, the exchange rate for any foreign currency is determined by the demand for and the supply of that currency. Exports from Canada create a demand for Canadian dollars (and a supply of foreign currency). Canadian imports create a supply of Canadian dollars (and a demand for foreign currency).

As Chapter 20 showed, large quantities of goods and services are traded across national boundaries. But there are also huge volumes of international transactions in such financial assets as stocks and bonds, in real assets such as land and capital goods; and there are gifts, remittances, and other transfers. A nation summarizes its transactions with the rest of the world in its balance of payments: a record of how it obtained foreign money during the year and what it did with this foreign money. Of course, all foreign money obtained was used for some purpose — it did not evaporate — and consequently the balance of payments always balances. However, various sections of the balance of payments need not balance, so one must be aware of the various definitions and usages in this area.

Probably the most difficult section of this chapter is concerned with balance of payments deficits and surpluses, the causes of these imbalances, and their economic implications. A deficit (surplus) exists when the receipts of foreign money are less (greater) than the payments of foreign money and the nation's official international reserves are reduced (expanded). The discussion of these topics is linked with explanations of exchange-rate determination under different systems, with emphasis on the flexible rate system. You should pay particular attention to the different ways in which a flexible exchange rate system and a fixed exchange rate system will correct balance of payments deficits and surpluses; and note the advantages and disadvantages of these two alternative methods of eliminating imbalances.

The last part of the chapter covers three historically important exchange-rate systems: the gold standard, the Bretton Woods system, and the managed floating rate. In the first two systems exchange rates are fixed; and, in the third system, exchange rates are fixed in the short run (to obtain the advantages of fixed exchange rates) and flexible in the long run (to enable nations to correct balance of payments deficits and surpluses).

■ CHECKLIST

When you have studied this chapter, you should be able to:

□ Explain how Canadian exports create a demand for Canadian dollars and generate a supply of foreign exchange; and how Canadian imports create a demand for foreign exchange and generate a supply of Canadian dollars.

□ Describe what is meant by the "foreign exchange market" and "foreign exchange rate."

□ Translate the Canadian dollar price of a unit of foreign currency into the foreign currency price of a dollar.

□ Explain how a nation's exports, in a sense, finance its imports.

□ Define each of the balances found in the balance of international payments; and distinguish between a surplus and deficit in each of the balances.

□ Explain how a nation finances a payments deficit and what it does with a payments surplus.

□ Show how a nation can export more goods and services than it imports and still have a balance of payments deficit; and how it can have a trade deficit and still have a balance of payments surplus.

□ Classify particular kinds of transactions by type of account.

□ Explain the relationship between the balances on the current account, capital accounts, and official settlements balance, and changes in official international reserves.

□ From the viewpoint of the Canadian economy, identify the different participants in the foreign exchange market who demand British pounds; identify the participants in the same foreign exchange market who supply pounds.

□ Explain, from a Canadian viewpoint, why the demand for pounds in the foreign exchange market is downsloping and the supply of pounds is upsloping.

□ Construct a numerical example to illustrate a depreciation of the Canadian dollar relative to the pound; and show the effect on the Canadian price of imports from Great Britain and the pound price of Canadian exports.

□ Identify the five principal determinants of the demand for and supply of a particular foreign money; and explain how a change in each of these determinants would affect the rate of exchange for that money.

□ Explain how flexible (floating) exchange rates operate to eliminate payments deficits and sur-

pluses; and give the three disadvantages of this method of correcting imbalances.

□ Enumerate the four means by which a nation may defend a fixed (or "pegged") foreign exchange rate.

□ Explain how a nation with a payments deficit might employ its international reserves to prevent a depreciation.

□ List the requirements that a nation had to fulfill to be on the gold standard; explain how gold flows operated to reduce payments deficits and surpluses; and identify two advantages and two drawbacks of the gold standard.

□ Explain how the Bretton Woods system stabilized exchange rates and attempted to provide for orderly changes in exchange rates to eliminate payments imbalances; and explain how it ended.

□ Explain what is meant by a system of managed floating exchange rates, how it currently operates in Canada; and enumerate its virtues and shortcomings.

■ CHAPTER OUTLINE

1. Trade between two nations differs from domestic trade because each nation uses a different currency. The problem is resolved by the existence of foreign exchange markets where the money used by one nation can be traded for the other nation's money.

(a) Canadian exports create a foreign demand for dollars, and the fulfillment of this demand increases the supply of foreign currency in the foreign exchange market. More foreign currency is now in Canadian banks and available to Canadian buyers.

(b) Canadian imports create a domestic demand for foreign currencies, and the fulfillment of this demand reduces the supply of foreign currency in the foreign-exchange market. Less foreign currency is now in Canadian banks and available to Canadian buyers.

2. A nation's balance of payments is an annual record of all transactions between its residents and residents of all other nations.

(a) The current account records the nation's trade in goods and services. Recorded as credits are: merchandise exports, exports of services, receipts of investment income, and receipts of transfers. Recorded as debits are: merchandise imports, imports of services, payments of investment income, and transfers paid out.

(1) The trade balance is equal to the difference between the exports and imports of goods. A nation is said to have a favourable trade balance if exports exceed imports.

(2) The balance on current account is equal to the balance on goods and services plus the nonmerchandise balance (balance on investment income and transfers).

(b) The capital account records the nation's trade in real and financial assets. Sales are counted as credits, and purchases are debits.

(1) The balance on capital account is a surplus (deficit) if its sales are greater (less) than its purchases of real and financial assets.

(c) The current and capital accounts are interrelated. A nation with a current account deficit can finance the deficit by borrowing or selling assets abroad (with a capital account surplus), and a nation with a current account surplus can lend or buy assets abroad (incur a capital account deficit).

(d) The official settlement account refers to the movement of official international reserves. When Canada has a net surplus on its current and capital accounts combined, our reserves of foreign currency will increase, and this will show in the balance of payments as a negative value on the official settlements account. When our current and capital accounts combine for a deficit, we will have used up some international reserves, and the official settlements account will show a positive value.

(e) Whenever the balance of payments is said to be in surplus or deficit, this refers to the net surplus or deficit before including the official settlements account. Canada has a balance of payments surplus (deficit) when the current and capital account combined balance is positive (negative) and the official reserves increase (decrease).

(f) A balance of payments deficit or surplus is not necessarily a bad or a good thing. However, a persistent balance of payments deficit is undesirable because the nation's official international reserves are limited, and once they are exhausted the nation may be required to take painful macroeconomic adjustments to correct the deficit.

3. These points can be illustrated using Canadian 1997 data. We had a current account deficit of $12.8 billion, so we had to obtain this amount either from reserves or foreign investors to finance the excess of current account spending of foreign currencies over earnings of foreign currencies. We also had a capital account surplus of $16.2 billion, meaning that this amount of investment flowed into Canada over and above the amount that flowed out. Or, we sold to foreigners more financial claims than we purchased from them. Overall, there was a net inflow of foreign currency equal to $3.4 billion (-$12.8 + $16.2), and this was added to our official reserves. It was recorded as -$3.4 billion on the official settlements account.

4. The adjustments a nation with a balance of payments deficit or surplus must make to correct the imbalance depends upon whether exchange rates are flexible (floating) or fixed.

(a) With floating rates, the demand for and the supply of foreign exchange determine exchange rates. The exchange rate for a currency is the rate at which the quantity demanded of that money is equal to the quantity supplied.

(b) A change in the demand or supply of a foreign money will cause the exchange rate for that money to rise or fall; and when there is a rise (fall) in the dollar price of one unit of a foreign money, it is said that the dollar has depreciated (appreciated) and that the foreign money has appreciated (depreciated).

(c) Changes in the demand for or supply of a foreign currency are caused by changes in tastes, relative income changes, relative price changes, relative interest rate changes, and speculation.

(d) Flexible exchange rates provide an automatic adjustment mechanism for balance of payments deficits or surpluses. When a nation has a payments deficit (surplus), its currency will depreciate (appreciate). This will make foreign goods and services more (less) expensive, decrease (increase) imports, make a nation's goods and services less (more) expensive for foreigners to buy, and increase (decrease) its exports. These adjustments correct the nation's payments deficit (surplus).

(e) Flexible exchange rates have three disadvantages: currency fluctuations create uncertainties for international traders and therefore tend to discourage trade; exchange rate changes also change the terms of trade; and exchange rate fluctuations can destabilize economies (by creating inflation or unemployment).

5. When a nation fixes (or "pegs") its exchange rate, its government must somehow prevent shortages and surpluses of their currency in the foreign exchange market. There are several ways to do this.

(a)   Using foreign exchange market intervention a government can stabilize the exchange rate by selling (buying) foreign money in exchange for its own money when there is a shortage (surplus) of the foreign money.

(b)   Using trade policies (such as import tariffs and quotas, and export subsidies) a nation with a payments deficit can discourage imports and encourage exports.

(c)   Using exchange controls a nation can deal with a payments deficit by requiring exporters who earn foreign exchange to sell it to the government. The government would then ration the available foreign exchange among importers to ensure that imports are not too high in relation to exports.

(d)   Using domestic stabilization policies (monetary and fiscal policies) a nation with a balance of payments deficit can reduce its national income and price level to stimulate net exports, and raise interest rates to attract capital inflows.

6. In recent times nations of the world have employed three different exchange-rate systems. From 1879 to 1934 the gold standard system kept exchange rates fairly stable.

(a)   A nation was on the gold standard when it: defined its currency in terms of a quantity of gold; maintained a fixed relationship between its stock of gold and its money supply; and allowed gold to be freely exported and imported.

(b)   Exchange rates between gold standard nations would fluctuate only within a narrow range (determined by the cost of shipping gold from country to country); and if an exchange rate rose (fell) to the upper (lower) limit of the range, gold would flow out of (into) a nation.

(c)   When a nation with a balance of payments deficit (surplus) began to lose (gain) gold, its money supply would decrease (increase). This would raise (lower) interest rates and reduce (expand) aggregate demand, domestic output, employment, and prices in that country; and the payments deficit (surplus) would be eliminated.

(d) The relative stability of exchange rates under the gold standard encouraged trade and automatically corrected payments deficits and surpluses. But it required that nations suffer unpleasant adjustments such as recession and inflation to eliminate their payments imbalances.

(e) During the worldwide Great Depression of the 1930s, many nations broke from the gold standard and devalued their currencies in hopes of selling more exports and boosting their employment and output.

7. From 1944 until 1971 most nations used an adjustable-peg system known as the Bretton Woods system. The International Monetary Fund (IMF) was created to manage this system that kept exchange rates relatively stable.

(a)   The system required each nation to define its currency in terms of gold or US dollars. This established fixed exchange rates.

(b)   A nation had to be prepared to use their international reserves to maintain their fixed exchange rate.

(c)   A nation could acquire reserves for protecting their exchange rates by selling foreign currencies, selling gold, or borrowing on a short-term basis from the IMF.

(d)   The system also provided for orderly changes in exchange rates to correct a fundamental imbalance (persistent and sizable balance of payments deficits) by allowing a nation to devalue its currency (increase its defined gold or dollar equivalent).

(e)   In the Bretton Woods system gold and US dollars came to be regarded as international reserves. For these reserves to grow, the United States had to continue to have balance of payments deficits; but to continue the policy of convertibility of dollars into gold at $35 per ounce, it had to reduce the deficits. This dilemma led the United States to suspend convertibility of the dollar in 1971, bringing an end to the Bretton Woods system, and beginning the era of floating exchange rates.

8. Exchange rates today are managed by individual nations to avoid short-term fluctuations and they are allowed to float in the long term to correct fundamental payments imbalances. Today the Bank of Canada intervenes regularly to smooth fluctuations in the Canadian dollar. This new system of managed floating exchange rates is favoured by some and criticized by others.

(a)   Proponents contend that the managed float system has allowed world trade to flourish and has enabled the world to adjust to severe economic shocks.

(b)   Critics argue that the system has increased the volatility of exchange rates and has not reduced payments deficits and surpluses; that it reinforces inflationary pressures in a nation; and that it is a "nonsystem" that a nation may employ to achieve its own domestic economic goals.

■   TERMS AND CONCEPTS

balance of payments	flexible or floating
balance of payments	exchange-rate
deficits and	system
surpluses	gold standard
balance on goods	International Monetary
and services	Fund
Bretton Woods System	managed floating
capital account	exchange rates
capital account	official international
balance	(foreign exchange)
current account	reserves
current account	purchasing power
balance	parity theory
devaluation	trade balance

■   HINTS AND TIPS

1.   This chapter is relatively long and difficult, and filled with new terms. Allocate your time accordingly. Some of the new terms are just special words used in international economics for concepts already familiar to you.

2.   It can be difficult to think about the "price" of a unit of money, even when that money is a unit of foreign currency. It may be helpful to remember that a peso or a franc is much like a pound of coffee or a bushel of wheat whose market price is determined by the forces of demand and supply.

3.   The terms *depreciate* and *appreciate* confuse many students. Here are some hints that may help. To depreciate means to decrease (and appreciate means to increase). If country A's currency depreciates, what decreases is the amount of country B's currency that a unit of A's currency will exchange for. If 1 dollar first bought 10 pesos, and later bought only 8 pesos, the dollar has depreciated.

4.   Capital flows can be tricky to classify as debits or credits. To keep this straight, think of merchandise trade. When Canada exports a snowmobile, money comes in from abroad so that is a credit for Canada. Similarly, when Canada exports a govern-

ment bond, or the title deed to an office building in Brampton, or shares in a Canadian software company, money comes in from abroad so that is also a credit for Canada.

■   FILL-IN QUESTIONS

1.   The rate of exchange for the French franc is the number of (francs, dollars) _____ that a Canadian must pay to obtain one (franc, dollar) _____.

2.   When the rate of exchange for 1 Saudi Arabian riyal is 34 Canadian cents, the rate of exchange for the Canadian dollar is _____ riyals.

3.   Canadian:
(a)   exports create a (demand for, supply of) _____ foreign money and generate a _____ dollars;
(b)   imports create a _____ foreign money and generate a _____ dollars.

4.   In addition to the demand for foreign exchange by Canadian firms that wish to import goods from foreign countries, Canadians also demand foreign money to purchase _____ and _____ and _____ services abroad and to pay _____ and _____ on foreign investments in Canada.

5.   On the balance of payments:
(a)   A transaction that earns foreign exchange for a nation is a (debit, credit) _____ and is shown with a (+, -) _____ sign.
(b)   A transaction that uses up foreign exchange is a _____ and is shown with a _____ sign.

6.   When a nation has a
(a)   deficit trade balance, its exports of _____ are (greater, less) _____ than its imports of _____.
(b)   current account deficit, its balance on goods and services plus its net _____ income and net _____ is (positive, negative) _____.

7.   The capital account records the capital inflows and capital outflows of a nation.
(a)   Capital inflows are the expenditures made (in that nation, abroad) _____ for _____ and _____ assets by residents of (that nation, other nations) _____; and capital outflows are the expenditures made

_____ by residents of _____ for _____ and _____ assets.

(b) A nation has a capital account surplus when its capital inflows are (greater, less) _____ than its outflows.

8. A nation may:

(a) finance a current account deficit by (buying, selling) _____ assets or by (borrowing, lending) _____ abroad; and

(b) use a current account surplus to (buy, sell) _____ assets or to (borrow, lend) _____ abroad.

9. (a) The official international reserves of a nation are the quantities of (foreign monies, its own money) _____ owned by its _____ bank.

(b) In the official settlements balance, if Canada has an entry with a + (plus) sign, this indicates that the Bank of Canada, on behalf of the government, has put (upward, downward) _____ pressure on the Canadian dollar by (buying, selling) _____ foreign exchange reserves.

(c) Thus a + (plus) on the official settlements balance means Canada has had a balance of payments (surplus, deficit) _____; and a - (minus) sign would mean Canada has had a payments _____.

10. If our dollar is floating freely, so the Bank of Canada (is, is not) _____ intervening in the foreign exchange market, and Canada is tending towards a balance of payments deficit:

(a) that dollar will (appreciate, depreciate) _____; and

(b) such a change in the exchange rate will cause our imports to (increase, decrease) _____, our exports to _____, and the size of our payments deficit will _____.

11. If the Canadian dollar appreciates relative to the US dollar, then the US dollar must _____ relative to the Canadian dollar.

12. The demand for US dollars in the foreign exchange market is downsloping because as the US dollar becomes less expensive American goods become _____ in Canadian dollars, and therefore Canadians will increase their purchases of these goods and services.

13. In general, the higher a nation's price level, the _____ is the amount of its currency that can be obtained for a unit of foreign currency. The _____ theory holds that exchange rates adjust to reflect differences in price levels in various countries.

14. There are three disadvantages of flexible exchange rates: (1) the risks and uncertainties associated with flexible rates tend to (expand, diminish) _____ trade between nations; (2) when a nation's currency depreciates, its terms of trade with other nations are (worsened, bettered) _____; and (3) fluctuating exports and imports can destabilize an economy and result in _____ or _____ in that economy.

15. To fix or "peg" the rate of exchange for the German mark when:

(a) the exchange rate for the mark is rising, Canada would (buy, sell) _____ marks in exchange for dollars;

(b) the exchange rate for the mark is falling, Canada would _____ marks in exchange for dollars.

16. A nation with a balance of payments deficit:

(a) might attempt to eliminate the deficit by (taxing, subsidizing) _____ imports or by _____ exports;

(b) might employ exchange controls and ration foreign exchange among those who wish to (export, import) _____ goods and services and require all those who _____ goods and services to sell the foreign exchange they earn to the _____.

17. A nation is on the gold standard when it: (1) defines its money in terms of _____; (2) maintains a fixed relationship between its _____ supply and gold _____; and (3) allows gold to be freely _____ from and _____ into the nation.

18. When the gold standard was in effect:

(a) exchange rates were relatively (stable, unstable) _____;

(b) but when a nation had a payments deficit, gold flowed (into, out of) _____ the nation, its money supply and price level (increased, decreased) _____, and its interest rates _____; and its payments deficit (rose, fell) _____, and it experienced (inflation, recession) _____.

19. The Bretton Woods system was established to bring about (flexible, fixed) _____ exchange rates; and, to accomplish this, it employed the _____ system of exchange rates. Under this system:

(a) a member nation defined its monetary unit in terms of _____ or _____;

(b) each member nation stabilized the exchange rate for its currency and prevented it from rising by (buying, selling) _____ foreign currency, which it obtained from its _____ fund, by (buying, selling) _____ gold, or by (borrowing from, lending to) _____ the International Monetary Fund;

(c) a nation with a deeply rooted payments deficit could (devalue, revalue) _____ its currency;

(d) official international reserves included both _____ and _____; and

(e) it was hoped that exchange rates in the short run would be (stable, flexible) _____ enough to promote international trade and in the long run would be _____ enough to correct balance of payments imbalances.

20. The system of exchange rates that developed since 1971 has been labelled a system of _____ exchange rates. This means that individual nations will:

(a) in the short term, buy and sell foreign exchange to keep exchange rates _____;

(b) in the long term, allow exchange rates to rise or fall to correct payments _____.

■ **PROBLEMS AND PROJECTS**

1. A Canadian exporter sells $3 million worth of wheat to an import firm in Colombia. If the exchange rate for the Colombian peso is $0.02 (two cents), the wheat has a total value of 150 million pesos.

(a) There are two ways the import firm in Colombia may pay for the wheat. It might write a cheque for 150 million pesos drawn on its bank in Bogota and send it to the Canadian exporter.

(1) The Canadian exporter would then sell the cheque to its bank in Regina where its demand deposit would increase by $_____ million.

(2) This Regina bank branch sells the cheque for 150 million pesos to its main branch, that is, the head office branch of the bank that keeps an account in the Bogota bank. The Regina bank's account in the main branch increases by _____ million (dollars, pesos) _____; and the main branch's account in the Bogota bank

increases by _____ million (pesos, dollars) _____.

(b) The second way for the importer to pay for the wheat is to buy from its bank in Bogota a draft on a Canadian bank for $3 million, pay for this draft by writing a cheque for 150 million pesos drawn on the Bogota bank, and send the cheque to the Canadian exporter.

(1) The Canadian exporter would then deposit the draft in its account in the Regina bank and its demand deposit account there would increase by $_____ million.

(2) The Regina bank collects the amount of the draft from the Canadian bank on which it is drawn through the clearinghouse. The account at the Bank of Canada of the bank of which the Regina branch forms a part increases by $_____ million; and the account of the bank on which the draft was drawn decreases by $_____ million.

(c) Regardless of the method employed by the Colombian importer to pay for the wheat,

(1) the export of the wheat created a (demand for, supply of) _____ dollars and a _____ pesos;

(2) the number of dollars owned by the Canadian exporter has (increased, decreased) _____ and the number of pesos owned by the Colombian importer has _____.

2. In 2005 Canada has a current account surplus of $27 billion, and a capital account deficit of $23 billion.

(a) In 2005, Canada has a balance of payments (deficit, surplus) _____ of $_____ billion.

(b) Accordingly, the official settlements balance would show an entry of $_____ billion. (Hint: specify the sign + or -)

(c) This entry means that Canada has (gained, lost) _____ this amount of foreign reserves.

3. Below are the supply and demand schedules for the British pound.

Qs of Pounds	Price per Pound ($)	Qd of Pounds
400	5.00	100
360	4.50	200
300	4.00	300
286	3.50	400
267	3.00	500
240	2.50	600
200	2.00	700

(a)   Assume that exchange rates are flexible.
(1) What will be the rate of exchange for the pound? $_____
(2) What will be the rate of exchange for the dollar? _____
(3) How many pounds will be purchased in the market? _____
(4) How many dollars will be purchased in the market? _____
(b)   If the Bank of Canada wished to fix or "peg" the price of the pound at $5.00, it would have to (buy, sell) _____ (how many) _____ pounds for $_____.

4. The exchange rate between the Canadian dollar and the US dollar is floating. What effect, if any, is each of the following events likely to have on the exchange rate, other things being equal? In the blanks, indicate "A" for appreciation of the Canadian $, "D" for depreciation, and "N" for no change.
(a)   ___ Canadian corporations make large payments to American bondholders.
(b)   ___ The rate of inflation in Canada increases relative to the US inflation rate.
(c)   ___ The Bank of Canada purchases Canadian dollars with US dollars to build its foreign exchange reserves.
(d)   ___ The US enters the recovery stage of the business cycle, while Canada remains mired in recession.
(e)   ___ The province of Ontario finances its deficit by borrowing in New York.
(f)   ___ Interest rates fall in Canada and remain constant in the United States.
(g)   ___ Falling unit labour costs in Canada increase the competitiveness of Canadian exports in the US market.
(h)   ___ An American-owned firm in Canada earns profits that are reinvested in Canada.
(i)   ___ Speculators anticipate a depreciation of the Canadian dollar relative to the US dollar.
(j)   ___ The demand by Americans for Canadian-produced forest products diminishes sharply.

■   **TRUE-FALSE**

Circle T if the statement is true, F if it is false.

1. The importation of goods by Canadians from abroad creates a supply of dollars in the foreign exchange market.   **T F**

2. The balance of international payments of Canada records all the payments its residents receive from and make to the residents of foreign nations.   **T F**

3. Exports are credits and imports are debits in the balance of payments of a nation.   **T F**

4. When a Canadian province sells bonds in Europe, the inflow of money shows up in the Canadian balance of payments in the capital account with a minus (-) sign attached.   **T F**

5. If a nation's exports of goods, services, and transfers are less than its imports of goods, services, and transfers, the nation's balance of payments will show a deficit in the current account.   **T F**

6. A country will have a favourable balance of trade whenever the value of exported goods is greater than the value of imported goods.   **T F**

7. If a resident of Germany buys a cottage on Salt Spring Island, B.C., this counts as a credit on Canada's capital account, and a debit on Germany's capital account.   **T F**

8. If the current account balance is $5 billion and the official settlements balance is -$4 billion, the capital account is in a deficit of $1 billion.   **T F**

9. Any nation running a balance of payments deficit is losing official international reserves.   **T F**

10. Suppose that Canadian $1.30 = US $1.00. Then it must also be true that US $0.70 = Canadian $1.00.   **T F**

11. The Canadian dollar has depreciated, relative to a foreign currency, whenever it takes more Canadian dollars to purchase a unit of the foreign currency.   **T F**

12. Whenever the Canadian dollar depreciates relative to the US dollar, the Canadian dollar price of American imports will rise.   **T F**

13. In a system of managed floating exchange rates, the central bank may have to intervene in the foreign exchange market.   **T F**

14. The quantity demanded of US dollars is downsloping because foreigners purchase greater quantities of American goods and require larger

quantities of US dollars as the US dollar becomes less expensive in foreign currency terms.   **T F**

15. When the Bank of Canada buys US dollars, it is putting upward pressure on the international value of the Canadian dollar.   **T F**

16. An increase in the number of dollars earned as dividends by Japanese investors in Canadian corporations will increase the demand for dollars and the supply of yen, and the price of the dollar will appreciate in Japan.   **T F**

17. Were Canada's terms of trade with Venezuela to worsen, Venezuela would obtain a greater quantity of Canadian goods and services for every barrel of oil it exported to Canada.   **T F**

18. To increase its official international reserves, a nation must have a balance of payments surplus.   **T F**

19. If Canada wishes to fix (or "peg") the value of the Canadian dollar in terms of the US dollar, the Bank of Canada must sell US dollars (in exchange for Canadian dollars) when the Canadian dollar is tending to depreciate.   **T F**

20. If country A defined its money as worth 100 grains of gold and country B defined its money as worth 20 grains of gold, then 5 units of country A's money would be worth 1 unit of country B's money.   **T F**

21. When nations were on the gold standard, exchange rates fluctuated only within limits determined by the cost of moving gold from one nation to another.   **T F**

22. In the Bretton Woods system, a nation was permitted to devalue its currency by as much as 10% in order to address a fundamental balance of payments deficit.   **T F**

23. One of the basic shortcomings of the Bretton Woods system was its inability to bring about the changes in exchange rates needed to correct persistent payments deficits and surpluses.   **T F**

24. Using the managed floating system of exchange rates, a nation with a persistent balance of payments surplus should allow the value of its currency to depreciate.   **T F**

25. The adjustable-peg system was intended to keep exchange rates nearly fixed, but also to avoid painful macroeconomic adjustments.   **T F**

■ **MULTIPLE-CHOICE**

Circle the letter that corresponds to the best answer.

1. If a Canadian could buy 25,000 British pounds for $100,000, the rate of exchange for the pound would be:
  (a) $40
  (b) $25
  (c) $4
  (d) $0.25

2. There is an increased demand for foreign currency (increased supply of Canadian dollars) when Canadians:
  (a) pay for goods and services imported from abroad
  (b) make payments of interest and dividends to foreign countries on their investments in Canada
  (c) make real and financial investments abroad
  (d) do all of the above

3. A nation's balance of trade is equal to its:
  (a) exports less its imports of merchandise (goods)
  (b) exports less its imports of goods and services
  (c) exports less its imports of goods and services plus its net investment income and transfers
  (d) exports less its imports of goods, services, and capital

4. A nation's balance on the current account is equal to its:
  (a) exports less its imports of merchandise (goods)
  (b) exports less its imports of goods and services
  (c) exports less its imports of goods and services plus its net investment income and net transfers
  (d) exports less its imports of goods, services, and capital

5. Capital flows into Canada include the purchase by foreign residents of:
  (a) a factory building owned by Canadians
  (b) shares of stock owned by Canadians

(c) bonds owned by Canadians

(d) all of the above

6. A Canadian current account deficit may be financed by:

(a) borrowing abroad

(b) selling real assets to foreigners

(c) selling financial assets to foreigners

(d) any of the above

7. Given the official settlements balance is zero, if Canada has a capital account surplus, it must also have a:

(a) current account surplus

(b) current account deficit

(c) balance of payments surplus

(d) balance of payments deficit

8. A nation may be able to correct or eliminate a persistent balance of payments deficit by:

(a) lowering the barriers on imported goods

(b) reducing the international value of its currency

(c) expanding its national income

(d) reducing its official international reserves

9. If exchange rates float freely, the exchange rate for any currency is determined by:

(a) the demand for it

(b) the supply of it

(c) the demand for and the supply of it

(d) the official reserves that "back" it

10. Under a floating exchange rate system, an increase in Canadian interest rates relative to US interest will:

(a) appreciate the Canadian dollar relative to the US dollar

(b) depreciate the Canadian dollar relative to the US dollar

(c) raise the price of US goods in Canadian dollars

(d) appreciate the US dollar relative to the Canadian dollar

11. If a Canadian province finances a deficit by borrowing abroad:

(a) Canadian interest rates will rise

(b) the Canadian dollar will depreciate

(c) the Canadian dollar will appreciate

(d) there will be an outflow of capital from Canada

12. If a nation had a balance of payments surplus and a floating exchange rate:

(a) its currency would appreciate, its exports would increase, and its imports would decrease

(b) its currency would appreciate, its exports would decrease, and its imports would increase

(c) its currency would depreciate, its exports would increase, and its imports would decrease

(d) its currency would depreciate, its exports would decrease, and its imports would increase

13. If exchange rates are flexible, which of the following would increase the dollar price of the Swedish krona?

(a) a rate of inflation greater in Sweden than in Canada

(b) real interest-rate increases greater in Sweden than in Canada

(c) national income increases greater in Sweden than in Canada

(d) expectations that the price of the krona will be lower in the future

14. Which of the following would be one of the results of using flexible exchange rates to correct a nation's balance of payments surplus?

(a) the nation's terms of trade with other nations would be worsened

(b) importers in the nation who had made contracts for the future delivery of goods would find that they had to pay a higher price than expected for the goods

(c) if the nation were at full employment, the decrease in exports and the increase in imports would be inflationary

(d) exporters in the nation would find their sales abroad had decreased

15. Disadvantages of a floating exchange rate system include all of the following except:

(a) uncertainty over future exchange rates

(b) instability in the macroeconomy caused by changing exchange rates

(c) decline in the terms of trade that accompany a currency depreciation

(d) an automatic adjustment mechanism for balance of payments problems

16. A nation with fixed exchange rates and a payments surplus might attempt to resolve the surplus by employing:

(a) import quotas

(b) higher tariffs

(c) subsidies on items the nation exports

(d) none of the above

17. Which one of the following conditions was a nation not required to meet to operate under the gold standard?

(a) use only gold as a medium of exchange

(b) maintain a fixed relationship between its gold stock and its money supply

(c) allow gold to be freely exported from and imported into the nation

(d) define its monetary unit in terms of a fixed quantity of gold

18. If the nations of the world were on the gold standard and one nation had a balance of payments surplus:

(a) foreign-exchange rates in that nation would rise toward the gold import point

(b) gold would tend to be imported into that nation

(c) the level of prices in that nation would tend to fall

(d) employment in that nation would tend to fall

19. Under the gold standard, a nation with a balance of payments deficit would experience all but one of the following. Which one?

(a) gold would flow out of the nation

(b) the nation's money supply would contract

(c) interest rates in the nation would fall

(d) real domestic output, employment, and prices in the nation would decline

20. Which of the following was the principal disadvantage of the gold standard?

(a) unstable foreign-exchange rates

(b) persistent payments imbalances

(c) the uncertainties and decreased trade that resulted from the depreciation of gold

(d) the domestic macroeconomic adjustments experienced by a nation with a payments imbalance

21. Which of the following was not among the elements of the adjustable-peg system of foreign exchange rates?

(a) each nation defined its monetary unit in terms of gold or dollars

(b) nations bought and sold their own currencies to stabilize exchange rates

(c) nations were allowed to devalue their currencies when faced with persistent payments deficits

(d) the deposit by all nations of their international reserves with the IMF

22. The dilemma created by the US payments deficits was that:

(a) to maintain the status of the dollar as an acceptable international monetary reserve the deficit had to be reduced, and to increase these reserves the deficits had to be continued

(b) to maintain the status of the dollar the deficit had to be continued, and to increase reserves the deficit had to be eliminated

(c) to maintain the status of the dollar the deficit had to be increased, and to expand reserves the deficit had to be reduced

(d) to maintain the status of the dollar the deficit had to be reduced, and to expand reserves the deficit had to be reduced

23. "Floating" the dollar means:

(a) the value of the dollar is to be determined by the demand for and the supply of the dollar

(b) the dollar price of gold is to be increased

(c) the price of the dollar is to be set by international agreement

(d) the gold content of the dollar is to be reduced

24. A system of managed floating exchange rates:

(a) allows nations to stabilize exchange rates in the short term

(b) requires nations to stabilize exchange rates in the long term

(c) entails stable exchange rates in both the short and long term

(d) none of the above

25. Floating exchange rates:

(a) tend to correct payments imbalances

(b) reduce the uncertainties and risks associated with international trade

(c) increase the world's need for official international reserves

(d) tend to expand the volume of world trade

■ DISCUSSION QUESTIONS

1. What is foreign exchange and the foreign exchange rate? Who are the demanders and suppliers of a particular foreign exchange, say, the French franc? Why is a buyer (demander) in the foreign exchange markets always a seller (supplier) also?

2. What does a nation's balance of payments summarize? What are the principal sections of a nation's balance of payments? What are the three kinds of items listed on each?

3. How does a nation finance a balance of payments deficit and what does it do with a balance of payments surplus?

4. Is it good or bad for a nation to have a balance of payments deficit or surplus?

5. In a flexible exchange rate system the exchange rate is determined by the forces of supply and demand. Use the balance of payments as given in Table 21-1 to enumerate the demanders and suppliers of foreign currencies.

6. What types of events cause the exchange rate for a foreign currency to appreciate or depreciate? How will each of these events affect the exchange rate for a nation's currency?

7. How can floating exchange rates eliminate balance of payments deficits and surpluses? What are the problems associated with this method of correcting payments imbalances?

8. How may a nation employ its foreign exchange reserves to fix or "peg" foreign-exchange rates? Be precise. How does a nation obtain or acquire these official international reserves?

9. What kinds of trade controls may nations with payments deficits employ to eliminate their deficits?

10. How can foreign exchange controls be used to overcome a payments deficit? Why do such exchange controls necessarily involve the rationing of foreign exchange?

11. If exchange rates are fixed, what kind of domestic macroeconomic adjustments are required to eliminate a payments deficit? To eliminate a payments surplus?

12. How did the gold standard operate? How did the gold standard correct payments imbalances? What were the disadvantages of this method of eliminating payments deficits and surpluses?

13. Why did the operation of the international gold standard ensure relatively stable exchange rates; that is, rates that fluctuate only within very narrow limits? What are the limits, and what are the advantages, of stable exchange rates?

14. What is the "critical difference" between the adjustment necessary to correct payments deficits and surpluses under the gold standard and those necessary when exchange rates are flexible? How did this difference lead to the demise of the gold standard during the 1930s?

15. Explain: (a) why the International Monetary Fund was established, and what the objectives of the adjustable-peg (or Bretton Woods) system were; (b) how the adjustable-peg system worked, and how it stabilized exchange rates in the short run; and (c) why and how the system was to allow for long-run exchange rate adjustments.

16. What was the role of the US dollar under the Bretton Woods system? Why was the dollar used by nations as an international money, and how could they acquire additional dollars?

17. Explain what is meant by a managed floating system of exchange rates. When are exchange rates managed, and when are they allowed to float?

18. Explain the arguments of the proponents and the critics of the managed floating system.

■ ANSWERS

FILL-IN QUESTIONS

1. dollars, franc

2. 2.94

3. (a) supply of, demand for; (b) demand for, supply of

4. tourism, freight, shipping, interest, dividends

5. (a) credit, +; (b) debit, -

6. (a) goods, less, goods; (b) investment, transfers, negative

7. (a) in that nation, real, financial, other nations, abroad, that nation, real, financial; (b) greater

8. (a) selling, borrowing; (b) buy, lend

9. (a) foreign monies, central; (b) upward, selling; (c) deficit, surplus

10. is not; (a) depreciate; (b) decrease, increase, decrease

11. depreciate

12. less expensive

13. greater; purchasing power parity

14. diminish; worsened; recession, inflation

15. (a) sell; (b) buy

16. (a) taxing, subsidizing; (b) import, export, government

17. (1) gold; (2) money, stock; (3) exported, imported

18. (a) stable; (b) out of, decreased, rose, fell, recession

19. fixed, adjustable-peg; (a) gold, US dollars; (b) selling, exchange-stabilization, selling, borrowing from; (c) devalue; (d) gold, US dollars; (e) stable, flexible

20. managed floating; (a) stable; (b) imbalances

PROBLEMS AND PROJECTS

1. (a) (1) 3, (2) 3, dollars, 150, pesos; (b) (1) 3, (2) 3, 3; (c) (1) demand for, supply of, (2) increased, decreased

2. (a) surplus, 4; (b) -4; (c) gained

3. (a) (1) 4.00, (2) 0.25 pounds, (3) 300, (4) 1200; (b) buy, 300, 1500

4. (a) D, (b) D, (c) A, (d) A, (e) A, (f) D, (g) A, (h) N, (i) D, (j) D

TRUE-FALSE

1. T	**2.** T	**3.** T	**4.** F	**5.** T	**6.** T
7. T	**8.** T	**9.** T	**10.** F	**11.** T	**12.** T
13. T	**14.** T	**15.** F	**16.** F	**17.** T	**18.** T
19. T	**20.** T	**21.** T	**22.** T	**23.** T	**24.** F
25. T					

MULTIPLE-CHOICE

1. (c)	**2.** (d)	**3.** (a)	**4.** (c)	**5.** (d)	**6.** (d)
7. (b)	**8.** (b)	**9.** (c)	**10.** (a)	**11.** (c)	**12.** (b)
13. (b)	**14.** (d)	**15.** (d)	**16.** (d)	**17.** (a)	**18.** (b)
19. (c)	**20.** (d)	**21.** (d)	**22.** (a)	**23.** (a)	**24.** (a)
25. (a)					

CHAPTER 22

The Economics of Developing Countries

Canada is among the world's richest nations, enjoying a GDP per capita many times greater than the GDP per capita in the world's poorest nations. This chapter assesses the facts of international income inequality, discusses the obstacles to growth in developing countries (DVCs), and examines what governments in these countries and governments in the industrially advanced countries (IACs) can do about the problem.

The level of disparity between nations can be measured by the percentage of world income going to the richest 20% (82.7% in 1992) compared to the percentage going to the poorest 20% (1.4% in 1992). Or it can be measured by comparing real per capita output figures (e.g., $39,640 in Japan, compared to $80 in Mozambique, in 1995). The absolute income gap between rich and poor nations is huge, and growing, which implies that DVCs must grow faster than IACs to close the gap. Such economic growth will require the DVCs to use existing resources more efficiently, and to expand their available supplies of resources. With respect to natural resources, the DVCs vary quite significantly, but there are common patterns with respect to human resources: DVCs tend to be overpopulated, suffer widespread unemployment and underemployment, and have low labour productivity.

DVCs can rarely expand land or natural resources, so they must improve their rates of capital accumulation, which would greatly improve the productivity of labour. Technological advance is another source of growth that may still have great potential. Unfortunately, DVCs are hindered by low savings rates, capital flight, and various sociocultural and institutional obstacles. These nations face a vicious circle of poverty: the consequences of today's poverty are also the causes of tomorrow's poverty. To break the cycle, capital accumulation and population control are crucial.

What is the role of government in fostering DVC growth? It is easy to identify positive roles such as establishing law and order, providing infrastructure, building effective social institution, etc. Yet, while there are many cases where government has contributed in such ways (e.g., Japan, South Korea, and Taiwan), there are also many cases where government corruption and ineptitude have stifled growth (e.g., Nicaragua, Haiti, and the Philippines).

Significant improvement in the DVCs seems unlikely without the support of IACs. The support could take the form of increased trade, foreign aid in grants and loans from governments, or flows of capital from private investors in developed nations. Each of these sources of assistance is subject to pitfalls. In the 1990s an increasing amount of the assistance for DVCs came as private capital flows. Many DVCs reformed their economies, typically to increase the role of markets in order to attract more direct investment, and to appease foreign lenders in hopes of averting debt crises. The revived flow of private capital has, however, not been enjoyed equally by all DVCs. African nations have seen particularly little assistance of this kind.

The chapter closes with a summary of the strategies that economists have suggested DVCs take to promote growth, and policies that IACs might adopt to foster DVC growth. Ultimately it is in the interests of the whole world to ensure that the citizens of all nations share in the benefits of income growth.

■ CHECKLIST

When you have studied this chapter, you should be able to:

233

☐ Describe the facts about income disparity between nations, and suggest ways of measuring income gaps.

☐ Distinguish between industrially advanced countries (IACs) and developing countries (DVCs) and describe the economic characteristics of the two groups.

☐ Explain why the gap in the standard of living between DVCs and IACs has widened.

☐ Identify the two basic avenues for economic growth in all nations.

☐ Discuss the human implications of poverty in the DVCs.

☐ Discuss natural resource problems in DVCs.

☐ Identify three specific problems related to human resources that plague most DVCs.

☐ Explain the problems that rapid population growth can create in DVCs.

☐ Describe the conditions of unemployment and underemployment in DVCs.

☐ State reasons for low labour productivity in DVCs.

☐ Present three reasons for the emphasis on capital formation in the DVCs.

☐ Explain the obstacles to saving and investment in DVCs.

☐ Explain why technological advancement is a promising source of growth for DVCs, yet one that might fail if inappropriate technologies are transferred from the IACs.

☐ List some sociocultural and institutional factors that inhibit growth in DVCs.

☐ Describe the "circle of poverty" in which many DVCs are caught.

☐ Discuss five areas in which DVC governments might play a positive role in fostering growth.

☐ Describe the problems with the role of the public sector in fostering economic development.

☐ Identify the three main types of assistance that IACs provide to DVCs.

☐ List nine DVC policies that could help to foster growth in DVCs.

☐ List five IAC policies that could help to foster growth in DVCs.

■ CHAPTER OUTLINE

1. There is considerable inequality in income among nations.

  (a) Nations can be classified into two major groups.

    (1) The 26 high-income nations are known as industrially advanced countries. IACs are characterized by high per capita incomes, large stocks of capital goods, advanced production technologies, and well-educated workers. Examples of IACs include Canada, the United States, and Japan.

    (2) The other 107 nations are the developing countries. DVCs have low incomes, are not industrialized, are heavily dependent on agriculture, have high population growth, and have low rates of literacy. About three-fourths of the world's population live in DVCs.

  (b) Some DVCs have achieved high annual growth rates in real GDP in recent decades, and a few have moved into the IAC group (e.g., South Korea, Singapore, Hong Kong). In contrast, some DVCs, such as those in sub-Saharan Africa, are not growing at all. Even if growth rates were the same for high and low-income nations, the absolute income gap would widen because of the higher income base in the IACs.

  (c) Compared with IACs, DVCs have lower per capita incomes, lower life expectancies, higher infant mortality, lower literacy rates, less food per person, and fewer nonhuman sources of energy.

2. Economic development requires that resources be used more efficiently, that the quantity of economic resources be increased, and that technology advance; but in DVCs there are many obstacles to development.

  (a) Many (but not all) DVCs possess inadequate natural resources, and the farm products that DVCs typically export are subject to wide fluctuation in prices.

  (b) Many DVCs are overpopulated, which usually causes a number of problems: food shortages, limited ability of families to save and invest, falling productivity, resource overuse, and urban problems.

  (c) DVCs tend also to have substantial unemployment, underemployment, and low labour productivity.

  (d) DVCs are short of capital goods because of low savings potential, the flight of capital to IACs, and the absence of investors and incentives to invest.

  (e) Technological knowledge is primitive in DVCs. Therefore, technology can be advanced fairly easily, but care must be taken to transfer from IACs technologies appropriate to the resource endowments and situations of the DVCs.

(f) The sociocultural and institutional environment in many DVCs is incompatible with rapid economic development.

3. DVCs save little, and therefore invest little in real and human capital, because they are poor. Because they do not invest, their outputs per capita remain low and they remain poor. Even if this vicious circle were to be broken, a rapid increase in population would leave the standard of living unchanged.

4. The appropriate role for government in fostering economic growth in DVCs is not entirely clear.

(a) One view is that government should play a positive role, especially in the initial stages of economic development in helping to overcome the lack of law and order, entrepreneurship, and infrastructure. Government policies may also assist capital formation and help to resolve social and institutional problems.

(b) Another view is that excessive and inappropriate government involvement hinders growth through bureaucratic impediments, corruption, bad administration, and the pursuit of political objectives over economic goals. The use of central planning restricts competition and individual incentives, which are ingredients in the growth process.

5. IACs can foster the development of the DVCs by providing three basic kinds of assistance.

(a) They can expand trade with DVCs by eliminating trade barriers that prevent the DVCs from selling their products in the IACs. Such assistance is problematic if prices of commodities exported by DVCs drop sharply, as often happens.

(b) Foreign aid in the form of loans and grants from governments and international organizations (including the World Bank) enable the DVCs to accumulate capital. Foreign aid is often criticized for breeding dependence, and for being misused due to inefficient or even corrupt bureaucracies.

(c) The flow of private capital from investors in IACs helps the DVCs to increase their productive capacities and per capita outputs.

6. In the 1980s, the large external debts of DVCs produced a debt crisis: they could not pay back their loans to foreign governments and foreign financial institutions.

(a) Several factors combined to create the crisis: soaring prices for imported oil, falling export revenues, currency depreciations that led to rising prices for import goods, and unproductive investments of the loan funds by the DVCs.

(b) Many of the debts were rescheduled or even written off, and eventually private capital flows to many DVCs began to increase in the 1990s. In order to attract the increased flows of direct foreign investment, many DVCs have undertaken broad economic reforms to increase the role of free markets, and reduce government involvement in the economy.

7. Economists suggest the following policies for a DVC that wants to promote growth: (1) establish the rule of law; (2) open the economy to international trade; (3) control population growth; (4) encourage foreign direct investment; (5) build human capital; (6) make peace with neighbouring nations; (7) establish an independent central bank; (8) establish a realistic exchange-rate policy; (9) privatize state industries.

8. Economists suggest the following as policies that IACs can undertake to promote growth in DVCs: (1) direct foreign aid to the poorest DVCs; (2) reduce barriers to trade with DVCs; (3) provide debt relief to DVCs; (4) allow in temporary workers while discouraging brain drain; (5) discourage arms sales to DVCs.

■ **TERMS AND CONCEPTS**

brain drain	**developing countries**
capital flight	**(DVCs)**
capital-saving	**direct foreign**
technological	**investment**
advance	**industrially advanced**
capital-using	**countries (IACs)**
technological	**land reform**
advance	**the will to develop**
capricious universe	**underemployment**
view	**vicious circle of**
demographic	**poverty**
transition view	**World Bank**

■ **HINTS AND TIPS**

1. There is no one factor that explains why some nations prosper while others do not. The chapter will give you a sense of the range of natural, human, social, and political factors that positively or negatively influence a nation's prospects for growth.

2.   Do not attempt to memorize the figures on the income disparity between rich and poor nations. But do look at these figures long enough to let the magnitude of the disparity sink in. Consider, for instance, how long you would have to work at the minimum wage in your province to earn as much as the average person in Ethiopia or Mozambique earns in a whole year (Table 22-2).

■   **FILL-IN QUESTIONS**

1. There is massive income inequality among nations. The richest 20% of the world's population receive about _____% of world income while the poorest 20% receive about _____% of world income.

2. (a) Nations can be classified as _____ countries (IACs) or as _____ countries (DVCs).
(b) IACs have a (higher, lower) _____ starting base for per capita income than DVCs, so the same percentage growth rate for both IACs and DVCs means an increase over time in the _____ income gap.

3. (a) The IACs have developed _____ economies based on large stocks of _____ goods, advanced production _____ and _____ labour forces.
(b) The economies of the DVCs tend to have low levels of _____, a large portion of the work force in the _____ industry, _____ population growth, _____ labour productivity, dated production _____, a small stock of capital _____, and exports consisting mainly of _____ or _____.

4. The process for economic growth involves more _____ use of existing resources and also increasing supplies of productive _____.

5. The standard of living can be calculated as the _____ divided by the _____.

6. Labour _____ is very low in most DVCs because these countries have been unable to invest in _____; and the so-called _____ contributes to declining skill levels as the best-trained workers leave DVCs to work in IACs.

7. Rapid population growth also creates problems for the transition to a productive modern economy because:
(a)   large families have low rates of _____ which restricts the accumulation of _____,
(b)   a growing population requires more investment to maintain the existing _____ to labour ratio,
(c)   a growing population may lead to the _____ of natural resources, and
(d)   the rapid growth of cities through migration can lead to massive _____ problems.

8. Technologies used in the IACs might be transferred to the DVCs; but the technologies used in the advanced nations are based upon a labour force that is (skilled, unskilled) _____, labour that is relatively (abundant, scarce) _____, and capital that is relatively _____, and their technologies tend to be (labour, capital) _____-using. DVCs would usually benefit more from the transfer of technologies that are _____.

9. The "will to develop" in DVCs involves a willingness to adjust the nations' _____ and _____ arrangements.

10. The three major ways in which IACs can assist economic development in the DVCs are by expanding _____, by giving _____, and by private _____.

11. The DVC debt crisis in the 1980s arose from the large (internal, external) _____ debts that had accumulated since the 1970s. The causes of the DVC debt crisis are given as follows:
(a)   Oil prices (increased, decreased) _____ during the 1970s and this event _____ the borrowing needs of DVCs to pay for imported oil.
(b)   In the early 1980s, the IACs had a (tight, easy) _____ monetary policy that (increased, decreased) _____ real interest rates and _____ the cost to DVCs of servicing debts. The recession of the early 1980s in the IACs also _____ the exports of farm products from DVCs to the industrialized nations.
(c)   The international value of the U.S. dollar (appreciated, depreciated) _____, which meant that DVCs had to pay (more, less) _____ for imports and receive _____ in return for exports.

12. In the 1990s the capital flowing into DVCs is largely from (private, public) _____ sources, and is provoking many DVCs to _____ their economies to promote growth and avert future _____ crises.

■ PROBLEMS AND PROJECTS

1. A developing country (DVC) has a real GDP per capita of $200, while an industrially advanced country (IAC) has a real GDP per capita of $4000. This DVC manages to get their economy growing at 7% per year, while the IAC grows at a steady 3.5% per year.

(a) Use the rule of 70 to fill in the first two blank columns.

(b) Fill in the third blank column calculated as the absolute gap between the DVC and IAC per capita GDP levels.

(c) Approximately how long will it be before the DVC catches up to the IAC in real GDP per capita?

Year	DVC $/capita	IAC $/capita	Absolute Gap $/capita
2000	200	4000	_____
2020	_____	_____	_____
2040	_____	_____	_____
2060	_____	_____	_____
2080	_____	_____	_____
2100	_____	_____	_____

2. While economic conditions are not identical in all developing nations, certain conditions are common to most of them. In the spaces after each of the following characteristics, indicate briefly the nature of this characteristic in most less-developed nations.

(a) Standard of living (per capita income) _____

(b) Average life expectancy _____

(c) Extent of unemployment _____

(d) Literacy _____

(e) Technology _____

(f) Percentage of the population working in agriculture _____

(g) Size of the population relative to the land and capital available _____

(h) The birth and death rates _____

(i) Quality of the labour force _____

(j) Amount of capital equipment relative to the labour force _____

(k) Level of saving _____

(l) Incentive to invest _____

(m) Amount of basic social capital _____

(n) Extent of industrialization _____

3. Suppose that it takes a minimum of 5 units of food to keep a person alive for a year, that the population can double itself every 10 years, and that the food supply can increase every 10 years by 200 units.

(a) Assume that both the population and the food supply grow at these rates. Complete the following table by computing the level of the population and the food supply in years 10 through 60.

Year	Food Supply	Population
0	200	20
10	_____	_____
20	_____	_____
30	_____	_____
40	_____	_____
50	_____	_____
60	_____	_____

(b) What happens to the relationship between the food supply and the population in the 30th year?

(c) What would actually prevent the population from growing at this rate following the 30th year?

(d) Assuming that the actual population growth in the years following the 30th does not outrun the food supply, what would be the size of the population in:

(1) Year 40: _____

(2) Year 50: _____

(3) Year 60: _____

(e) Why does the standard of living fail to increase in the years following the 30th, even though the food supply increased by 75% between years 30 and 60?

■ TRUE-FALSE

Circle T if the statement is true, F if it is false.

1. About three-fourths of the world's population lives in less-developed countries. **T F**

2. The annual per capita GNP growth rate in the IACs in recent years has been higher than that recorded in the DVCs. **T F**

3. The difference between the per capita incomes in the DVCs and the per capita incomes in the IACs is decreasing, albeit slowly.   **T   F**

4. No nation has achieved a high standard of living without a large supply of natural resources.   **T   F**

5. In 1995 per capita GDP in Canada was over 200 times as high as in Mozambique.   **T   F**

6. A factor preventing the elimination of unemployment in the DVCs is that migration to the cities exceeds the number of job openings available in the cities.   **T   F**

7. Saving in DVCs is a larger percentage of national output than in IACs, and this is a main reason total saving in DVCs is small.   **T   F**

8. Once initiated, the process of capital accumulation can allow for enough income growth to permit the higher rate of savings to finance yet higher rates of capital accumulation.   **T   F**

9. Lack of adequate infrastructure is a barrier to achieving adequate levels of private investment in DVCs.   **T   F**

10. Technological knowledge from the IACs is readily transferable to the DVCs.   **T   F**

11. When technological advances are capital-saving, it is possible for an economy to increase its productivity without any net investment in capital goods.   **T   F**

12. Labour-saving and capital-using technologies are typically appropriate to DVCs.   **T   F**

13. Emancipation from custom and tradition is often a fundamental prerequisite of economic development.   **T   F**

14. The capricious universe view is that there is little or no correlation between an individual's activities and the outcomes that person experiences. **T   F**

15. DVCs would benefit if the IACs would reduce tariffs and eliminate import quotas on the goods that DVCs export.   **T   F**

16. Capital flight harms domestic growth by diverting savings out of the country.   **T   F**

17. An increase in the output and employment of Canada would benefit DVCs by providing them with a larger market for their exports.   **T   F**

18. The purpose of the World Bank is to collect on loans that banks and governments in the IACs have made to DVCs.   **T   F**

19. The "brain drain" refers to the large flows of talented and educated people leaving IACs to take better opportunities in DVCs.   **T   F**

20. One reason that foreign aid is viewed as harmful is that it tends to promote dependency and reduce the effectiveness of market incentives.   **T   F**

21. In virtually all DVCs, governments are working actively and positively towards the goals of economic growth and development.   **T   F**

22. The IACs could help the DVCs grow by discouraging arms sales to the DVCs because spending on arms diverts spending from infrastructure and education.   **T   F**

■   **MULTIPLE-CHOICE**

Circle the letter that corresponds to the best answer.

1. Which of the following would be considered a DVC?
  (a)   China
  (b)   Kuwait
  (c)   Taiwan
  (d)   New Zealand

2. If per capita income is $600 a year in a DVC and per capita income is $12,000 in an IAC, then a 2% growth rate increases the absolute income gap by how much in one year?
  (a) $120
  (b) $228
  (c) $240
  (d) $252

3. When the average annual rate of growth in per capita GNP in a DVC is 1%, approximately how many years will it take for the standard of living to double?
  (a)   27 years
  (b)   35 years

(c) 57 years
(d) 70 years

4. Which of the following is high in the DVCs?
(a) life expectancy
(b) infant mortality
(c) literacy
(d) per capita energy consumption

5. Which of the following is an obstacle to economic growth in DVCs?
(a) the supply of natural resources
(b) the size and quality of the labour force
(c) the supply of capital equipment
(d) all of the above

6. The DVCs are characterized by all of the following, with the exception of:
(a) high proportion of the labour force in agriculture
(b) dated production techniques
(c) high unemployment
(d) high capital to labour ratio

7. The demographic transition view holds that:
(a) rising GDP per capita leads to more rapid population growth
(b) rising GDP per capita must be achieved before population growth will slow down
(c) increasing numbers of people will migrate from DVCs to IACs
(d) increasing numbers of people will migrate from IACs to DVCs

8. An increase in the total output of food and consumer goods in a DVC may not raise the standard of living because:
(a) of diminishing returns
(b) it may provoke an increase in the population
(c) of disguised unemployment
(d) the skill level of the labour force is low

9. Which of the following best describes the unemployment found in the DVCs?
(a) the result of cyclical fluctuations in aggregate demand
(b) the agricultural workers who have migrated to urban areas and failed to find employment
(c) the workers in excess of the optimum population
(d) workers whose productivity is subject to diminishing returns

10. Which of the following is not a reason for placing special emphasis on capital accumulation in DVCs?
(a) the inflexible supply of arable land
(b) the low productivity of workers
(c) the low marginal contribution of capital equipment
(d) the possibility that capital accumulation will be "cumulative"

11. Which of the following is not a factor limiting saving in DVCs?
(a) the output of the economy is too low to permit a large volume of saving
(b) those who do save do not make their saving available to their own economies
(c) the highly unequal distribution of income
(d) the low marginal contribution of capital equipment to production

12. When citizens of DVCs transfer savings or invest savings in IACs, it is referred to as:
(a) brain drain
(b) capital flight
(c) savings potential
(d) in-kind investment

13. Which of the following is not an example of sociocultural obstacles to development often found in DVCs?
(a) tribal and ethnic conflicts
(b) a strong tradition of private property rights
(c) allocation of jobs based on caste or social standing rather than ability or merit
(d) religious beliefs may restrict the length of the workday or divert resources to ceremonial uses

14. Which of the following is an example of infrastructure?
(a) a steel plant
(b) a highway
(c) a farm
(d) a casino

15. Which of the following is not a factor leading to low productivity in the DVCs?
(a) low investment in human capital
(b) low marginal propensity to consume
(c) the absence of an entrepreneurial class
(d) low levels of physical capital per worker

16. Assume the total real output of a DVC increases from $100 billion to $115.5 billion, while its population expands from 200 million to 210 million people. Real income per capita has, as a result, increased by:

(a) $50
(b) $100
(c) $150
(d) $200

17. The government often has a major role in the early stages of economic development. Which one of the following is not one of the reasons?

(a) the government must establish an independent central bank

(b) the government can encourage foreign direct investment

(c) the government must ensure that property rights are clearly defined and enforced

(d) the government must fix the value of the currency at a high level

18. The technology used in IAC countries may not be appropriate for DVCs due to:

(a) a higher rate of population growth in the DVCs

(b) lower per capita income in the DVCs

(c) higher per capita energy consumption in the IACs

(d) differences in factor endowments in the IACs and the DVCs

19. An event that occurred during the 1970s or early 1980s that contributed to the DVC debt crisis was:

(a) a sharp decline in the price of oil charged by OPEC nations

(b) a depreciation in the international value of the U.S. dollar

(c) a tight monetary policy and recession in the IACs

(d) a rise in net export earnings of the DVCs

20. Which of the following is not among the common criticisms of foreign aid?

(a) countries receiving aid tend to become dependent on the aid

(b) aid is often given only to nations whose politics are compatible with the donor nations

(c) aid tends to create overly rapid growth in countries receiving the aid

(d) due to corruption, aid often fails to reach its intended target

21. Which one of the following is not one of the ways that IACs could help the DVCs to foster growth?

(a) raising tariffs and quotas on labour-intensive products

(b) provide debt relief to DVCs by renegotiating or cancelling some of the loans

(c) eliminate the OPEC cartel which keeps oil price artificially high

(d) discourage "brain drains"

22. The institution primarily responsible for the plan to prevent the financial collapse of the Mexican economy was:

(a) the World Bank

(b) the Canadian International Development Agency

(c) the Bank of Canada

(d) the International Monetary Fund

■ **DISCUSSION QUESTIONS**

1. What is the degree of income inequality among nations of the world? Classify nations into two groups and describe this inequality. How do the levels of GDP per capita and their growth rates compare among rich nations and poor nations?

2. What are the "human implications" of poverty found in DVCs?

3. Describe the basic avenues of economic growth. Do these avenues differ for IACs and DVCs?

4. How would you describe the natural resource situation for DVCs? How do price fluctuations affect DVC exports? Is a weak natural resource base necessarily an obstacle to economic growth?

5. What are the implications of a high rate of growth in population? Can the standard of living be raised by merely increasing the output of consumer goods in DVCs?

6. What obstacles do the human resources of DVCs place in the path of economic development? What are the reasons for the low level of labour productivity in DVCs? How does "brain drain" affect DVCs?

7. Why do we emphasize capital accumulation as a means of promoting economic growth in DVCs?

Why do DVCs struggle to achieve adequate saving rates, and to mobilize their savings into domestic capital accumulation? What obstacles limit the flow of foreign capital into DVCs? How is infrastructure important for capital formation?

8. How might the DVCs improve their technology without engaging in slow and expensive research? What are the risks to acquiring technology in this way?

9. What is meant by the "will to develop"? How is it related to social and institutional change in DVCs?

10. Explain the "vicious circle" of poverty found in the DVCs. How does population growth make an escape from this vicious circle difficult?

11. Why is the role of government expected to be a positive one in the early phases of development in DVCs? What have been the problems with the involvement of government in economic development?

12. How can Canada help DVCs? What types of aid can be offered? Can Canada assist DVCs without any spending on "foreign aid"? Can this type of aid ensure rapid and substantial development in DVCs?

13. What are the purposes and activities of the World Bank?

14. How did the DVC debt crisis arise? Explain the economic consequences for DVCs and IACs of the debt crisis.

15. What is the nature of most of the capital flows into DVCs in the 1990s? Why do some nations receive more of such flows than other nations?

■ ANSWERS

FILL-IN QUESTIONS

1. 83, 1

2. (a) industrially advanced, developing; (b) higher, absolute

3. (a) market, capital, technologies, well-educated; (b) industrialization, agricultural, rapid, low, technology, equipment, agricultural commodities, raw materials

4. efficient, resources

5. consumer goods (food), population

6. productivity, human capital, brain drain

7. (a) savings, capital; (b) capital; (c) depletion; (d) urban

8. skilled, scarce, abundant, capital; capital-saving (or labour-using)

9. social, institutional

10. trade, foreign aid, capital flows (investment spending)

11. external, (a) increased, increased; (b) tight, increased, increased; decreased; (c) appreciated, more, less

12. private, reform, debt

PROBLEMS AND PROJECTS

1. (a) DVC: 200, 800, 3200, 12,800, 51,200, 204,800; IAC: 4000, 8000, 16,000, 32,000, 64,000, 128,000; (b) Gap: 3800, 7200, 12,800, 19,200, 12,800, -76,800; (c) between 80 and 100 years

2. (a) low; (b) short; (c) widespread; (d) low; (e) primitive; (f) large; (g) large; (h) high; (i) poor; (j) small (k) low; (l) absent; (m) small; (n) small

3. (a) Food supply: 400, 600, 800, 1000, 1200, 1400; Population: 40, 80, 160, 320, 640, 1280; (b) The food supply is just able to support the population; (c) The inability of the food supply to support a population growing at this rate; (d) (1) 200, (2) 240, (3) 280; (e) The population increased as rapidly as the food supply.

TRUE-FALSE

1. T	**2.** F	**3.** F	**4.** F	**5.** T	**6.** T
7. F	**8.** T	**9.** T	**10.** F	**11.** T	**12.** F
13. T	**14.** T	**15.** T	**16.** T	**17.** T	**18.** F
19. F	**20.** T	**21.** F	**22.** T		

MULTIPLE-CHOICE

1. (a)	**2.** (b)	**3.** (d)	**4.** (b)	**5.** (d)	**6.** (d)
7. (b)	**8.** (b)	**9.** (b)	**10.** (c)	**11.** (d)	**12.** (b)
13. (b)	**14.** (b)	**15.** (b)	**16.** (a)	**17.** (d)	**18.** (d)
19. (c)	**20.** (c)	**21.** (a)	**22.** (d)		

CHAPTER 23

Transition Economies: Russia and China

Among the most important developments in recent world history is the evolution from communism to market system in Russia and China. On the spectrum of economic systems, both China and Russia (part of the former Soviet Union) are shifting away from their traditional command systems, and towards more market-based systems. Chapter 23 describes how the command system known as central planning worked in the Soviet Union and China, the ideological foundations underlying that system, the factors that moved these nations towards a market system, and the challenges that still face these societies in transition.

Just as the market system in Canada is supported by our prevailing capitalist ideology, the former command economies in the former Soviet Union and China were founded on a Marxian ideology. At the core of these beliefs was the labour theory of value, which traced all commodity values back to labour, holding that the income of capitalists is surplus value expropriated from workers. Under communism, property resources (including land, factories, etc.) were owned and controlled by the state. Resource allocation decisions were made by central planning, rather than in a decentralized fashion responding to market forces.

The goals of central planning included rapid industrialization, economic growth, and military strength. Planners set quotas of outputs that each industry was responsible for producing, and set quotas of inputs that should be supplied to each industry. Between the 1930s and 1950s these economies mobilized resources very effectively and were successful relative to their stated goals. But by the 1970s Soviet growth was lagging behind growth in the major market economies, and by the late 1980s Soviet output was falling, and crisis was unavoidable. In 1991 the Soviet Union broke apart into several separate nations, Russia being the largest. China has taken a decidedly different path in its quest to improve economic performance. Since 1978, the Communist Party has gradually reformed the Chinese economy through selective introductions of free markets.

The economic reforms in China and the former Soviet Union that seem so opposite to Marxist ideology were caused by problems inherent in central planning. In the market system millions of decisions by resource suppliers, producers, and consumers are coordinated in a spontaneous and decentralized manner. Under central planning the coordination must be done by the bureaucracy. This becomes increasingly difficult as an economy becomes larger, more modern, and more specialized. In market systems prices and profits provide incentives and serve as clear signals of success. Centrally planned systems are woefully lacking in appropriate incentives and success indicators. Over time these limitations took a toll in the Soviet Union and China. The quality and availability of consumer goods were miserable, and became less and less tolerable to citizens who had endured prolonged sacrifices with the expectation that they would eventually enjoy higher living standards. Under these strains, a collapse was inevitable unless there was drastic reform.

Since Boris Yeltsin became leader in 1992, Russia has committed to making the transition to a market economy. Private property has been established, and many previously state-owned enterprises have been privatized. Most price controls have been removed, including the control on the ruble's foreign exchange rate. Allowing prices to adjust freely has helped to alleviate drastic shortages, but has also been highly inflationary. While the old system has been torn apart, the new system is not yet complete. Among other problems, the decline in real output and living standards that started at the end of the 1980s accelerated during the reforms. At this point, the future of Russia is unclear. Some analysts predict that the current problems and instability will drive the society back to communism. Others believe that progress is continuing towards a functioning market economy.

China has initiated gradual reforms under the direction of its Communist Party. Land reform has given tenant-farmers some profit incentive. State-owned enterprises have been given some authority to determine their output levels, and to sell some of their outputs for profits. Special economic zones have been created to foster investment and exports. China's real output growth has been impressive, but China is a long way from being an industrially advanced nation. Many of the reforms have been only partial; property rights are incomplete, trade with other nations is still very restricted, some regions have hardly developed at all, and the whole nation is vulnerable to macroeconomic instability.

Russia and China make an interesting comparison. Russia's transition has certainly been more troubled, but it may in the long run be more lasting and more fruitful because more fundamental freedoms now exist in Russia than in China.

■ CHECKLIST

When you have studied this chapter, you should be able to:
☐ Outline the key elements of Marxian ideology.
☐ Identify two outstanding institutions of the communist economies.
☐ Make seven generalizations about the functioning of central economic planning.
☐ Compare how the coordination problem and the incentive problems are handled in a market economy and in a centrally planned economy.
☐ Describe the deteriorating economic performance of the former Soviet economic system, and identify six factors that contributed to its collapse.
☐ Explain the role of privatization, private property rights, and price reform in Russia's transition to a market economy.
☐ Describe the effects of reducing monopoly power and promoting competition in Russian markets.
☐ Use a supply and demand graph to discuss the difficulties posed by price reforms in Russia's transition.

☐ Explain the importance of Russia joining the world economy.
☐ Describe the causes and effects of Russia's problems with inflation.
☐ Discuss the two other major problems Russia has encountered in the transition.
☐ State an optimistic and a pessimistic view of the future prospects for economic reforms in Russia.
☐ Explain the strategy behind the Chinese government's gradual introduction of reforms.
☐ Discuss the main elements of economic reform in China.
☐ Describe the positive outcomes of Chinese economic reforms as well as the remaining problems.
☐ State an optimistic and a pessimistic view of the future prospects for economic reforms in China.

■ CHAPTER OUTLINE

1. The economies of China and the former Soviet Union were previously based on Marxist ideology.

(a) The Soviet government was viewed as a dictatorship of the proletariat (or working class) under Lenin and Stalin, and the Chinese economy was a dictatorship under Mao Zedong.

(b) The Marxian concept of a labour theory of value held that only labour creates value in production, and that profits are a surplus value expropriated from workers by capitalists, who because of the institution of private property, were able to control the means of production (capital goods).

(c) The communist system of the former Soviet Union and China sought to end this exploitation of workers by eliminating private property and creating a classless society.

(d) The two major institutional features of these two economies were state ownership of property resources and central economic planning.

2. Central planning was especially prevalent in the Soviet Union, but was also used in China. The operation of central planning exhibited seven features:

(a) the attachment of great importance to military strength and industrialization;

(b) the overcommitment of available resources and inability to meet planning targets;

(c) achievement of increased production through mobilizing more resources rather than increasing productivity;

(d) resource allocation by directives rather than by markets and prices;

(e)   price controls imposed by government;

(f)   an emphasis on the self-sufficiency of the nation; and

(g)   passive use of monetary and fiscal policies.

3. Central planning has proven to be fraught with fundamental difficulties.

(a)   The basic chore of coordinating millions upon millions of resource allocation decisions overwhelms the bureaucracy that is responsible. In the market system coordination is handled in a decentralized and spontaneous fashion, and this works much better in a complex, modern economy.

(b)   The price mechanism provides incentives to produce goods that consumers want, to produce as efficiently as possible, and to provide good quality and good service. Central planning lacks any comprehensive incentive mechanisms; production quotas are not enough.

4. The Soviet economy collapsed, and the once great nation broke into several smaller republics, Russia being the largest. Many factors contributed to the collapse.

(a)   Economic growth declined, and real output fell sharply.

(b)   Technology lagged by western standards and manufactured goods were of poor quality.

(c)   Promises to consumers that consumer goods would eventually become abundant were broken.

(d)   The large financial burden for military expenditures diverted resources from the production of consumer and capital goods.

(e)   Inefficiencies in agriculture acted as a drag on economic growth and hurt productivity in other sectors of the economy.

5. Though reforms commenced in 1986, under Gorbachev, dramatic changes took place after Yeltsin came to power in 1992.

(a)   Private property rights were established, and much government property has been privatized to encourage entrepreneurship.

(b)   Price controls that were intended to keep the cost of living down, also had the effect of stifling incentives to produce more and better products that would match consumer demands. Most price controls were lifted under sweeping reforms.

(c)   Along with privatizing state enterprises, Russian reformers are trying to instill competition in Russian industries.

(d)   Russia has made the ruble a fully convertible currency to help Russia trade more effectively with other nations.

(e)   Hyperinflation followed the early price reforms, in part because households had large savings of rubles from the days when there were no goods to buy, and because governments dealt with their deficits by issuing vast amounts of new money.

6. Two other significant problems have plagued Russia's transition to a market economy:

(a)   Political and economic reforms have been so extreme that they have significantly set back Russia's real output and the living standards of its citizens. Real GDP shrank every year between 1991 and 1996.

(b)   Income inequality has risen because market reforms have created some "big winners" whereas others have suffered. Crime has grown, corruption is rampant, and health care and education have deteriorated.

7. The prospects for Russia's transition to a market economy are still uncertain. The pessimistic view is that the government will remain weak with a mounting public debt, minimal control of inflation, and an inability to provide basic public services. These destabilizing conditions could lead to the return of hyperinflation and collapse of the economy. The more optimistic view is that real output has stopped falling and the rate of inflation will fall. Market reforms are now taking hold and the economy will prosper. Although the transition will continue for at least another decade, an economic collapse and return to socialism is unlikely given the progress that has been made.

8. China's Communist Party has chosen a very different route to reform: a gradual, piecemeal approach that would avoid political upheaval.

(a)   In agriculture, individual farmers can now lease land (decollectivization). Though they must still sell a certain amount of their output to the government at set prices, they can sell the remainder at market prices (two-track price system). Productivity in agriculture is much higher, freeing up labour to reallocate to township and village enterprises.

(b)   State-owned enterprises (SOEs) in urban areas have been granted more authority in production and employment decisions, and are permitted to retain some of their profits. Urban collectives owned by managers and workers are encouraged.

(c)   Special economic zones have been created to attract foreign investment, private ownership and international trade. "Near-capitalism" is booming in these zones.

(d)   China has developed some of the institutions needed to support a market system: a central bank, an enterprise tax system, a mechanism for exchanging currencies, and a stock market.

(e)   In the 1990s China tried to make SOEs more "corporate-like." A 1997 plan calls for consolidation of major SOEs into 1,000 large enterprises operating with the government as majority shareholder, but having shares also owned by the public. About 300,000 smaller SOEs would be sold to private individuals, or allowed to go bankrupt.

9. China has achieved impressive growth rates during the 1990s (averaging about 9% annually). This has boosted domestic saving and investment, foreign investment and capital accumulation. Per capita incomes have risen despite population problems. Yet China still faces problems in making a full transition to a market system:

(a)   Property rights are incomplete, leading to incentive problems which retard productivity growth.

(b)   Investment spending is volatile, leaving China very vulnerable to macroeconomic instability.

(c)   China is not fully integrated with the global economy, and many of its policies and practices (e.g., intellectual property rights) are unacceptable to other nations.

(d)   There is great regional unevenness in China's economic development.

10. China and Russia have taken different paths in their transition to market systems. China's transition to date has been smoother, but Russia's may be more likely to succeed ultimately because in China the state has retained more of its powers and controls. The real test of China's acceptance of the market system may come when China must confront demands for the political freedoms that normally accompany the economic freedoms that China is gradually allowing.

■ TERMS AND CONCEPTS

central economic planning	state ownership
coordination problem	state-owned enterprises
incentive problem	surplus value
labour theory of value	township and village enterprises
special economic zones	urban collectives

■ HINTS AND TIPS

1.   View this chapter not only as a study of Russia and China, but as a contrast with Canada's economy. Thinking about this gives you a chance to review, apply, and integrate many of the economic concepts and ideas you've learned about how the market system works. In particular, it is easy to overlook the institutional framework which allows the market system to work as well as it does in Canada. Studying the economic history of these societies that have habitually lacked private property rights and incentive systems is a good way to see the importance of these factors.

■ FILL-IN QUESTIONS

1. China and the former Soviet Union both formed _____ economies based on _____ ideology. They believed that:

(a)   the value of any commodity is determined by the amount of _____ required to produce it;

(b)   in capitalist economies, because capital is (privately, publicly) _____ owned, capitalists exploit workers by paying them a wage that is equal to the _____ wage and obtain _____ value at the expense of workers; and

(c)   in a communist economy, capital and other property resources will be _____ owned, and society will be governed by the Communist Party as a dictatorship of the _____.

2. The two major institutions of the former Soviet Union and China are the ownership of _____ resources by the _____ and central economic _____.

3. Economic planning in the former Soviet Union functioned in several ways.

(a)   The Soviet five-year plans sought to achieve rapid _____ and _____ strength, but these policies created an (over, under) _____-commitment of resources and resulted in an _____-production of goods for consumers.

(b)   Early economic growth was achieved by _____ resources and reallocating surplus labour from _____ to industry.

(c) The government allocated inputs among industries by planning _____.

(d)   The Soviet Union considered itself to be a (capitalist, socialist) _____ nation surrounded by _____ nations, and central plans were designed to achieve economic _____ sufficiency.

(e)   Monetary and fiscal policies in the Soviet Union were (active, passive)_____. Prices were _____ by government.

4. Decision-making in a market economy is (centralized, decentralized) _____, but in the Soviet economy it was _____. The market system tends to produce a reasonably (efficient, inefficient) _____ allocation of resources, but central planning in the Soviet economy was _____ and resulted in production bottlenecks and failures to meet many production targets.

5.   There are a number of reasons for the collapse of communism and the failure of the Soviet economy.

(a)   There was a large _____ burden on the economy that diverted resources from the production of investment and consumer goods.

(b) Agriculture was (efficient, inefficient) _____ and (helped, hurt) _____ economic growth and productivity in other sectors of the economy.

(c)   There were continual (surpluses, shortages) _____ of consumer goods, and the goods available were often of _____ quality.

(d)   Central planning became (more, less) _____ complex and difficult as the economy grew and became more sophisticated.

(e)   Measures of economic performance were (adequate, inadequate) _____ for determining the success or failure of economic activities.

(f)   Economic incentives were (effective, ineffective) _____ for encouraging work or for giving signals for efficient allocation of resources in the economy.

6. The economic reforms in Russia have several elements.

(a)   One of the most important changes is the establishment of _____ rights and the transfer of government property to _____ ownership.

(b)   Under central planning, many input and output prices were set too (high, low) _____, resulting in (surpluses, shortages) _____. The removal of price controls created a serious (deflation, inflation) _____ problem.

(c)   The economy must also promote _____ by splitting up the large state-owned enterprises so that there is more than one business producing each good or service, and potential for _____ power is reduced.

(d)   To help Russia to join the international economy, the ruble has been made a fully _____ currency on international markets.

(e)   Stabilization of the _____ level requires that the government cease financing deficits by increasing the supply of _____. Russia has also established an independent _____.

7. At this point in the transition to a market economy Russia is facing huge problems. Large declines in real GDP have lowered citizens' _____. Because there have been gainers and losers in the economic restructuring, and because of corruption and illegal activities, economic _____ has increased.

8. Significant differences exist between China's transition experience and Russia's. So far, China's government has largely (kept, lost) _____ its power and control, and real GDP per capita has (fallen, grown) _____.

9. Reforms in China include the following elements:

(a)   Agricultural reform in China has included _____, whereby land is leased to individual farmers. These farmers must produce some output to sell to _____ at controlled prices, but are allowed to sell any extra output in markets at _____-determined prices.

(b)   Urban industries have been reformed by granting _____-owned enterprises more autonomy, and giving them some profit incentive. Government has also encouraged the formation of _____ collectives — enterprises owned jointly by managers and their workers.

(c)   To attract foreign investment, private ownership and international trade, _____ zones have been established.

(d)   A stock market, a central bank, and a currency exchange are examples of _____being developed to help the transition to a market system.

(e) More recently, the government is seeking to consolidate the major _____ into 1,000 large enterprises, and to sell off any smaller _____ that are still viable.

10. The positive results of China's reforms include impressive rates of _____ and rising _____ incomes, despite continued population growth. China still has problems to solve before their transition is really successful:
(a) _____ are still incomplete;
(b) the country is very vulnerable to _____ instability;
(c) the country is still not fully integrated with the _____ economy; and
(d) the development so far is geographically _____.

■ **PROBLEMS AND PROJECTS**

1. The table below lists key institutions and characteristics of the Canadian economy in the left column and of the former Soviet Union in the right column. Match the Canadian and Soviet institutions or characteristics.

Canadian institution or characteristic	Soviet institution or characteristic
1. private property	a. state enterprises
2. profit	b. labour theory of value
3. entrepreneurial freedom	c. state ownership of resources
4. supply and demand	d. communism
5. democracy	e. surplus value
6. capitalism	f. party dictatorship
7. corporations	g. central planning

2. Answer the next set of questions based on the table below. In the table are the columns for the price, quantity demanded (Q_d) by consumers, and a fixed quantity supplied by government (Q_{s1}) for a product in the former Soviet Union. The column for (Q_{s2}) shows the supply curve for the product after privatization in the industry producing the product.

Price (in rubles)	Q_d	Q_{s1}	Q_{s2}
90	25	25	55
80	30	25	50
70	35	25	45
60	40	25	40
50	45	25	35
40	50	25	30
30	55	25	25

(a) What are the equilibrium price and quantity when only the government supplies the product (as per Q_{s1} schedule)? Price = _____, Quantity = _____.
(b) If the government tries to make the product more accessible to lower-income consumers by setting the price at 30 rubles, what is the result? Q_d = _____, Q_s = _____, and Shortage = _____.
(c) If the government decontrols prices but does not privatize industry, what will price and output be? Price = _____, Quantity = _____.
(d) With privatization, the supply becomes schedule Q_{s2}. What are the resulting price and quantity? Price = _____, Quantity = _____.

■ **TRUE-FALSE**

Circle T if the statement is true, F if it is false.

1. The labour theory of value is the Marxian idea that the exchange value of a product is determined by the supply and demand of labour resources. **T F**

2. Surplus value in Marxian ideology is the value of a commodity at equilibrium in a competitive market. **T F**

3. The Soviet economy was characterized by both state ownership of resources and decentralized economic decision-making. **T F**

4. Soviet and Chinese governments both relied on central planning to determine which goods to produce, and what quantities to produce. **T F**

5. Historically, the Soviet Union placed emphasis on rapid industrialization and economic self-sufficiency. **T F**

6. Economic resources tended to be undercommitted in the Soviet economy. **T F**

7. China actively used monetary and fiscal policies to manipulate aggregate levels of employment, output, and prices. **T F**

8. In the few years before the breakup of the Soviet Union real output increased significantly. **T F**

9. Greater productivity and technological progress in the civilian sector were often sacrificed or limited by the demands to support a large military in the Soviet Union. **T F**

10. The problems of central planning became easier and less complex as the Soviet economy grew over time, but the economy was undermined by calls for democratic reform.   **T F**

11. In the Communist system one of the key incentives was to move up the political hierarchy within the party.   **T F**

12. "Decollectivization" refers to a reform of the taxation system in China.   **T F**

13. The transition to a market economy in Russia requires the breakup of large industries and actions to promote competition.   **T F**

14. SOEs have been given profit incentives in China.   **T F**

15. SEZs have been established in Russia to stimulate foreign trade and investment.   **T F**

16. China still has not created a central bank to regulate its money supply.   **T F**

17. One of the major accomplishments of Russian economic reform has been limited inflation because of the reduction in the ruble overhang and tight control of the money supply.   **T F**

18. One of the major problems still facing China is to find ways to prevent and deal with macroeconomic instability.   **T F**

■ **MULTIPLE-CHOICE**

Circle the letter that corresponds to the best answer.

1. Which of the following was an element in the ideology of China and the Soviet Union?
  (a) dictatorship over the business class
  (b) the creation of surplus value by government
  (c) the labour theory of value
  (d) the private ownership of property

2. Marxian (or communist) ideology in the Soviet Union was highly critical of capitalist societies because in those societies:
  (a) capitalists own the machinery and equipment necessary for production
  (b) capitalists pay workers a wage that is less than the value of their production

  (c) capitalists expropriate the surplus value of workers
  (d) all of the above are true

3. The institution that was most characteristic of the Soviet Union and China was:
  (a) private ownership of property
  (b) authoritarian central planning
  (c) a system of markets and prices
  (d) consumer sovereignty

4. Industrialization and rapid economic growth in China were initially achieved by:
  (a) the mobilization of economic resources
  (b) the overcommitment of economic resources
  (c) price controls and price fixing
  (d) active use of fiscal policy by the government

5. The Soviet Union viewed itself historically as a single socialist nation surrounded by hostile capitalist nations, and as a consequence central planning stressed the need for:
  (a) consumer sovereignty
  (b) economic self-sufficiency
  (c) allocation by directive
  (d) all of the above

6. In the system of central planning, the outputs of some industries become the inputs for other industries, but a failure of one industry to meet its target would cause:
  (a) inflation in wholesale and retail prices
  (b) the decay of the infrastructure
  (c) a chain reaction of production problems and bottlenecks
  (d) widespread unemployment among workers

7. Which of the following is evidence of the economic failure of communism in the Soviet Union?
  (a) lagging technology compared to Western standards
  (b) an inability to supply consumer goods that people wanted
  (c) the poor quality of consumer goods
  (d) all of the above

8. Which of the following was a cause of low productivity in agriculture in the Soviet Union?
  (a) inability to make productive use of the abundance of good farmland in the country
  (b) the failure to construct an effective incentive system for agriculture

(c) an increase in the length of the growing season

(d) the overuse of certain chemical fertilizers on crops

9. What was the major success indicator for Soviet enterprises?
(a) maximizing profits
(b) keeping prices to a minimum
(c) meeting production targets
(d) maximizing worker incomes

10. Which of the following is **not** one of the components of the most recent and sweeping reform effort in Russia?
(a) privatization
(b) promotion of competition
(c) an increased role for government
(d) more participation in the world economy

11. The effect of price controls on most consumer goods in the Soviet Union was that:
(a) shortages developed because quantity demanded was greater than the quantity supplied by the competitive market at the controlled price set by government
(b) prices rose because the quantity demanded by consumers was greater than the quantity supplied by government
(c) prices fell because the quantity supplied by the competitive market was greater than the quantity demanded by consumers
(d) shortages developed because the quantity demanded by consumers was greater than the quantity supplied by the government at the price set by government

12. What does "ruble overhang" refer to?
(a) currency and deposits hoarded by households
(b) excessive money supply growth
(c) accumulated government debt
(d) international lack of confidence in the ruble

13. Which is considered a major accomplishment of economic reforms in Russia in the 1990s?
(a) greater income equality
(b) an increase in price controls
(c) elimination of corruption and black markets
(d) reduction in the rate of inflation

14. Decontrol of prices has had what effect in markets for consumer goods in Russia?

(a) rising prices
(b) creation of shortages
(c) creation of surpluses
(d) less efficient allocation of resources

15. Agricultural and rural reform in China was primarily intended to:
(a) increase the number of workers in the agricultural sector
(b) increase productivity in agriculture
(c) avoid having population move to the cities
(d) none of the above

16. Reforms of state-owned enterprises in China gave these enterprises:
(a) greater autonomy in determining output levels
(b) greater autonomy in employment decisions
(c) some profit incentive
(d) all of the above

17. China's Special economic zones have:
(a) stimulated foreign investment in China
(b) increased Chinese exports
(c) undercut support for central planning
(d) all of the above

18. As part of its reform package, China has established:
(a) complete property rights for landowners
(b) a central bank
(c) strong intellectual property rights
(d) membership in the World Trade Organization

■ **DISCUSSION QUESTIONS**

1. What are the essential features of Marxian ideology on which the command economy of the Soviet Union and China were based?

2. What were the two principal economic institutions of communist economies? How do these compare with Canada's institutions?

3. Describe how central planning functioned historically. What generalizations can you make about resource use, directives, prices, self-sufficiency, and macroeconomic policies?

4. Why does central planning result in a coordination problem, and an incentive problem? Compare the operation of central planning with the use of markets and prices for economic decision-making.

5. What main factors contributed to the collapse of the Soviet economy?

6. What were the key elements of Russia's transition to a market system?

7. What reasons were there for decontrolling prices in Russia, and what were the short-term problems caused by this?

8. Discuss what must be done in Russia to promote competition. Why are state monopolies a problem?

9. What steps were taken in Russia to achieve stable prices?

10. Describe the major accomplishments to date of economic reform in Russia. What major problems remain for Russia? What are Russia's prospects for making successful and lasting economic transformation?

11. What general strategy has China taken in reforming its economy to include elements of a market system?

12. What were the key elements of agricultural and urban industrial reforms in China? How are state-owned enterprises being treated, and what difference is it making?

13. What other institutional changes has China undertaken to support the functioning of a market system?

14. In what respects is China's transition still incomplete, and what are the risks for the current Chinese government, and for Chinese citizens?

■ ANSWERS

FILL-IN QUESTIONS

1. communist, Marxist; (a) labour; (b) privately, subsistence, surplus; (c) publicly, people

2. property, state, planning

3. (a) industrialization, military, over, under; (b) mobilizing, agriculture; (c) targets; (d) socialist, capitalist, self; (e) passive, controlled

4. decentralized, centralized; efficient, inefficient

5. (a) military; (b) inefficient, hurt; (c) shortages, poor; (d) more; (e) inadequate; (f) ineffective

6. (a) property, private; (b) low, shortages; inflation; (c) competition, monopoly; (d) convertible; (e) price, money; central bank.

7. living standards; inequality

8. kept, grown

9. (a) decollectivization; government, market; (b) state, urban; (c) special economic; (d) support institutions; (e) SOEs, SOEs.

10. economic growth, real per capita; (a) property rights; (b) macroeconomic; (c) global; (d) uneven

PROBLEMS AND PROJECTS

1. 1-c, 2-e, 3-g, 4-b, 5-f, 6-d, 7-a.

2. (a) 90, 25; (b) 55, 25, 30; (c) 90, 25; (d) 60, 40

TRUE-FALSE

1. F	**2.** F	**3.** F	**4.** T	**5.** T	**6.** F
7. F	**8.** F	**9.** T	**10.** F	**11.** T	**12.** F
13. T	**14.** T	**15.** F	**16.** F	**17.** T	**18.** T

MULTIPLE-CHOICE

1. (c)	**2.** (d)	**3.** (b)	**4.** (a)	**5.** (b)	**6.** (c)
7. (d)	**8.** (b)	**9.** (c)	**10.** (c)	**11.** (d)	**12.** (a)
13. (d)	**14.** (a)	**15.** (b)	**16.** (d)	**17.** (d)	**18.** (b)

Answers to Key Questions

CHAPTER 1

1-1 This behaviour can be explained in terms of marginal costs and marginal benefits. At a standard restaurant, items are priced individually — they have a positive marginal cost. If you order more, it will cost you more. You order until the marginal benefit from the extra food no longer exceeds the marginal cost. At a buffet you pay a flat fee no matter how much you eat. Once the fee is paid, additional food items have a zero marginal cost. You therefore continue to eat until your marginal benefit becomes zero.

1-5 Economic theory consists of factually supported generalizations about economic behaviour. Economists use two methods to obtain sound theory: induction and deduction. In *deduction* the economist starts with a hypothesis and tests it for accuracy by gathering and examining facts. In *induction*, the economist starts by gathering facts and then examines their relationships, so as to extract a cause and effect pattern: a theory. Regardless of how derived, economic theory enables policy makers to formulate economic policy relevant to real-world goals and problems.

As for the quotation, the opposite is true; any theory not supported by facts is not a good theory. Good economic theory is empirically grounded; it is based on facts and so is highly practical.

1-7 (a), (d), and (f) are macro; (b), (c), and (e) are micro.

1-8 (a) and (c) are positive; (b) and (d) are normative.

1-9 (a) The fallacy of composition is the mistake of believing that something true for an individual part is necessarily true for the whole. Example: A single auto producer can increase its profits by lowering its price and taking business away from its competitors. But matched price cuts by all auto manufacturers will not necessarily yield higher industry profits.

(b) The "after this, therefore because of this" fallacy is incorrectly reasoning that when one event precedes another, the first event *necessarily* caused the second. Example: Interest rates rise, followed by an increase in the rate of inflation, leading to the erroneous conclusion that the rise in interest rates caused the inflation. Actually, higher interest rates slow inflation.

Cause-and-effect relationships are difficult to isolate because "other things" are continually changing.

Appendix 1-2 (a) More tickets are bought at each price; the line shifts to the right. (b) and (c) Fewer tickets are bought at each price; the line shifts to the left.

Appendix 1-3 Income column: $0; $5,000; $10,000, $15,000; $20,000. Saving column: $–500; 0; $500; $1,000; $1,500. Slope = 0.1 (= $1,000 – $500)/$15,000 – $10,000). Vertical intercept = $–500. The slope shows the amount saving will increase for every $1 increase in income; the intercept shows the amount of saving (dissaving) occurring when income is zero. Equation: $S = $–500 + 0.1Y$ (where S is saving and Y is income). Saving will be $750 at the $12,500 income level.

Appendix 1-6 Slopes: at $A = +4$; at $B = 0$; at $C = –4$.

2-5 Economics deals with the "limited resources — unlimited wants" problem. Unemployment represents valuable resources that could have been used to produce more goods and services — to meet more wants and ease the economizing problem.

Allocative efficiency means that resources are being used to produce the goods and services most wanted by society. The economy is then located at the optimal point on its production possibilities curve where marginal benefit equals marginal cost for each good. *Productive efficiency* means the least costly production techniques are being used to produce wanted goods and services. Example: manual typewriters produced using the least-cost techniques but for which there is no demand.

2-6   (a) See curve *EDCBA* below. The assumptions are full employment and productive efficiency, fixed supplies of resources, and fixed technology.

(b) 4.5 rockets; .33 automobiles, as determined from the table. Increasing opportunity costs are reflected in the concave-from-the-origin shape of the curve. This means the economy must give up larger and larger amounts of rockets to get constant added amounts of automobiles — and vice versa.

(c) It must obtain full employment and productive efficiency.

Question 2-6

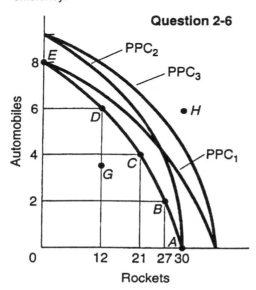

2-9   The marginal benefit curve is downsloping; MB falls as more of a product is consumed because additional units of a good yield less satisfaction than previous units. The marginal cost curve is upsloping; MC increases as more of a product is produced because additional units require the use of increasingly unsuitable resources. The optimal amount of a particular product occurs where MB equals MC. If MC exceeds MB, fewer resources should be allocated to this use. The resources are more valuable in some alternative use (as reflected in the higher MC) than in this use (as reflected in the lower MB).

2-10   See the answer for Question 2-6. *G* indicates unemployment, productive inefficiency, or both. *H* is at present unattainable. Economic growth — through more inputs, better inputs, improved technology — must be achieved to attain *H*.

2-11   See the answer for Question 2-6. PPC₁ shows improved rocket technology. PPC₂ shows improved auto technology. PPC₃ shows improved technology in producing both products.

■ CHAPTER 3

3-2   "Roundabout" production means using capital goods in the production process, enabling producers to obtain more output than through direct production. The direct way to produce a corn crop is to scatter seed about in an unplowed field. The roundabout way is to plow, fertilize, harrow, and till the field using machinery and then use a seed drill to sow the seeds in rows at the correct depth. The higher yield per acre will more than compensate the farmer for the cost of using the capital goods.

To increase the capital stock at full employment, the current production of consumer goods must decrease. Moving along the production possibilities curve toward more capital goods comes at the expense of current consumption.

No, it can use its previously unemployed resources to produce more capital goods, without sacrificing consumption goods. It can move from a point inside the curve to a point on it, thus obtaining more capital goods.

3-9   The quest for profit led firms to produce these goods. Producers looked for and found the least-cost combination of resources in producing their output. Resource suppliers, seeking income, made these resources available. Consumers, through their dollar votes, ultimately decide on what will continue to be produced.

■ CHAPTER 4

4-2   Demand increases in (a), (c), (e), and (f); decreases in (b) and (d).

4-5   Supply increases in (a), (d), (e), and (g); decreases in (b), (c), and (f).

4-7   Data, from top to bottom: −13; −7; 0; +7; +14; and +21.
(a) P_e = $4.00; Q_e = 75,000. Equilibrium occurs where there is neither a shortage nor surplus of wheat. At the immediately lower price of $3.70, there is a shortage of 7,000 bushels. At the immediately higher price of $4.30, there is a surplus of 7,000 bushels.

(b)

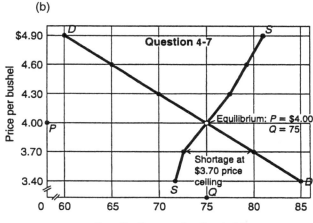

Quantity (thousands of bushels)

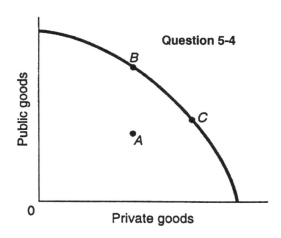

(c)   Because at $3.40 there will be a 13,000 bushel shortage that will drive the price up. Because at $4.90 there will be a 21,000 bushel surplus that will drive the price down. Quotation is incorrect; just the opposite is true.
(d)   A $3.70 ceiling causes a persistent shortage. Government might want to suppress inflation.

4-8   (a)   Price up: quantity down; (b) Price down; quantity down; (c) Price down; quantity up; (d) Price indeterminate; quantity up; (e) Price up; quantity up; (f) Price down; quantity indeterminate; (g) Price up; quantity indeterminate; (h) Price indeterminate and quantity down.

■ CHAPTER 5

5-3   Public goods are indivisible (they are produced in such large units that they cannot be sold to individuals) and the exclusion principle does not apply to them (once the goods are produced nobody — including free riders — can be excluded from the goods' benefits). The free-rider problem explains the significance of the exclusion principle. The exclusion principle separates goods and services that private firms will supply (because those who do not pay for them can be excluded from their benefits) and goods and services that government must supply (because people can obtain the benefits without paying). Government must levy taxes to get revenues to pay for public goods.

5-4   On the curve, the only way to obtain more public goods is to reduce the production of private goods (from C to B.).

An economy operating inside the curve can expand the production of public goods without sacrificing private goods (say, from A to B) by making use of unemployed resources.

■ CHAPTER 6

6-3   Greater exporting increases domestic output and thus increases revenues to domestic exporting firms. Because these firms would employ more resources, household income would rise. Households would then use part of their greater income to buy more imported goods (imports would rise).

Canadian exports in 1997 were $301.1 billion (flow 13) and imports were $276.8 billion (flow 16).

Flow 14 must equal flow 13. Flow 15 must equal flow 16.

6-4   (a)   Yes, because the opportunity cost of radios is less (1R = 1C) in South Korea than in Canada (1R = 2C). South Korea should produce radios and Canada should produce chemicals.
(b)   If they spe....lize, Canada can produce 20 tonnes of chemicals and South Korea can produce 30,000 radios. Before specialization South Korea produced alternative B and Canada alternative D for a total of 28,000 radios (24,000 + 4,000) and 18 tonnes of chemicals (6 tonnes + 12 tonnes). The gain is 2,000 radios and 2 tonnes of chemicals.
(c)   The limits of the terms of trade are determined by the comparative cost conditions in each country before trade: 1R = 1C in South Korea and 1R = 2C in Canada. The terms of trade must be somewhere between these two ratios for trade to occur.

If the terms of trade are 1R = 1 1/2 C, South Korea would end up with 26,000 radios (= 30,000 − 4,000) and 6 tonnes of chemicals. Canada would have 4,000 radios and 14 tonnes of chemicals (= 20 − 6). South Korea has gained 2,000 radios. Canada has gained 2 tonnes of chemicals.

(d)   Yes, the world is obtaining more output from its fixed resources.

6-6   The first part of this statement is incorrect. Canadian exports create a domestic *supply* of foreign currencies, not a domestic demand for them. The second part of the statement is accurate. The foreign demand for dollars (from Canadian exports) generates a supply of foreign currencies to Canadians.

A decline in Canadian incomes or a weakening of Canadian preferences for foreign goods would reduce our imports, reducing our demand for foreign currencies. These currencies would depreciate (the dollar would appreciate). Dollar appreciation means Canadian exports will decline and Canadian imports will rise.

6-10   GATT is the General Agreement on Tariffs and Trade. It affects nearly everyone around the globe because its trade liberalization applies to 120 nations. Major outcomes: reduced tariffs and quotas; liberalized trade in services; lower agricultural subsidies; enhanced protection of intellectual property rights; creation of the World Trade Organization. The EU and NAFTA are free-trade blocs. GATT reduces tariffs and liberalizes trade from nearly *all* nations. The ascendancy of the EU and the passage of NAFTA undoubtedly encourage nations to reach the latest GATT agreement. The tariff reductions within the EU and NAFTA apply only to sellers from other nations in the blocs. The GATT provisions reduce trade barriers facing *all* exporting nations, including those outside the trade blocs.

■   **CHAPTER 7**

7-3   They are excluded because the dollar value of final goods includes the dollar value of intermediate goods. If intermediate goods were counted, then multiple counting would occur. The value of steel (intermediate good) used in autos is included in the price of the auto (the final product).

This value is not included in GDP because such sales and purchases simply transfer the ownership of existing assets; such sales and purchases are not themselves (economic) investment and thus should not be counted as production of final goods and services.

Used furniture was produced in some previous year; it was counted as GDP then. Its resale does not measure new production.

7-6   When gross investment exceeds depreciation, net investment is positive and production capacity expands; the economy ends the year with more physical capital than it started with. When gross investment equals depreciation, net investment is zero and production capac-

ity is said to be static; the economy ends the year with the same amount of physical capital. When depreciation exceeds gross investment, net investment is negative and production capacity declines; the economy ends the year with less physical capital.

The first statement is wrong. Just because *net* investment was a minus $324 million in 1933 does not mean the economy produced no new capital goods in that year. It simply means depreciation exceeded gross investment by $324 million. So the economy ended the year with $324 million less capital.

The second statement is correct. If only one $20 spade is bought by a construction firm in the entire economy in a year and no other physical capital is bought, then gross investment is $20 — a positive amount. This is true even if *net* investment is highly negative because depreciation is well above $20. If not even this $20 spade has been bought, then gross investment would have been zero. But gross investment can never be less than zero.

7-8   (a)   GDP = $215
            (b)   NDI = $174

7-11   Price index for 1984 = 62.5; 60 percent; real GDP for 1984 = $112,000 and real GDP for 1992 = $352,000.

7-12   Values for real GDP, top to bottom of the column $53.8 (inflating); $38.4 (inflating); $187.4 (inflating); $353.7 (inflating); $616.8 (inflating); $744.4 (deflating); $769.5 (deflating).

■   **CHAPTER 8**

8-1   The four phases of a typical business cycle, starting at the bottom, are trough, recovery, peak, and recession.   As seen in Figure 8-1, the length of a complete cycle varies from about 2 to 3 years to as long as 15 years.

Normally there is a pre-Christmas spurt in production and sales and a January slackening. This normal seasonal variation does not signal boom or recession. From decade to decade, the long-term trend (the secular trend) of the Canadian economy has been upward. A period of no GDP growth thus does not mean that all is normal but that the economy is operating below its trend growth of output.

Because durable goods last, consumers can postpone buying replacements. This happens when people are worried about a recession and whether there will be a paycheque next month. And firms will soon stop producing what people are not buying. Durable goods industries therefore suffer large output declines during recessions. In contrast, consumers cannot long postpone the buying of nondurables such as food; therefore recessions only slightly reduce nondurable output.

8-3 Labour force = 230 [= 500 − (120 + 150)]; official unemployment rate = 10% [= (23/230) x 100].

8-5 GDP gap = 8% [= (9 − 5) x 2]; forgone output = $40 billion (=8% of $500 billion).

8-7 This year's rate of inflation is 10% or [(121 − 110)/110] x 100.

Dividing 70 by the annual percentage rate of increase of any variable (for instance, the rate of inflation or population growth) will give the approximate number of years for doubling of the variable.

(a) 35 years (= 70/2); (b) 14 years (=70/5); (c) 7 years (=70/10).

■ CHAPTER 9

9-6 Data for completing the table (top to bottom). Consumption: $244; $260; $276; $292; $308; $324; $340; $356; $32. APC: 1.02; 1.00; .99; .97; .96; .95; .94; .94; .93. APS: −.02; .00; .01; .03; .04; .05; .06; .06; .07. MPC: .80 throughout. MPS: .20 throughout.

(a) See the graphs below.

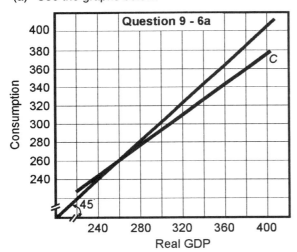

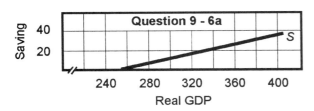

(b) Break-even income = $260. Households dissave borrowing or using past savings.

(c) Technically, the APC diminishes and the APS increases because the consumption and saving schedules have positive and negative vertical intercepts respectively. (Appendix to Chapter 1). MPC and MPS measure *changes* in consumption and saving as income changes; they are the *slopes* of the consumption and saving schedules. For straight-line consumption and saving schedules, these slopes do not change as the level of income changes; the slopes and thus the MPC and MPS remain constant.

9-8 See the graph. Aggregate investment: (a) $20 billion; (b) $30 billion; (c) $40 billion. This is the investment-demand curve because we have applied the rule of undertaking all investment up to the point where the expected rate of return, r, equals the interest rate, *i*.

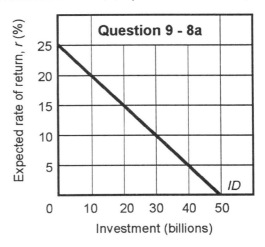

9-10 Saving data for completing the table (top to bottom): $−4; $0; $4; $8; $12; $16; $20; $24; $28.

Equilibrium GDP = $340 billion, determined where (1) aggregate expenditures equal GDP (C of $324 billion + I of $16 billion = GDP of $340 billion); or (2) where planned I = S (I of $16 billion = S of $16 billion). Equilibrium level of employment = 65 million; MCP = .8; MPS = .2.

9-11 At the $380 billion level of GDP, planned saving = $24 billion; planned investment = $16 billion (from the question). This deficiency of $8 billion of planned investment causes an unplanned $8 billion *increase* in inventories. Actual investment is $24 billion (= $16 billion of planned investment *plus* $8 billion of unplanned inventory investment), matching the $24 billion of actual saving.

At the $300 billion level of GDP, saving = $8 billion; planned investment = $16 billion (from the question). This excess of $8 billion of planned investment causes an unplanned $8 billion *decline* in inventories. Actual investment is $8 billion (= $16 billion of planned investment *minus* $8 billion of unplanned inventory disinvestment) matching the actual saving of $8 billion.

When unplanned investments in inventories occur, as at the $380 billion level of GDP, businesses revise their production plans downward and GDP falls. When unintended disinvestments in inventories occur, as at the

$300 billion level of GDP; businesses revise their production plans upward and GDP rises. Equilibrium GDP — in this case, $340 billion — occurs where planned investment equals saving.

■ CHAPTER 10

10-2 The multiplier effect is the magnified increase in equilibrium GDP that occurs when any component of aggregate expenditures changes. The greater the MPC (the smaller the MPS), the greater the multiplier.

MPS = 0, multiplier = infinity; MPS = .4, multiplier = 2.5; MPS = .6, multiplier = 1.67; MPS = 1, multiplier = 1.

MPC = 1; multiplier = infinity; MPC = .9, multiplier = 10; MPC = .67; multiplier = 3; MPC = .5, multiplier = 2; MPC = 0, multiplier = 1.

MPC = .8: Change in GDP = $40 billion (= $8 billion × multiplier of 5); MPC = .67: Change in GDP = $24 billion ($8 billion × multiplier of 3). The simple multiplier takes account of only the leakage of saving. The complex multiplier also takes account of leakages of taxes and imports, making the complex multiplier less than the simple multiplier.

10-5 (a) $400
(b) Net exports: $2, –$2, –$6, –$10, –$14, –$18, –$22, –$26. Aggregate expenditures, open economy: $242, $278, $314, $350, $386, $422, $458, $494. Equilibrium GDP: $350. Equilibrium GDP is lower because of imports.
(c) $300; $400; level of imports and equilibrium GDP are inversely related.
(d) Open economy multiplier = 1/(MPS + MPM) = 1/(0.2 + 0.08) = 3.57.

10-8 The addition of government through equal increases of G and T of $100 billion increases equilibrium GDP from $340 billion to $440 billion. This is the balanced-budget multiplier at work. It comes about because the effect of an increase in taxes on AE is not direct, as is an increase in G. Increased taxes work through their effect on C. When MPC is 0.8, increased T of $100 billion results in a decreased C of $80 billion [= 0.8($100 billion)] (with the balance of the tax increase being paid through a $20 million decrease in saving [= 0.2 ($100 billion)]).

With a multiplier of 5 = 1/(1 – 0.8), an $80 billion decrease in C causes a $400 billion decline in equilibrium GDP. But the $100 billion increase in G causes a $500 billion increase in equilibrium GDP, which therefore, with the two effects at work, increases by $100 billion (= $500 – $400 billion).

10-10 (a) Recessionary gap. Equilibrium GDP is $600 billion, while full employment GDP is $700 billion. Employment will be 2 million less than at full employment. Aggregate expenditures will have to in-

crease by $20 million at each level of GDP to eliminate the recessionary gap.
(b) Inflationary gap. Aggregate expenditures are excessive, causing demand-pull inflation. Aggregate expenditures will have to fall by $20 billion at each level of GDP to eliminate the inflationary gap.

■ CHAPTER 11

11-4 (a) See the graph. Equilibrium price level = 200. Equilibrium real output = $300 billion. No, the full-capacity level of GDP is $400 billion, where the AS curve becomes vertical.
(b) At a price level of 150, real GDP supplied is a maximum of $200 billion, less than the real GDP demanded of $400 billion. The shortage of real output will drive the price level up. At a price level of 250, real GDP supplied is $400 billion, which is more than the real GDP demanded of $200 billion. The surplus of real output will drive down the price level. Equilibrium occurs at the price level at which AS and AD intersect.
(c) See the graph. Increases in consumer, investment, government, or net export spending might shift the AD curve rightward. New equilibrium price level = 250. New equilibrium GDP = $400 billion. The intermediate range.

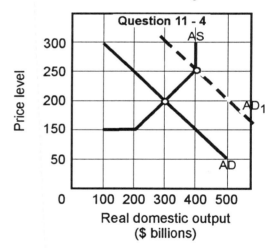

11-5 (a) Productivity = 2.67(= 300/112.5). (b) Per-unit cost of production = $.75 (= $2 × 112.5/300). (c) New per-unit production cost = $1.13. The AS curve would shift leftward. The price level would rise and real output would decrease. (d) New per-unit cost of production = $0.375 ($2 × 112.5/600). AS curve shifts to the right; price level declines and real output increases.

11-7 (a) AD curve left; (b) AD curve right; (c) AS curve left; (d) AD curve right; (e) AD curve left; (f) AD curve right; (g) AS curve right; (h) AD curve right; (i) AS curve right; (j) AS curve left; (k) AD curve right; AS curve left; (l) AD curve left; (m) AS curve right.

11-9 (a) Price level rises and no change in real output; (b) price level drops and real output increases; (c) price level does not change, but real output rises; (d) price level does not change, but real output declines; (e) price level increases, but the change in real output is indeterminate; (f) price level drops, and real output declines.

11-15 (a) $280; $220. When the price level rises from 100 to 125 [in aggregate supply schedule AS(P_{100})], producers experience higher prices for their products. Because nominal wages are constant, profits rise and producers increase output to Q = $280. When the price level decreases from 100 to 75, profits decline and producers adjust their output to Q = $75. These are short-run responses to changes in the price level.
(b) $250; $250. In the long run, a rise in the price level to 125 leads to nominal wage increases. The AS(P_{100}) schedule changes to AS(P_{125}) and Q returns to $250, now at a price level of 125. In the long run, a decrease in price level to 75 leads to lower nominal wages, yielding aggregate supply schedule AS(P_{75}). Equilibrium Q returns to $250, now at a price level of 75.
(c) Graphically, the explanation is identical to Figure 11-10. Short-run AS : P_1 = 100; P_2 = 125; P_3 = 75; and Q_1 = $250; Q_2 = $280; and Q_3 = $220. Long-run aggregate supply = Q_1 = $250 at each of the three price levels.

■ CHAPTER 12

12-1 Reduce government spending, increase taxes, or some combination of both. In the real world, the goal is to reduce *inflation* — to keep prices from rising so rapidly — not to reduce the *price level*. A "conservative" economist might favour cuts in government spending, since this would reduce the size of government. A "liberal" economist might favour a tax hike; it would preserve government spending programs.

12-5 The *cyclically adjusted budget* indicates what the federal budgetary deficit or surplus would be if the economy were at full employment throughout the year. This budget is a useful measure of fiscal policy. If the cyclically adjusted budget is moving towards deficit, fiscal policy is expansionary. If the full-employment budget is moving towards surplus, fiscal policy is contractionary. The actual budget compares G and T for the year and is an unreliable indicator of the government's fiscal policy. It does not account for shortfalls of tax revenues arising from less than full-employment output. A *structural deficit* is the difference between G and T when the economy is

at full employment. A *cyclical deficit* is the difference between G and T caused by tax revenues being below those accruing when the economy is at full employment.
At GDP_f, the structural deficit is *ab* and the cyclical deficit is zero. Government should raise T or reduce G to eliminate this deficit but it may want to take this action over several years to avoid pushing the economy into recession.

12-7 It takes time to ascertain the direction in which the economy is moving (recognition lag), to get a fiscal policy enacted into law (administrative lag), and for the policy to have its full effect on the economy (operational lag). Meanwhile, other factors may change, rendering inappropriate a particular fiscal policy. Nevertheless, discretionary fiscal policy is a valuable tool in preventing severe recession or severe demand-pull inflation.
A political business cycle is the concept that politicians are more interested in re-election than in stabilizing the economy. Before the election, they enact tax cuts and spending increases even though this may fuel inflation. After the election, they apply the brakes to restrain inflation. The economy will slow and unemployment will rise. In this view the political process creates economic instability.
The crowding-out effect is the reduction in investment spending caused by the increase in interest rates arising from an increase in government spending, financed by borrowing. The increase in G was designed to increase AD but the resulting increase in interest rates may decrease I. Thus the impact of the expansionary fiscal policy may be reduced.
The next export effect also arises from the higher interest rates accompanying expansionary fiscal policy. The higher interest rates make Canadian bonds more attractive to foreign buyers. The inflow of foreign currency to buy dollars to purchase the bonds drives up the international value of the dollar, making imports less expensive for Canadians and Canadian exports more expensive for people abroad. Net exports in Canada decline, and like the crowding-out effect, diminish the expansionary fiscal policy.

■ CHAPTER 13

13-4 $M1$ = currency (in circulation) + chequable deposits. The largest component of $M1$ is chequable deposits. If the face value of a coin were not greater than its intrinsic (metallic) value, people would remove coins from circulation and sell them for their metallic content. $M2$ = $M1$ + personal savings deposits and nonpersonal (business) notice deposits. M2+ = M2+ deposits at trust and mortgage loan companies, and deposits at *caisses populaires* and credit unions, plus money market mutual funds, and deposits at other institutions.
Near-monies represent wealth; the more wealth people have, the more they are likely to spend out of current income. Also, the fact that near-monies are liquid adds

to potential economic instability. People may cash in their near-monies and spend the proceeds while the monetary authorities are trying to stem inflation by reducing the money supply. Finally, near-monies can complicate monetary policy because $M1$, $M2$, and $M2+$ do not always change in the same direction.

The argument for including nonchequable savings deposits in a definition of money is that saving deposits can quickly be transferred to a chequing account or withdrawn as cash and spent.

13-6 In the first case, the value of the dollar (in year 2, relative to year 1) is $.80 (= 1/1.25); in the second case the value is $2 (= 1/.50). Generalization: The price level and the value of the dollar are inversely related.

■ CHAPTER 14

14-2 Reserves are assets to chartered banks in that they are cash that belongs to these banks: either cash with which the bank started operations, or profits, or money deposited in the bank by its customers and for which the bank has created in exchange a deposit liability. Excess reserves are cash owned by a chartered bank over and above what it desires to hold as its cash reserves to meet its customers' demand. Excess reserves may safely be lent by the chartered bank; when they are, the money supply increases by the amount of the loan.

14-4 Banks create or add to chequing, or demand, account balances when they make loans; these demand deposits are part of the money supply. People pay off loans by writing cheques. Demand deposits fall, meaning the money supply drops. Money is "destroyed."

14-8

Assets				Liabilities and net worth			
	(1)	(2)			(1)	(2)	
Reserves	$22,000	$22,000	$ 6,250	Demand deposits	$100,000	$115,750	$100,000
Securities	$38,000	$38,000	$38,000				
Loans	$40,000	$55,750	$55,750				

Desired reserves are 6.25% of $100,000 = $6,250.
Actual reserves = $22,000
Desired reserves = $6,250
Excess reserves = $15,750
(a) The maximum amount of new loans the bank may make is $15,750. The new balance sheet is shown in column 1 above.
(b) The money supply has increased by $15,750, since this is the amount by which demand deposits have increased, and demand deposits are part of the money supply.
(c) After cheques are drawn for the entire amount of the loan and cleared against this bank, its balance sheet will appear as column 2 above.

(d) Desired reserves are now $10,000 (–10% of $100,000). Excess reserves are now $12,000 ($22,000 – $10,000), which this bank may safely lend. When it does so, the money supply increases by $12,000.

Questions (a) and (b) are answered below, with the change in the desired reserve ratio factored in.

Assets				Liabilities and net worth			
	(1)	(2)			(1)	(2)	
Reserves	$22,000	$22,000	$ 10,000	Demand deposits	$100,000	$112,000	$100,000
Securities	$38,000	$38,000	$38,000				
Loans	$40,000	$52,000	$52,000				

14-13

Assets			Liabilities and net worth		
	(1)			(1)	
Reserves	$ 6.1	$ 6.1	Demand deposits	$150	$152.5
Securities	20	20			
Loans	123.9	126.4			

(a) Desired reserves are $6 billion (= 4% of $150 billion). Excess reserves are $0.1 billion (= $6.1 – $6.0 billion). The maximum amount the banking system might lend is $2.5 billion (= $0.1 billion × 25), as shown on the balance sheet above.
(b) Desired reserves are $7.5 billion (= 5% of $150 billion). Excess reserves are $–1.4 billion (= $6.1 – $7.5 billion). The banking system must recall loans of $28 billion (=$–1.4 billion × 20).

Assets			Liabilities and net worth		
	(1)			(1)	
Reserves	$ 6.1	$ 6.1	Demand deposits	$150	$122
Securities	20	20			
Loans	123.9	95.9			

The increase in the desired reserve ratio changes the banking system's excess reserves from $0.1 to a shortfall of $1.4 billion and decreases the money multiplier from 25 to 20.

■ CHAPTER 15

15-3 (a) and (b)
Consolidated Balance Sheet
All Chartered Banks (billions of dollars)

	(1)	(2)
Assets:		
Reserves	$4.8	$4.7	$5.0
Securites	20.0	20	19.8
Loans	71.2	71.2	71.2
Liabilities:		
Deposits	$96.0	$95.9	$96.0
Advances from Bank of Canada	0.0	0.0	0.0

Balance Sheet
Bank of Canada (billions of dollars)

		(1)	(2)
Assets			
Securites	$15.8	$15.7	$16.0
Advances to Chartered Banks	0.0	0.0	0.0
Liabilities			
Reserves of Chartered Banks	$4.8	$4.7	$5.0
Government of Canada Deposits	0.1	0.1	0.1
Notes in circulation	10.9	10.9	10.9

(c) (1) Money supply (deposits) *directly* changes only in (a); in this case, it decreases by $0.1 billion.
(2) See balance sheets.
(3) Money-creating potential of the banking system decreases by $2 billion in (a), and increases by $4 billion in (b).

15-4 (a) The level of nominal GDP. The higher this level, the greater the amount of money demanded for transactions. (b) The interest rate. The higher the interest rate, the smaller the amount of money demanded as an asset.

On a graph measuring the interest rate vertically and the amount of money demanded horizontally, the two demand-for-money curves can be summed horizontally to get the total demand for money. This total demand shows the total amount of money demanded at each interest rate. The equilibrium interest rate is determined at the intersection of the total demand for money curve and the supply of money curve.

(a) Expanded use of credit cards: transaction demand for money declines; total demand for money declines; interest rate falls. (b) Shortening of worker pay periods: transaction demand for money declines; total demand for money declines; interest rate falls. (c) Increase in nominal GDP: transaction demand for money increases; total demand for money increases; interest rate rises.

15-8 (a) Sell government securities in the open market. This would immediately decrease the money supply by the amount of the securities sales. If the banks had been fully loaned up, they would now have to decrease their loans by a multiple (because of the money multiplier) of their bond sales. This would force up interest rates (this, added to the immediate effect of the bond sales, would tend to drive down their prices, that is, drive interest rates up), and decrease aggregate expenditures.
(b) Switching government deposits from the chartered banks will reduce excess reserves, thus banks could loan out fewer funds, thereby decreasing the money supply.

15-9 The basic objective of monetary policy is to assist the economy in achieving a full employment, noninflationary level of total output. Changes in the money supply affect interest rates, which affect investment spending and therefore aggregate demand.

(a) A steep demand curve for money makes monetary policy more effective since the steepness of the curve means that only a relatively small change in the money supply is needed to produce large changes in interest rates. A relatively flat investment demand curve aids monetary policy since it means that only a small change in the interest rate is sufficient to change investment sharply. (b) A high MPC (low MPS) yields a large income multiplier, meaning that a relatively small initial change in spending will multiply into a larger change in GDP.

An easy money policy increases the money supply. The increase in GDP resulting from an easy money policy will also increase the transactions demand for money, partially offsetting the reduction in the interest rate associated with the initial increase in the money supply. Overall, investment spending, aggregate demand, and GDP will not rise by as much. The reverse is true for a tight money policy.

15-10 The intent of a contractionary monetary policy would be shown as a leftward shift of the aggregate demand curve and a decline in the price level (or, in the real world, a reduction in the rate of inflation). In an open economy, the interest rate hike resulting from the tight money policy would entice people abroad to buy Canadian securities. Because they would need Canadian dollars to buy these securities, the international demand for dollars would rise, causing the dollar to appreciate. Net exports would fall, pushing the aggregate demand curve farther leftward than in the closed economy.

■ CHAPTER 16

16-1 (a) See Figure 16-2 in the chapter. Short run: The aggregate supply curve shifts to the left, the price level rises, and real output declines. Long run: The aggregate supply curve shifts back rightward (due to declining nominal wages), the price level falls, and real output increases.
(b) See Figure 16-1. Short run: The aggregate demand curve shifts to the right, and both the price level and real output increase. Long run: The aggregate supply curve shifts to the left (due to higher nominal wages), the price level rises, and real output declines.
(c) See Figure 16-3. Short run: The aggregate demand curve shifts to the left, both the price level and real output decline. Long run: The ag-

gregate supply curve shifts to the right, the price level falls further, and real output increases.

16-3 Adaptive expectations: People form their expectations of future inflation on the basis of previous and present rates of inflation and only gradually change their expectations as experience unfolds. Rational expectations: People form their expectations by predicting what inflation will be in the future.

With adaptive expectations, an increase in inflation reduces the unemployment rate since prices rise but nominal wages for a time stay constant; thus higher inflation is associated with lower unemployment rates. This is not possible with rational expectations since workers anticipate the higher inflation and immediately take action to increase their nominal wages to avoid suffering a decline in real wages.

Both types of expectations result in a vertical long-run Phillips curve because workers either *eventually* (adaptive expectations) or *immediately* (rational expectations) adjust their expectations of inflation to the actual rate of inflation. Therefore, no trade-off between inflation and the unemployment rate exists in the long run.

16-5 Taxes and transfers reduce incentives to work; the economy is overregulated. The Laffer curve relates tax revenues to tax rates and suggests that tax revenues first rise as tax rates increase, reach a maximum at some particular tax rate, and then decline as tax rates further increase. This curve reflects the supply-side tenet that high taxes create disincentives to work and thus to earn income; reduced income reduces income tax revenue.

■ **CHAPTER 17**

17-1 (a) Classical economists envisioned the AS curve as being perfectly vertical. When prices fall, real profits do not decrease because wage rates fall in the same proportion. With constant real profits, firms have no reason to change the quantities of output they supply. Keynesians viewed the AS curve as being horizontal at outputs less than the full employment output. Declines in aggregate demand in this range do not change the price level because wages and prices are assumed to be inflexible downward.

(b) Classical economists viewed AD as stable so long as the monetary authorities hold the money supply constant. Therefore inflation and deflation are unlikely. Keynesians viewed the AD curve as unstable — even if the money supply is constant — since investment spending is volatile. Decreases in AD can cause a recession; rapid increases in AD can cause demand-pull inflation.

The Keynesian view seems more consistent with the facts of the Great Depression; in that period, real output

declined significantly in Canada and remained low for a decade.

17-4 Velocity = 3.5. They will cut back on their spending to try to restore their desired ratio of money to other items of wealth. Nominal GDP will have to fall to $266 billion (= $76 billion of money supply x 3.5) to restore equilibrium.

17-7 See the graph and the decline in aggregate demand from AD_1 to AD_2. RET view: The economy anticipates the decline in the price level and immediately moves from a to d. Mainstream view: The economy first moves from a to b and then to c. In view of historical evidence, the mainstream view seems more plausible to us than the RET view; only when aggregate demand shifts from AD_2 to AD_1 will full employment output Q_1 be restored.

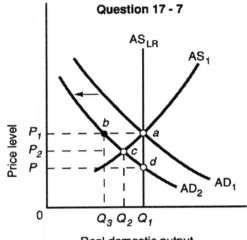

Question 17 - 7

Real domestic output

17-13 (a) RET;
(b) MAIN;
(c) MON;
(d) MAIN;
(e) MON.

■ **CHAPTER 18**

18-2 There are four supply factors, a demand factor, and an efficiency factor in explaining economic growth. (1) Supply factors: the quantity and quality of natural resources, the quantity and quality of human resources, the stock of capital goods, and technology. (2) Demand factor: maintaining full employment. (3) Efficiency factor: productive and allocative efficiency.

In the long run, a nation must expand its production capacity in order to grow (supply side). But aggregate demand must also expand (demand side) or the extra capacity will stand idle. Economic growth depends on an enhanced ability to produce *and* a greater willingness to buy.

The supply side of economic growth is illustrated by the outward expansion of the production possibilities curve, as from *AB* to *CD* in Figure 18-1. The demand side of economic growth is shown by the movement from a point on *AB* to an optimal point on *CD*, as from *a* to, say, *b* in the figure.

18-3   Growth rate of real GDP = 4 percent = ($31,200 - $30,000)/$30,000). GDP per capita in year 1 = $300 = ($30,000/100). GDP per capita in year 2 = $305.88 = ($31,200/102). Growth rate of GDP per capita is 1.96 percent = ($305.88 - $300)/300).

In the graph, AD_1 and AS_1 intersect for 1949 at a price level of 100 and GDP of 100. The 1997 AD_2 and AS_2 intersect at a price level of 706 (an increase of 606 percent) and at a real GDP of $615 (an increase of 515 percent).

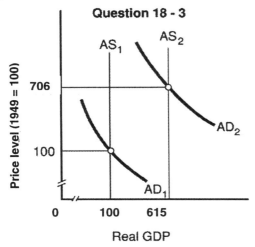

Question 18 - 3

"One Possible Graphical Solution"

18-5   Refer to Table 18-2. Between 1961 and 1996 44.5% of Canada's growth came from increased quantities of capital, 29% from increased quantities of labour, and the remaining 26.7% attributed to aggregate total factor productivity. Among the key factors contributing to TFP are technological advance, improved education and training of the work force, greater exploitation of economies of scale, and better allocation of resources.

18-8   The most commonly proposed explanations for Canada's productivity slowdown since 1975 include: falling rates of investment, sharply increased energy prices, faltering technological progress, a slowdown in the improvement of labour quality, and dismal growth of productivity in the service sector. A slowdown in productivity will cause Canada's standard of living to improve more slowly (or even to fall if population growth outstrips our real GDP growth). Other potential impacts of productivity slowdown are rising unit labour costs and rising rates of

inflation along with declining Canadian competitiveness in world markets. A low rate of productivity growth also makes it difficult for an economy to afford the investment, education, R&D, and other activities necessary to raise the rate of productivity growth. It remains to be seen whether Canada is experiencing a lasting resurgence in productivity growth through the emergence of a "new economy."

■   **CHAPTER 19**

19-1   a)   There is practically no potential for using fiscal policy as a stabilization tool under an annually balanced budget. In an economic downturn, tax revenues fall. To keep the budget in balance, fiscal policy would require the government to reduce its spending or increase its tax rates, adding to the deficiency in spending and accelerating the downturn. If the economy were booming and tax revenues were mounting, to keep the budget balanced fiscal policy would have to increase government spending or reduce taxes, thus adding to the already excessive demand and accelerating the inflationary pressures. An annually balanced budget would intensify cyclical ups and downs.

(b)   A cyclically balanced budget would be countercyclical, as it should be, since it would bolster demand by lowering taxes and increasing government spending during a recession and restrain demand by raising taxes and reducing government spending during an inflationary boom. However, because boom and bust are not always of equal intensity and duration, budget surpluses during the upswing need not automatically match budget deficits during the downswing. Requiring the budget to be balanced over the cycle may necessitate inappropriate changes in tax rates or levels of government expenditures.

(c)   Functional finance pays no attention to the balance of deficits and surpluses annually or over the cycle. What counts is the maintenance of a noninflationary full-employment level of spending. Balancing the economy is what counts, not the budget.

19-3   Two ways of measuring the public debt: (1) measure its absolute size; (2) measure its size as a percentage of GDP.

An internally held debt is one in which the bondholders live in the nation having the debt; an externally held debt is one in which the bondholders are citizens of other nations. Paying off an internally held debt would involve boosting taxes or reducing other government spending and using the proceeds to buy the government bonds. This would present a problem of income distribution because holders of the government bonds generally have higher incomes than the average taxpayer. But paying off an internally held debt would not burden the economy as a whole — the money used to pay off the debt would stay within the domestic economy.

In paying off an externally held debt people abroad would use the proceeds of the bond sales to buy goods from the country paying off its external debt. That nation would have to send some of its output abroad to be consumed by others (with no imported goods in exchange).

Refinancing the public debt simply means rolling over outstanding debt—selling "new" bonds to retire maturing bonds.

19-7 Economists do not, in general, view the large public debt as a burden for future generations. Future generations not only inherit the public debt, they inherit the bonds that constitute the public debt. They also inherit public capital goods, some of which were financed by the debt.

There is one way the debt can be a burden to future generations. Unlike tax financing, debt financing may drive up interest rates since government must compete with private firms for funds in the bond market. Higher interest rates will crowd out some private investment, resulting in a smaller stock of future capital goods and thus a less productive economy for future generations to inherit.

19-8 Cause and effect chain: Government borrowing to finance the debt competes with private borrowing and drives up the interest rate; the higher interest rate induces an inflow of foreign money to buy the now higher-return Canadian bonds; to buy the bonds the foreign financiers must first buy Canadian dollars; the demand for dollars rises and the dollar appreciates; Canada's exports fall and imports rise; a Canadian trade deficit results.

The Canadian public often blames the large trade deficits on the trade policies of other countries — particularly the United States. But, as noted in the scenario just described, a substantial portion of the large Canadian *trade* deficits may have resulted from Canada running large *budget* deficits for the past decade or more.

■ **CHAPTER 20**

20-4 (a) New Zealand's cost ratio is 1 plum = 4 apples (or 1 apple = 1/4 plum). Spain's cost ratio is 1 plum = 1 apple (or 1 apple = 1 plum). See the graphs.
(b) New Zealand should specialize in apples, Spain in plums.
(c) See the graphs.

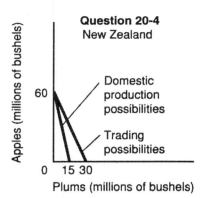

Question 20-4
New Zealand

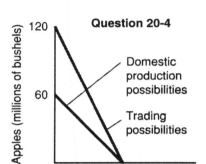

Question 20-4

(d) Total production before specialization and trade: 40 apples (20 + 20) and 50 plums (10 + 40). After specialization and trade: 60 apples and 60 plums. Gain = 20 apples and 10 plums.

20-6

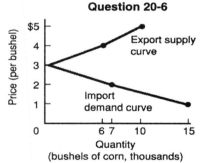

Question 20-6

At $1: import 15,000. At $2: import 7,000. At $3: no imports or exports. At $4: export 6,000. At $5: export 10,000.

Canada will export corn, France will import it.

20-7

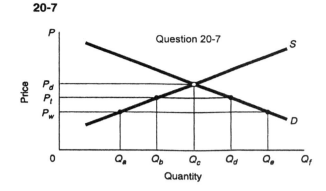

See the graph. Canada does not have a comparative advantage in this product because the world price P_w is below the Canadian domestic price of P_d. Imports will reduce the price of P_w, increasing consumption from nontrade Q_c to Q_e and decreasing domestic production from Q_c to Q_a. See the graph. A tariff of P_wP_t (a) harms domestic consumers by increasing price from P_w to P_t and decreasing consumption from Q_e to Q_d; (b) aids domestic producers through the increase in price from P_w to P_t and the expansion of domestic production from Q_a to Q_b; (c) harms foreign exporters by decreasing exports from Q_aQ_e to Q_bQ_d.

An import quota of Q_bQ_d would have the same effects as the tariff, but there would be no tariff revenues to government from these imports; this revenue would in effect be transferred to foreign producers.

20-11 The major cost of trade protection is reduced efficiency borne price increases by consumers. Prices of imported goods rise, decreasing levels of competition for domestic firms producing similar goods and allowing them to increase their prices. Prices of products using these goods as imports also rise. Prices of all other goods increase as consumer spending patterns change. Also, resources are reallocated from more efficient to less efficient domestic industries.

The main benefit of protectionist policies is greater profits for the protected firms. Government also benefits from tariff revenues. But empirical studies find that the costs of protectionism greatly exceed the benefits, resulting in a large net cost — or efficiency loss — to society.

■ CHAPTER 21

21-2 A demand for francs is created in (a), (c), and (f). A supply of francs is created in (b), (d), (e), and (g).

21-3 Balance of trade = $10 billion surplus (= exports of goods of $40 billion minus imports of goods of $30 billion). Balance on goods and services = $15 billion surplus (= $55 billion of exports of goods and services minus $40 billion of imports of goods and services).

Balance on current account = $20 billion surplus (= credits of $65 billion minus debits of $45 billion). Balance on capital account = $30 billion deficit (= Foreign purchases of assets in Canada of $10 billion minus Canadian purchases of assets abroad of $40 billion). Balance of payments = $10 billion deficit.

21-6 The Canadian demand for pesos is downsloping: When the peso depreciates in value (relative to the dollar) Canadians find that Mexican goods and services are less expensive in dollar terms and purchase more of them, demanding a greater quantity of pesos in the process. The supply of pesos to Canada is upsloping: As the peso appreciates in value (relative to the dollar), Canadian goods and services become cheaper to Mexicans in peso terms. Mexicans buy more dollars to obtain more Canadian goods, supplying a larger quantity of pesos.

The peso appreciates in (a), (f), (g), and (h) and depreciates in (b), (c), (d), and (e).

21-10 See the graph illustrating the market for Zees.

(a) The decrease in demand for Zees from D_1 to D_2 will create a surplus (ab) of Zees at the $5 price. To maintain the $5 to Z1 exchange rate, Canada must undertake policies to shift the demand-for-Zee curve rightward or shift the supply-of-Zee curve leftward. To increase the demand for Zees, Canada could use dollars or gold to buy Zees in the foreign exchange market; employ trade policies to increase imports from Zeeonia; or enact expansionary fiscal and monetary policies to increase Canadian domestic output and income, thus increasing imports from Zeeonia. Expansionary monetary policy would also reduce the *supply* of Zees: Zeeons would respond to the resulting lower Canadian interest rates by reducing their financial investing in Canada. Therefore, they would not supply as many Zees to the foreign exchange market.

(b) Under a system of flexible exchange rates, the ab surplus of Zees (the Canadian balance of payments surplus) will cause the Zee to depreciate and the dollar to appreciate until the surplus is eliminated (at the $4 = Z1 exchange rate shown in the figure).

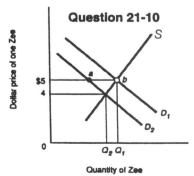

■ CHAPTER 22

22-3 Rise in per capita output gap = $135 (= 3% × $5,000 − 3% × $500).

22-6 Demographic transition view: Expanded output and income in developing countries result in lower birthrates and slower growth of population. As incomes of primary family members expand, they begin to see the marginal cost of a larger family exceeding the marginal benefit. The policy emphasis should therefore be on economic growth. Traditional view: Developing nations should reduce population growth as a first priority. Slow population growth enables the growth of per capita income.

22-7 Capital earns a higher return where it is scarce, *other things equal*. But when comparing investment opportunities between IACs and DVCs, other things are not equal. Advanced factories filled with specialized equipment require a productive work force. IACs have an abundance of educated, experienced workers; these workers are scarce in DVCs. Also, IACs have extensive public infrastructures that increase the returns on private capital. Example: a network of highways makes it more profitable to produce goods that need to be widely transported. Finally, investment returns must be adjusted for risk. IACs have stable governments and "law and order," reducing the risk of capital being "nationalized" or pilfered by organized crime.

22-13 To describe countries such as Japan and South Korea, we would need to change labels on three boxes, leading to a change in the "results" boxes. "Rapid" population growth would change to "low" rate of population growth; "low" level of saving would change to "high" level of saving; "low" levels of investment in physical and human capital would change to "high" levels of investment in physical and human capital. These three changes would result in higher productivity and higher per capita income, which would produce a rising level of demand. Other factors: stable national government; homogeneous population; extensive investment in infrastructure; "will to develop"; and strong private incentives.

■ CHAPTER 23

23-5 See Figure 23-1. Because Russia and China set prices and did not allow them to change as supply or demand shifted, prices were below the equilibrium price for most goods and services. When the fixed price, P_f is below the equilibrium price, P_e, there will be a shortage since the quantity demanded will exceed the quantity supplied.

Black markets are common where prices are fixed below equilibrium levels. People can buy goods at the fixed government prices (or pay off clerks to save such goods to sell to them), and because of the shortages at the low fixed price, resell these goods at a much higher price to those unable to find the goods in government stores at the controlled prices. This reselling is said to occur on the black market.

23-6 Privatization of state-owned businesses; market-determined prices; promotion of competition; integration with the world economy; and price-level stabilization. These reforms are referred to as shock therapy because they were dramatic and quick rather than phased in over many years or decades. Russia's reform has been successful in privatizing the economy, establishing market-determined prices, and setting the stage for future prosperity. But the transition has resulted in declining living standards for many and increasing income inequality.

23-8 (a) Leasing of land resulted in individually operated rather than collectivized farms; this greatly increased production incentives and boosted farm output. (b) Price reform established market-based prices. These higher-than-government prices provided incentives for enterprises to expand output; they also enabled market-determined allocation of resources to replace inefficient central planning. (c) Private rural and urban enterprises absorbed workers released by greater productivity in China's agricultural sector and established competition for China's state-owned enterprises. (d) The special economic zones — with their private corporations, free trade, and foreign investment — established the workability and benefits of "near-capitalism." (e) Corporatization focused the goals of state-owned enterprises on providing the high-quality, minimum per-unit cost goods desired by consumers.